THE ADVENTURES OF Dr. McNinja
Night Powers

Written and Penciled by **Chris Hastings**
Inked by **Kent Archer**
Cover by **Carly Monardo**

Monster Mart
Colored by **Carly Monardo**

Death Volley
Colored by **Carly Monardo** and **Anthony Clark**

Doc Gets Rad
Colored by **Anthony Clark**

Beyond Winter Wonderdome
Written by **Benito Cereno**
Drawn by **Les McClaine**

Introduction by **Kate Beaton**

DARK HORSE BOOKS

To Carly, the woman whose
laughter means the most to me.

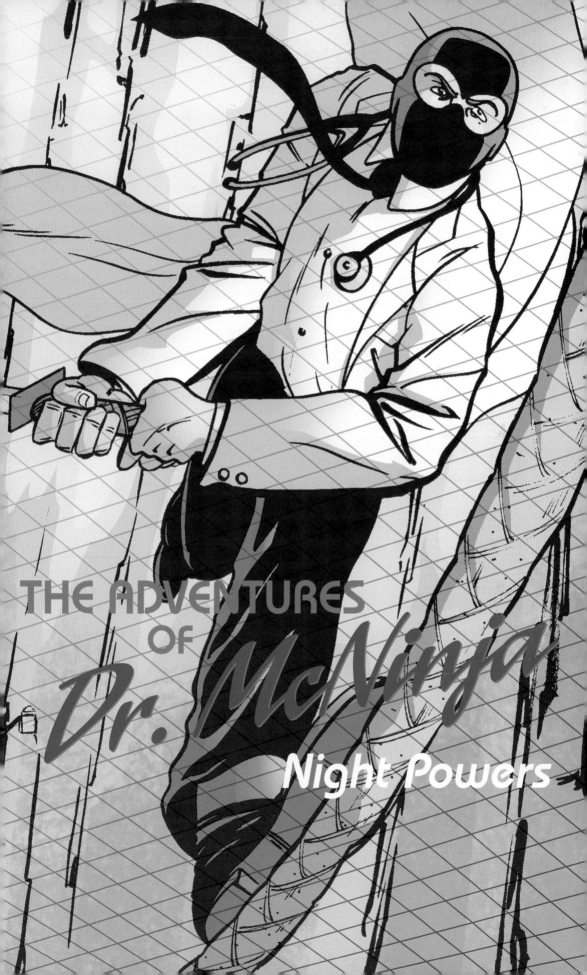

THE ADVENTURES OF Dr. McNinja

Night Powers

Publisher
Mike Richardson

Editor
Rachel Edidin

Assistant Editor
John Schork

Art Director
Lia Ribacchi

Designer
Aimee Danielson-Germany

Special thanks to **Cary Grazzini**.

Published by Dark Horse Books
A division of Dark Horse Comics, Inc.
10956 SE Main St.
Milwaukie, OR 97222

DarkHorse.com
DrMcNinja.com

First Edition: May 2011
ISBN: 978-1-59582-709-8

10 9 8 7 6 5 4 3 2

Printed by Midas Printing International, Ltd., Huizhou, China.

CONTENTS

INTRODUCTION

by Kate Beaton

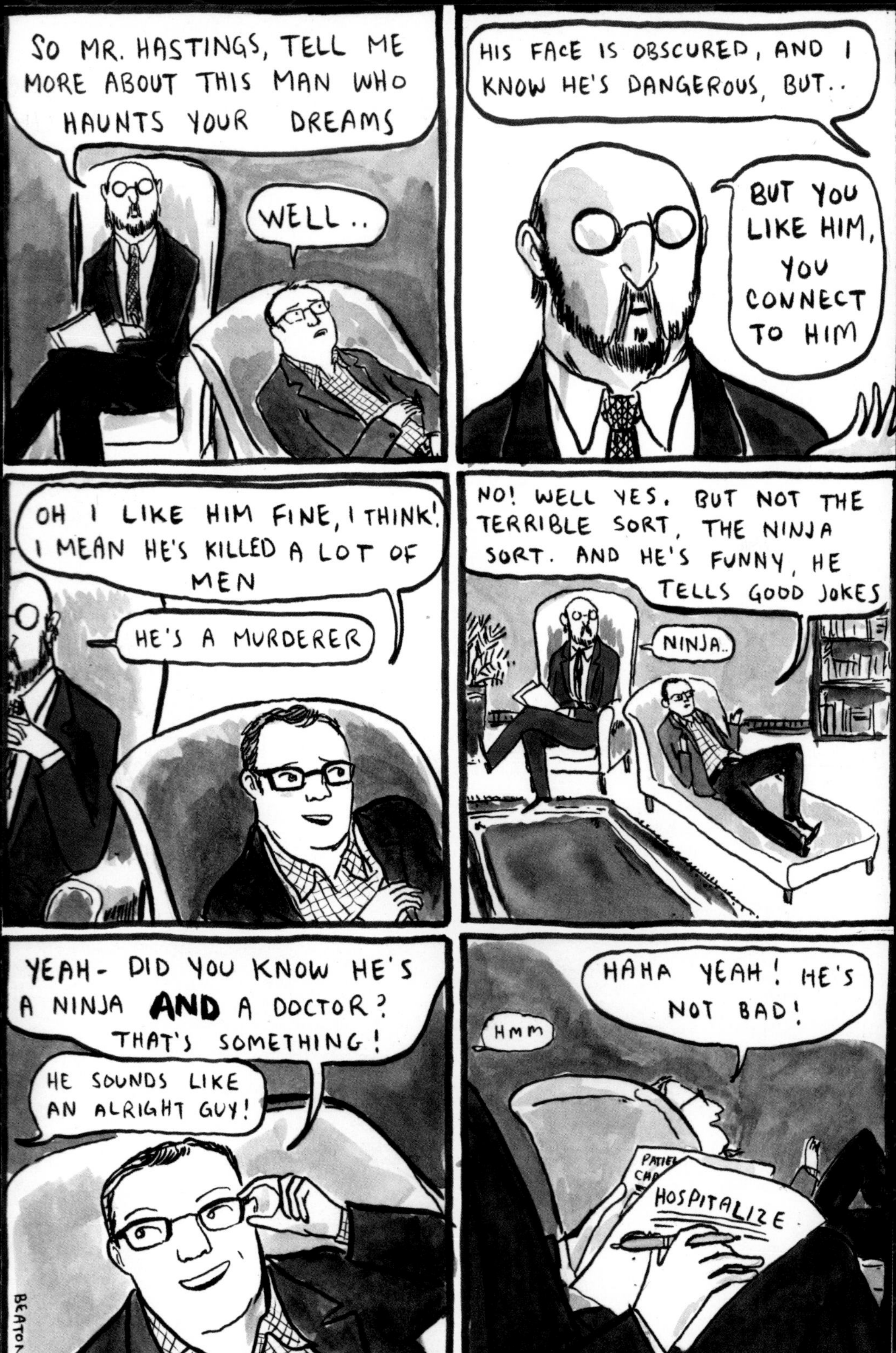
SO MR. HASTINGS, TELL ME MORE ABOUT THIS MAN WHO HAUNTS YOUR DREAMS
WELL..
HIS FACE IS OBSCURED, AND I KNOW HE'S DANGEROUS, BUT..
BUT YOU LIKE HIM, YOU CONNECT TO HIM
OH I LIKE HIM FINE, I THINK! I MEAN HE'S KILLED A LOT OF MEN
HE'S A MURDERER
NO! WELL YES. BUT NOT THE TERRIBLE SORT, THE NINJA SORT. AND HE'S FUNNY, HE TELLS GOOD JOKES
NINJA..
YEAH- DID YOU KNOW HE'S A NINJA **AND** A DOCTOR? THAT'S SOMETHING!
HE SOUNDS LIKE AN ALRIGHT GUY!
BEATON
HMM
HAHA YEAH! HE'S NOT BAD!
HOSPITALIZE

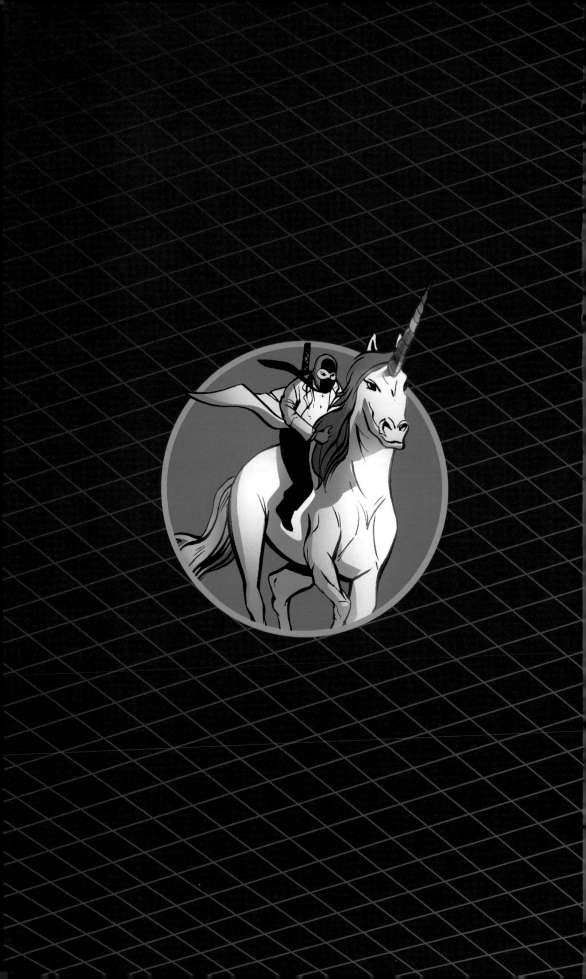

BORN TO A FAMILY OF NINJA.

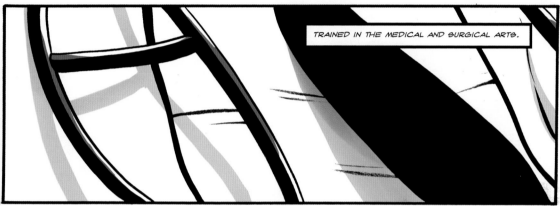

TRAINED IN THE MEDICAL AND SURGICAL ARTS.

HE KILLS WITH ONE HAND AND HEALS WITH THE OTHER.

THESE ARE...

Remember that discussion on whether the comic should be digitally shaded or in pure black and white? I thought of a third option. . .

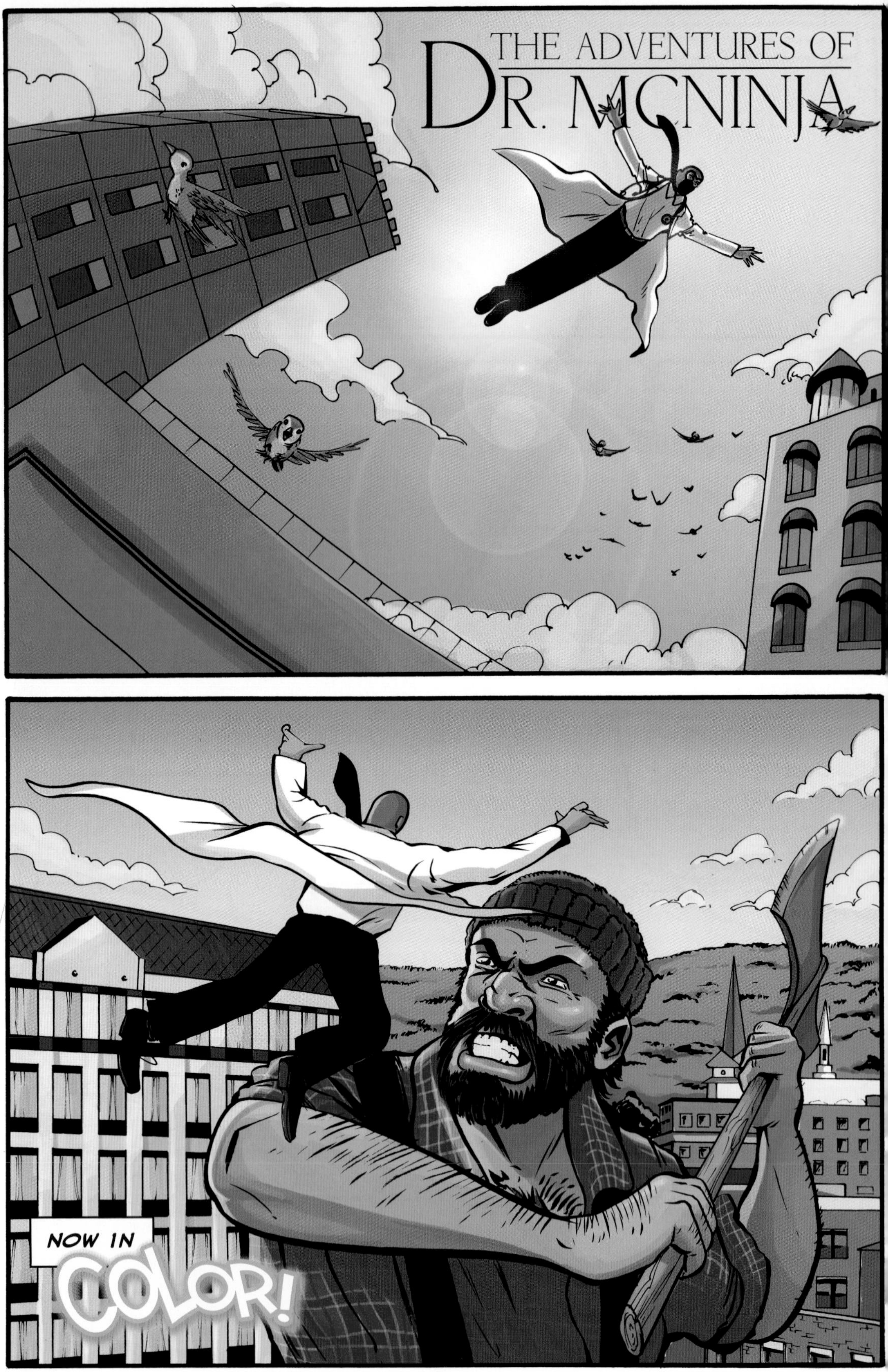

THE ADVENTURES OF
DR. MCNINJA
NOW IN
COLOR!

Dr. McNinja in color: Showing you where lens flare is appropriate since 2008.

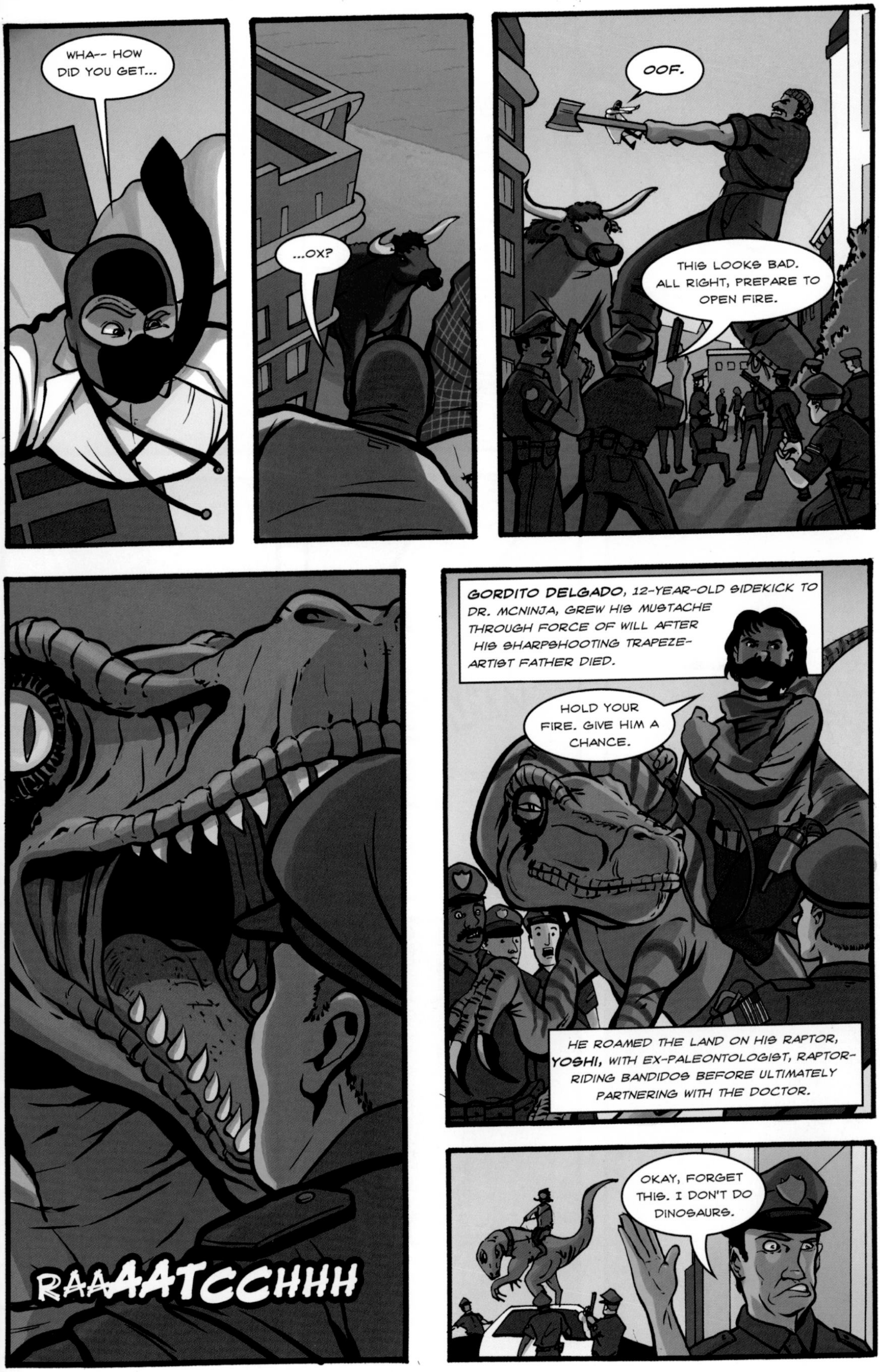
WHA-- HOW DID YOU GET...
...OX?
OOF.
THIS LOOKS BAD. ALL RIGHT, PREPARE TO OPEN FIRE.
RAAAATCCHHH
GORDITO DELGADO, 12-YEAR-OLD SIDEKICK TO DR. MCNINJA, GREW HIS MUSTACHE THROUGH FORCE OF WILL AFTER HIS SHARPSHOOTING TRAPEZE-ARTIST FATHER DIED.
HOLD YOUR FIRE. GIVE HIM A CHANCE.
HE ROAMED THE LAND ON HIS RAPTOR, YOSHI, WITH EX-PALEONTOLOGIST, RAPTOR-RIDING BANDIDOS BEFORE ULTIMATELY PARTNERING WITH THE DOCTOR.
OKAY, FORGET THIS. I DON'T DO DINOSAURS.

Ninjas, zombies, giant lumberjacks, SURE. I signed up for that! But I draw the line at dinosaurs.

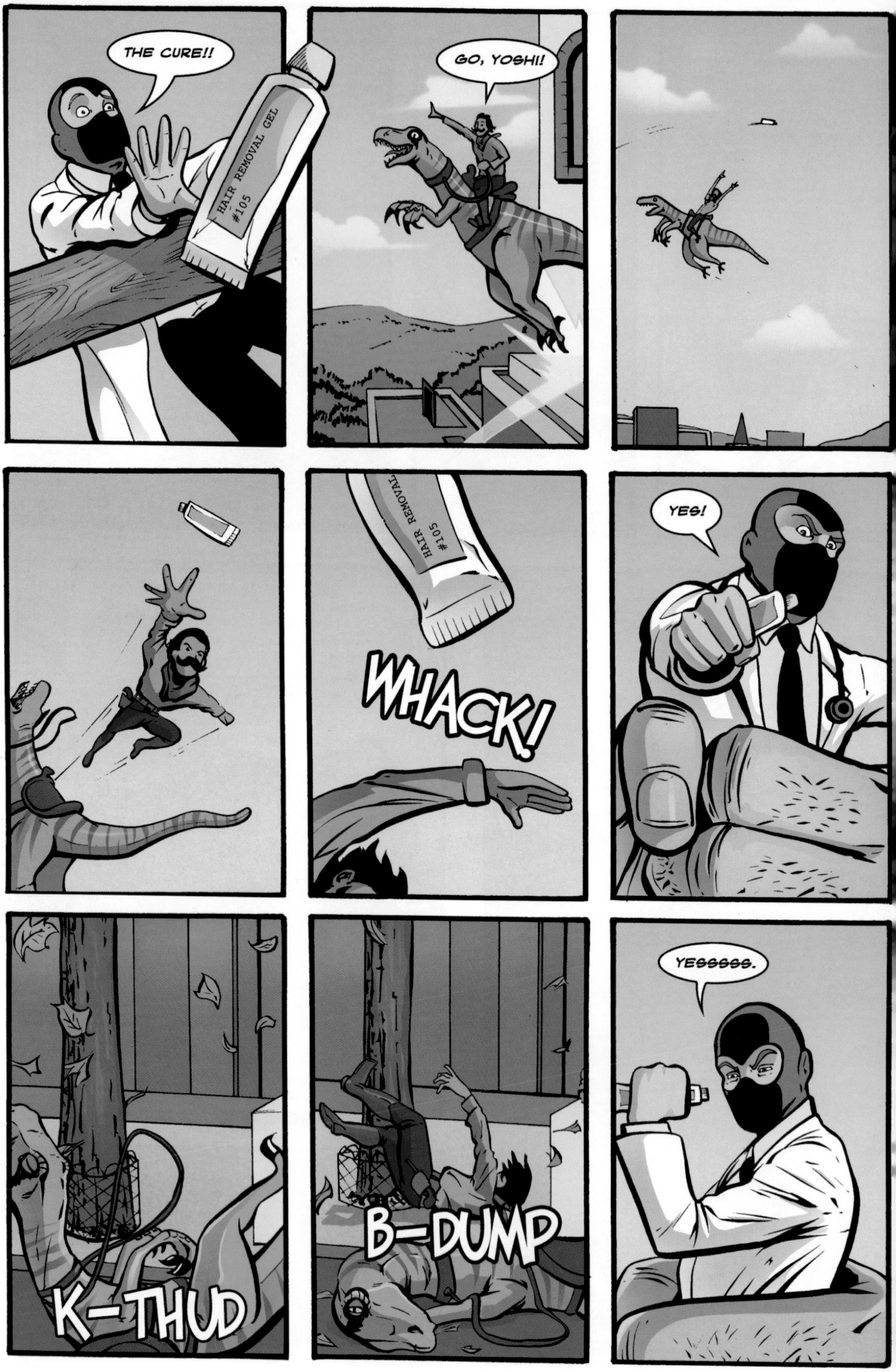
THE CURE!!
HAIR REMOVAL GEL
#105
GO, YOSHI!
HAIR REMOVAL
#105
WHACK!
YES!
K-THUD
B-DUMP
YESSSSS.

A classic maneuver.

LET'S SEE HOW BRAWNY YOU ARE WITHOUT THAT BEARD!
RRAAAGGHH!!!
MY BABY!
AND SHE'LL NEVER HAVE TO WORRY ABOUT FACIAL HAIR EVER AGAIN. THE CREAM IS PERMAN--
I SEE, YOU DON'T CARE ABOUT A WORD I'M SAYING. NO, WHY SHOULD YOU. I'M JUST THE DOCTOR.
OH, HONEY. I WAS SO SCARED FOR YOU.
YAP YAP YAP.

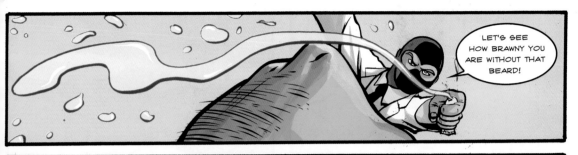

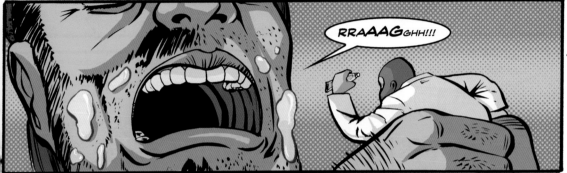

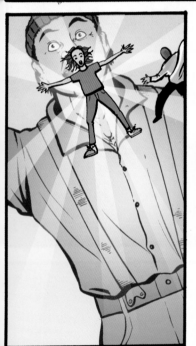

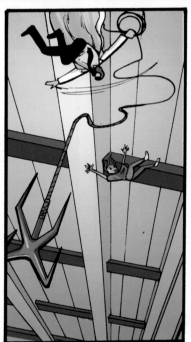

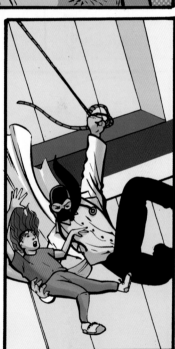

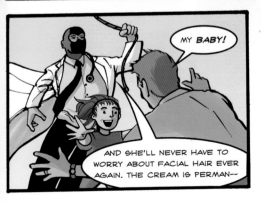

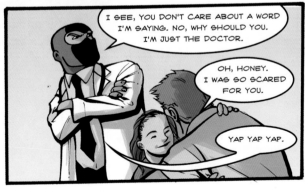

He's mad the concerned father doesn't care that his daughter will never have to wax her upper lip. And you know what, he's RIGHT.

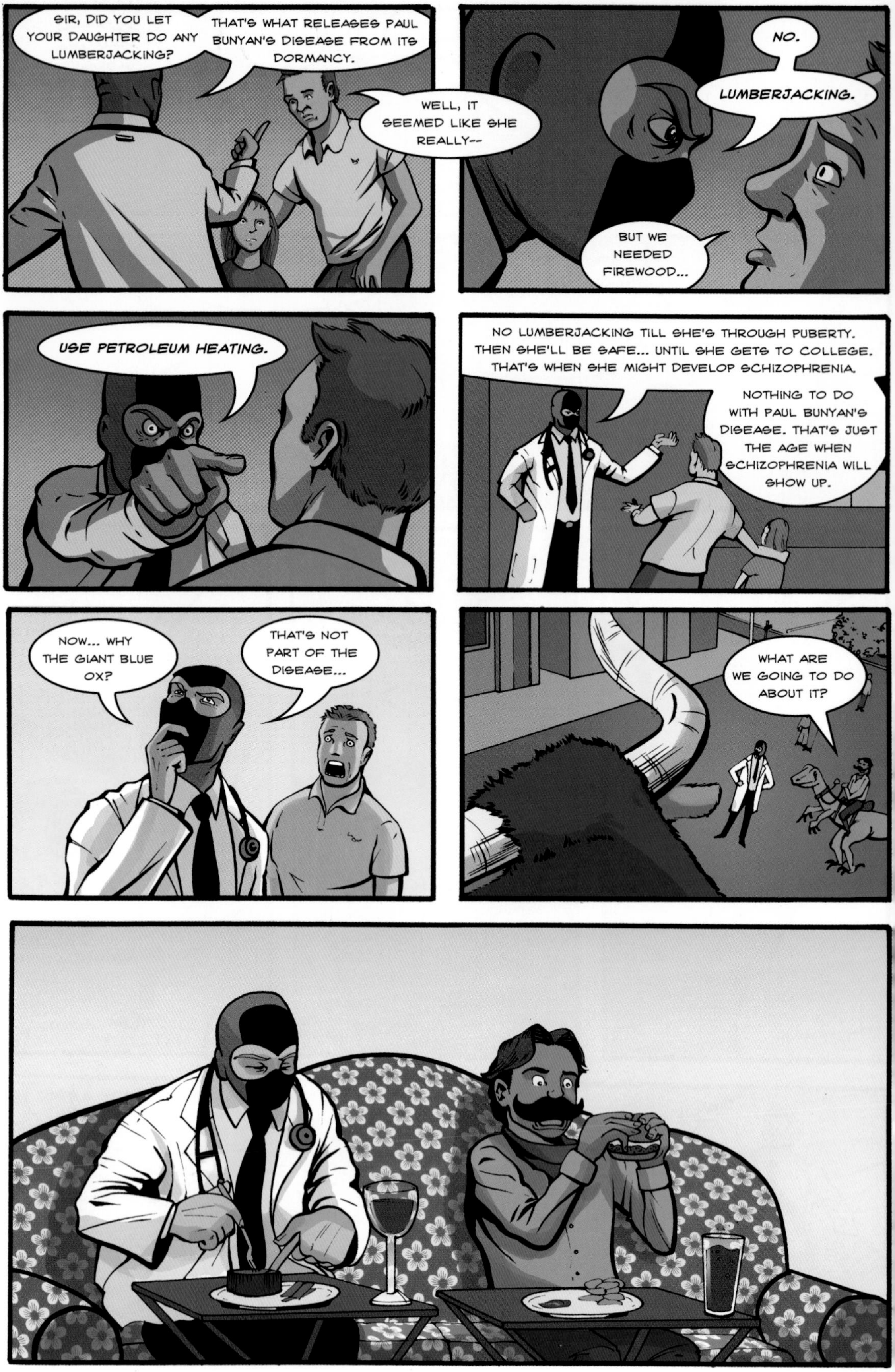
SIR, DID YOU LET YOUR DAUGHTER DO ANY LUMBERJACKING?
THAT'S WHAT RELEASES PAUL BUNYAN'S DISEASE FROM ITS DORMANCY.
WELL, IT SEEMED LIKE SHE REALLY--
NO.
LUMBERJACKING.
BUT WE NEEDED FIREWOOD...
USE PETROLEUM HEATING.
NO LUMBERJACKING TILL SHE'S THROUGH PUBERTY. THEN SHE'LL BE SAFE... UNTIL SHE GETS TO COLLEGE. THAT'S WHEN SHE MIGHT DEVELOP SCHIZOPHRENIA.
NOTHING TO DO WITH PAUL BUNYAN'S DISEASE. THAT'S JUST THE AGE WHEN SCHIZOPHRENIA WILL SHOW UP.
NOW... WHY THE GIANT BLUE OX?
THAT'S NOT PART OF THE DISEASE...
WHAT ARE WE GOING TO DO ABOUT IT?

We're going to sell it to the circus, and then dye our dinner blue.

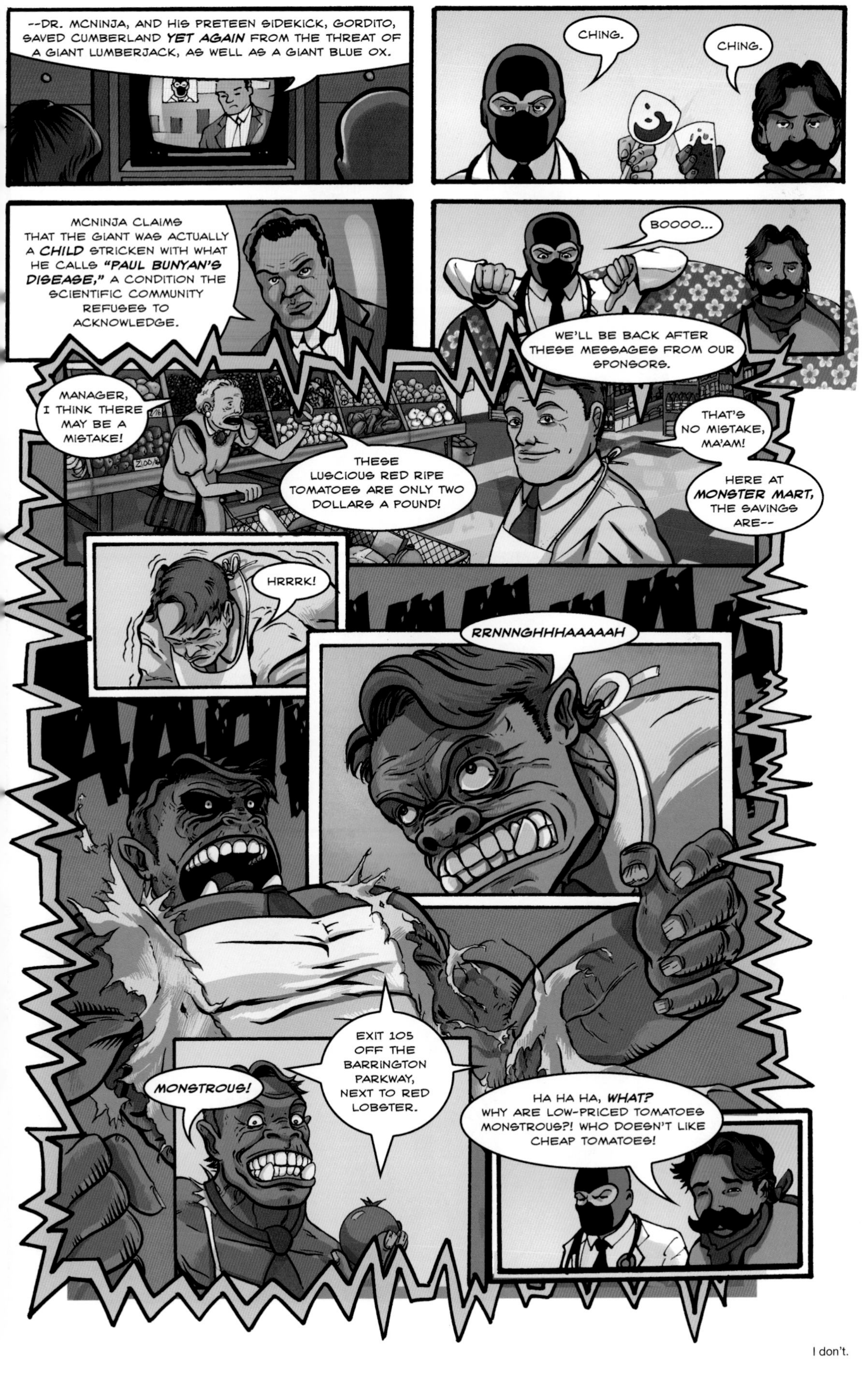
--DR. MCNINJA, AND HIS PRETEEN SIDEKICK, GORDITO, SAVED CUMBERLAND YET AGAIN FROM THE THREAT OF A GIANT LUMBERJACK, AS WELL AS A GIANT BLUE OX.
CHING.
CHING.
MCNINJA CLAIMS THAT THE GIANT WAS ACTUALLY A CHILD STRICKEN WITH WHAT HE CALLS "PAUL BUNYAN'S DISEASE," A CONDITION THE SCIENTIFIC COMMUNITY REFUSES TO ACKNOWLEDGE.
BOOOO...
WE'LL BE BACK AFTER THESE MESSAGES FROM OUR SPONSORS.
MANAGER, I THINK THERE MAY BE A MISTAKE!
THESE LUSCIOUS RED RIPE TOMATOES ARE ONLY TWO DOLLARS A POUND!
THAT'S NO MISTAKE, MA'AM!
HERE AT MONSTER MART, THE SAVINGS ARE--
HRRRK!
RRNNNGHHHAAAAAH
MONSTROUS!
EXIT 105 OFF THE BARRINGTON PARKWAY, NEXT TO RED LOBSTER.
HA HA HA, WHAT? WHY ARE LOW-PRICED TOMATOES MONSTROUS?! WHO DOESN'T LIKE CHEAP TOMATOES!

I don't.

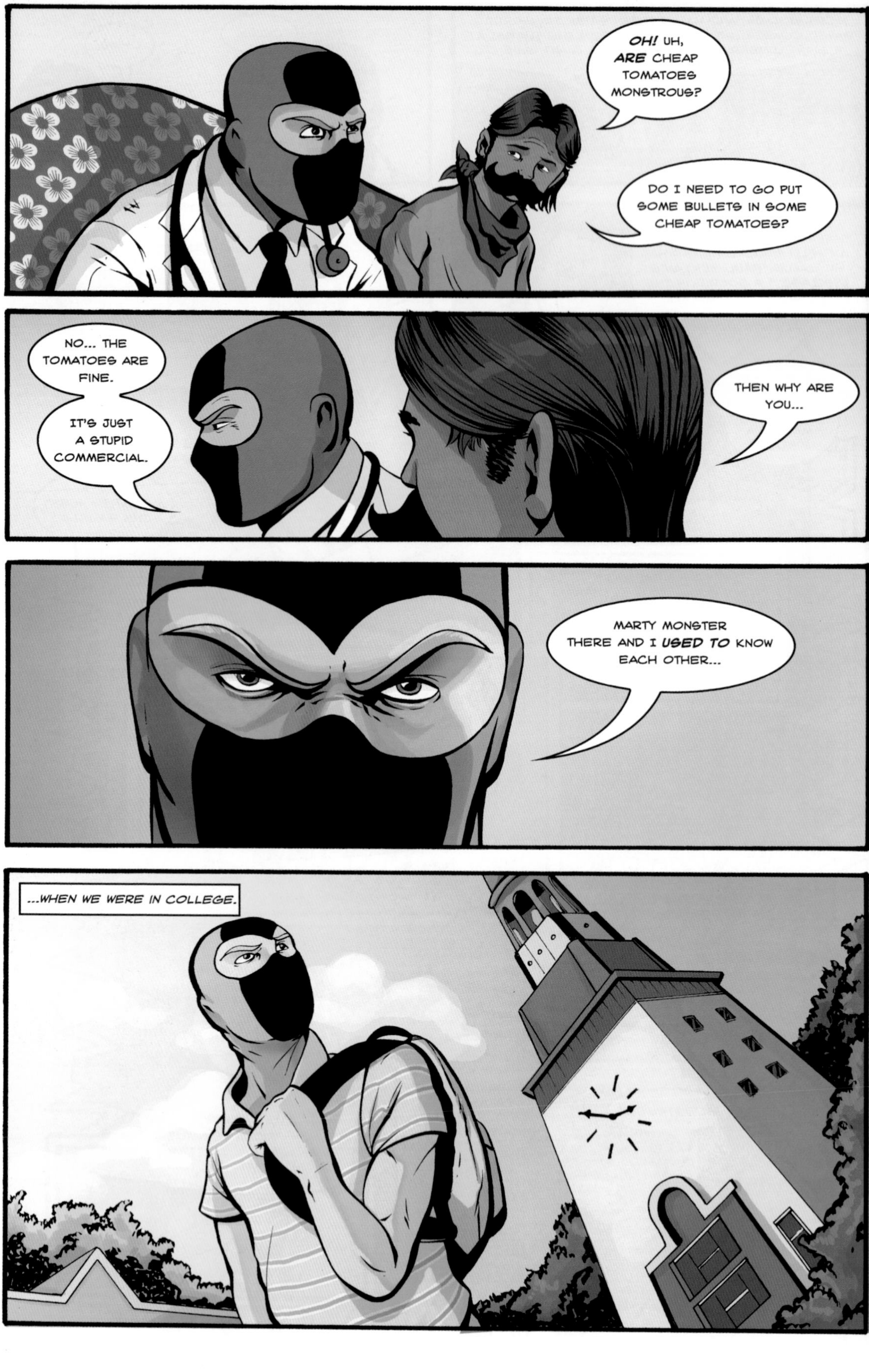
OH! UH, ARE CHEAP TOMATOES MONSTROUS?
DO I NEED TO GO PUT SOME BULLETS IN SOME CHEAP TOMATOES?
NO... THE TOMATOES ARE FINE.
IT'S JUST A STUPID COMMERCIAL.
THEN WHY ARE YOU...
MARTY MONSTER THERE AND I USED TO KNOW EACH OTHER...
...WHEN WE WERE IN COLLEGE.

I wore bright colors because I was a young, cocky ninja. And because it was 1989.

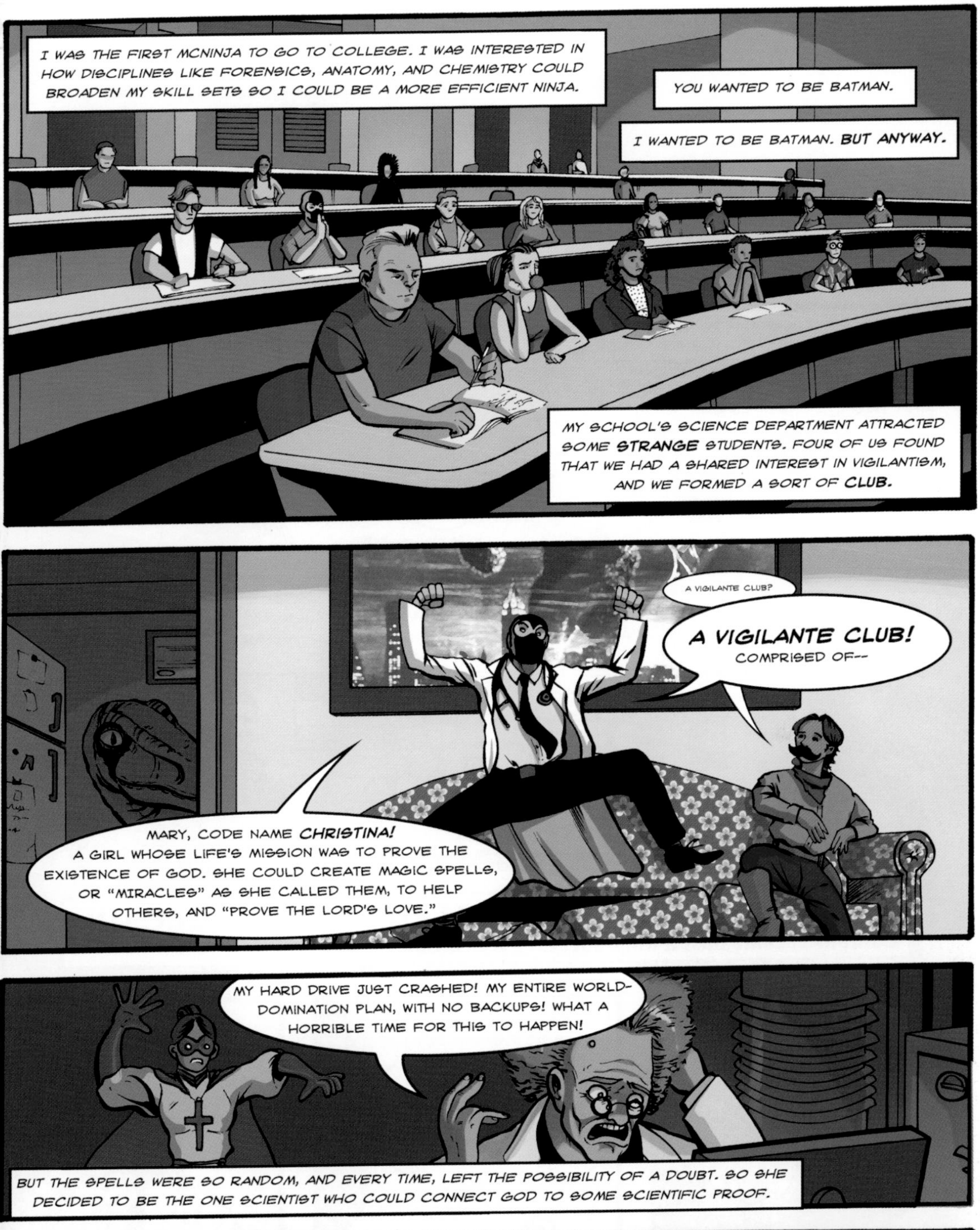
I WAS THE FIRST MCNINJA TO GO TO COLLEGE. I WAS INTERESTED IN HOW DISCIPLINES LIKE FORENSICS, ANATOMY, AND CHEMISTRY COULD BROADEN MY SKILL SETS SO I COULD BE A MORE EFFICIENT NINJA.
YOU WANTED TO BE BATMAN.
I WANTED TO BE BATMAN. BUT ANYWAY.
MY SCHOOL'S SCIENCE DEPARTMENT ATTRACTED SOME STRANGE STUDENTS. FOUR OF US FOUND THAT WE HAD A SHARED INTEREST IN VIGILANTISM, AND WE FORMED A SORT OF CLUB.
A VIGILANTE CLUB?
A VIGILANTE CLUB! COMPRISED OF--
MARY, CODE NAME CHRISTINA! A GIRL WHOSE LIFE'S MISSION WAS TO PROVE THE EXISTENCE OF GOD. SHE COULD CREATE MAGIC SPELLS, OR "MIRACLES" AS SHE CALLED THEM, TO HELP OTHERS, AND "PROVE THE LORD'S LOVE."
MY HARD DRIVE JUST CRASHED! MY ENTIRE WORLD-DOMINATION PLAN, WITH NO BACKUPS! WHAT A HORRIBLE TIME FOR THIS TO HAPPEN!
BUT THE SPELLS WERE SO RANDOM, AND EVERY TIME, LEFT THE POSSIBILITY OF A DOUBT. SO SHE DECIDED TO BE THE ONE SCIENTIST WHO COULD CONNECT GOD TO SOME SCIENTIFIC PROOF.
JAMES! THE LEADER OF OUR GROUP.
HE INVENTED JET BOOTS, AND HE USED THEM TO KICK PEOPLE.
HA!
UAAAGHH!

Judy HATES that poster.

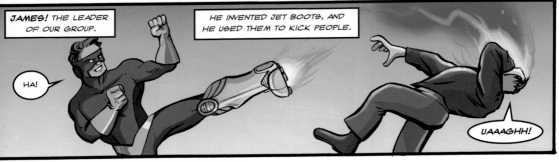

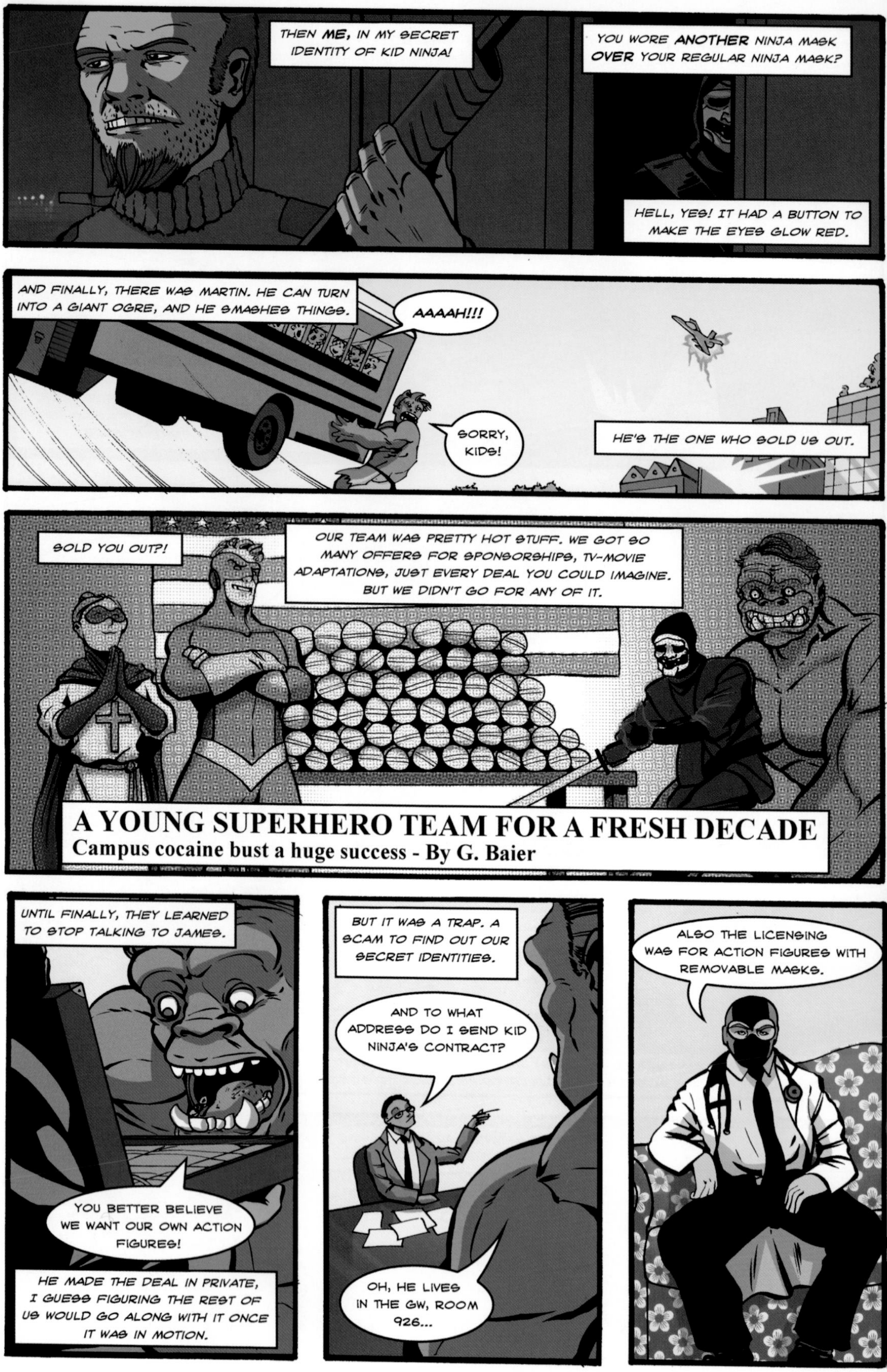
THEN ME, IN MY SECRET IDENTITY OF KID NINJA!
YOU WORE ANOTHER NINJA MASK OVER YOUR REGULAR NINJA MASK?
HELL, YES! IT HAD A BUTTON TO MAKE THE EYES GLOW RED.
AND FINALLY, THERE WAS MARTIN. HE CAN TURN INTO A GIANT OGRE, AND HE SMASHES THINGS.
AAAAH!!!
SORRY, KIDS!
HE'S THE ONE WHO SOLD US OUT.
SOLD YOU OUT?!
OUR TEAM WAS PRETTY HOT STUFF. WE GOT SO MANY OFFERS FOR SPONSORSHIPS, TV-MOVIE ADAPTATIONS, JUST EVERY DEAL YOU COULD IMAGINE. BUT WE DIDN'T GO FOR ANY OF IT.
A YOUNG SUPERHERO TEAM FOR A FRESH DECADE
Campus cocaine bust a huge success - By G. Baier
UNTIL FINALLY, THEY LEARNED TO STOP TALKING TO JAMES.
YOU BETTER BELIEVE WE WANT OUR OWN ACTION FIGURES!
HE MADE THE DEAL IN PRIVATE, I GUESS FIGURING THE REST OF US WOULD GO ALONG WITH IT ONCE IT WAS IN MOTION.
BUT IT WAS A TRAP. A SCAM TO FIND OUT OUR SECRET IDENTITIES.
AND TO WHAT ADDRESS DO I SEND KID NINJA'S CONTRACT?
OH, HE LIVES IN THE GW, ROOM 926...
ALSO THE LICENSING WAS FOR ACTION FIGURES WITH REMOVABLE MASKS.

To whomever reads this and is astounded because THEY live in the GW, room 926 . . . Open your door, and look in the hole in the door frame. There is a secret there.

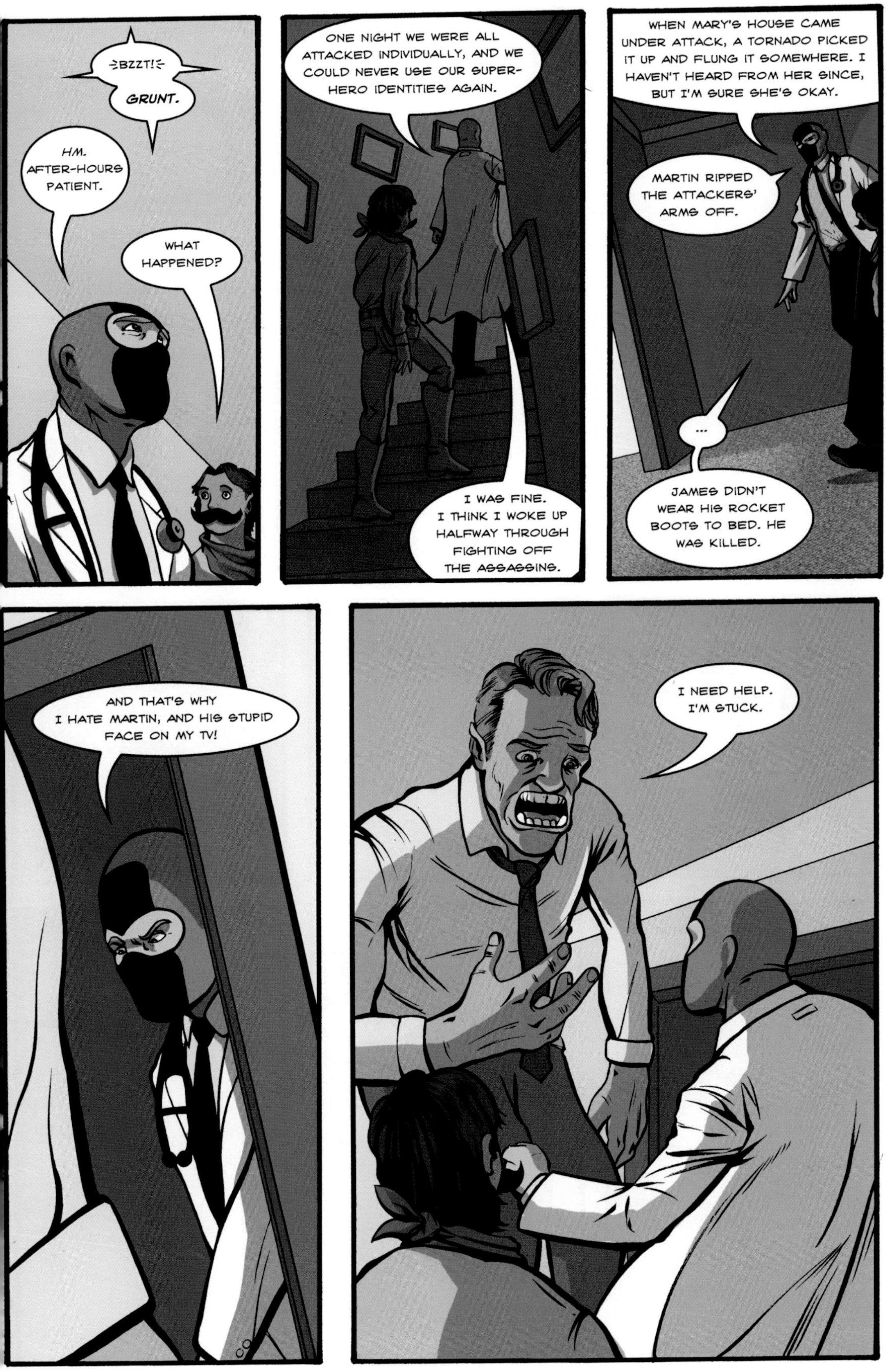
⋦BZZT!⋧
GRUNT.
HM. AFTER-HOURS PATIENT.
WHAT HAPPENED?
ONE NIGHT WE WERE ALL ATTACKED INDIVIDUALLY, AND WE COULD NEVER USE OUR SUPER-HERO IDENTITIES AGAIN.
I WAS FINE. I THINK I WOKE UP HALFWAY THROUGH FIGHTING OFF THE ASSASSINS.
WHEN MARY'S HOUSE CAME UNDER ATTACK, A TORNADO PICKED IT UP AND FLUNG IT SOMEWHERE. I HAVEN'T HEARD FROM HER SINCE, BUT I'M SURE SHE'S OKAY.
MARTIN RIPPED THE ATTACKERS' ARMS OFF.
...
JAMES DIDN'T WEAR HIS ROCKET BOOTS TO BED. HE WAS KILLED.
AND THAT'S WHY I HATE MARTIN, AND HIS STUPID FACE ON MY TV!
I NEED HELP. I'M STUCK.

Always wear your rocket boots to bed.

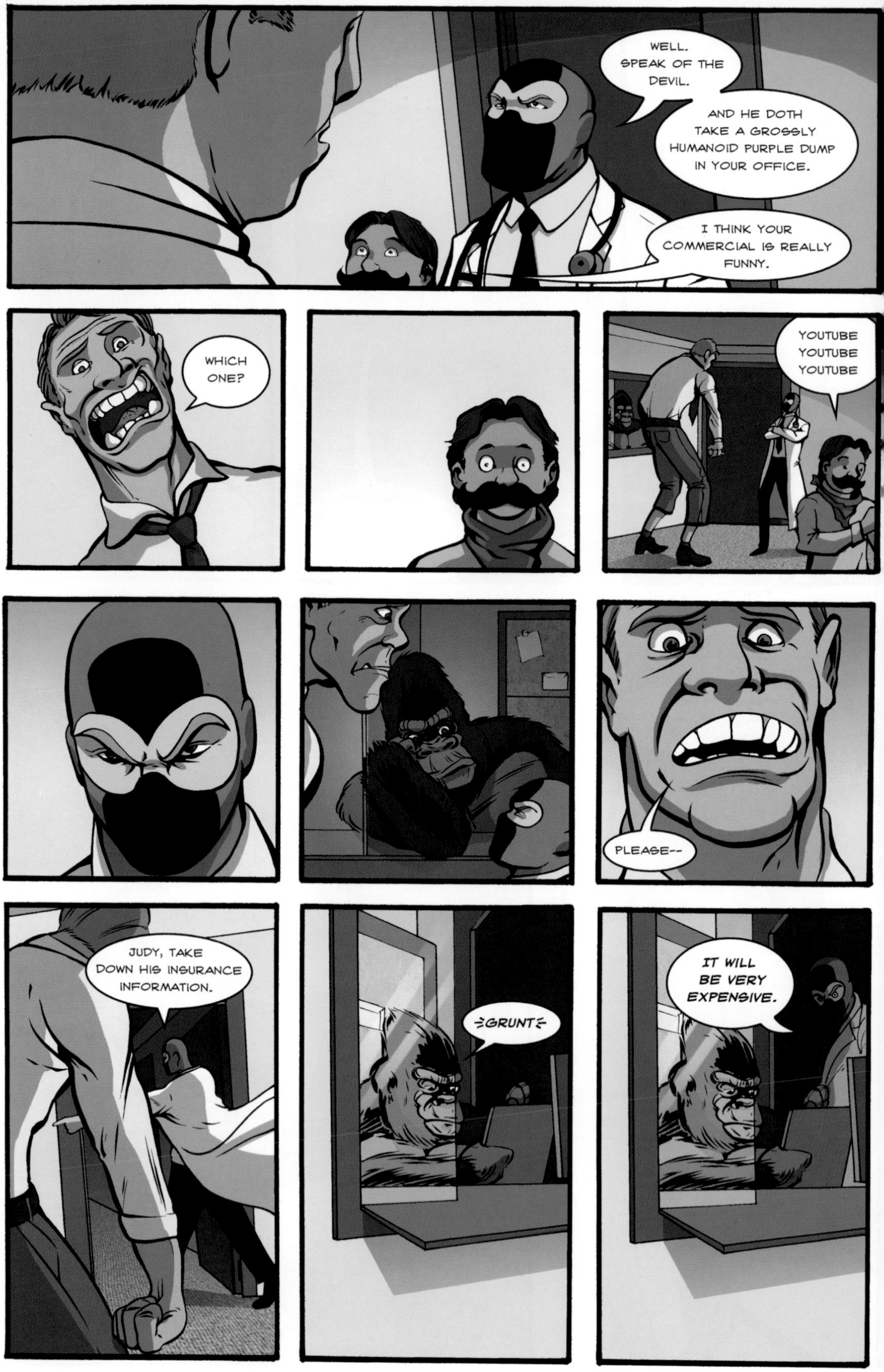
WELL. SPEAK OF THE DEVIL.
AND HE DOTH TAKE A GROSSLY HUMANOID PURPLE DUMP IN YOUR OFFICE.
I THINK YOUR COMMERCIAL IS REALLY FUNNY.
WHICH ONE?
YOUTUBE YOUTUBE YOUTUBE
PLEASE--
JUDY, TAKE DOWN HIS INSURANCE INFORMATION.
GRUNT
IT WILL BE VERY EXPENSIVE.

Gordito got so excited, he ran in a straight line to his laptop. But there are a few walls in the way, so he got knocked down before he remembered about doors and hallways.

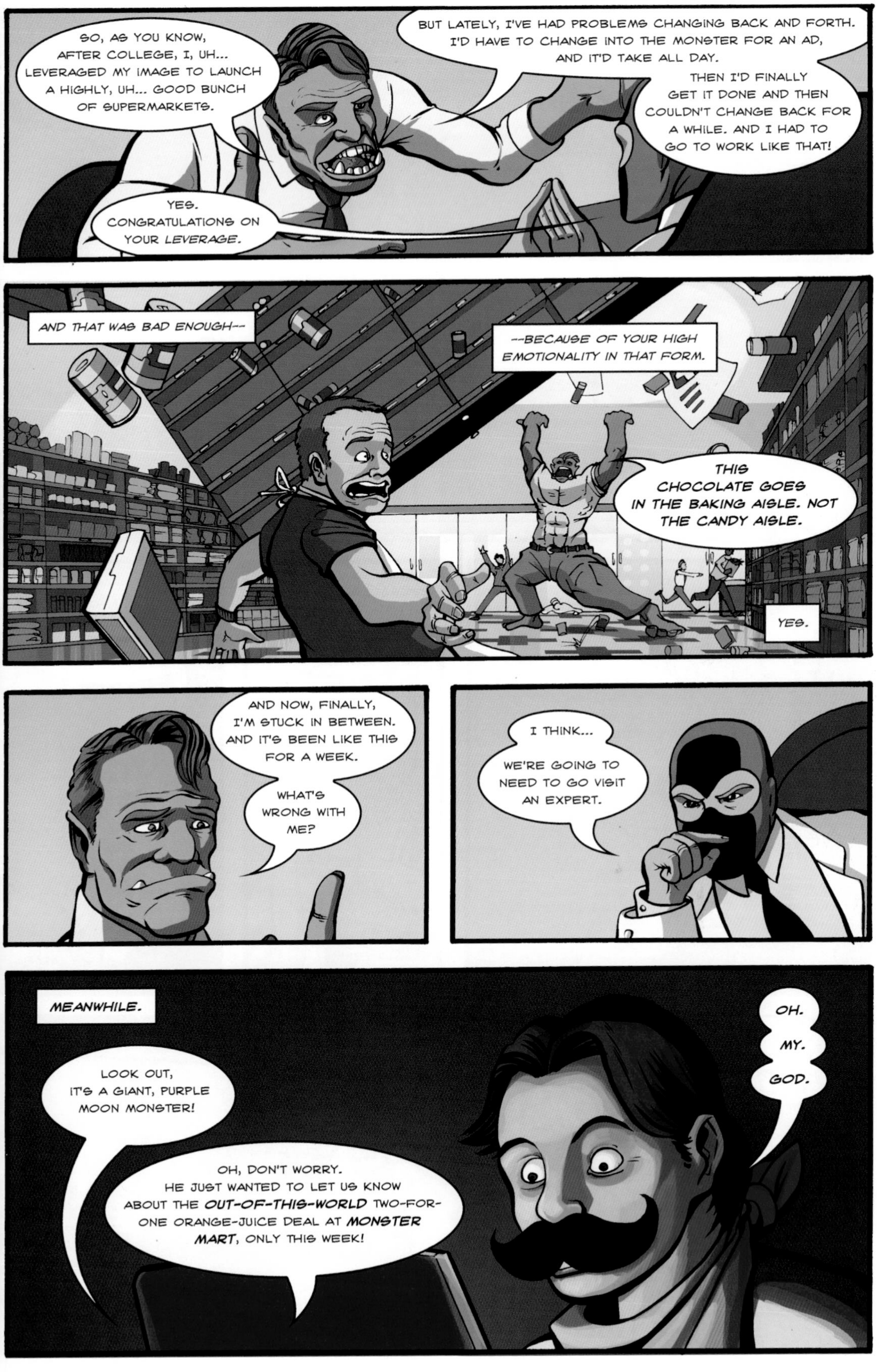
SO, AS YOU KNOW, AFTER COLLEGE, I, UH... LEVERAGED MY IMAGE TO LAUNCH A HIGHLY, UH... GOOD BUNCH OF SUPERMARKETS.
BUT LATELY, I'VE HAD PROBLEMS CHANGING BACK AND FORTH. I'D HAVE TO CHANGE INTO THE MONSTER FOR AN AD, AND IT'D TAKE ALL DAY.
THEN I'D FINALLY GET IT DONE AND THEN COULDN'T CHANGE BACK FOR A WHILE. AND I HAD TO GO TO WORK LIKE THAT!
YES. CONGRATULATIONS ON YOUR LEVERAGE.
AND THAT WAS BAD ENOUGH--
--BECAUSE OF YOUR HIGH EMOTIONALITY IN THAT FORM.
THIS CHOCOLATE GOES IN THE BAKING AISLE. NOT THE CANDY AISLE.
YES.
AND NOW, FINALLY, I'M STUCK IN BETWEEN. AND IT'S BEEN LIKE THIS FOR A WEEK.
WHAT'S WRONG WITH ME?
I THINK...
WE'RE GOING TO NEED TO GO VISIT AN EXPERT.
MEANWHILE.
LOOK OUT, IT'S A GIANT, PURPLE MOON MONSTER!
OH, DON'T WORRY. HE JUST WANTED TO LET US KNOW ABOUT THE OUT-OF-THIS-WORLD TWO-FOR-ONE ORANGE-JUICE DEAL AT MONSTER MART, ONLY THIS WEEK!
OH.
MY.
GOD.

Yes, that is the same supermarket where Ben Franklin first encountered the spooky horse.

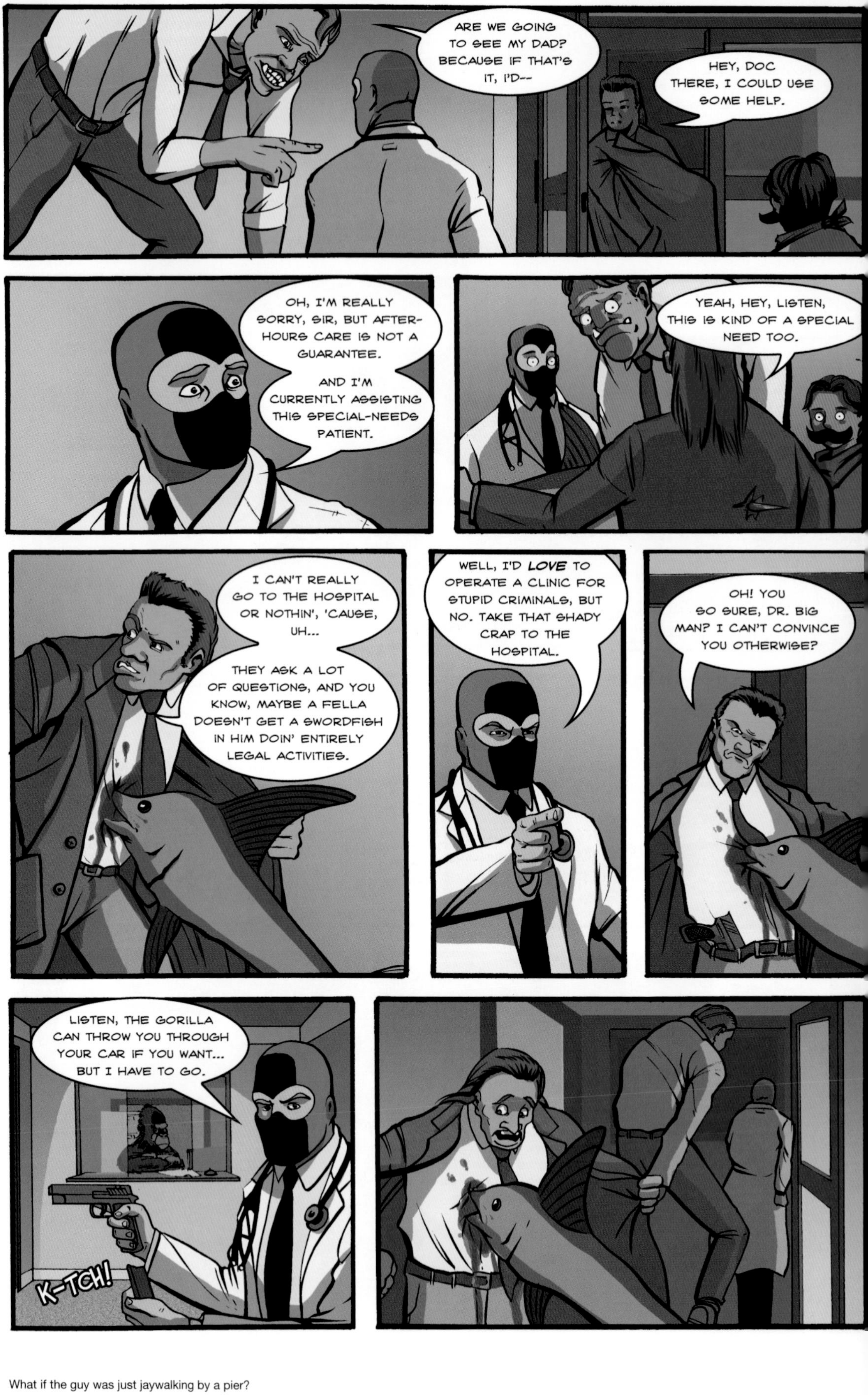

ARE WE GOING TO SEE MY DAD? BECAUSE IF THAT'S IT, I'D--
HEY, DOC THERE, I COULD USE SOME HELP.
OH, I'M REALLY SORRY, SIR, BUT AFTER-HOURS CARE IS NOT A GUARANTEE.
AND I'M CURRENTLY ASSISTING THIS SPECIAL-NEEDS PATIENT.
YEAH, HEY, LISTEN, THIS IS KIND OF A SPECIAL NEED TOO.
I CAN'T REALLY GO TO THE HOSPITAL OR NOTHIN', 'CAUSE, UH...
THEY ASK A LOT OF QUESTIONS, AND YOU KNOW, MAYBE A FELLA DOESN'T GET A SWORDFISH IN HIM DOIN' ENTIRELY LEGAL ACTIVITIES.
WELL, I'D LOVE TO OPERATE A CLINIC FOR STUPID CRIMINALS, BUT NO. TAKE THAT SHADY CRAP TO THE HOSPITAL.
OH! YOU SO SURE, DR. BIG MAN? I CAN'T CONVINCE YOU OTHERWISE?
LISTEN, THE GORILLA CAN THROW YOU THROUGH YOUR CAR IF YOU WANT... BUT I HAVE TO GO.
K-TCH!

What if the guy was just jaywalking by a pier?

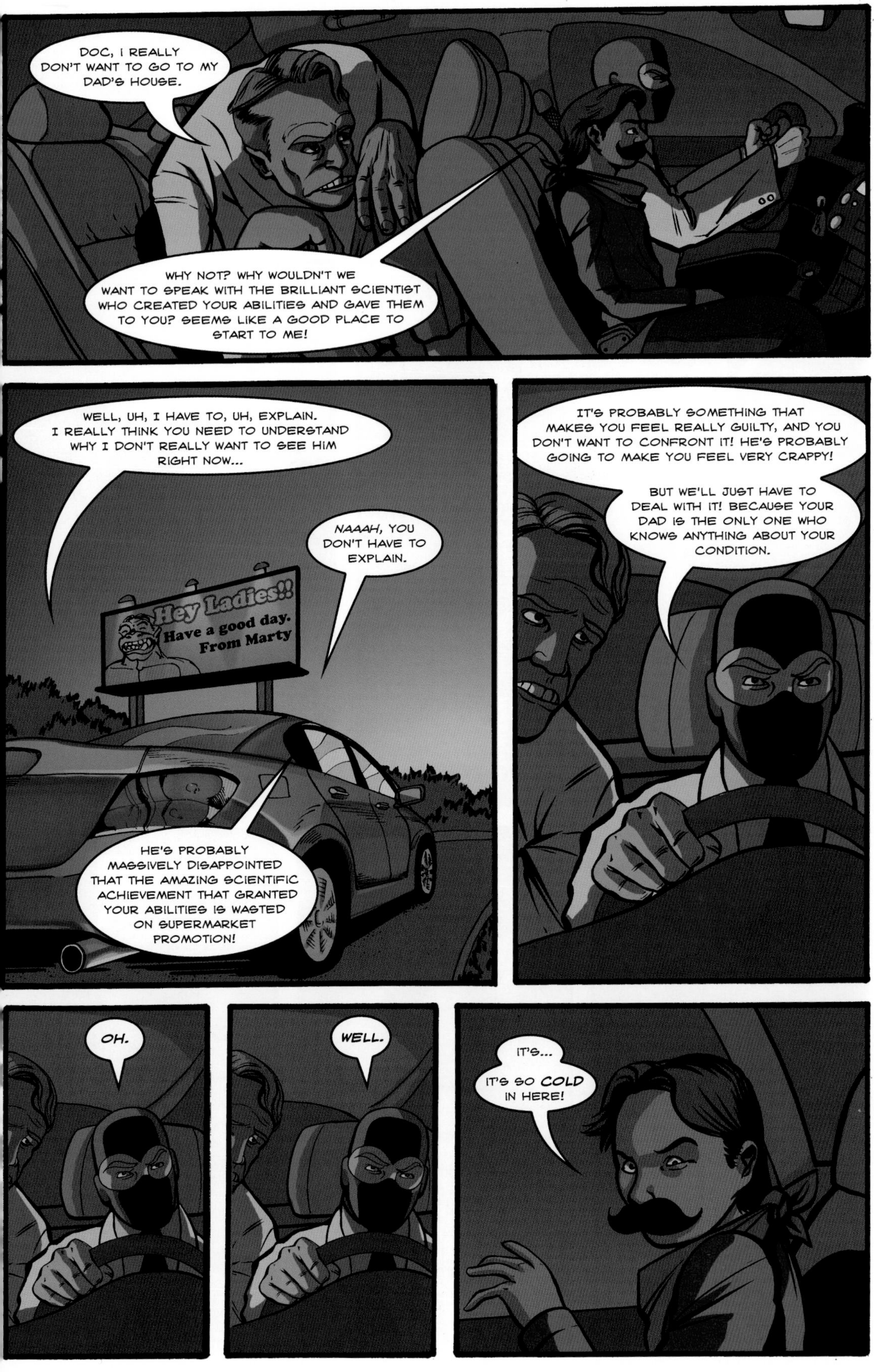
DOC, I REALLY DON'T WANT TO GO TO MY DAD'S HOUSE.
WHY NOT? WHY WOULDN'T WE WANT TO SPEAK WITH THE BRILLIANT SCIENTIST WHO CREATED YOUR ABILITIES AND GAVE THEM TO YOU? SEEMS LIKE A GOOD PLACE TO START TO ME!
WELL, UH, I HAVE TO, UH, EXPLAIN. I REALLY THINK YOU NEED TO UNDERSTAND WHY I DON'T REALLY WANT TO SEE HIM RIGHT NOW...
NAAAH, YOU DON'T HAVE TO EXPLAIN.
Hey Ladies!! Have a good day. From Marty
HE'S PROBABLY MASSIVELY DISAPPOINTED THAT THE AMAZING SCIENTIFIC ACHIEVEMENT THAT GRANTED YOUR ABILITIES IS WASTED ON SUPERMARKET PROMOTION!
IT'S PROBABLY SOMETHING THAT MAKES YOU FEEL REALLY GUILTY, AND YOU DON'T WANT TO CONFRONT IT! HE'S PROBABLY GOING TO MAKE YOU FEEL VERY CRAPPY!
BUT WE'LL JUST HAVE TO DEAL WITH IT! BECAUSE YOUR DAD IS THE ONLY ONE WHO KNOWS ANYTHING ABOUT YOUR CONDITION.
OH.
WELL.
IT'S...
IT'S SO COLD IN HERE!

Copy-paste art is fun sometimes.

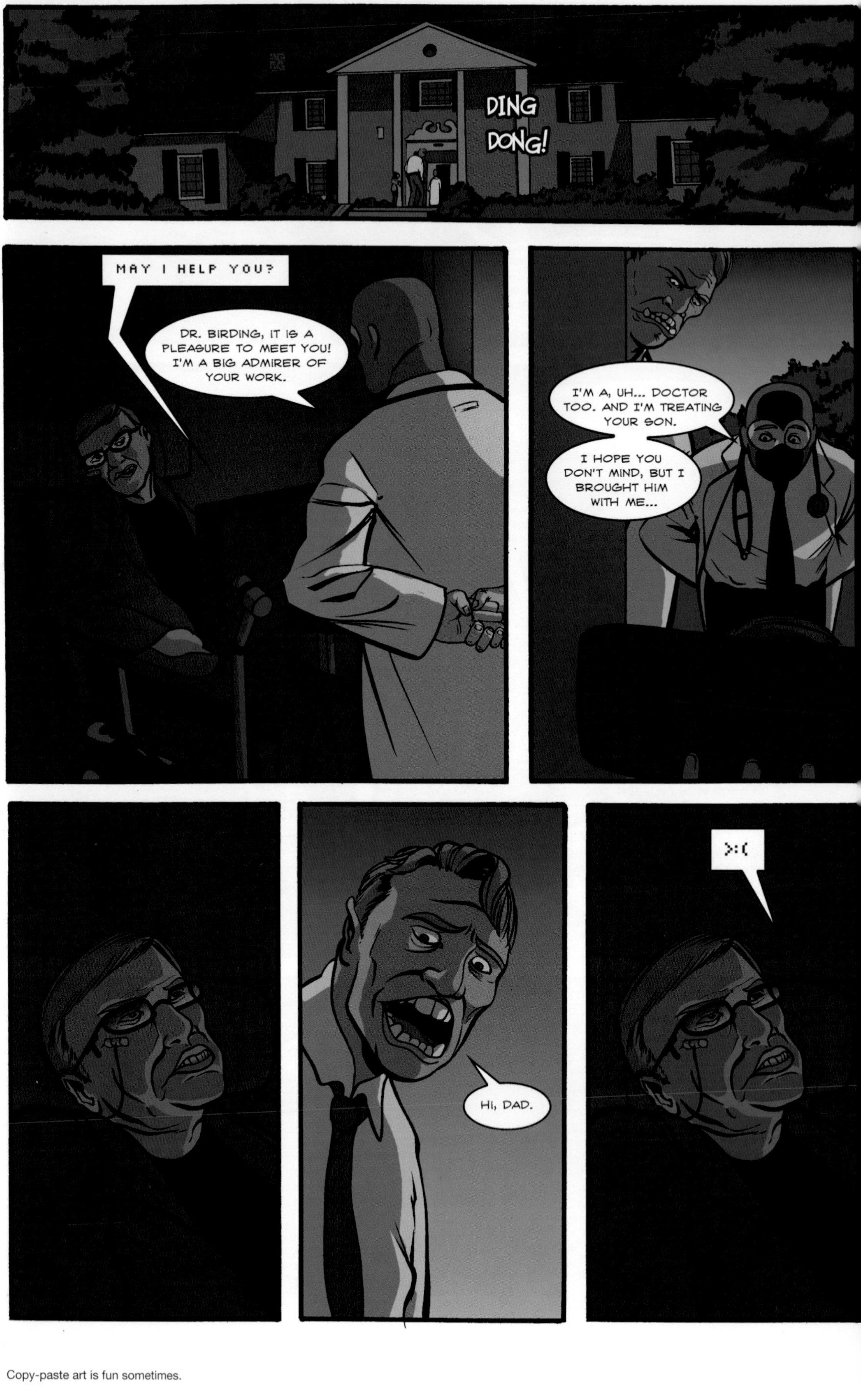
DING
DONG!
MAY I HELP YOU?
DR. BIRDING, IT IS A PLEASURE TO MEET YOU! I'M A BIG ADMIRER OF YOUR WORK.
I'M A, UH... DOCTOR TOO. AND I'M TREATING YOUR SON.
I HOPE YOU DON'T MIND, BUT I BROUGHT HIM WITH ME...
HI, DAD.
>:(

Copy-paste art is fun sometimes.

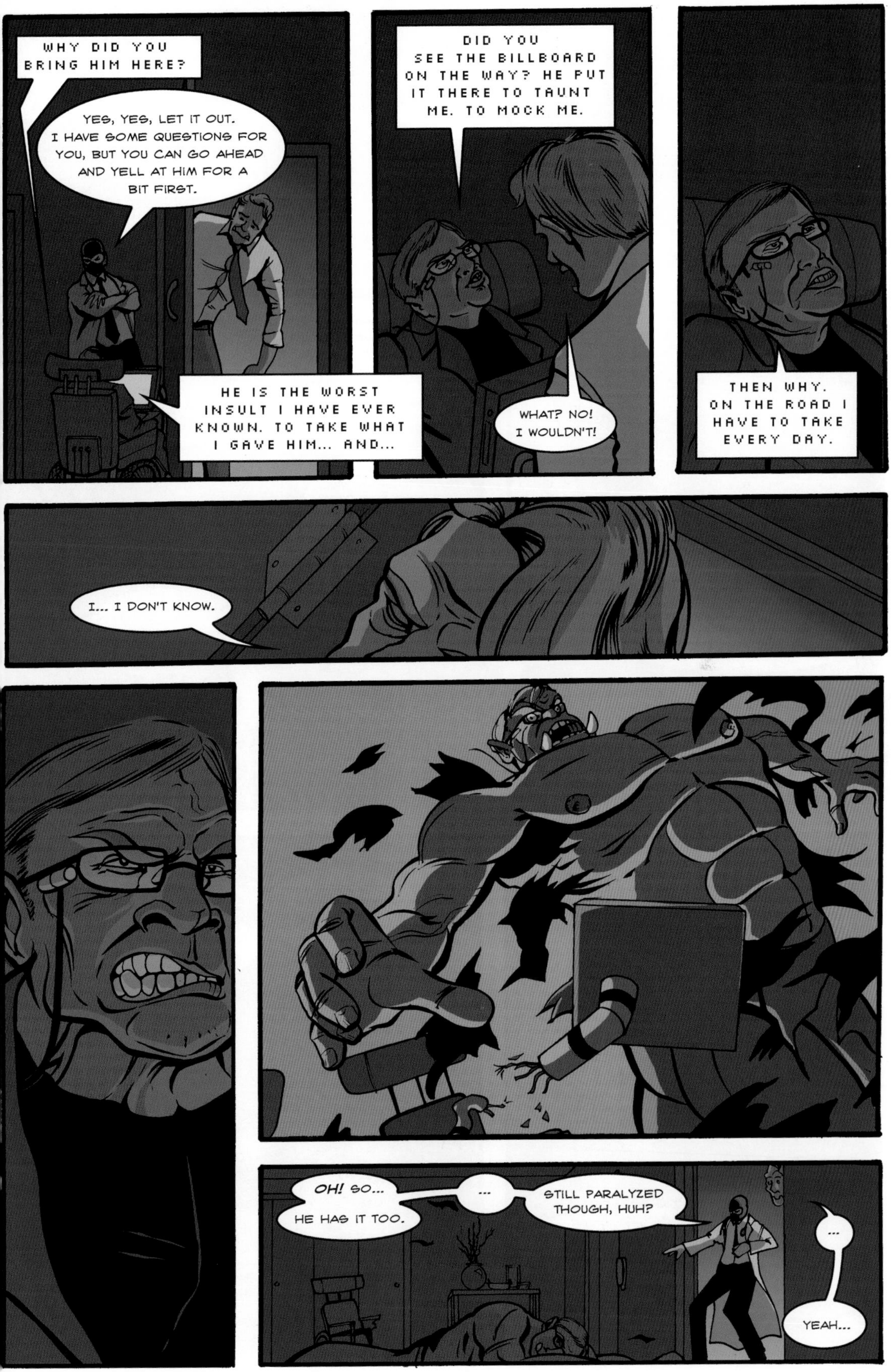
WHY DID YOU BRING HIM HERE?
YES, YES, LET IT OUT. I HAVE SOME QUESTIONS FOR YOU, BUT YOU CAN GO AHEAD AND YELL AT HIM FOR A BIT FIRST.
HE IS THE WORST INSULT I HAVE EVER KNOWN. TO TAKE WHAT I GAVE HIM... AND...
DID YOU SEE THE BILLBOARD ON THE WAY? HE PUT IT THERE TO TAUNT ME. TO MOCK ME.
WHAT? NO! I WOULDN'T!
THEN WHY. ON THE ROAD I HAVE TO TAKE EVERY DAY.
I... I DON'T KNOW.
OH! SO...
HE HAS IT TOO.
...
STILL PARALYZED THOUGH, HUH?
...
YEAH...

My color notes for Carly: "Make sure to give him good purple nurples."

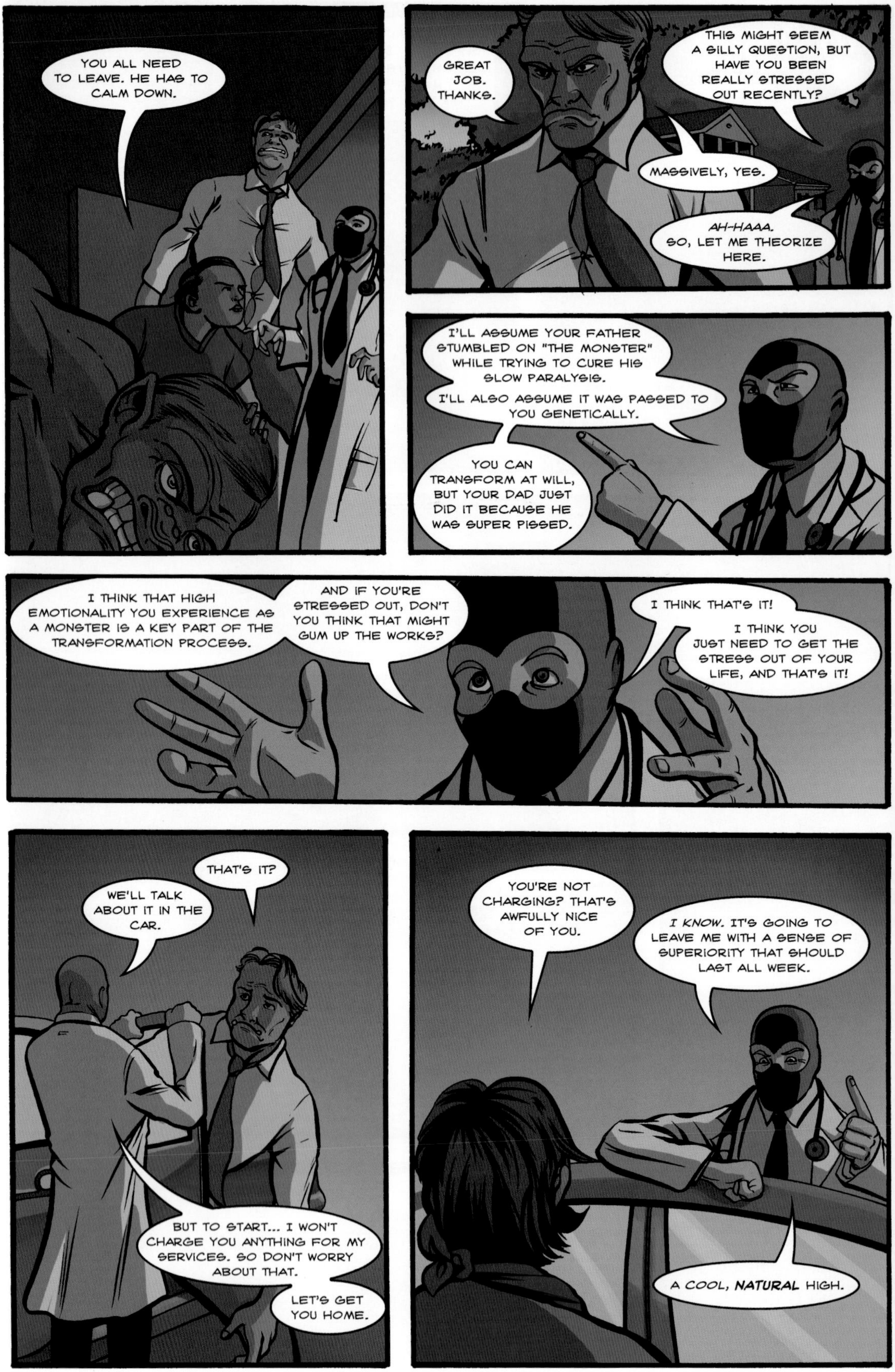
YOU ALL NEED TO LEAVE. HE HAS TO CALM DOWN.
GREAT JOB. THANKS.
THIS MIGHT SEEM A SILLY QUESTION, BUT HAVE YOU BEEN REALLY STRESSED OUT RECENTLY?
MASSIVELY, YES.
AH-HAAA. SO, LET ME THEORIZE HERE.
I'LL ASSUME YOUR FATHER STUMBLED ON "THE MONSTER" WHILE TRYING TO CURE HIS SLOW PARALYSIS.
I'LL ALSO ASSUME IT WAS PASSED TO YOU GENETICALLY.
YOU CAN TRANSFORM AT WILL, BUT YOUR DAD JUST DID IT BECAUSE HE WAS SUPER PISSED.
I THINK THAT HIGH EMOTIONALITY YOU EXPERIENCE AS A MONSTER IS A KEY PART OF THE TRANSFORMATION PROCESS.
AND IF YOU'RE STRESSED OUT, DON'T YOU THINK THAT MIGHT GUM UP THE WORKS?
I THINK THAT'S IT!
I THINK YOU JUST NEED TO GET THE STRESS OUT OF YOUR LIFE, AND THAT'S IT!
WE'LL TALK ABOUT IT IN THE CAR.
THAT'S IT?
BUT TO START... I WON'T CHARGE YOU ANYTHING FOR MY SERVICES. SO DON'T WORRY ABOUT THAT.
LET'S GET YOU HOME.
YOU'RE NOT CHARGING? THAT'S AWFULLY NICE OF YOU.
I KNOW. IT'S GOING TO LEAVE ME WITH A SENSE OF SUPERIORITY THAT SHOULD LAST ALL WEEK.
A COOL, NATURAL HIGH.

Oh, wait, no. I'm thinking of skateboard tricks. Skateboard tricks get you high.

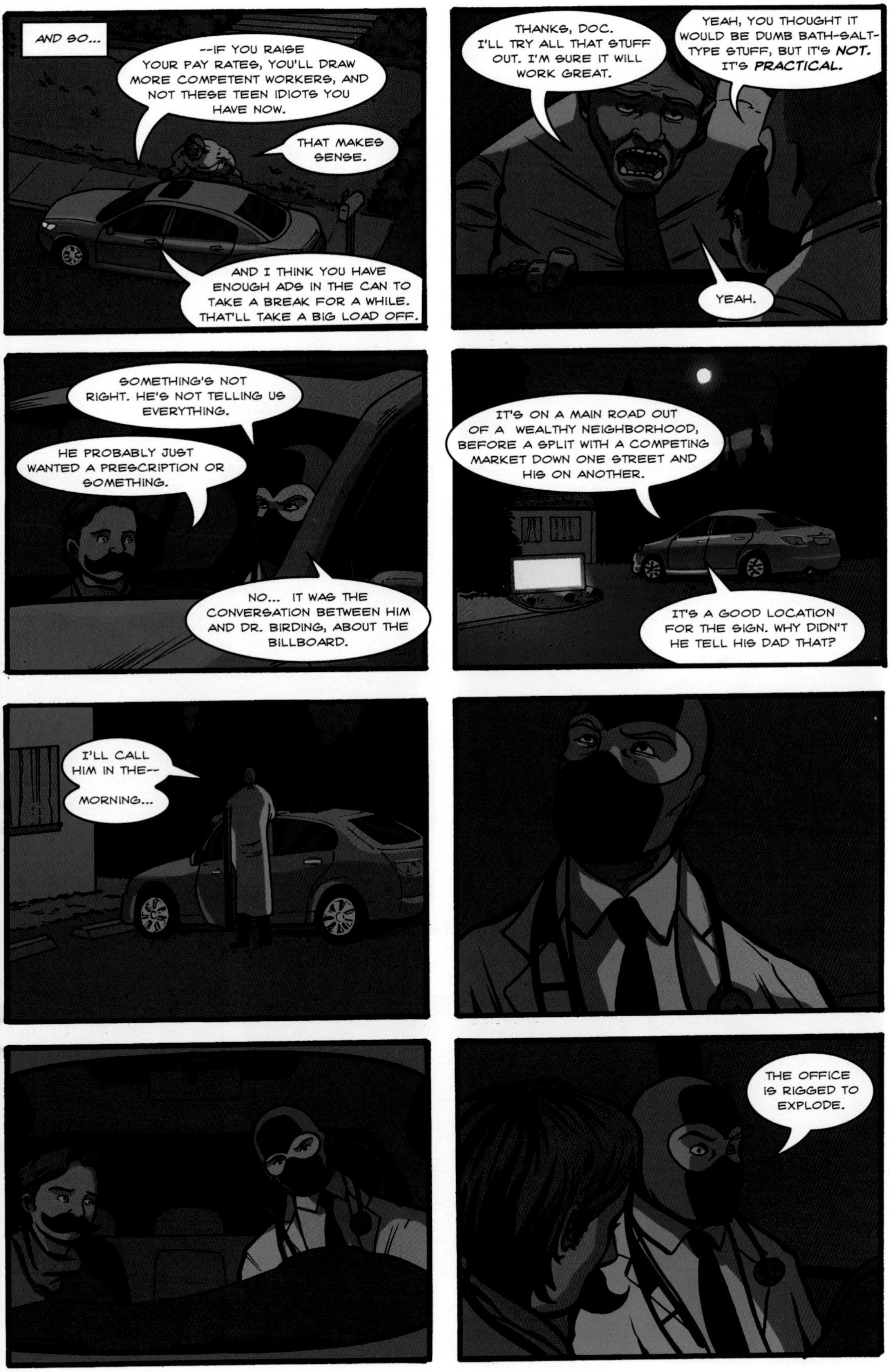
AND SO...
--IF YOU RAISE YOUR PAY RATES, YOU'LL DRAW MORE COMPETENT WORKERS, AND NOT THESE TEEN IDIOTS YOU HAVE NOW.
THAT MAKES SENSE.
AND I THINK YOU HAVE ENOUGH ADS IN THE CAN TO TAKE A BREAK FOR A WHILE. THAT'LL TAKE A BIG LOAD OFF.
THANKS, DOC. I'LL TRY ALL THAT STUFF OUT. I'M SURE IT WILL WORK GREAT.
YEAH, YOU THOUGHT IT WOULD BE DUMB BATH-SALT-TYPE STUFF, BUT IT'S NOT. IT'S PRACTICAL.
YEAH.
SOMETHING'S NOT RIGHT. HE'S NOT TELLING US EVERYTHING.
HE PROBABLY JUST WANTED A PRESCRIPTION OR SOMETHING.
NO... IT WAS THE CONVERSATION BETWEEN HIM AND DR. BIRDING, ABOUT THE BILLBOARD.
IT'S ON A MAIN ROAD OUT OF A WEALTHY NEIGHBORHOOD, BEFORE A SPLIT WITH A COMPETING MARKET DOWN ONE STREET AND HIS ON ANOTHER.
IT'S A GOOD LOCATION FOR THE SIGN. WHY DIDN'T HE TELL HIS DAD THAT?
I'LL CALL HIM IN THE--
MORNING...
THE OFFICE IS RIGGED TO EXPLODE.

It boggles my mind that if a bath SMELLS GOOD ENOUGH, it will make you less worried about things.

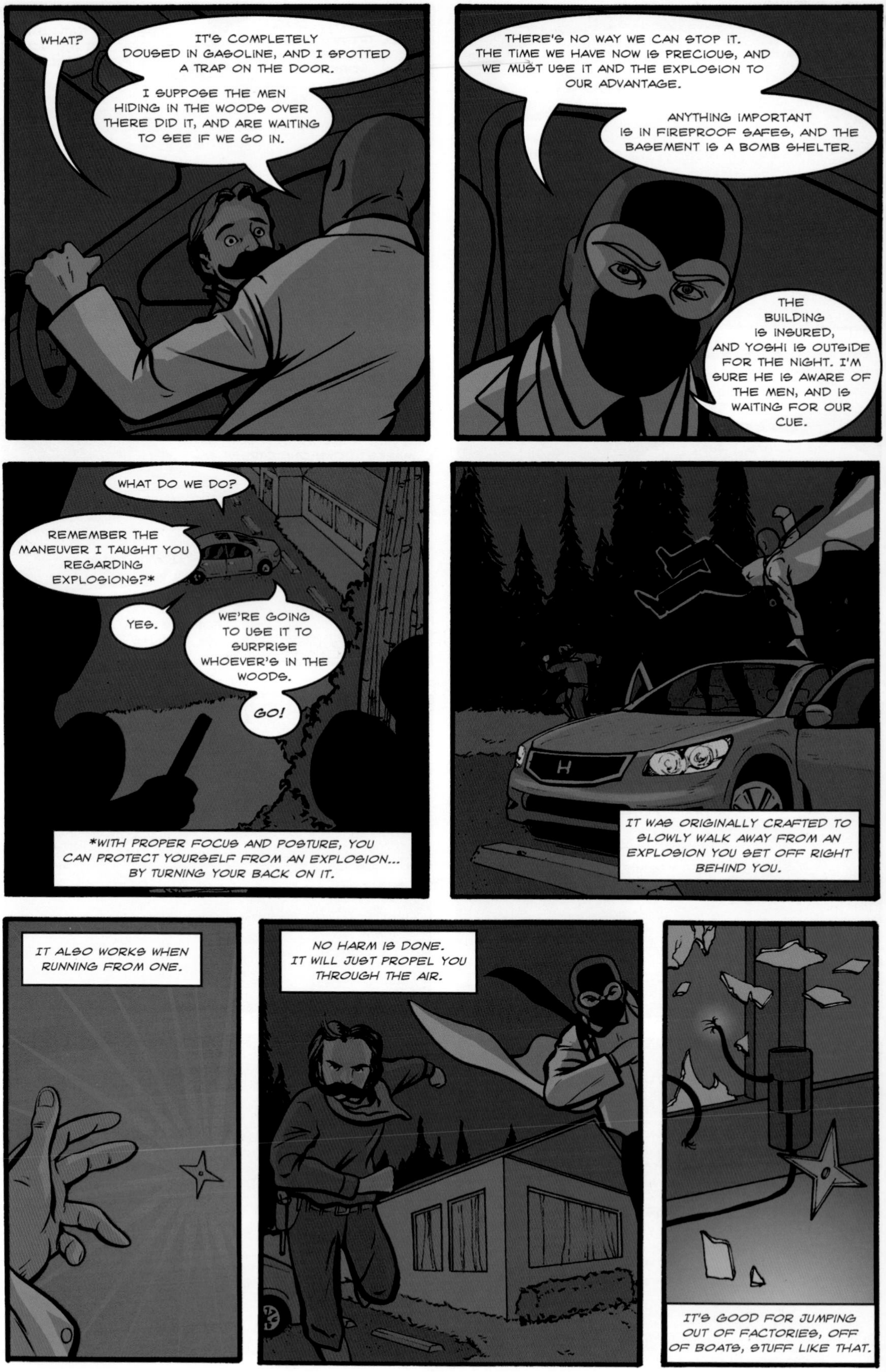
WHAT?
IT'S COMPLETELY DOUSED IN GASOLINE, AND I SPOTTED A TRAP ON THE DOOR.
I SUPPOSE THE MEN HIDING IN THE WOODS OVER THERE DID IT, AND ARE WAITING TO SEE IF WE GO IN.
THERE'S NO WAY WE CAN STOP IT. THE TIME WE HAVE NOW IS PRECIOUS, AND WE MUST USE IT AND THE EXPLOSION TO OUR ADVANTAGE.
ANYTHING IMPORTANT IS IN FIREPROOF SAFES, AND THE BASEMENT IS A BOMB SHELTER.
THE BUILDING IS INSURED, AND YOSHI IS OUTSIDE FOR THE NIGHT. I'M SURE HE IS AWARE OF THE MEN, AND IS WAITING FOR OUR CUE.
WHAT DO WE DO?
REMEMBER THE MANEUVER I TAUGHT YOU REGARDING EXPLOSIONS?*
YES.
WE'RE GOING TO USE IT TO SURPRISE WHOEVER'S IN THE WOODS.
GO!
*WITH PROPER FOCUS AND POSTURE, YOU CAN PROTECT YOURSELF FROM AN EXPLOSION... BY TURNING YOUR BACK ON IT.
IT WAS ORIGINALLY CRAFTED TO SLOWLY WALK AWAY FROM AN EXPLOSION YOU SET OFF RIGHT BEHIND YOU.
IT ALSO WORKS WHEN RUNNING FROM ONE.
NO HARM IS DONE. IT WILL JUST PROPEL YOU THROUGH THE AIR.
IT'S GOOD FOR JUMPING OUT OF FACTORIES, OFF OF BOATS, STUFF LIKE THAT.

Judy is at pottery class.

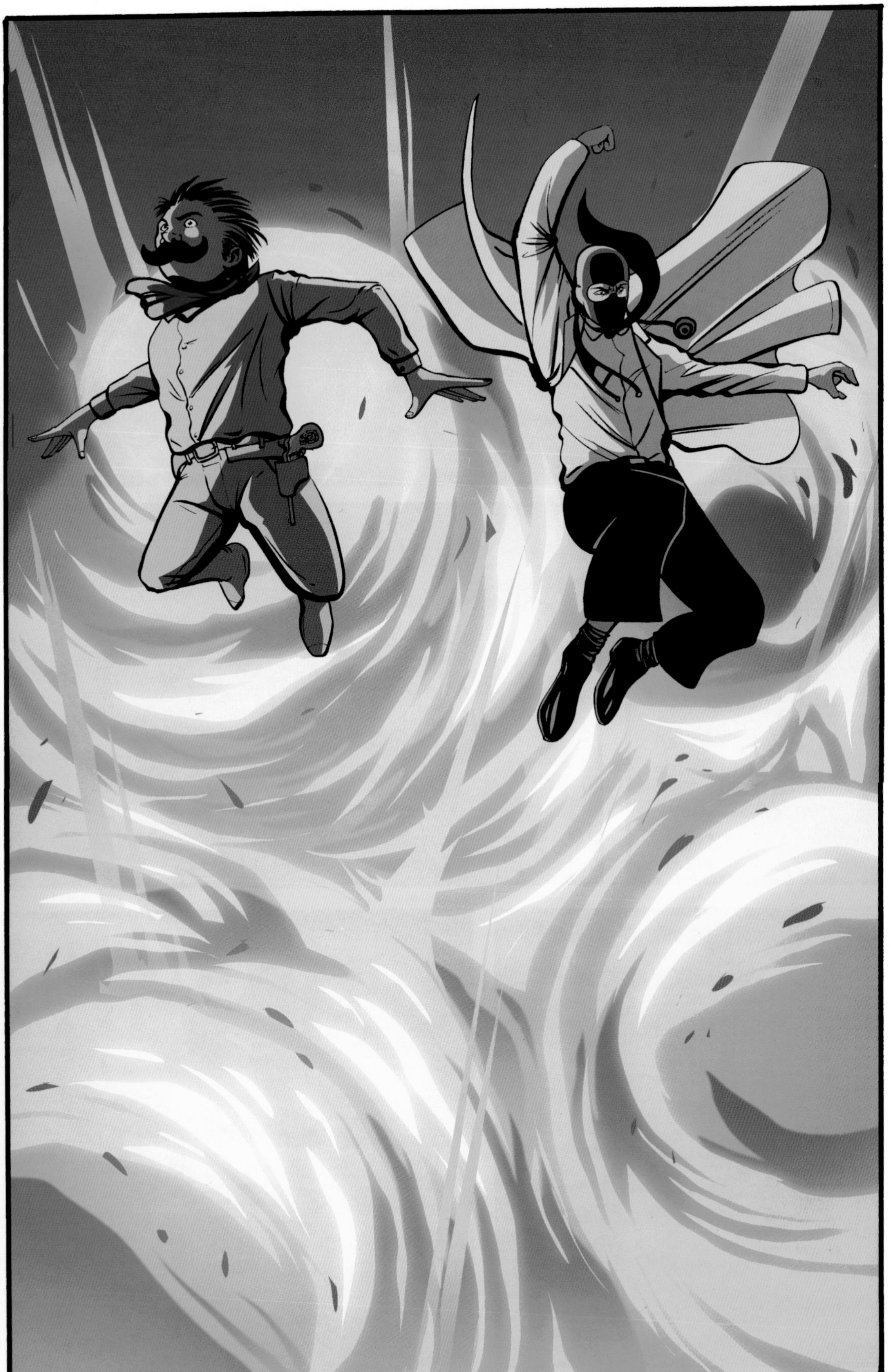

Happy third anniversary, Dr. McNinja! You don't have an office anymore.

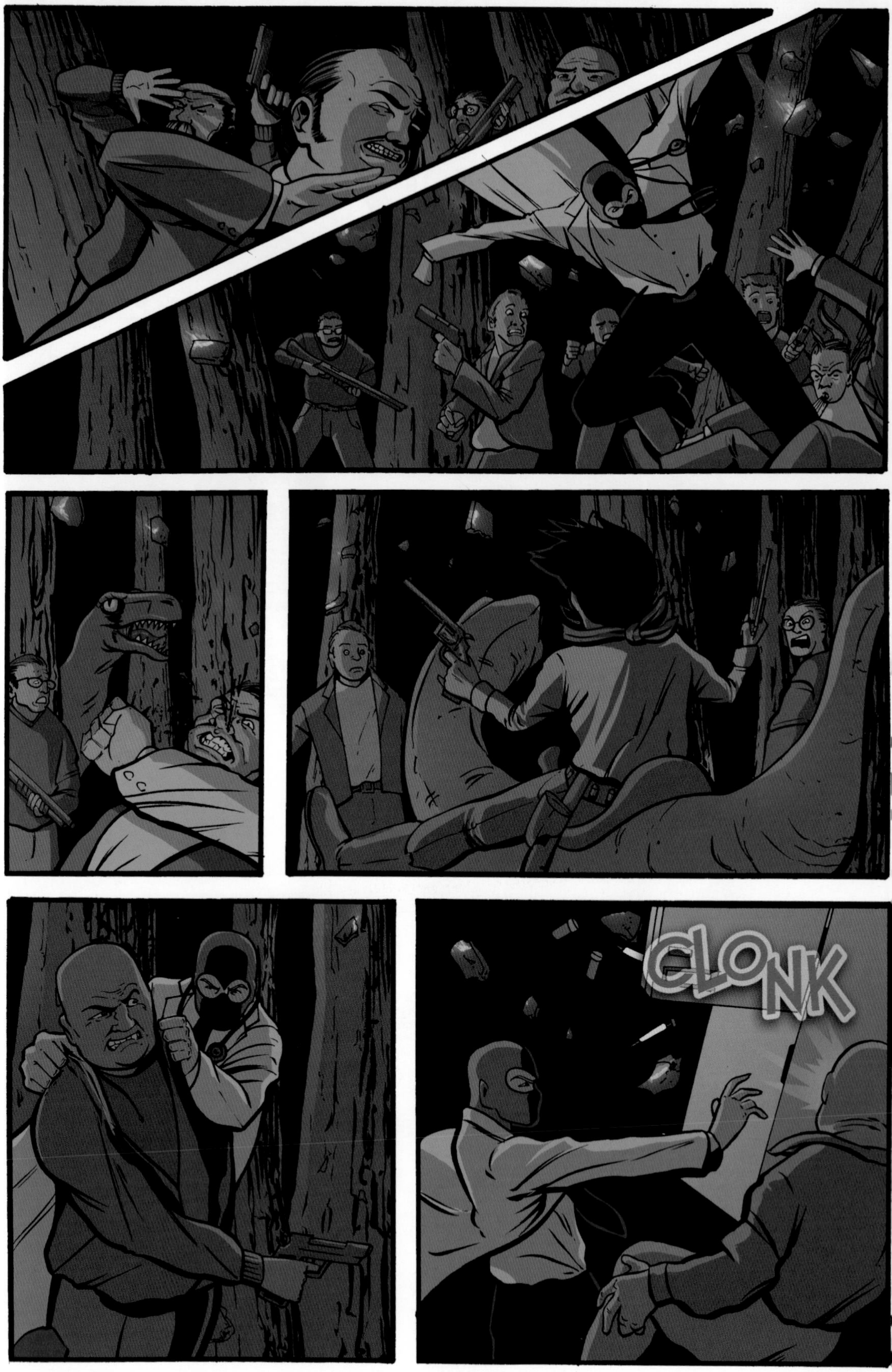
CLONK

And then Indiana Jones climbs out of the fridge.

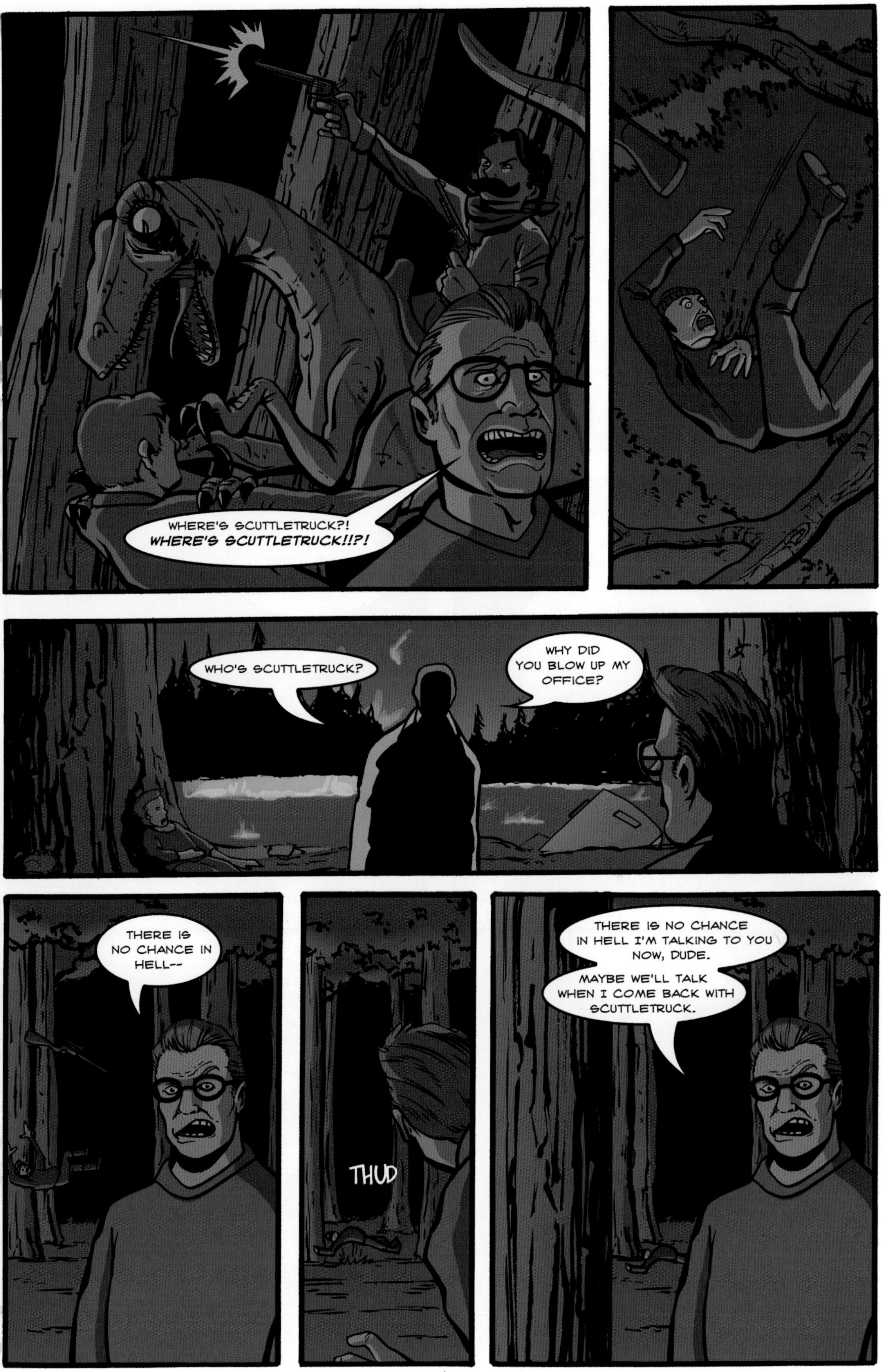
WHERE'S SCUTTLETRUCK?!
WHERE'S SCUTTLETRUCK!!?!
WHO'S SCUTTLETRUCK?
WHY DID YOU BLOW UP MY OFFICE?
THERE IS NO CHANCE IN HELL--
THUD
THERE IS NO CHANCE IN HELL I'M TALKING TO YOU NOW, DUDE.
MAYBE WE'LL TALK WHEN I COME BACK WITH SCUTTLETRUCK.

I had to remind myself to draw the guys with guns so they at least seemed VAGUELY threatening.

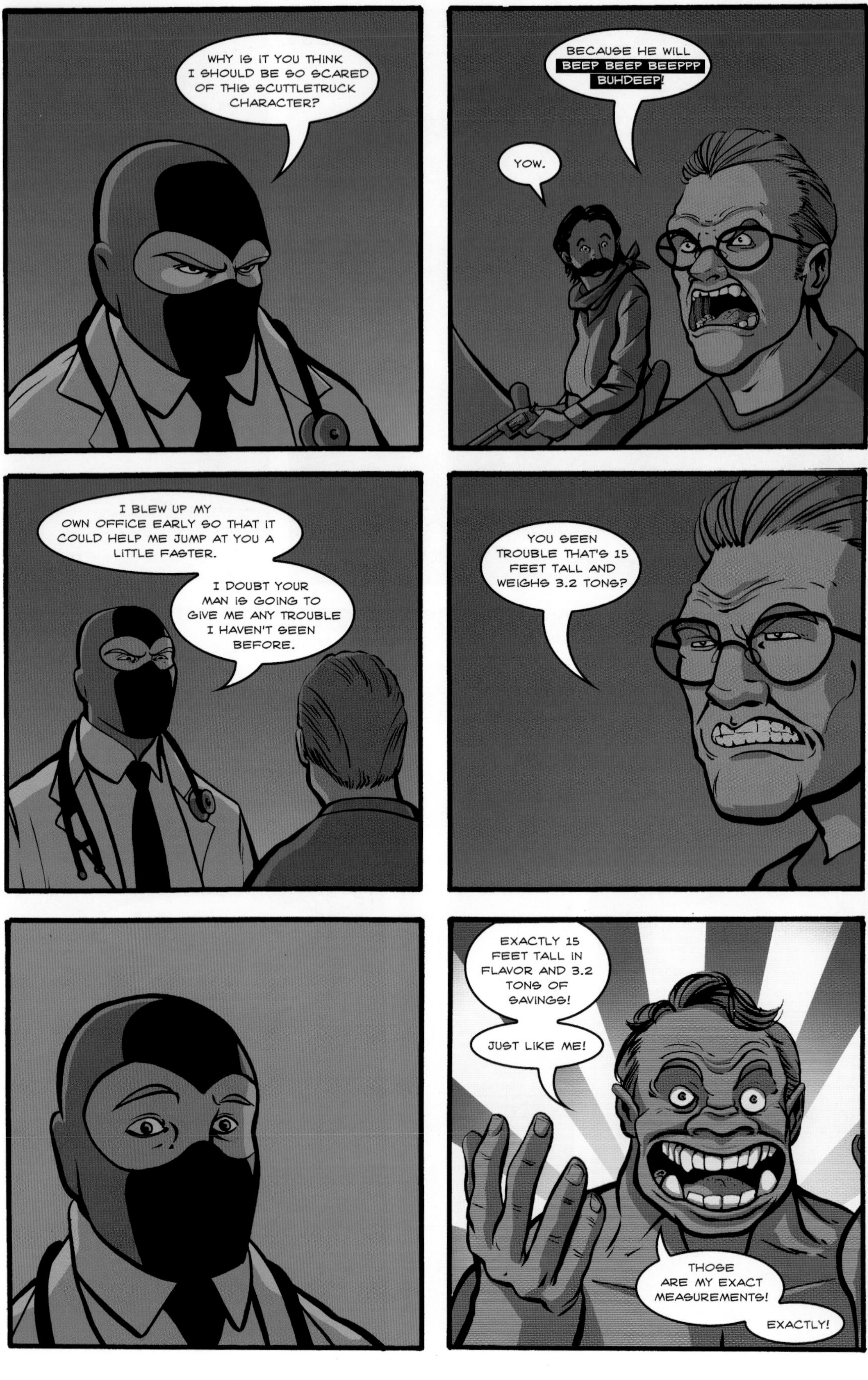
WHY IS IT YOU THINK I SHOULD BE SO SCARED OF THIS SCUTTLETRUCK CHARACTER?
BECAUSE HE WILL BEEP BEEP BEEPPP BUHDEEP!
YOW.
I BLEW UP MY OWN OFFICE EARLY SO THAT IT COULD HELP ME JUMP AT YOU A LITTLE FASTER.
I DOUBT YOUR MAN IS GOING TO GIVE ME ANY TROUBLE I HAVEN'T SEEN BEFORE.
YOU SEEN TROUBLE THAT'S 15 FEET TALL AND WEIGHS 3.2 TONS?
EXACTLY 15 FEET TALL IN FLAVOR AND 3.2 TONS OF SAVINGS!
JUST LIKE ME!
THOSE ARE MY EXACT MEASUREMENTS!
EXACTLY!

JUDY UPDATE: She has picked out a VERY nice glaze.

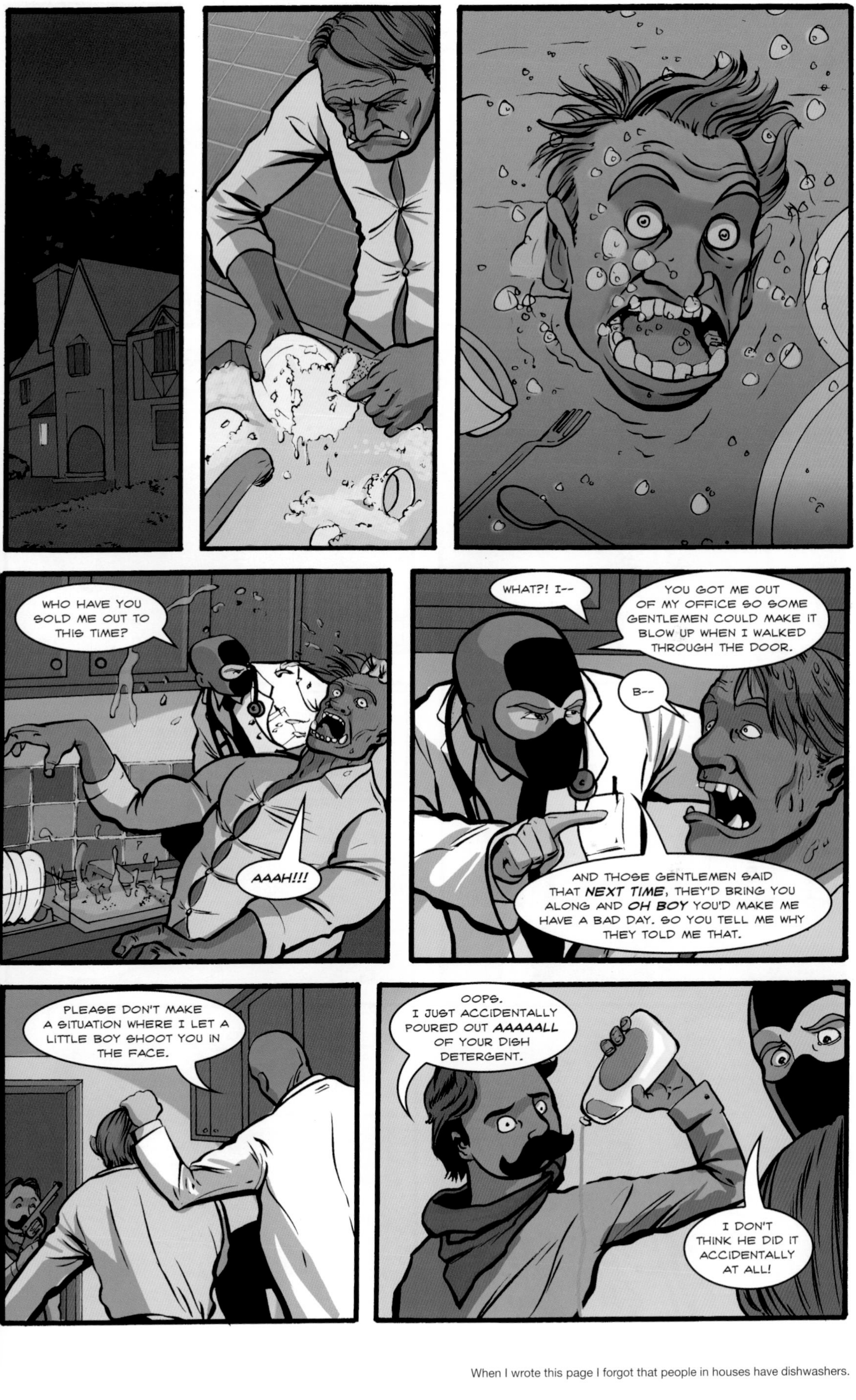
WHO HAVE YOU SOLD ME OUT TO THIS TIME?
AAAH!!!
WHAT?! I--
YOU GOT ME OUT OF MY OFFICE SO SOME GENTLEMEN COULD MAKE IT BLOW UP WHEN I WALKED THROUGH THE DOOR.
B--
AND THOSE GENTLEMEN SAID THAT NEXT TIME, THEY'D BRING YOU ALONG AND OH BOY YOU'D MAKE ME HAVE A BAD DAY. SO YOU TELL ME WHY THEY TOLD ME THAT.
PLEASE DON'T MAKE A SITUATION WHERE I LET A LITTLE BOY SHOOT YOU IN THE FACE.
OOPS. I JUST ACCIDENTALLY POURED OUT AAAAALL OF YOUR DISH DETERGENT.
I DON'T THINK HE DID IT ACCIDENTALLY AT ALL!

When I wrote this page I forgot that people in houses have dishwashers.

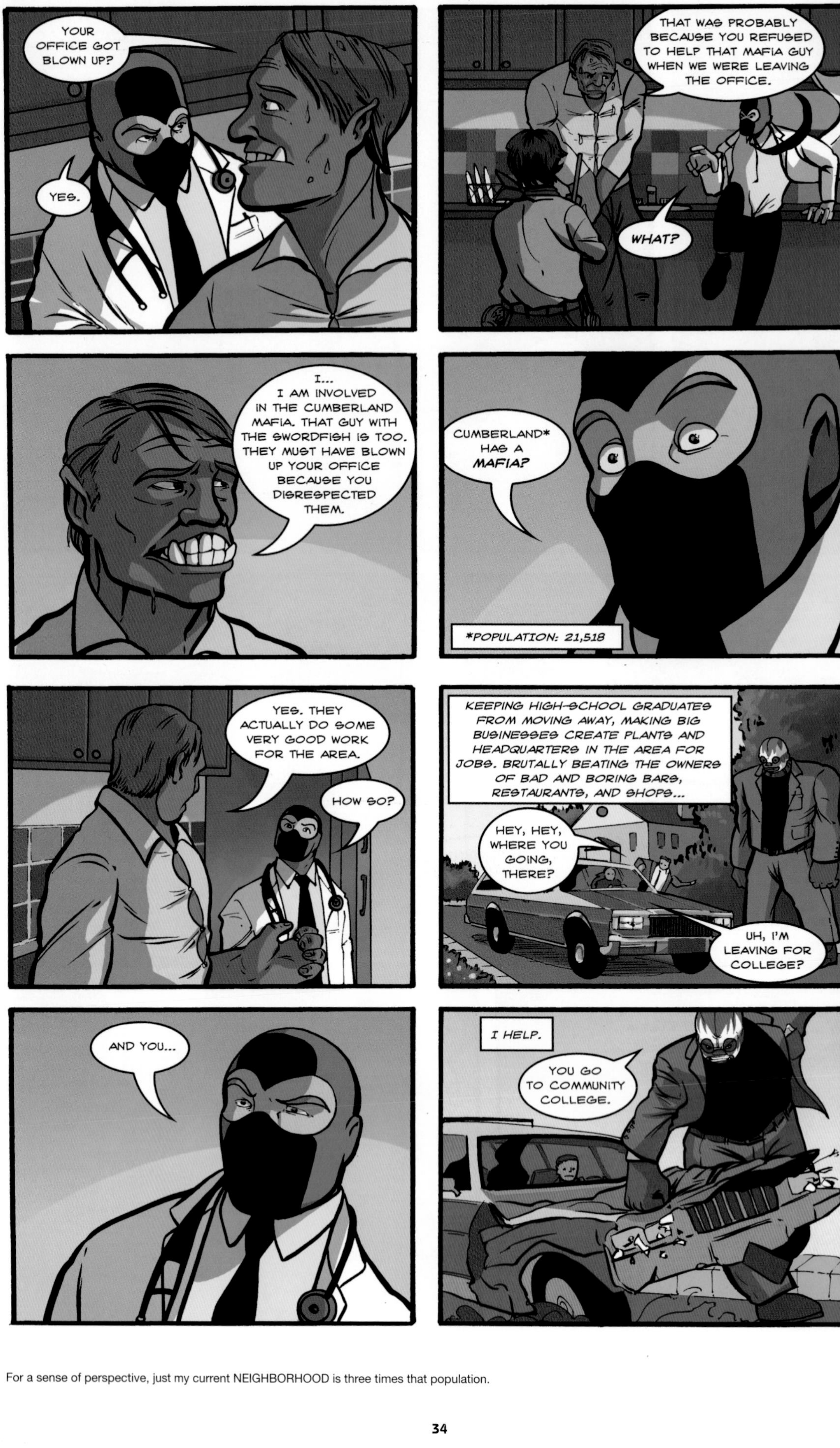
YOUR OFFICE GOT BLOWN UP?
YES.
THAT WAS PROBABLY BECAUSE YOU REFUSED TO HELP THAT MAFIA GUY WHEN WE WERE LEAVING THE OFFICE.
WHAT?
I... I AM INVOLVED IN THE CUMBERLAND MAFIA. THAT GUY WITH THE SWORDFISH IS TOO. THEY MUST HAVE BLOWN UP YOUR OFFICE BECAUSE YOU DISRESPECTED THEM.
CUMBERLAND* HAS A MAFIA?
*POPULATION: 21,518
YES. THEY ACTUALLY DO SOME VERY GOOD WORK FOR THE AREA.
HOW SO?
KEEPING HIGH-SCHOOL GRADUATES FROM MOVING AWAY, MAKING BIG BUSINESSES CREATE PLANTS AND HEADQUARTERS IN THE AREA FOR JOBS. BRUTALLY BEATING THE OWNERS OF BAD AND BORING BARS, RESTAURANTS, AND SHOPS...
HEY, HEY, WHERE YOU GOING, THERE?
UH, I'M LEAVING FOR COLLEGE?
AND YOU...
I HELP.
YOU GO TO COMMUNITY COLLEGE.

For a sense of perspective, just my current NEIGHBORHOOD is three times that population.

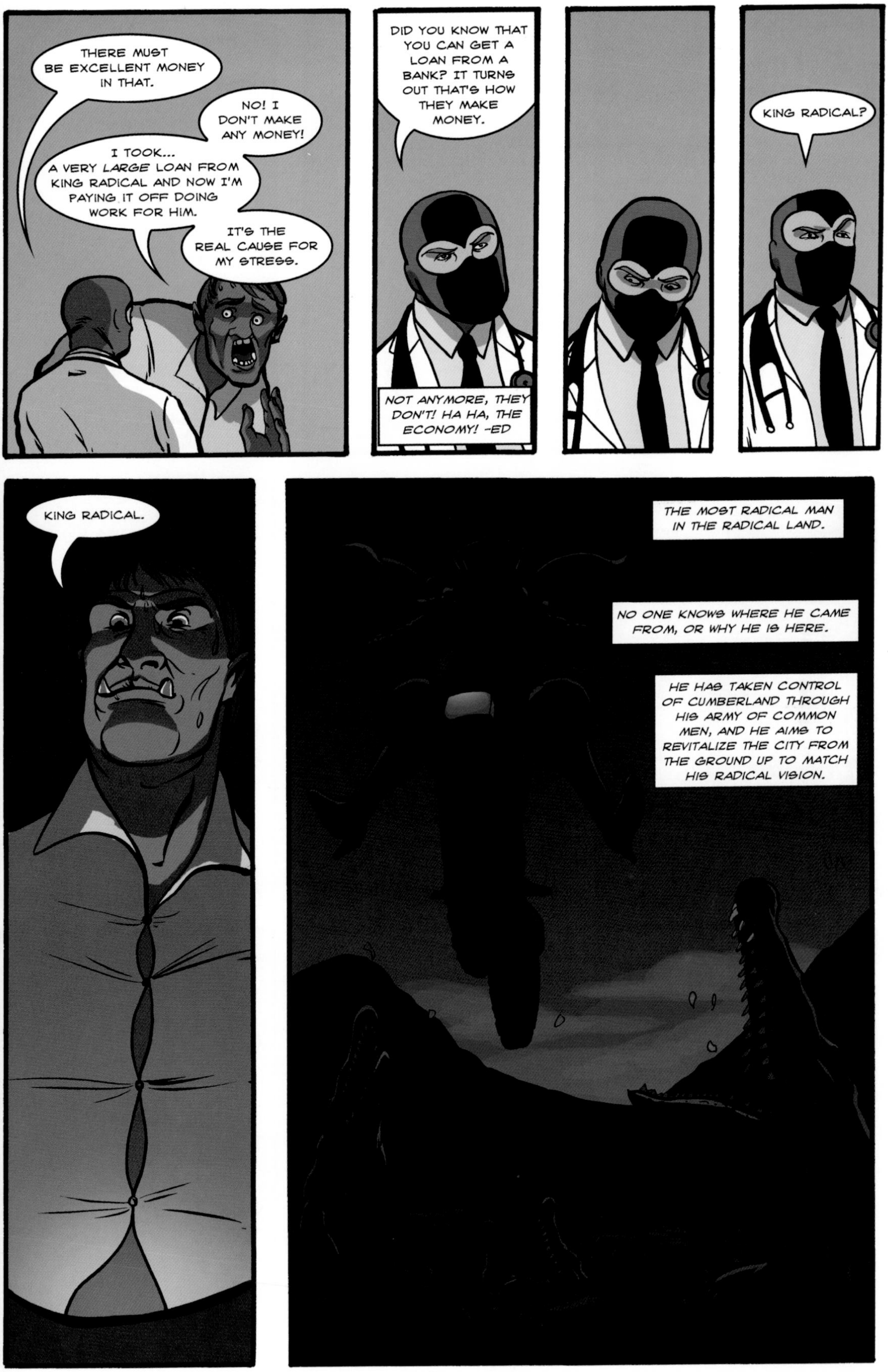
THERE MUST BE EXCELLENT MONEY IN THAT.
NO! I DON'T MAKE ANY MONEY!
I TOOK... A VERY *LARGE* LOAN FROM KING RADICAL AND NOW I'M PAYING IT OFF DOING WORK FOR HIM.
IT'S THE REAL CAUSE FOR MY STRESS.
DID YOU KNOW THAT YOU CAN GET A LOAN FROM A BANK? IT TURNS OUT THAT'S HOW THEY MAKE MONEY.
NOT ANYMORE, THEY DON'T! HA HA, THE ECONOMY! -ED
KING RADICAL?
KING RADICAL.
THE MOST RADICAL MAN IN THE RADICAL LAND.
NO ONE KNOWS WHERE HE CAME FROM, OR WHY HE IS HERE.
HE HAS TAKEN CONTROL OF CUMBERLAND THROUGH HIS ARMY OF COMMON MEN, AND HE AIMS TO REVITALIZE THE CITY FROM THE GROUND UP TO MATCH HIS RADICAL VISION.

So . . . radical . . .

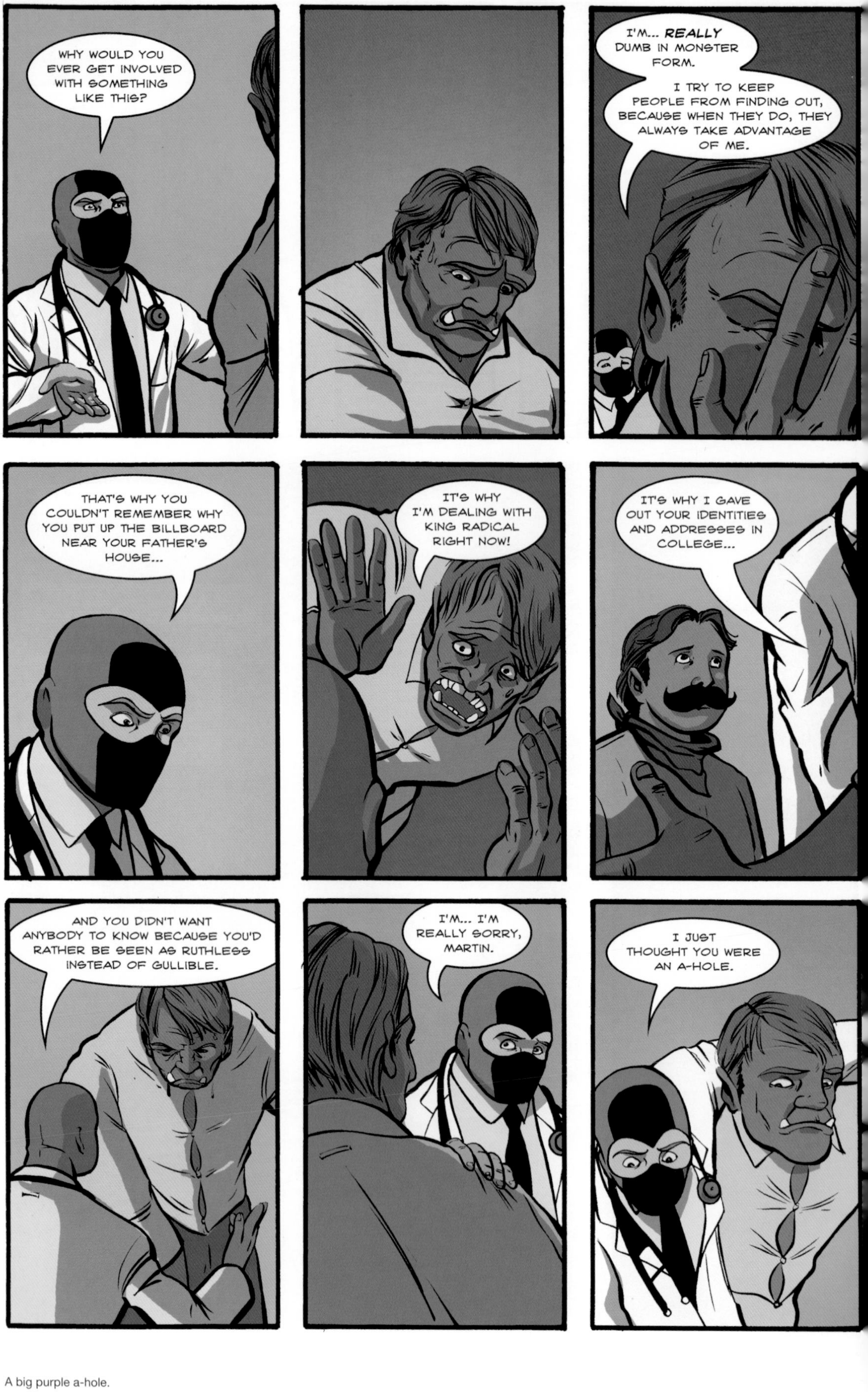
WHY WOULD YOU EVER GET INVOLVED WITH SOMETHING LIKE THIS?
I'M... REALLY DUMB IN MONSTER FORM.
I TRY TO KEEP PEOPLE FROM FINDING OUT, BECAUSE WHEN THEY DO, THEY ALWAYS TAKE ADVANTAGE OF ME.
THAT'S WHY YOU COULDN'T REMEMBER WHY YOU PUT UP THE BILLBOARD NEAR YOUR FATHER'S HOUSE...
IT'S WHY I'M DEALING WITH KING RADICAL RIGHT NOW!
IT'S WHY I GAVE OUT YOUR IDENTITIES AND ADDRESSES IN COLLEGE...
AND YOU DIDN'T WANT ANYBODY TO KNOW BECAUSE YOU'D RATHER BE SEEN AS RUTHLESS INSTEAD OF GULLIBLE.
I'M... I'M REALLY SORRY, MARTIN.
I JUST THOUGHT YOU WERE AN A-HOLE.

A big purple a-hole.

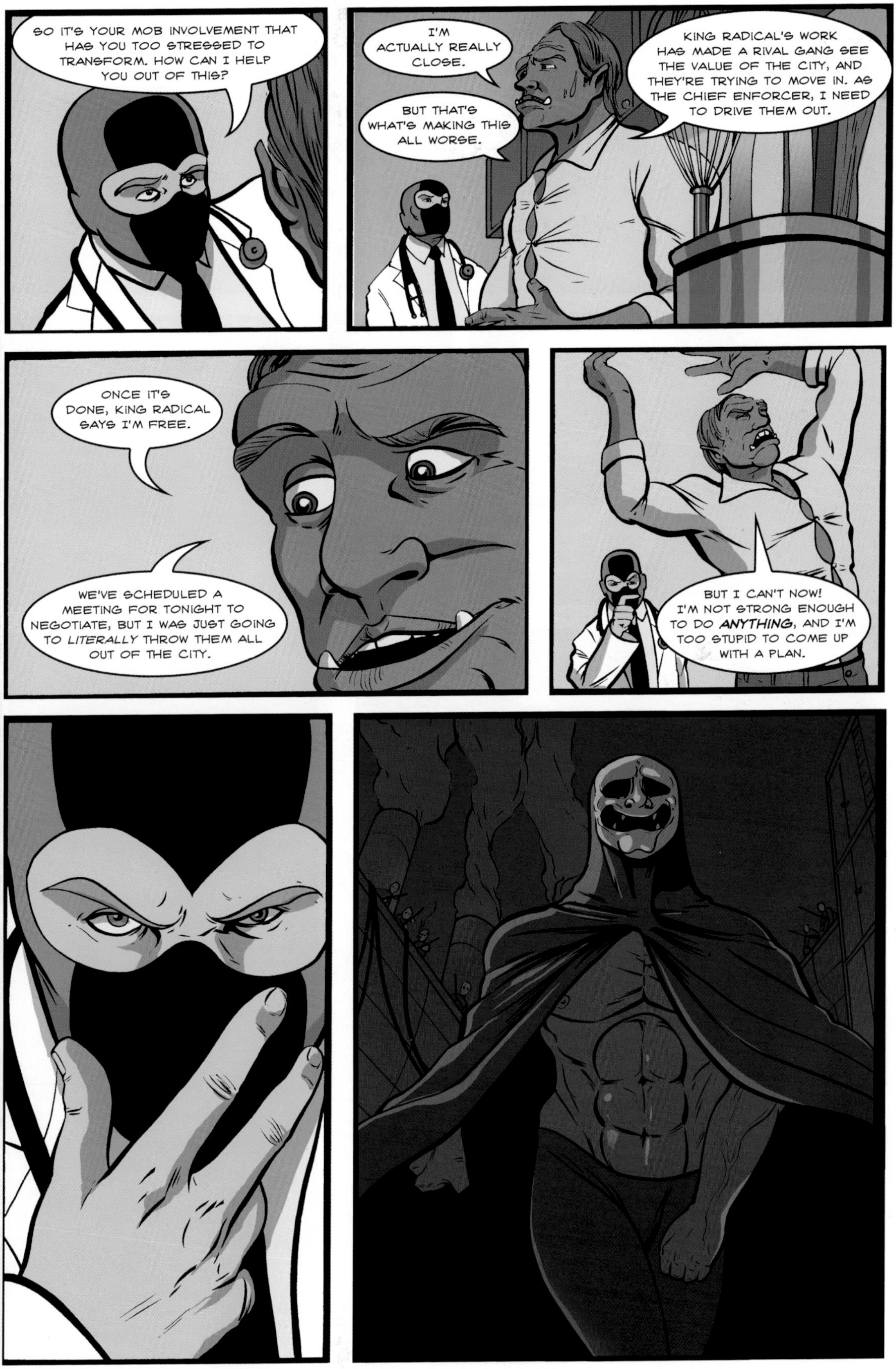
SO IT'S YOUR MOB INVOLVEMENT THAT HAS YOU TOO STRESSED TO TRANSFORM. HOW CAN I HELP YOU OUT OF THIS?
I'M ACTUALLY REALLY CLOSE.
BUT THAT'S WHAT'S MAKING THIS ALL WORSE.
KING RADICAL'S WORK HAS MADE A RIVAL GANG SEE THE VALUE OF THE CITY, AND THEY'RE TRYING TO MOVE IN. AS THE CHIEF ENFORCER, I NEED TO DRIVE THEM OUT.
ONCE IT'S DONE, KING RADICAL SAYS I'M FREE.
WE'VE SCHEDULED A MEETING FOR TONIGHT TO NEGOTIATE, BUT I WAS JUST GOING TO *LITERALLY* THROW THEM ALL OUT OF THE CITY.
BUT I CAN'T NOW! I'M NOT STRONG ENOUGH TO DO ***ANYTHING***, AND I'M TOO STUPID TO COME UP WITH A PLAN.

So step one of the plan is walk down by the docks with your shirt off.

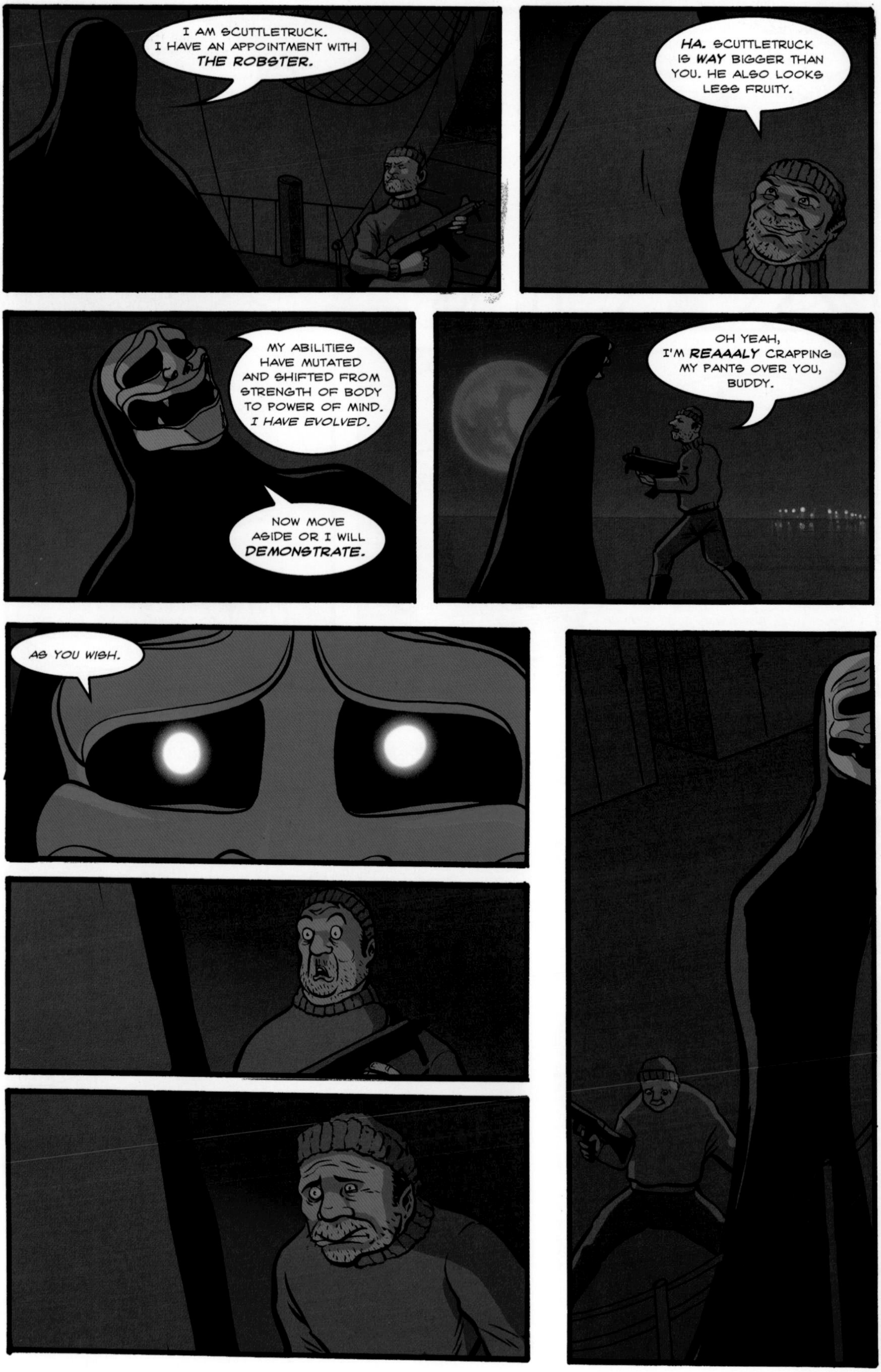
I AM SCUTTLETRUCK. I HAVE AN APPOINTMENT WITH THE ROBSTER.
HA. SCUTTLETRUCK IS WAY BIGGER THAN YOU. HE ALSO LOOKS LESS FRUITY.
MY ABILITIES HAVE MUTATED AND SHIFTED FROM STRENGTH OF BODY TO POWER OF MIND. I HAVE EVOLVED.
NOW MOVE ASIDE OR I WILL DEMONSTRATE.
OH YEAH, I'M REAAALY CRAPPING MY PANTS OVER YOU, BUDDY.
AS YOU WISH.

Yes, the gentleman's feet are tastefully cropped so that you can't see anything coming out of the legs of the pants.

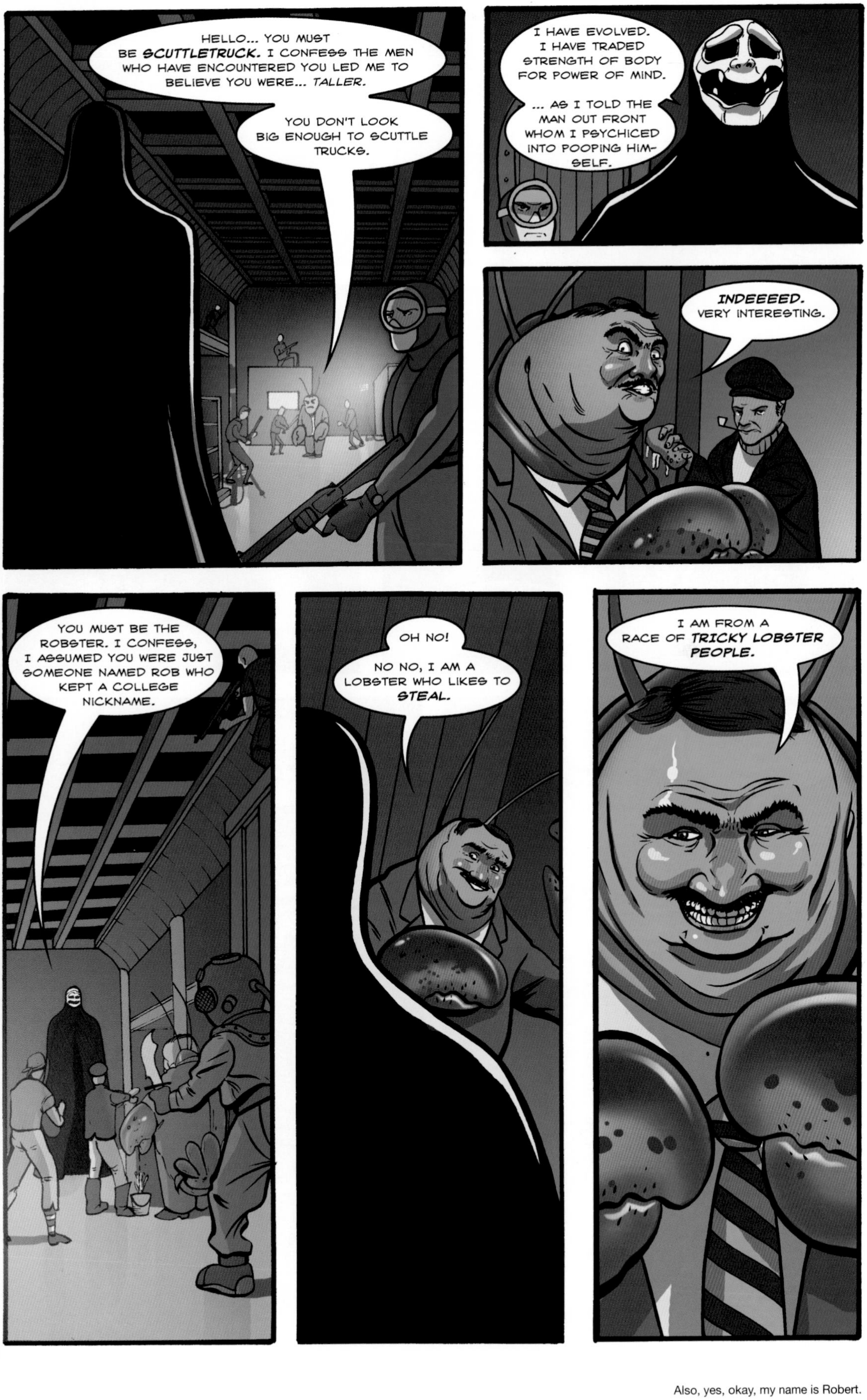
HELLO... YOU MUST BE SCUTTLETRUCK. I CONFESS THE MEN WHO HAVE ENCOUNTERED YOU LED ME TO BELIEVE YOU WERE... TALLER.
YOU DON'T LOOK BIG ENOUGH TO SCUTTLE TRUCKS.
I HAVE EVOLVED. I HAVE TRADED STRENGTH OF BODY FOR POWER OF MIND.
... AS I TOLD THE MAN OUT FRONT WHOM I PSYCHICED INTO POOPING HIM-SELF.
INDEEEEED. VERY INTERESTING.
YOU MUST BE THE ROBSTER. I CONFESS, I ASSUMED YOU WERE JUST SOMEONE NAMED ROB WHO KEPT A COLLEGE NICKNAME.
OH NO!
NO NO, I AM A LOBSTER WHO LIKES TO STEAL.
I AM FROM A RACE OF TRICKY LOBSTER PEOPLE.

Also, yes, okay, my name is Robert.

DOWN TO BUSINESS. YOU ARE A REPRESENTATIVE OF KING RADICAL.
GASP!
GASP!
KING RADICAL!
YOU'VE BEEN ASSIGNED TO DRIVE MY OPERATION OUT OF TOWN.
CORRECT. BUT I HAVE AN OFFER. WHAT PERCENTAGE OF YOUR MEN DO YOU HAVE IN HERE, RIGHT NOW... TO PROTECT YOU FROM ME.
ONLY THE BEST. ABOUT A THIRD OF THEM.
IF I CAN TAKE THEM ALL OUT, RIGHT NOW, WITH MY PSYCHIC POWERS, YOU'LL CUT YOUR LOSSES, TAKE YOUR REMAINING TWO-THIRDS, AND LEAVE.
YOU KNOW, I WAS GOING TO PROPOSE THE SAME THING! SORT OF!
I WAS JUST GOING TO HAVE THEM ALL SHOOT YOU, AND IF YOU SURVIVED I'D PROBABLY RUN AWAY, YEAH.
I WOULD EXPECT NO LESS FROM A TRICKY LOBSTER MAN.

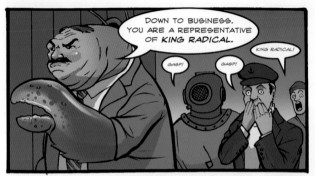

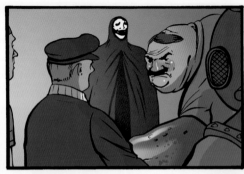

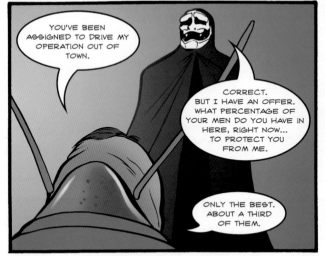

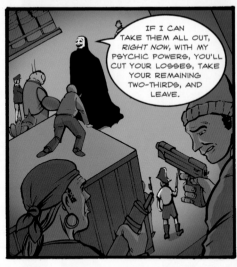

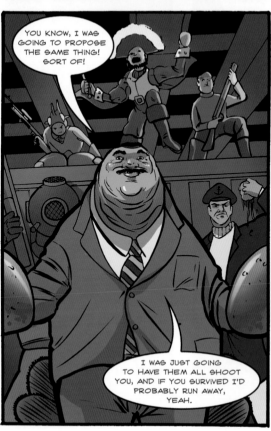

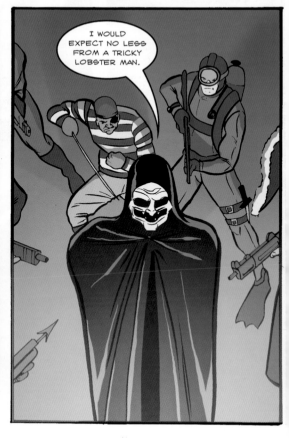

Man, when lobster people turn out to be real, I am going to have to do some pretty quick editing here.

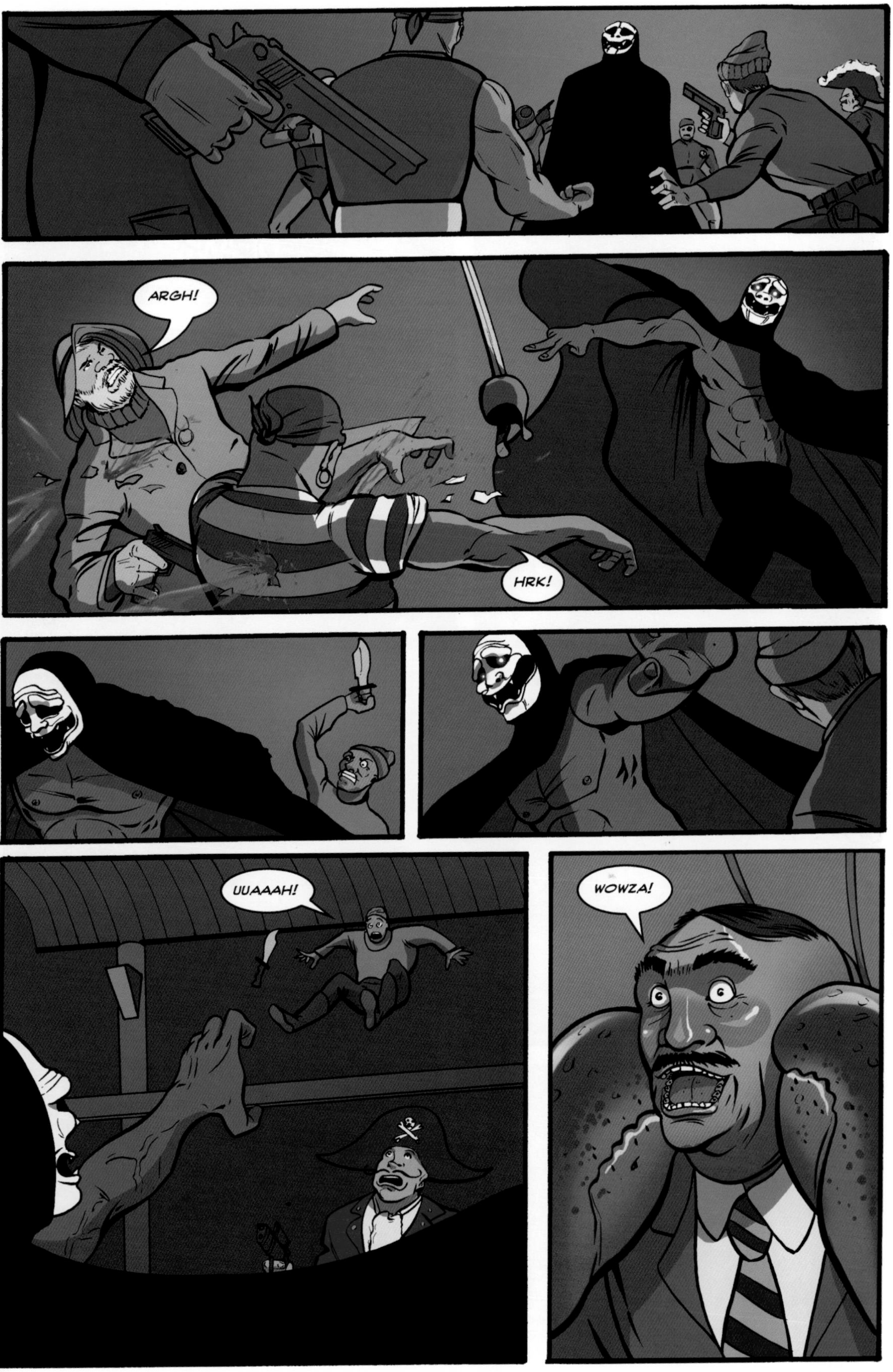
ARGH!
HRK!
UUAAAH!
WOWZA!

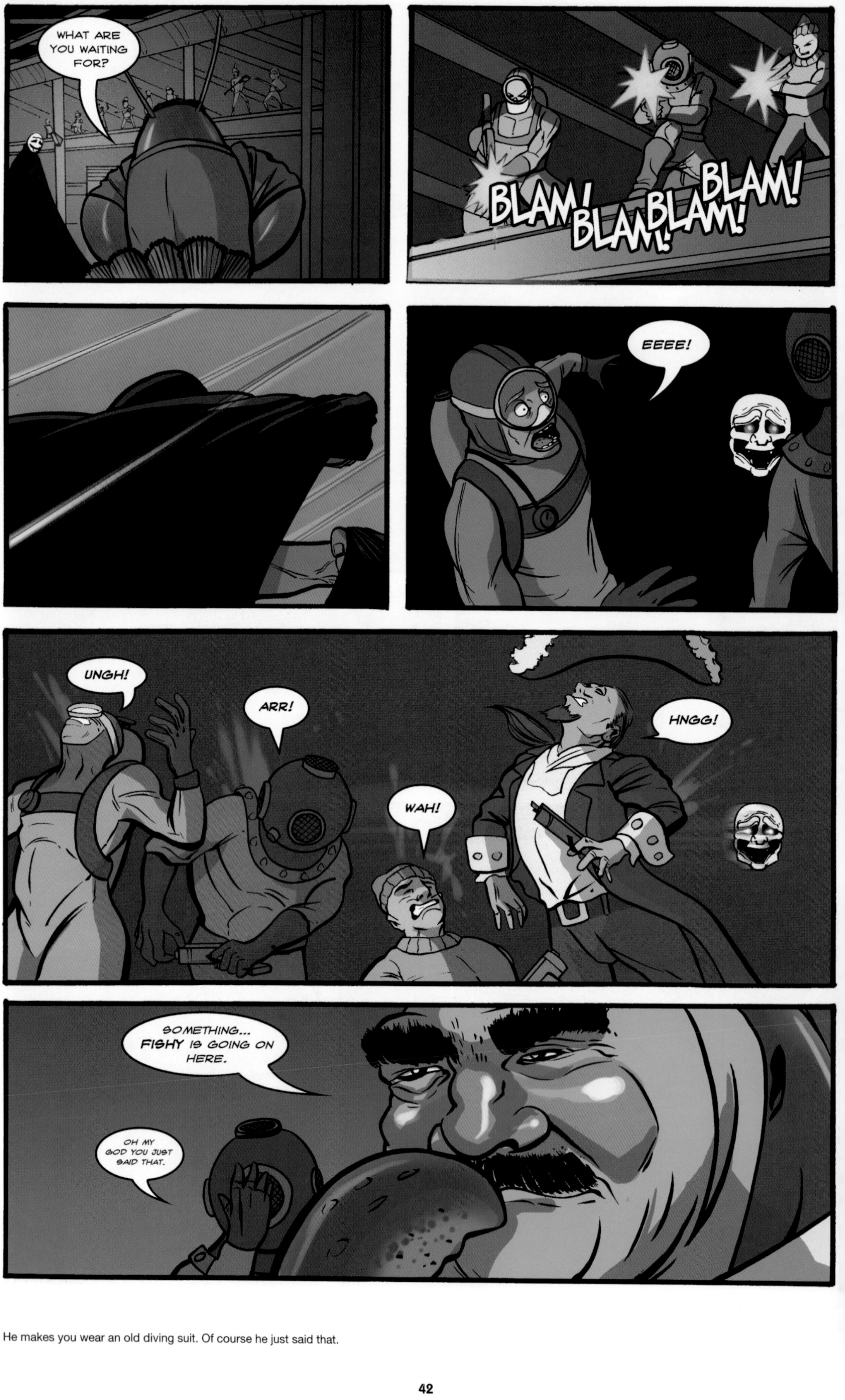
WHAT ARE YOU WAITING FOR?
BLAM! BLAM! BLAM! BLAM!
EEEE!
UNGH!
ARR!
WAH!
HNGG!
SOMETHING... FISHY IS GOING ON HERE.
OH MY GOD YOU JUST SAID THAT.

He makes you wear an old diving suit. Of course he just said that.

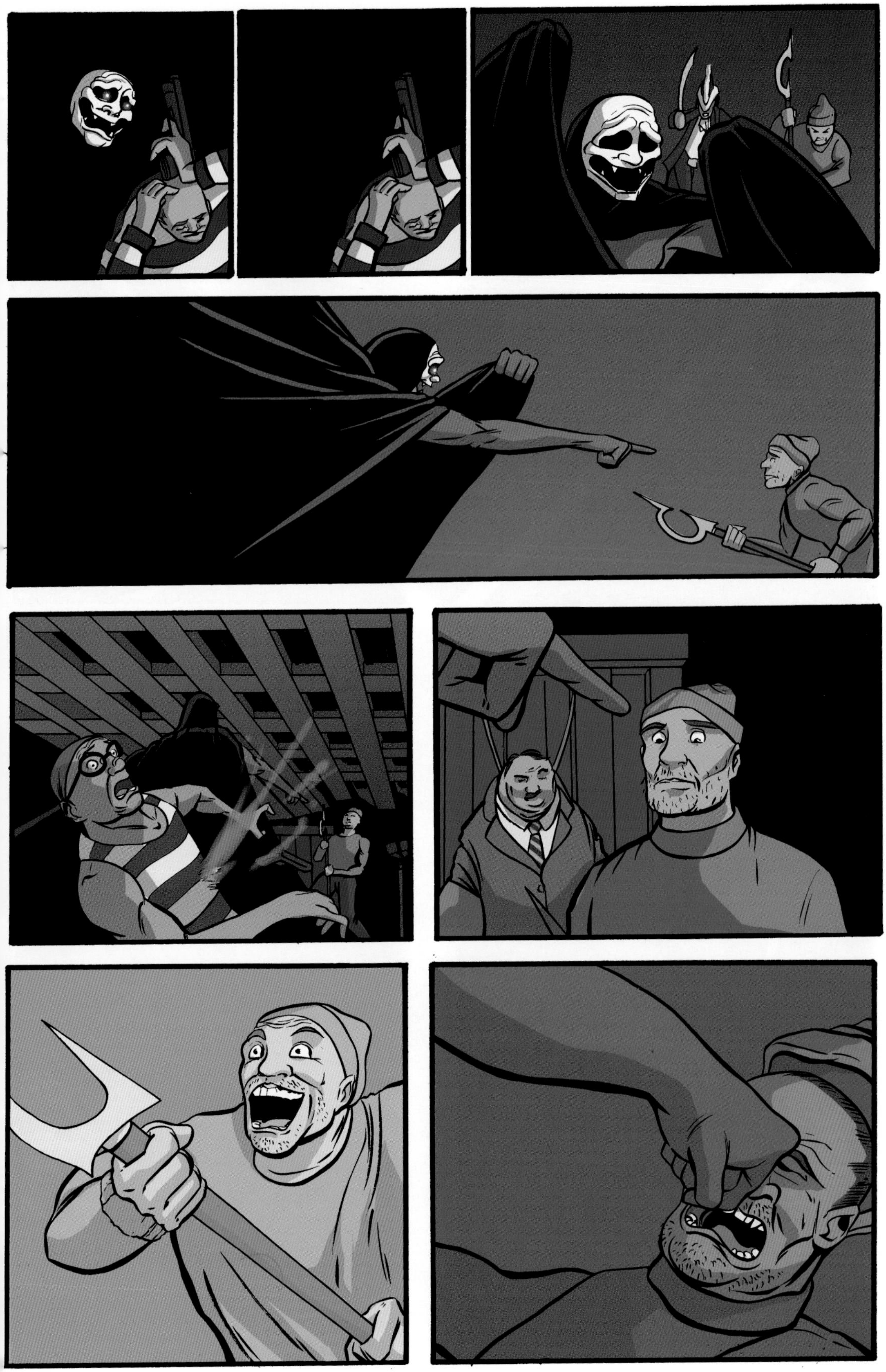

Bonk.

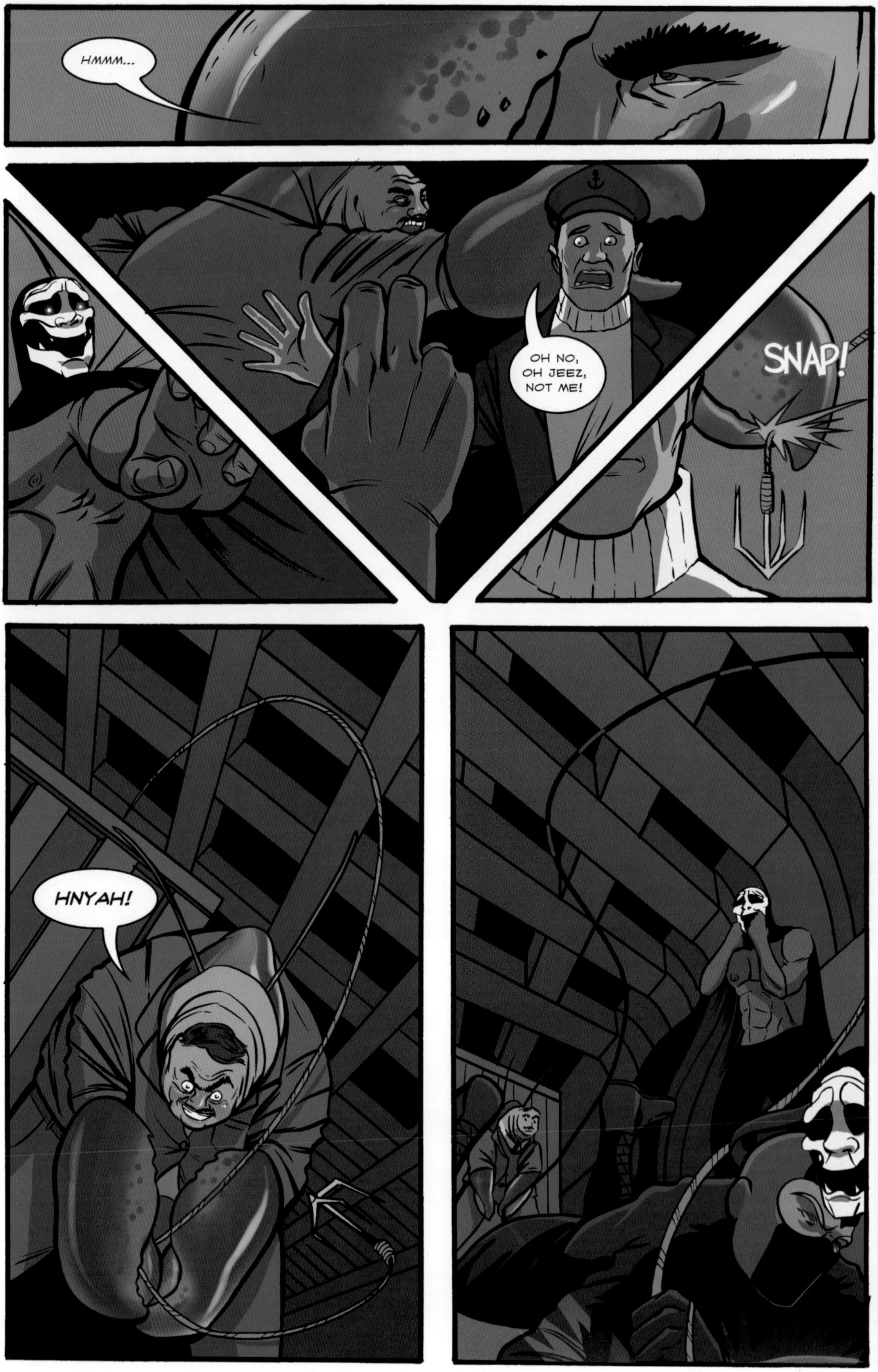
HMMM...
OH NO, OH JEEZ, NOT ME!
SNAP!
HNYAH!

Yeah, I don't know how he gets the suit on over the claws.

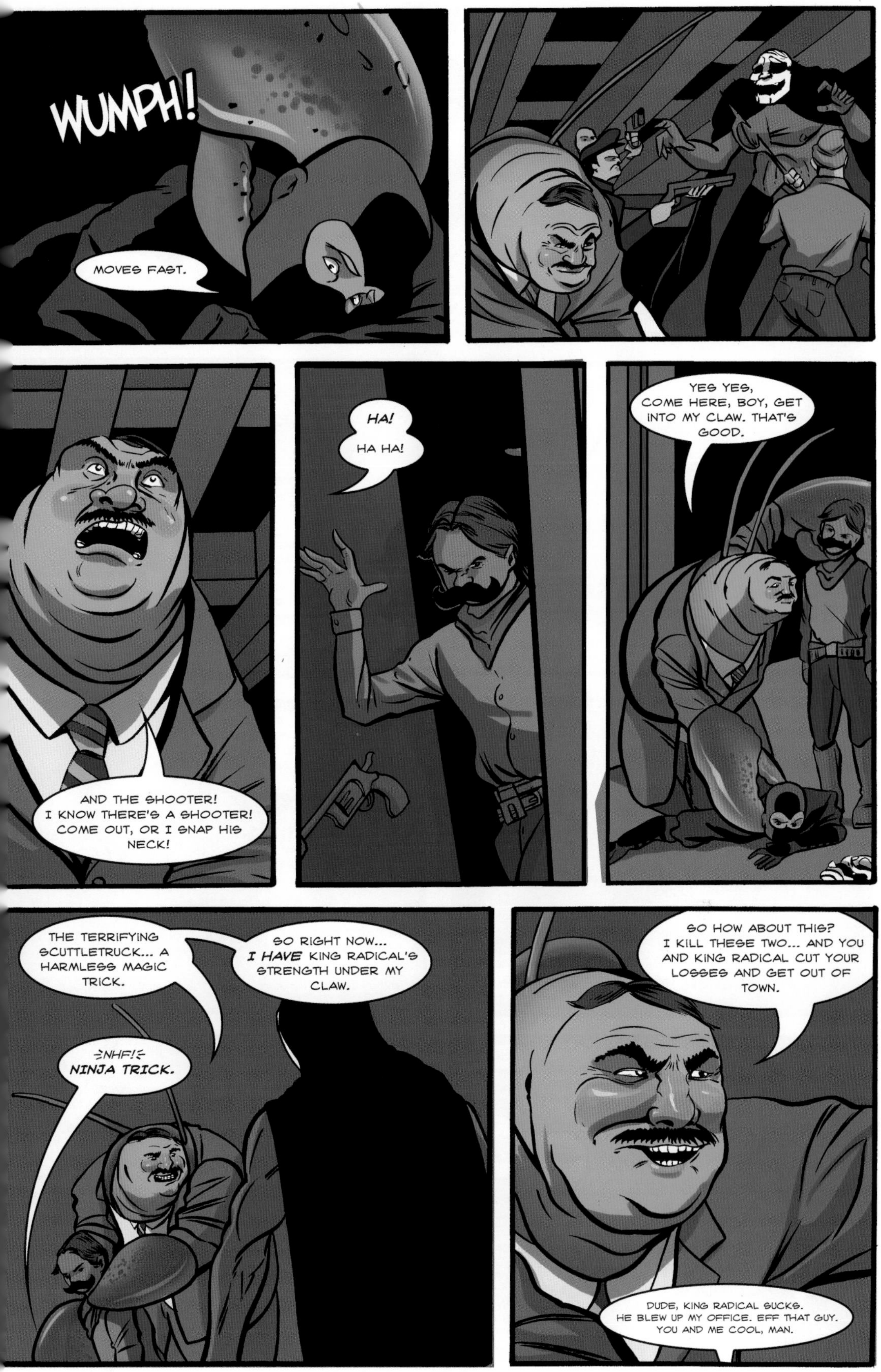
WUMPH!
MOVES FAST.
AND THE SHOOTER! I KNOW THERE'S A SHOOTER! COME OUT, OR I SNAP HIS NECK!
HA! HA HA!
YES YES, COME HERE, BOY, GET INTO MY CLAW. THAT'S GOOD.
THE TERRIFYING SCUTTLETRUCK... A HARMLESS MAGIC TRICK.
SO RIGHT NOW... I HAVE KING RADICAL'S STRENGTH UNDER MY CLAW.
NHF! NINJA TRICK.
SO HOW ABOUT THIS? I KILL THESE TWO... AND YOU AND KING RADICAL CUT YOUR LOSSES AND GET OUT OF TOWN.
DUDE, KING RADICAL SUCKS. HE BLEW UP MY OFFICE. EFF THAT GUY. YOU AND ME COOL, MAN.

Gordito is just so annoyed. SO ANNOYED.

IF YOU LEAVE BY THE COUNT OF FIVE, YOU CAN GO TELL RADICAL HOW THINGS WENT HERE.
OTHERWISE, I'LL JUST SEND HIM A LETTER TELLING HIM TO PICK UP THREE BODIES.
FIVE.
FOUR.
A C- IN BIOLOGY. YOU MAKE ME WISH MY BROKEN BODY COULD CRY.
SHE WAS TAKEN BY A TORNADO BECAUSE OF YOU! YOU MONSTER!
THREE.
TWO.
SORRY, EVERYBODY! WE'LL HAVE TO DO ANOTHER TAKE!
THE RETARD FORGOT HIS LINE AGAIN!
IT WILL BE VERY EXPENSIVE.
I WON'T CHARGE YOU ANYTHING FOR MY SERVICES.
ONE.
I THINK YOUR COMMERCIAL IS REALLY FUNNY.
HOW CAN I HELP YOU OUT OF THIS?

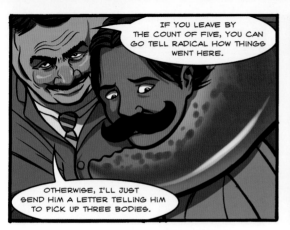

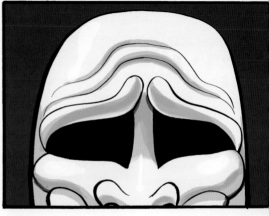

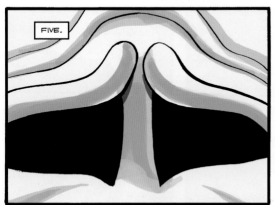

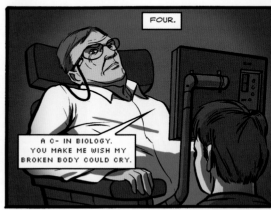

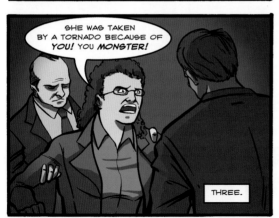

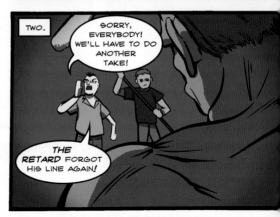

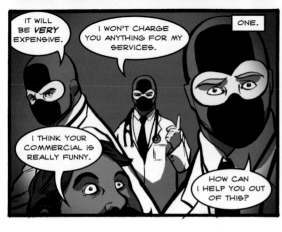

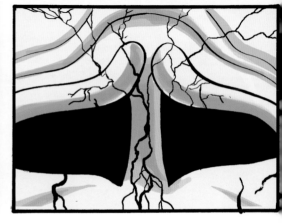

Ha ha, okay, Mr. Big Shot Local Cable Commercial Director.

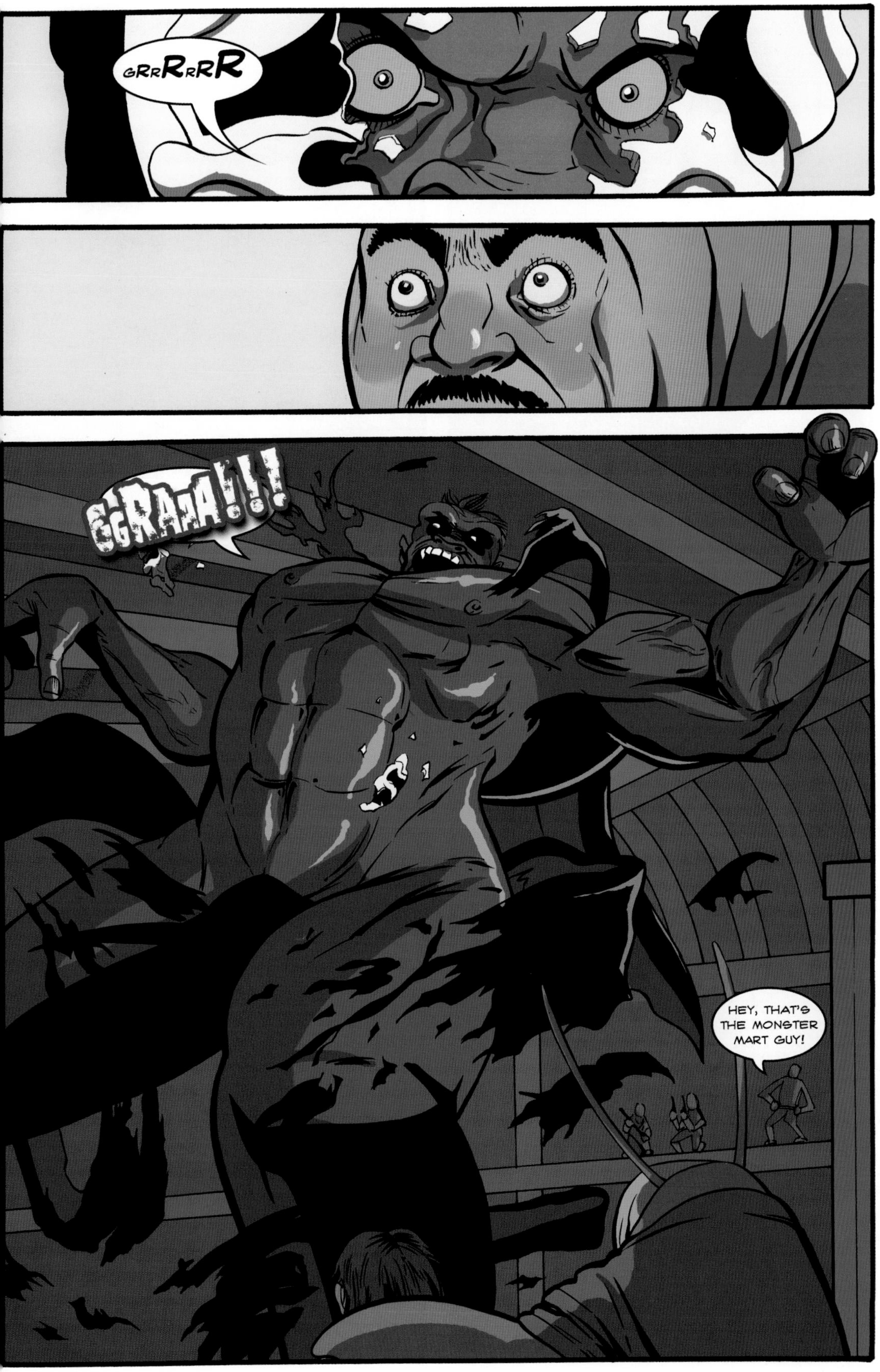
GRRRRRR
GGRAAAA!!!
HEY, THAT'S THE MONSTER MART GUY!

The pants aren't stretchy.

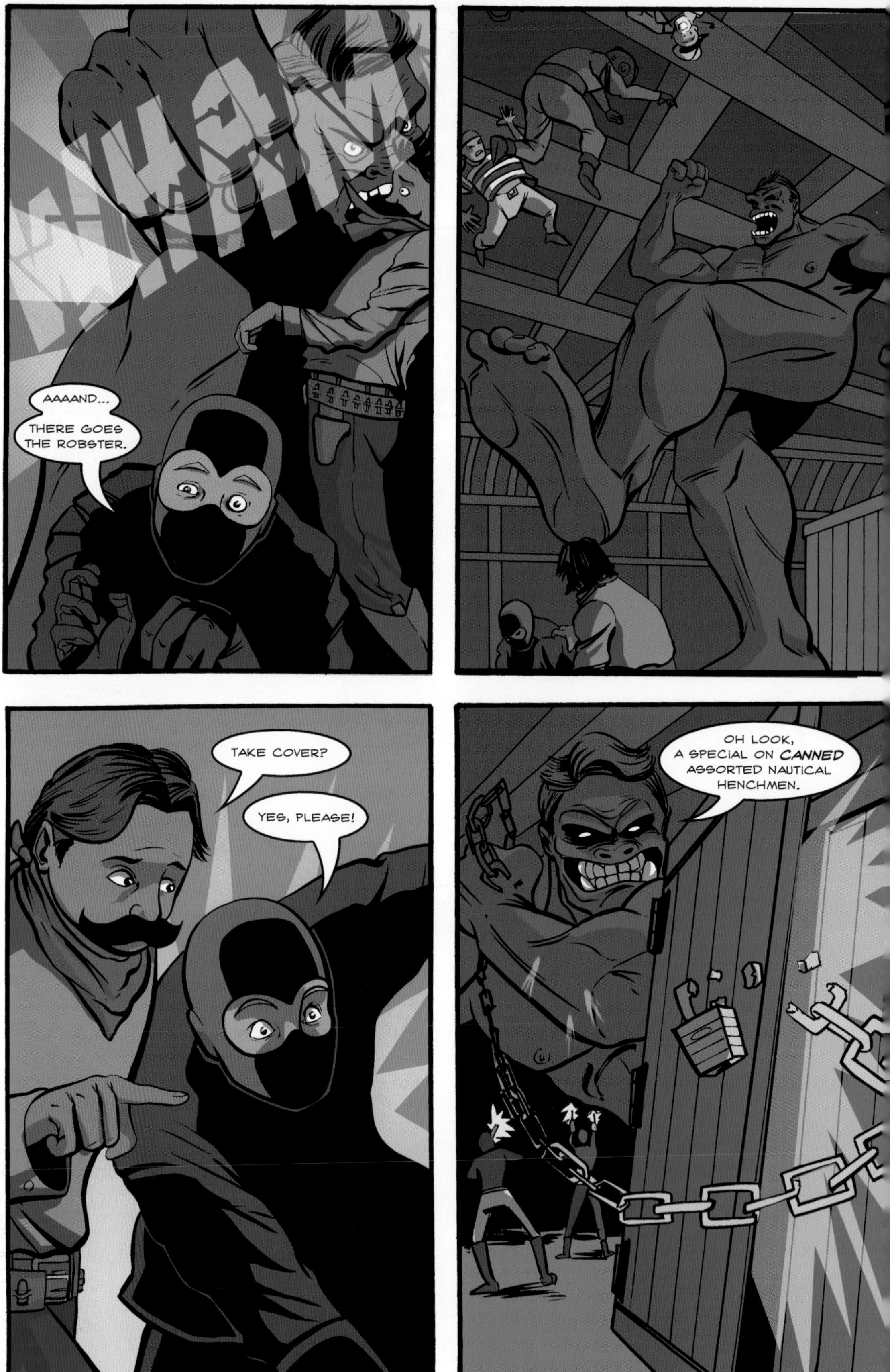
AAAAND...
THERE GOES THE ROBSTER.
TAKE COVER?
YES, PLEASE!
OH LOOK, A SPECIAL ON *CANNED* ASSORTED NAUTICAL HENCHMEN.

Martin thinks everybody calls shipping containers like that "cans" because of the second season of *The Wire*.

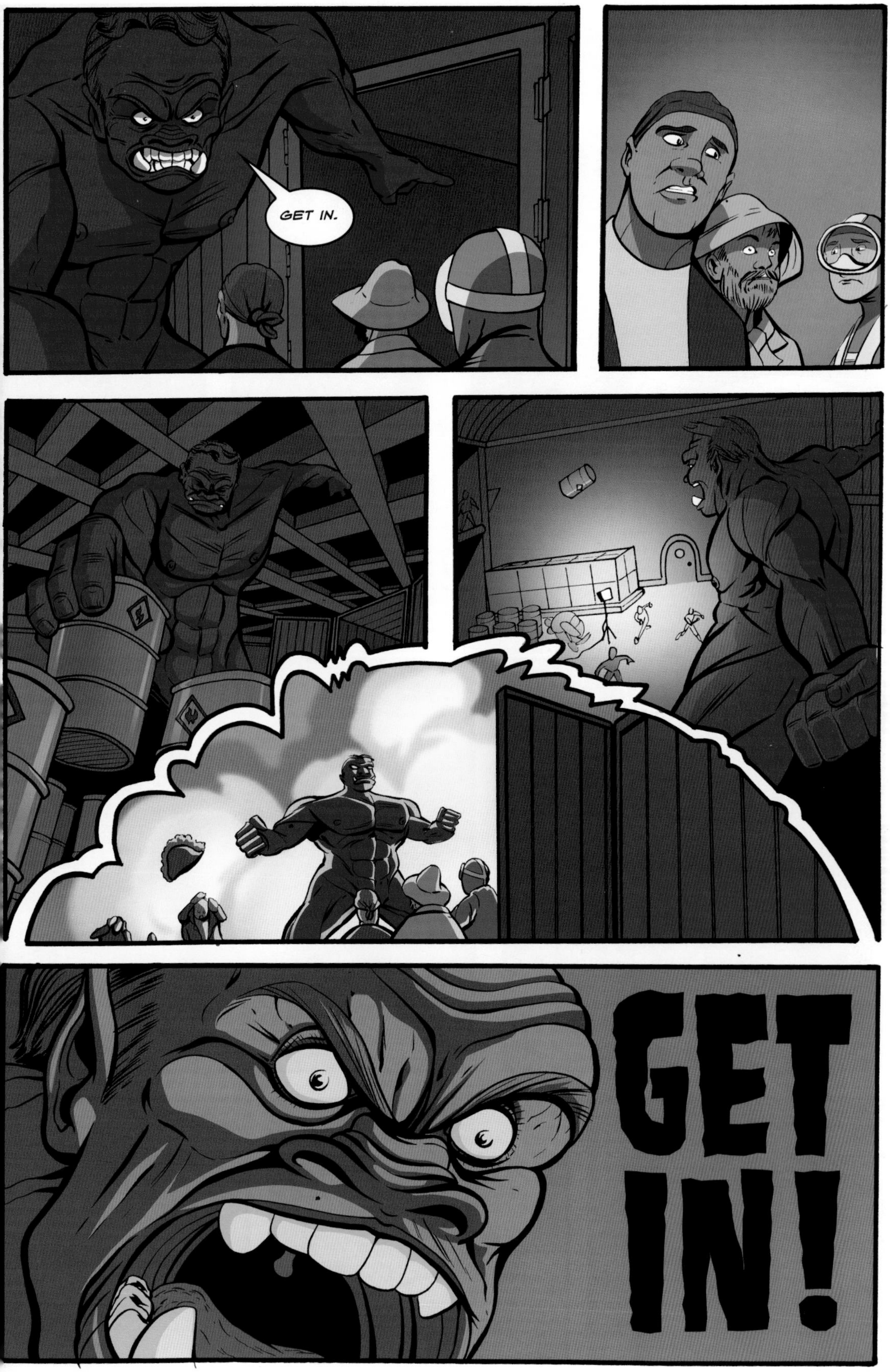
GET IN.
GET IN!

You may begin to notice that the world of Dr. McNinja is very similar to that of video-game shooters. Flammable barrels are everywhere.

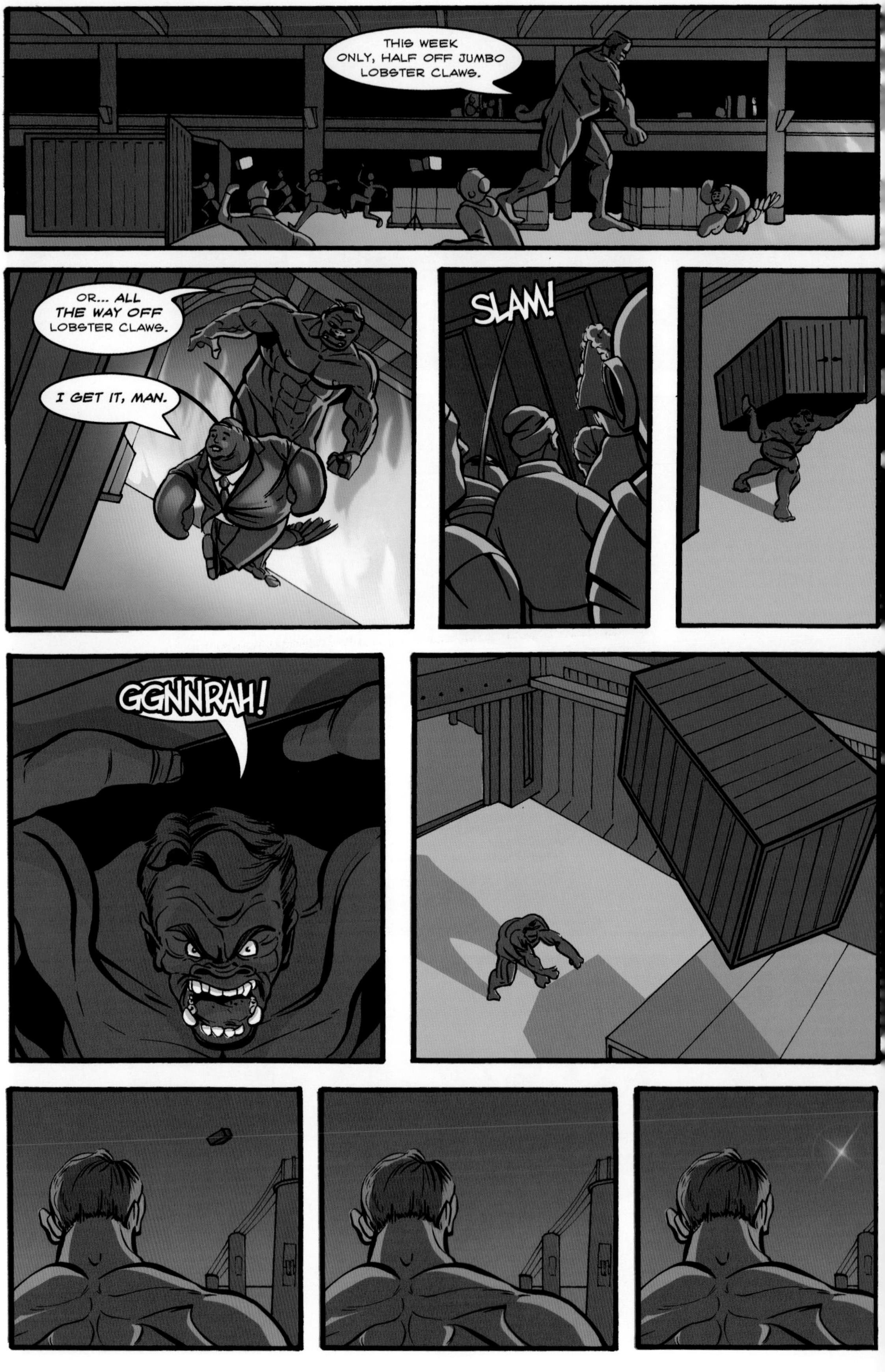
THIS WEEK ONLY, HALF OFF JUMBO LOBSTER CLAWS.
OR... ALL THE WAY OFF LOBSTER CLAWS.
I GET IT, MAN.
SLAM!
GGNNRAH!

JUDY UPDATE: Judy thinks how nice her new pottery will look on her desk. She doesn't know yet.

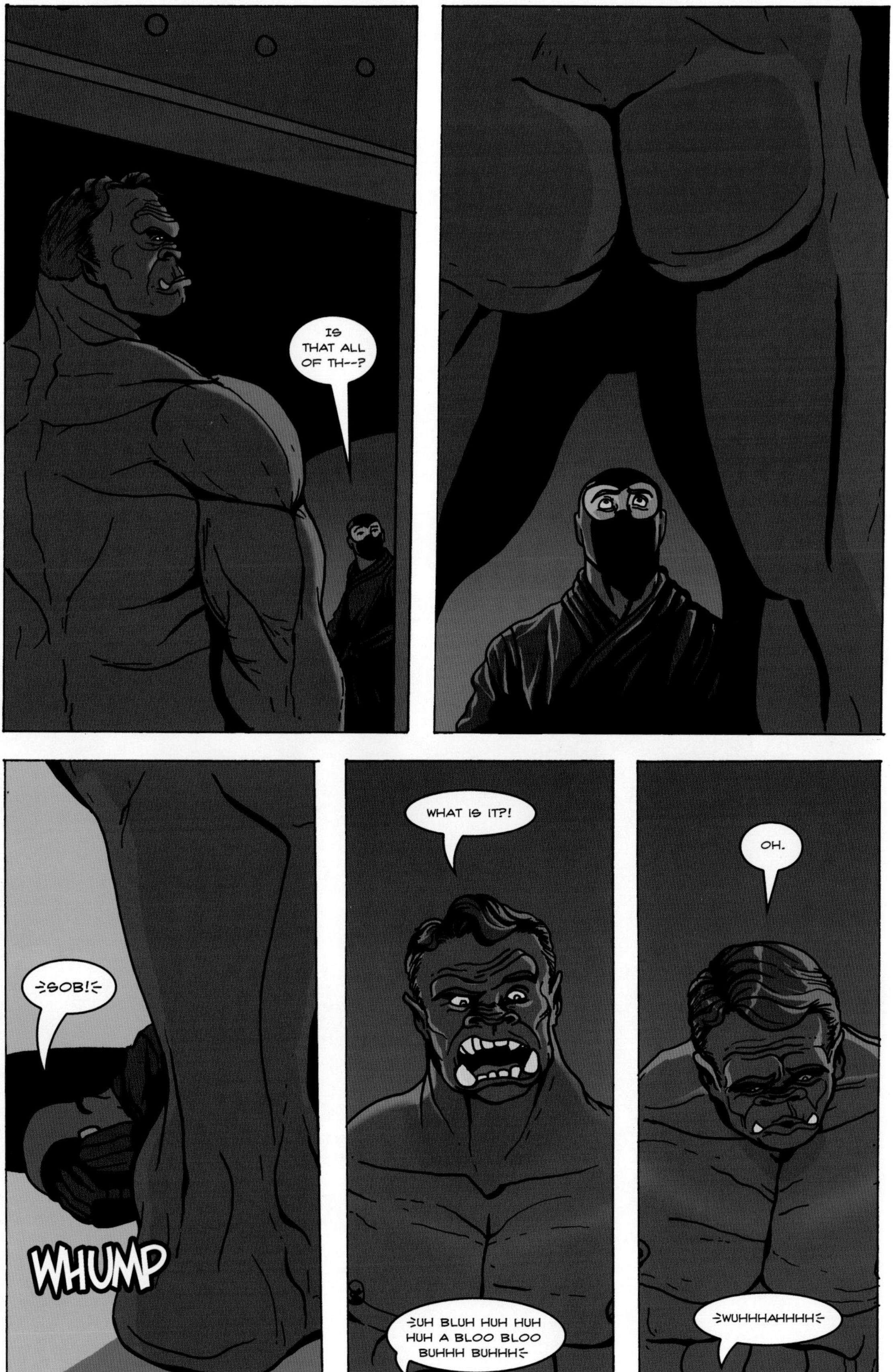
IS THAT ALL OF TH--?
=SOB!=
WHUMP
WHAT IS IT?!
=UH BLUH HUH HUH HUH A BLOO BLOO BUHHH BUHHH=
OH.
=WUHHHAHHHH=

A medical professional.

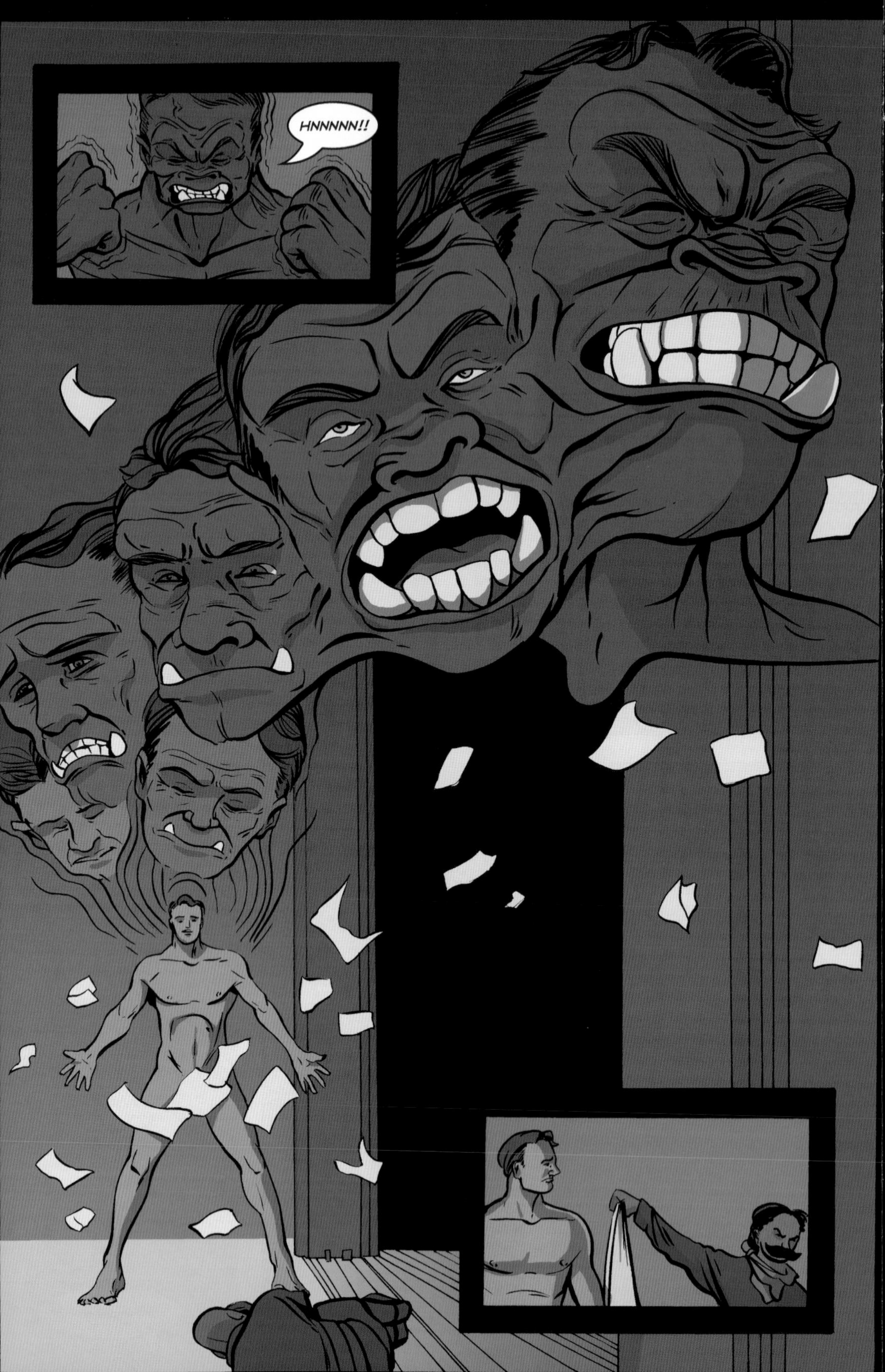
HNNNNN!!

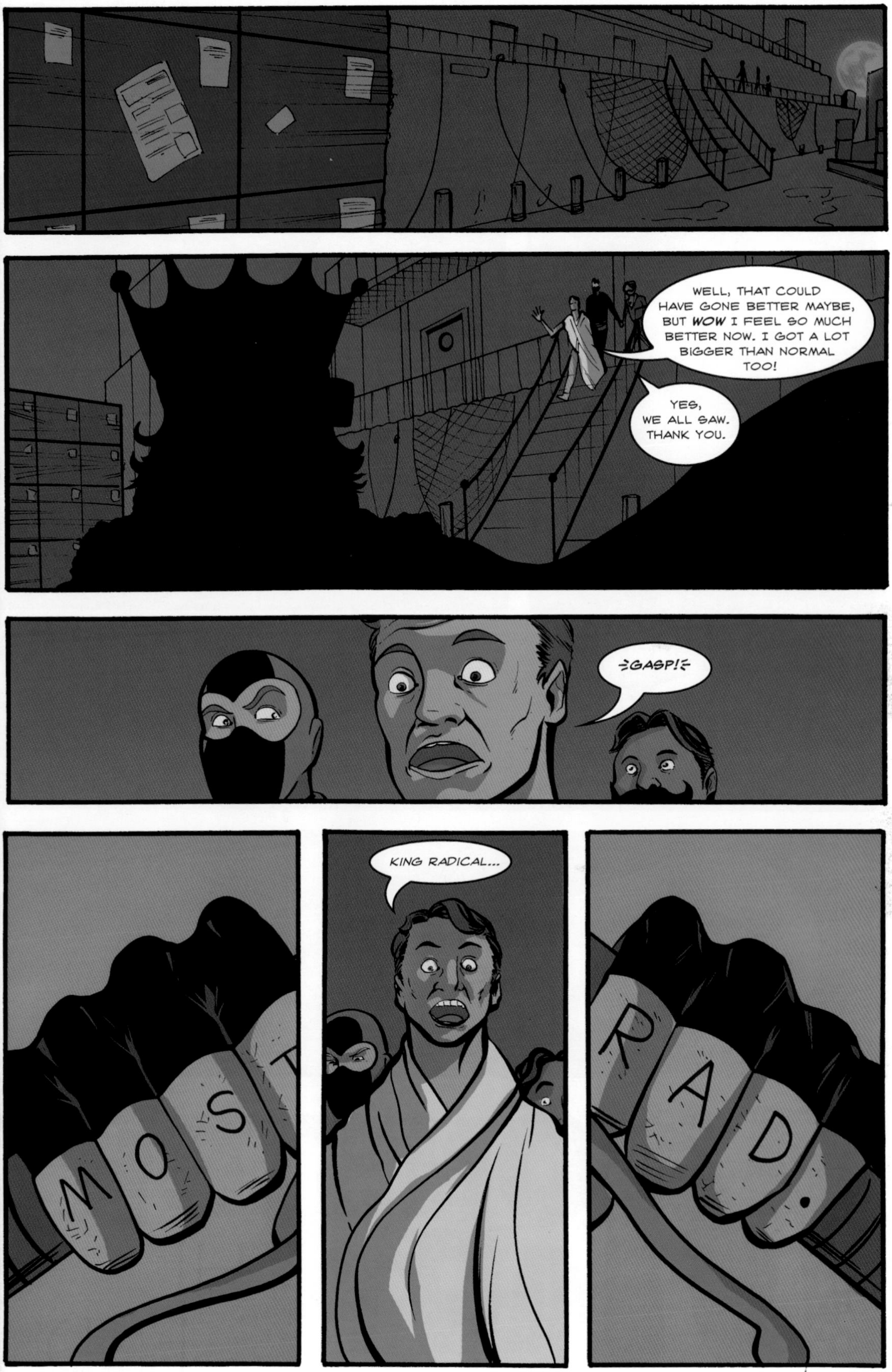
WELL, THAT COULD HAVE GONE BETTER MAYBE, BUT WOW I FEEL SO MUCH BETTER NOW. I GOT A LOT BIGGER THAN NORMAL TOO!
YES, WE ALL SAW. THANK YOU.
GASP!
MOST
KING RADICAL...
RAD.

Next time I should give him some trumpeters that ride skateboards, to announce his presence.

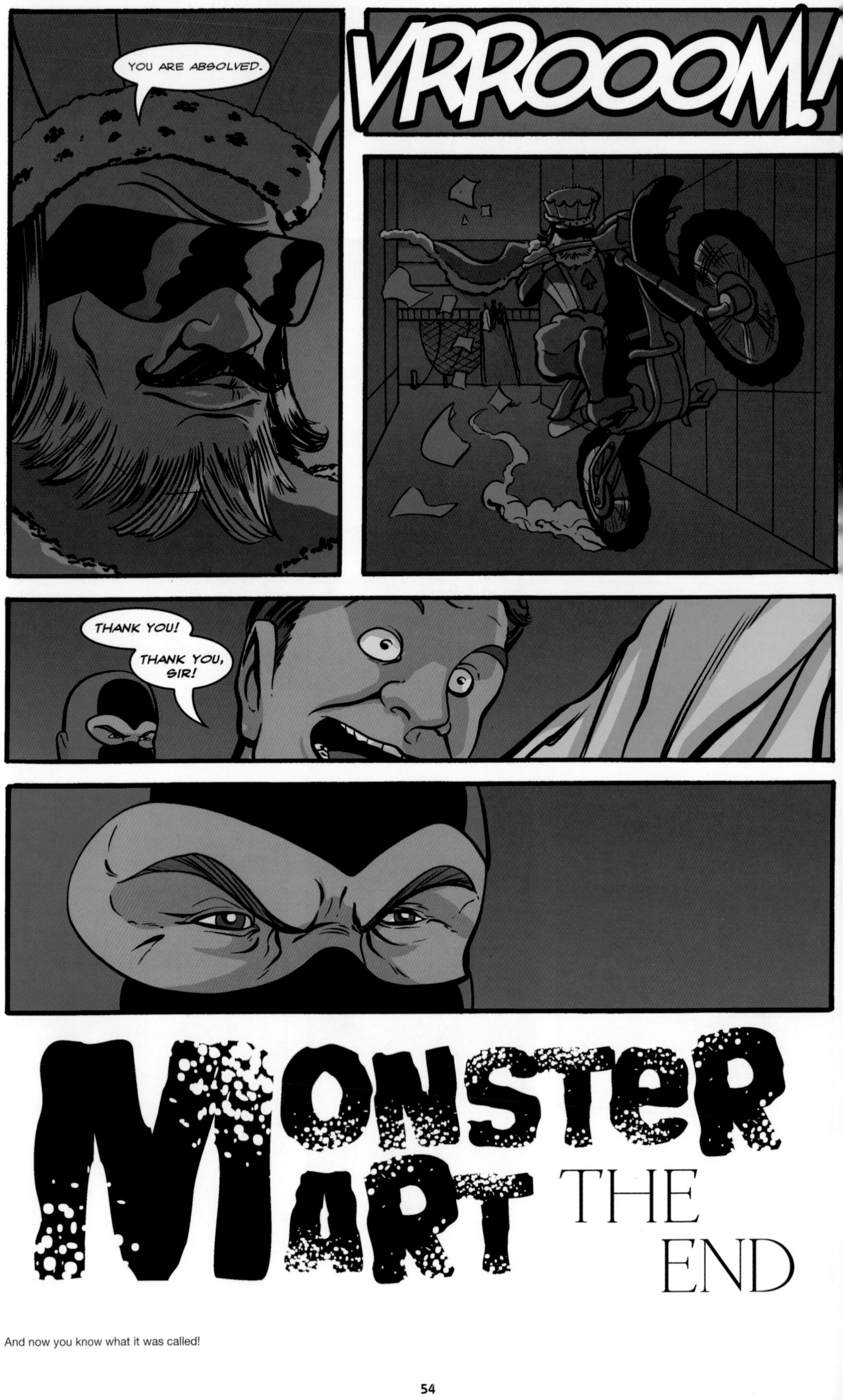
YOU ARE ABSOLVED.
VRROOOM!
THANK YOU!
THANK YOU, SIR!

MONSTER MART THE END

And now you know what it was called!

DR. MCNINJA'S FINAL THOUGHTS

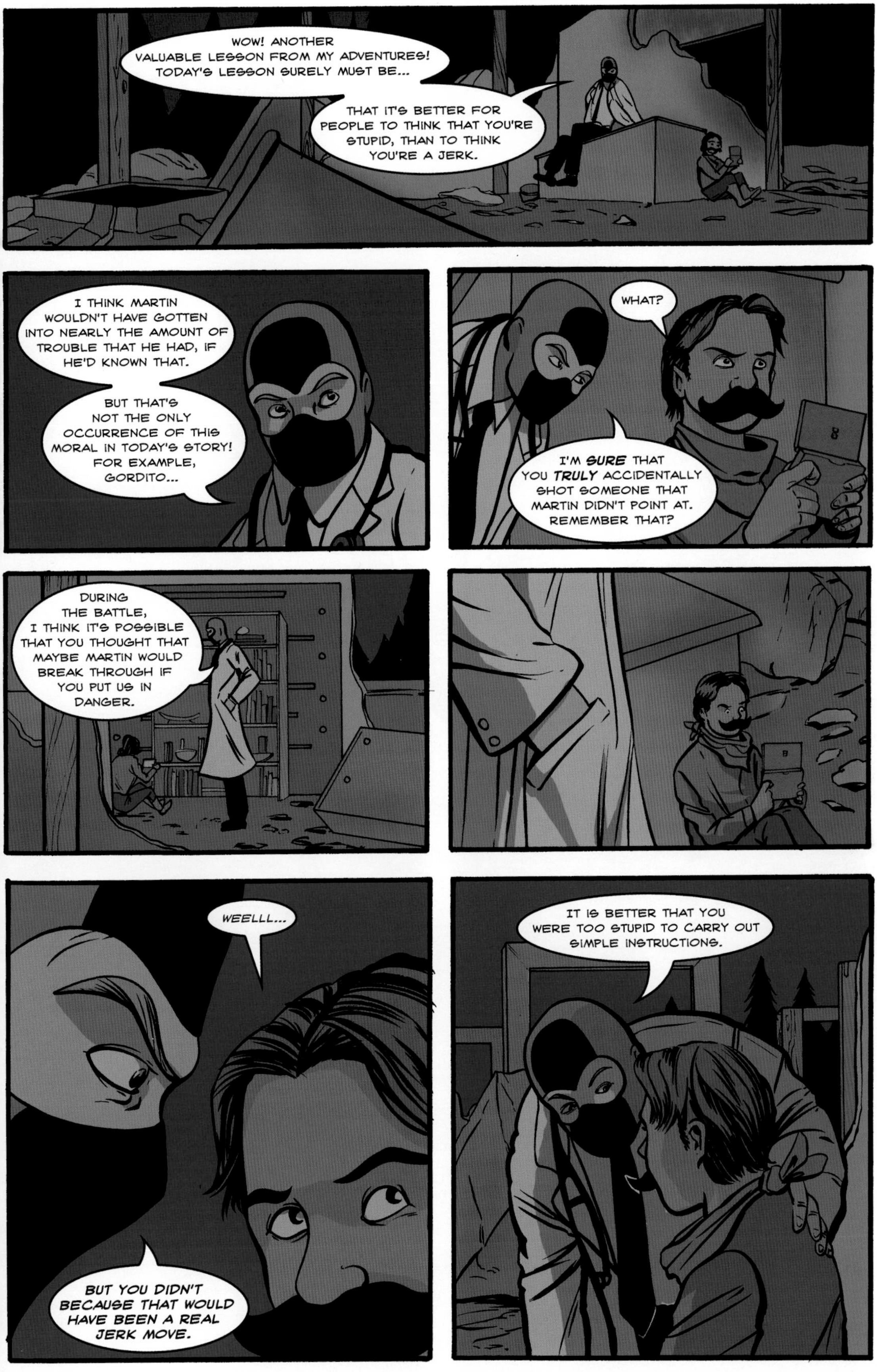

WOW! ANOTHER VALUABLE LESSON FROM MY ADVENTURES! TODAY'S LESSON SURELY MUST BE...
THAT IT'S BETTER FOR PEOPLE TO THINK THAT YOU'RE STUPID, THAN TO THINK YOU'RE A JERK.
I THINK MARTIN WOULDN'T HAVE GOTTEN INTO NEARLY THE AMOUNT OF TROUBLE THAT HE HAD, IF HE'D KNOWN THAT.
BUT THAT'S NOT THE ONLY OCCURRENCE OF THIS MORAL IN TODAY'S STORY! FOR EXAMPLE, GORDITO...
WHAT?
I'M *SURE* THAT YOU *TRULY* ACCIDENTALLY SHOT SOMEONE THAT MARTIN DIDN'T POINT AT. REMEMBER THAT?
DURING THE BATTLE, I THINK IT'S POSSIBLE THAT YOU THOUGHT THAT MAYBE MARTIN WOULD BREAK THROUGH IF YOU PUT US IN DANGER.
WEELLL...
BUT YOU DIDN'T BECAUSE THAT WOULD HAVE BEEN A REAL JERK MOVE.
IT IS BETTER THAT YOU WERE TOO STUPID TO CARRY OUT SIMPLE INSTRUCTIONS.

Gordito clearly finds the stylus gimmicky, but enjoys the device nonetheless.

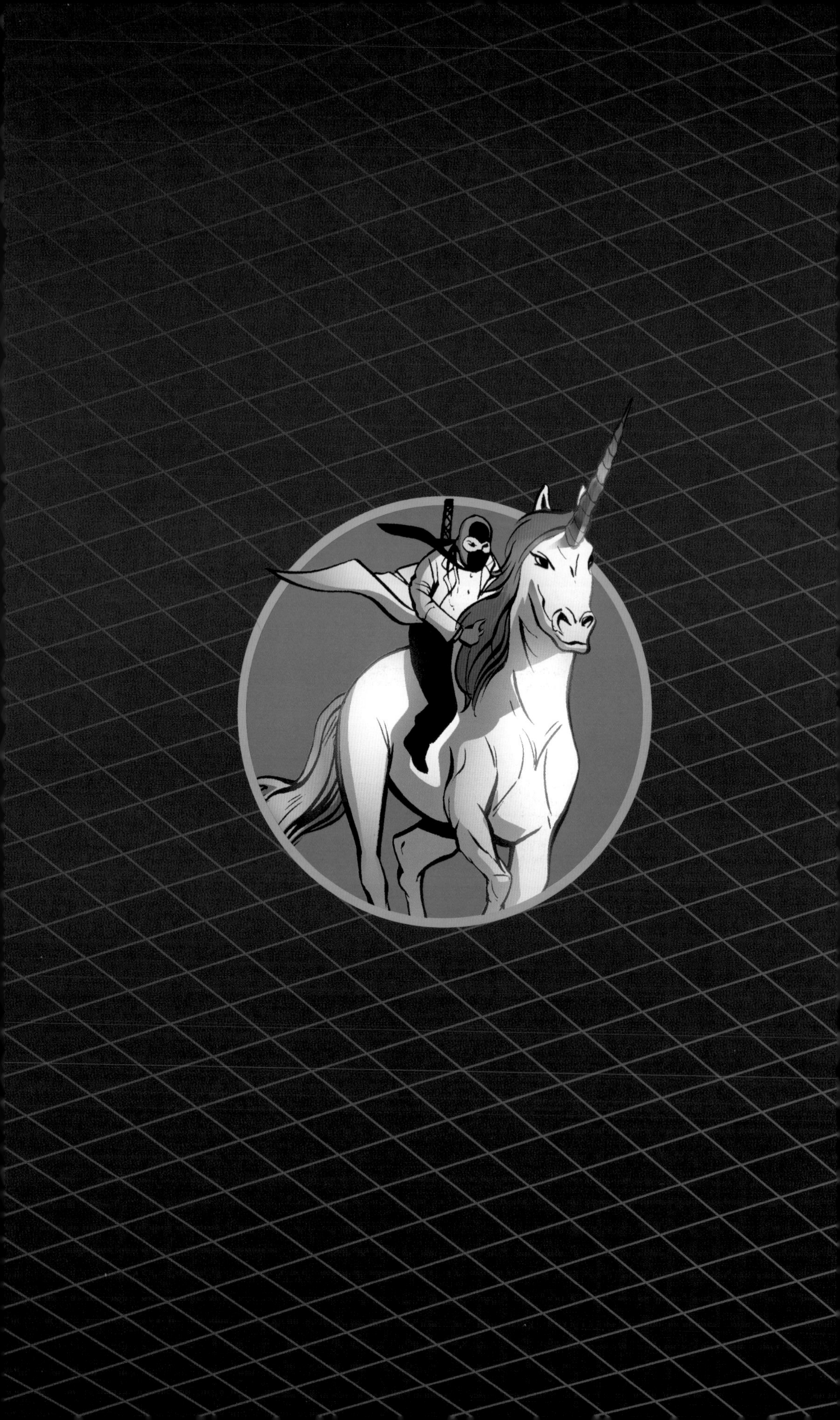

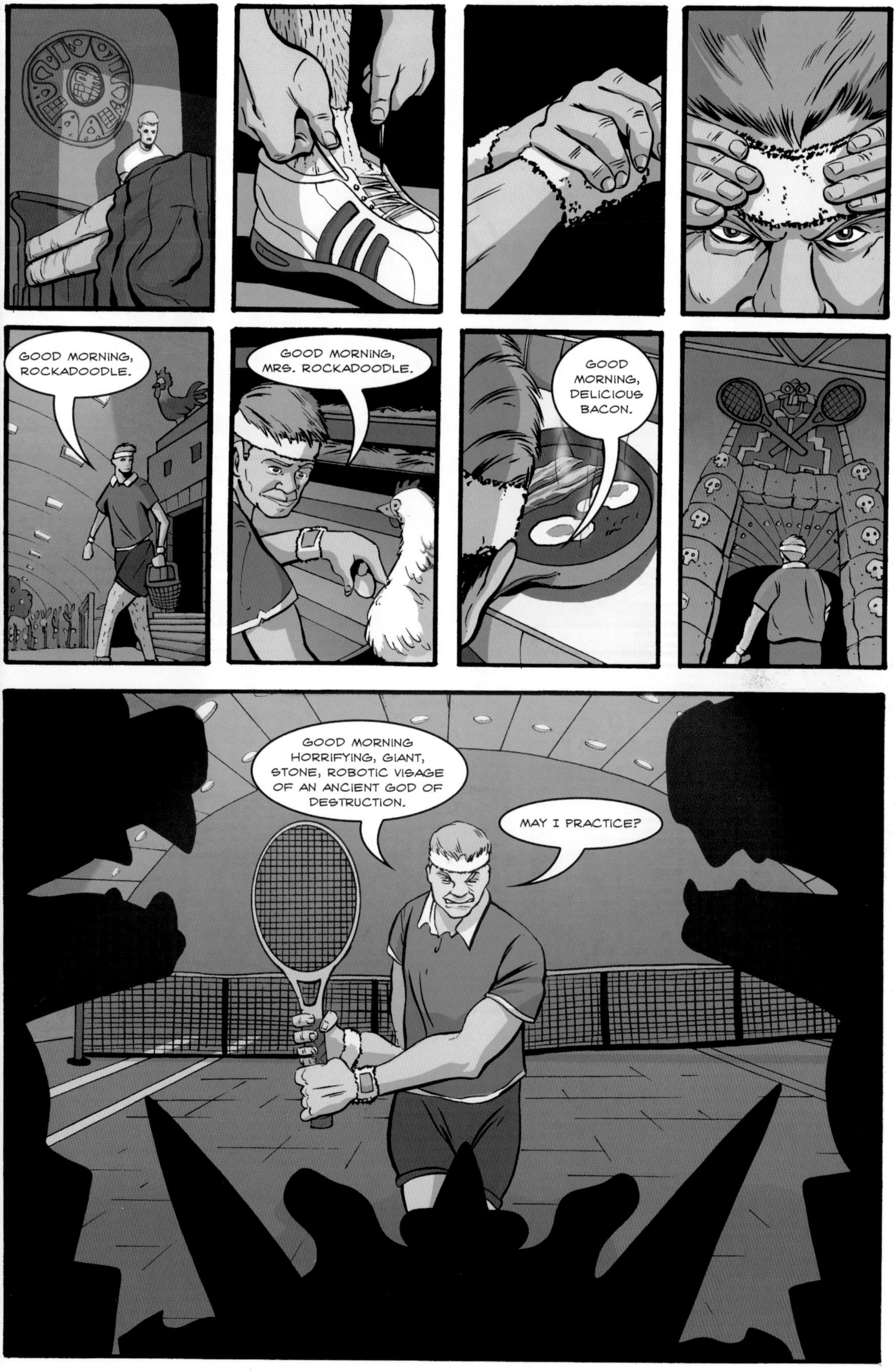
GOOD MORNING, ROCKADOODLE.
GOOD MORNING, MRS. ROCKADOODLE.
GOOD MORNING, DELICIOUS BACON.
GOOD MORNING HORRIFYING, GIANT, STONE, ROBOTIC VISAGE OF AN ANCIENT GOD OF DESTRUCTION.
MAY I PRACTICE?

Hey, remember Rockadoodle? Chris Hastings does.

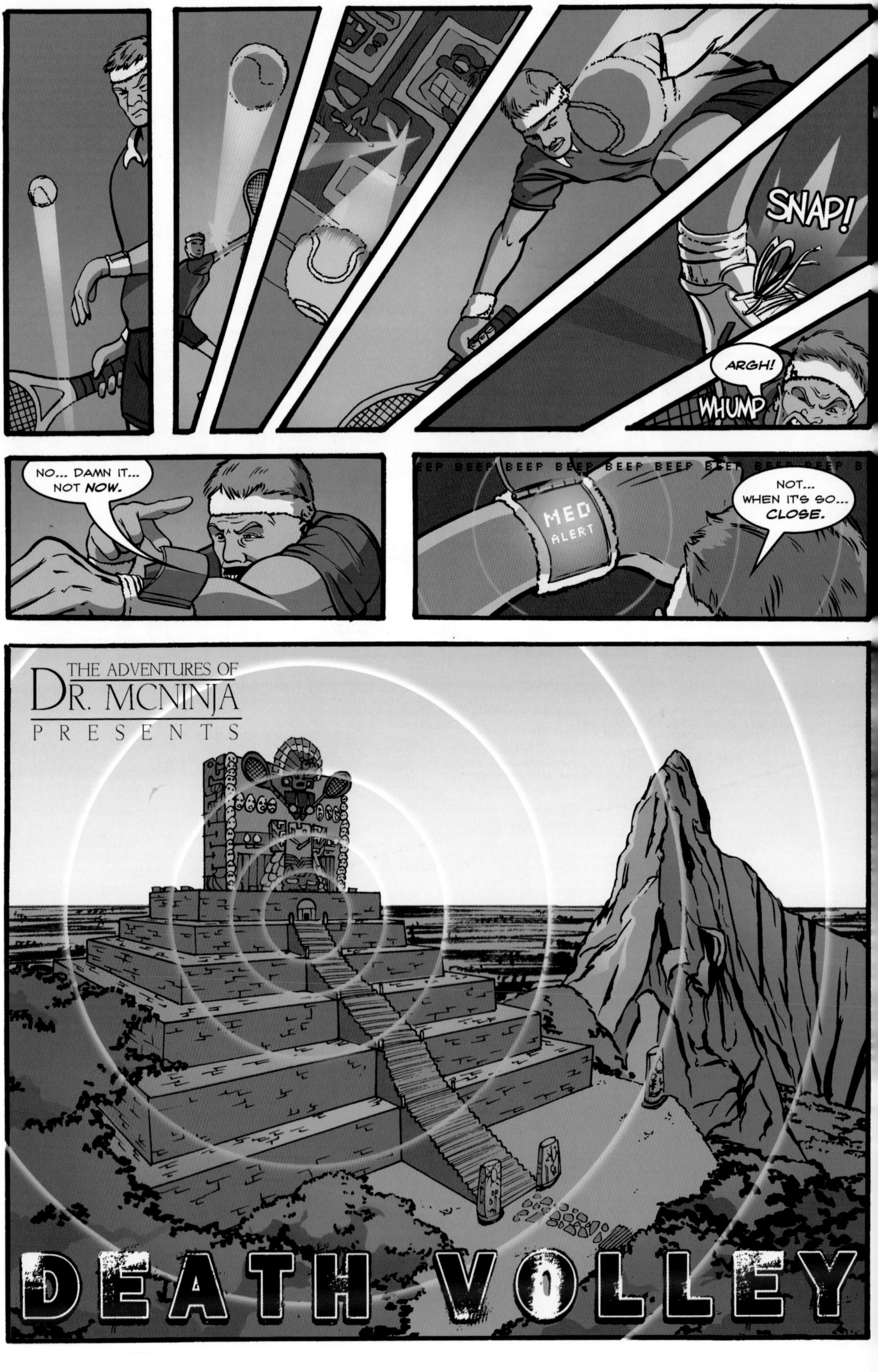
SNAP!
ARGH!
WHUMP
NO... DAMN IT... NOT NOW.
BEEP BEEP BEEP BEEP BEEP BEEP BEEP BEEP BEEP
MED ALERT
NOT... WHEN IT'S SO... CLOSE.
THE ADVENTURES OF DR. MCNINJA PRESENTS
DEATH VOLLEY

Maybe my favorite story title yet.

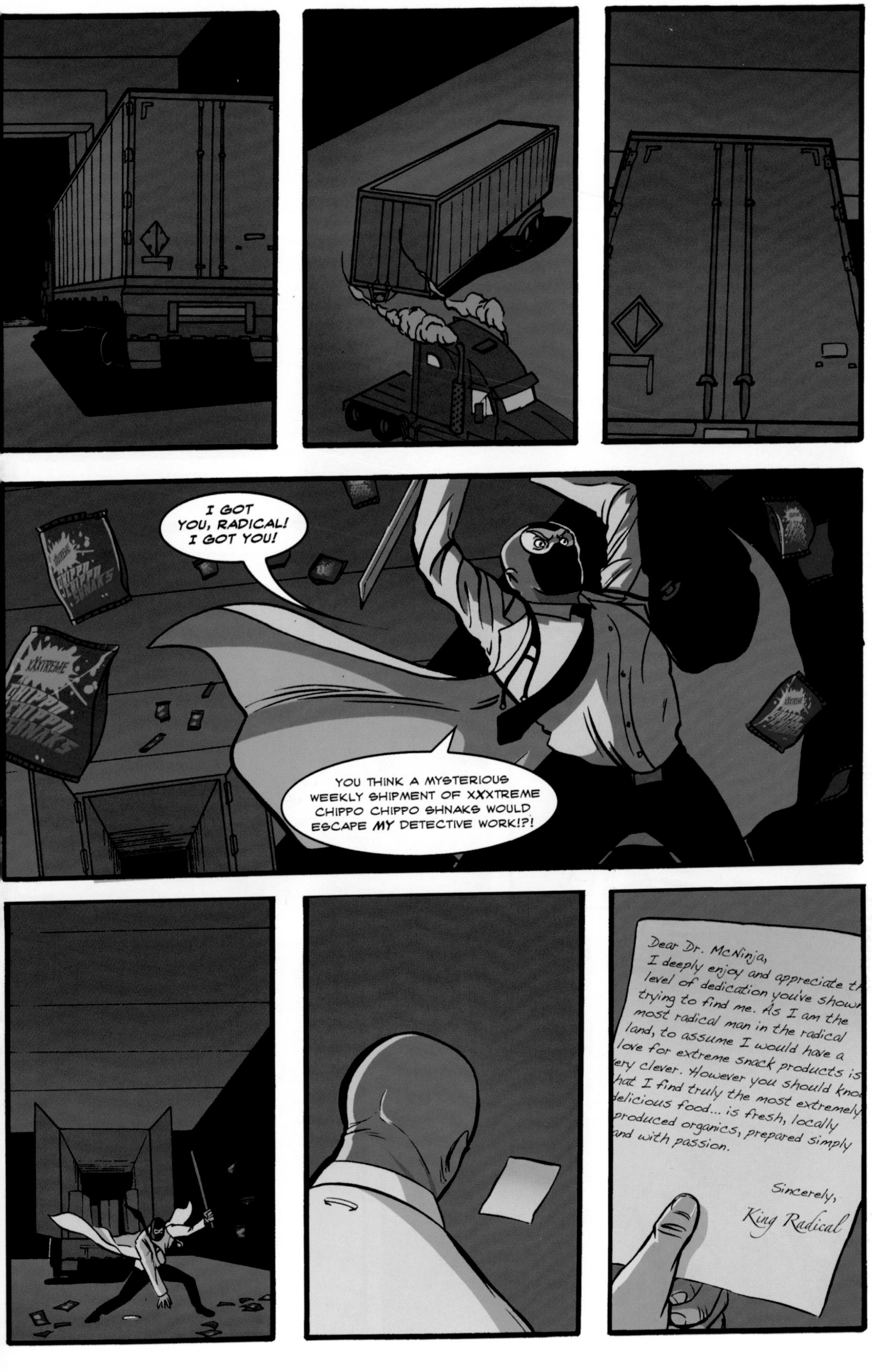
I GOT YOU, RADICAL! I GOT YOU!
XXXTREME CHIPPO CHIPPO SHNAKS
YOU THINK A MYSTERIOUS WEEKLY SHIPMENT OF XXXTREME CHIPPO CHIPPO SHNAKS WOULD ESCAPE *MY* DETECTIVE WORK!?!
Dear Dr. McNinja,
I deeply enjoy and appreciate th
level of dedication you've shown
trying to find me. As I am the
most radical man in the radical
land, to assume I would have a
love for extreme snack products is
ery clever. However you should kno
hat I find truly the most extremely
delicious food... is fresh, locally
produced organics, prepared simply
and with passion.
Sincerely,
King Radical

Could King Radical be GORDON RAMSAY?!!?

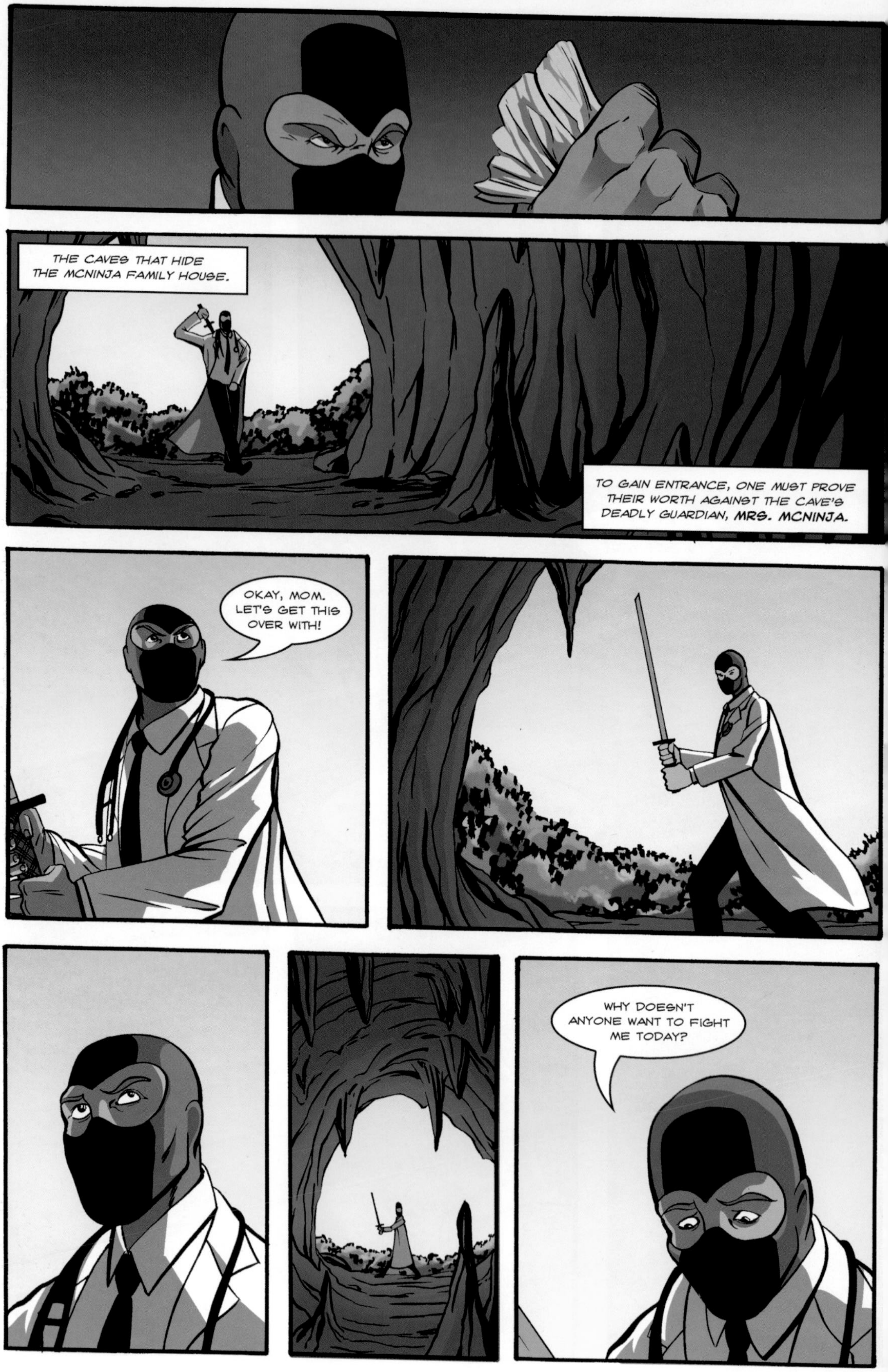
THE CAVES THAT HIDE THE MCNINJA FAMILY HOUSE.
TO GAIN ENTRANCE, ONE MUST PROVE THEIR WORTH AGAINST THE CAVE'S DEADLY GUARDIAN, MRS. MCNINJA.
OKAY, MOM. LET'S GET THIS OVER WITH!
WHY DOESN'T ANYONE WANT TO FIGHT ME TODAY?

'CAUSE YOU STANK.

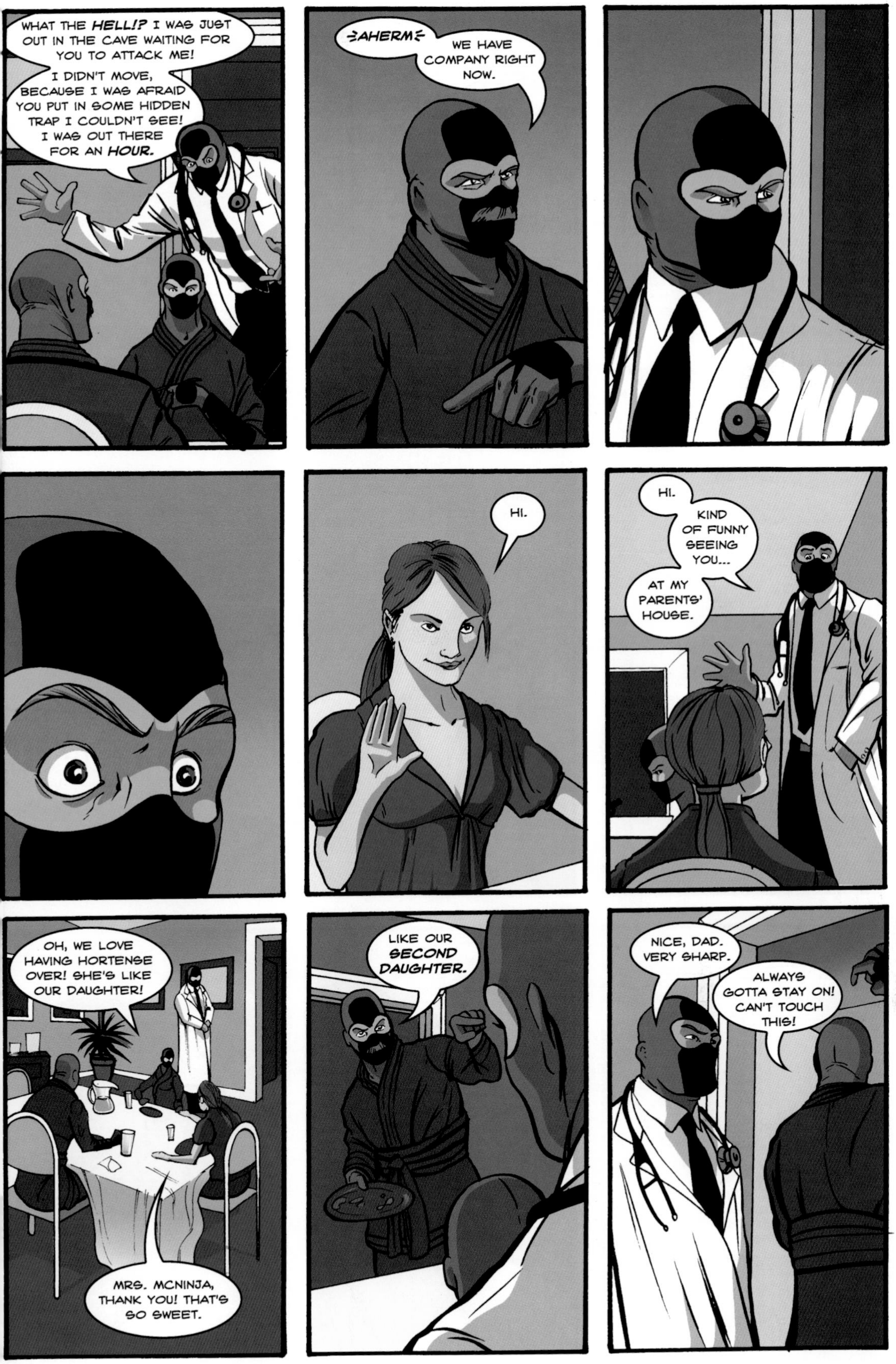
WHAT THE HELL!? I WAS JUST OUT IN THE CAVE WAITING FOR YOU TO ATTACK ME!
I DIDN'T MOVE, BECAUSE I WAS AFRAID YOU PUT IN SOME HIDDEN TRAP I COULDN'T SEE! I WAS OUT THERE FOR AN HOUR.
AHERM
WE HAVE COMPANY RIGHT NOW.
HI.
HI.
KIND OF FUNNY SEEING YOU...
AT MY PARENTS' HOUSE.
OH, WE LOVE HAVING HORTENSE OVER! SHE'S LIKE OUR DAUGHTER!
MRS. MCNINJA, THANK YOU! THAT'S SO SWEET.
LIKE OUR SECOND DAUGHTER.
NICE, DAD. VERY SHARP.
ALWAYS GOTTA STAY ON! CAN'T TOUCH THIS!

Seconds after I typed that line, THE SONG CAME ON THE RADIO. It was amazing.

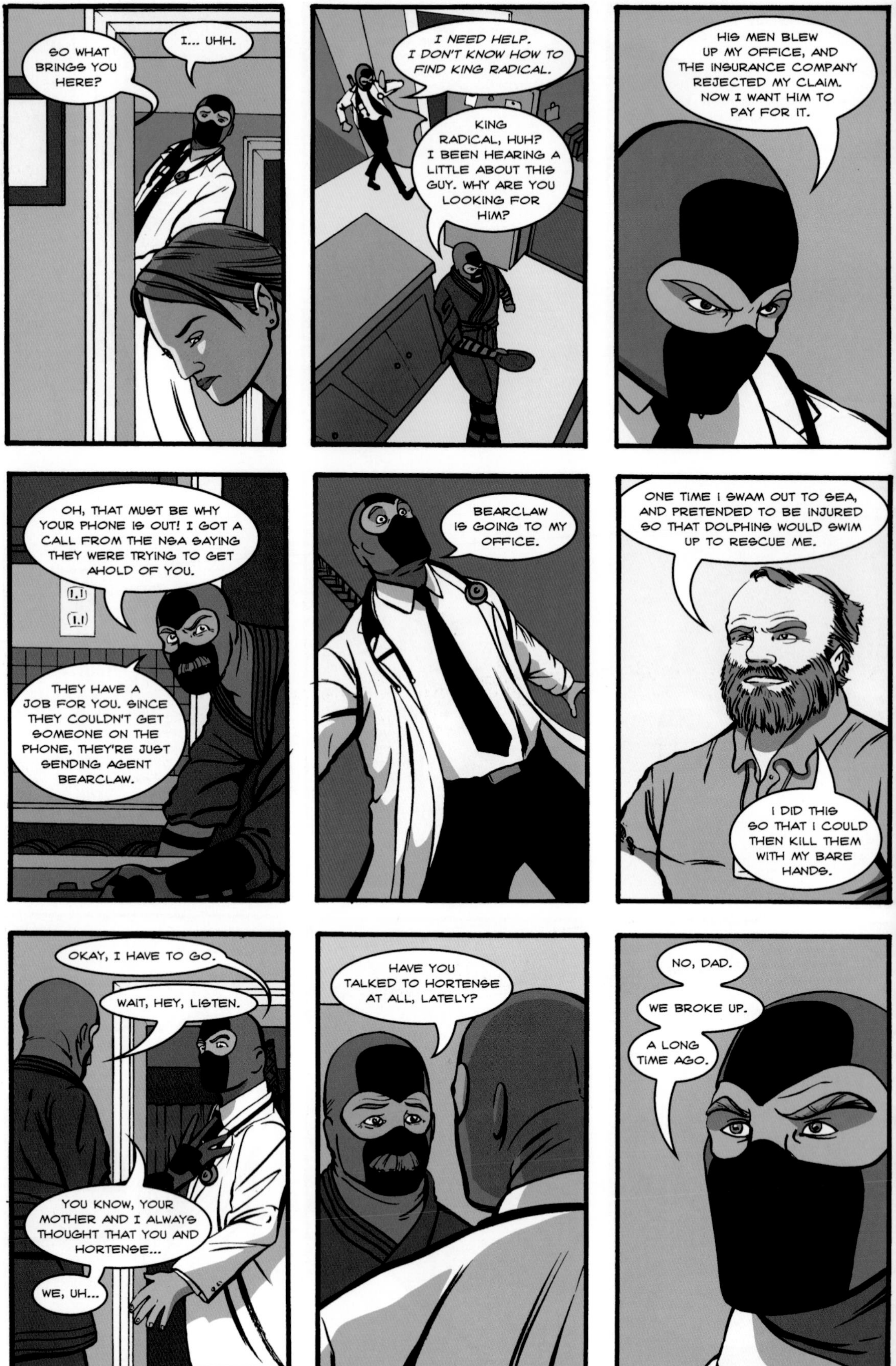
SO WHAT BRINGS YOU HERE?
I... UHH.
I NEED HELP. I DON'T KNOW HOW TO FIND KING RADICAL.
KING RADICAL, HUH? I BEEN HEARING A LITTLE ABOUT THIS GUY. WHY ARE YOU LOOKING FOR HIM?
HIS MEN BLEW UP MY OFFICE, AND THE INSURANCE COMPANY REJECTED MY CLAIM. NOW I WANT HIM TO PAY FOR IT.
OH, THAT MUST BE WHY YOUR PHONE IS OUT! I GOT A CALL FROM THE NSA SAYING THEY WERE TRYING TO GET AHOLD OF YOU.
THEY HAVE A JOB FOR YOU. SINCE THEY COULDN'T GET SOMEONE ON THE PHONE, THEY'RE JUST SENDING AGENT BEARCLAW.
BEARCLAW IS GOING TO MY OFFICE.
ONE TIME I SWAM OUT TO SEA, AND PRETENDED TO BE INJURED SO THAT DOLPHINS WOULD SWIM UP TO RESCUE ME.
I DID THIS SO THAT I COULD THEN KILL THEM WITH MY BARE HANDS.
OKAY, I HAVE TO GO.
WAIT, HEY, LISTEN.
YOU KNOW, YOUR MOTHER AND I ALWAYS THOUGHT THAT YOU AND HORTENSE...
WE, UH...
HAVE YOU TALKED TO HORTENSE AT ALL, LATELY?
NO, DAD.
WE BROKE UP.
A LONG TIME AGO.

I'm not really sure what look I was going for when I gave Bearclaw a polo shirt with torn sleeves.

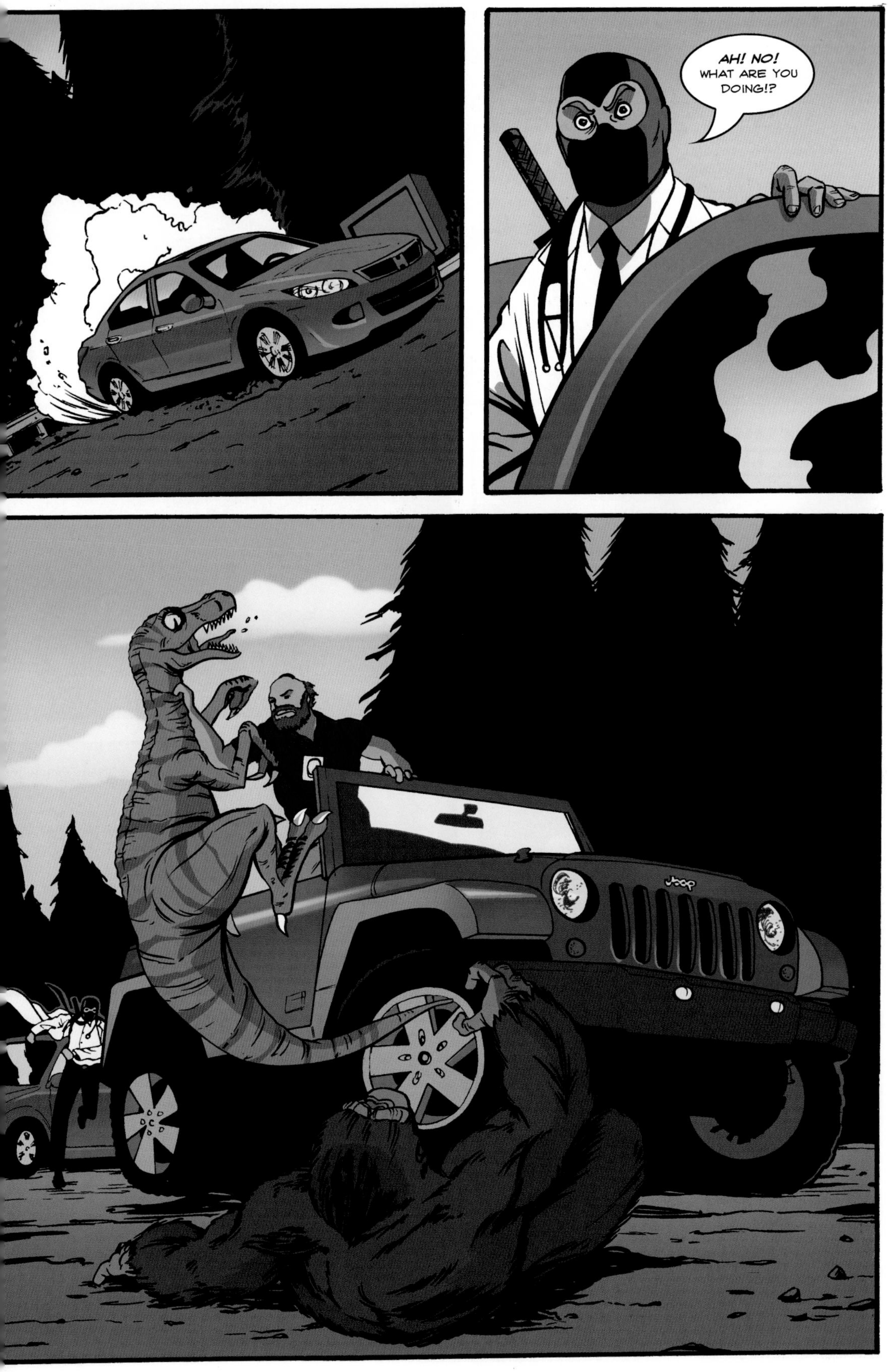
AH! NO! WHAT ARE YOU DOING!?

Bearclaw kind of gets bounced around from agency to agency because of stunts like this.

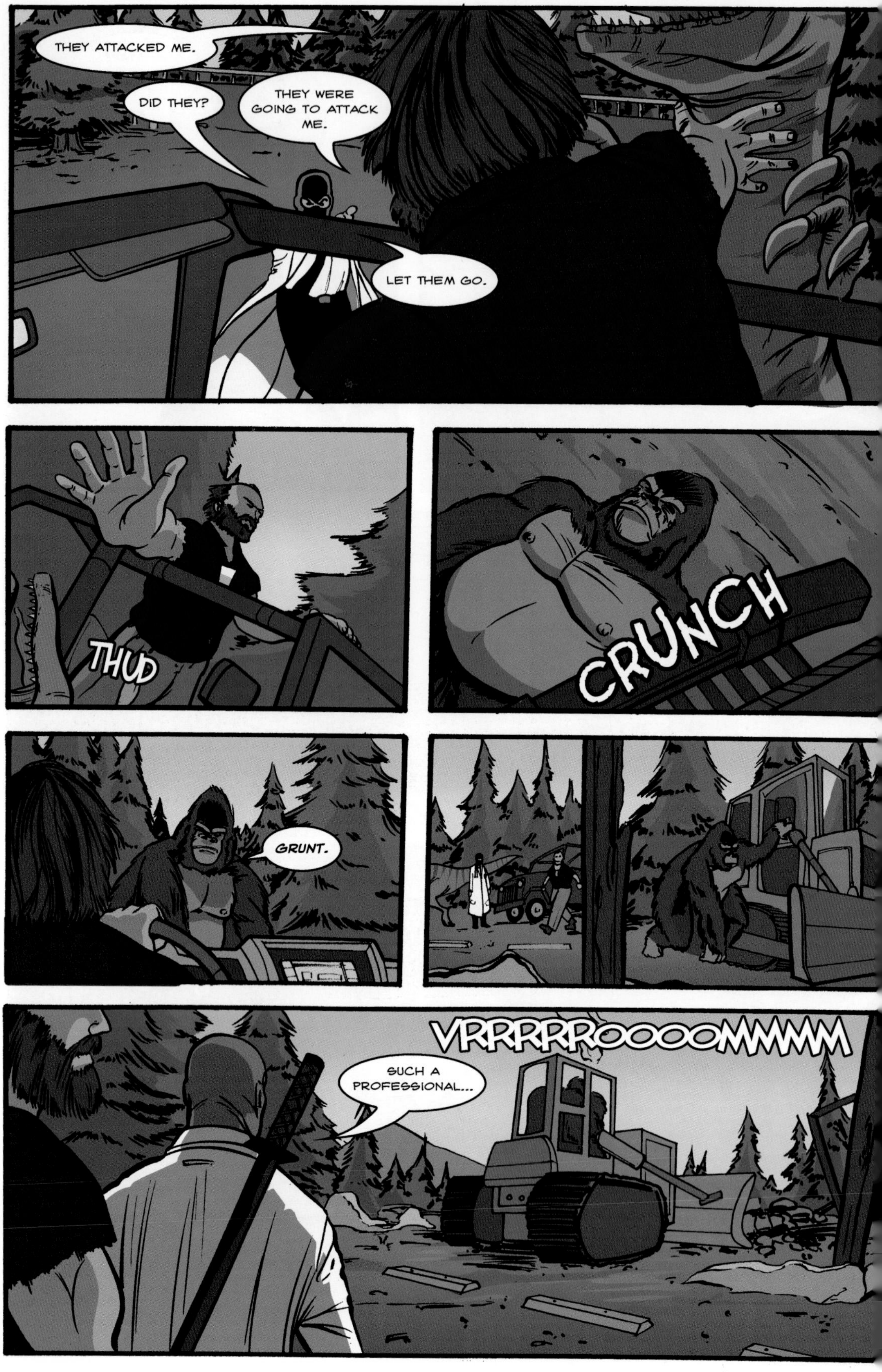
THEY ATTACKED ME.
DID THEY?
THEY WERE GOING TO ATTACK ME.
LET THEM GO.
THUD
CRUNCH
GRUNT.
VRRRRROOOOOMMMM
SUCH A PROFESSIONAL...

I should probably start to explore WHY Judy puts up with all of it. Life debt? Sent from the future to protect Doc from robots? Is actually a robot HERSELF?!

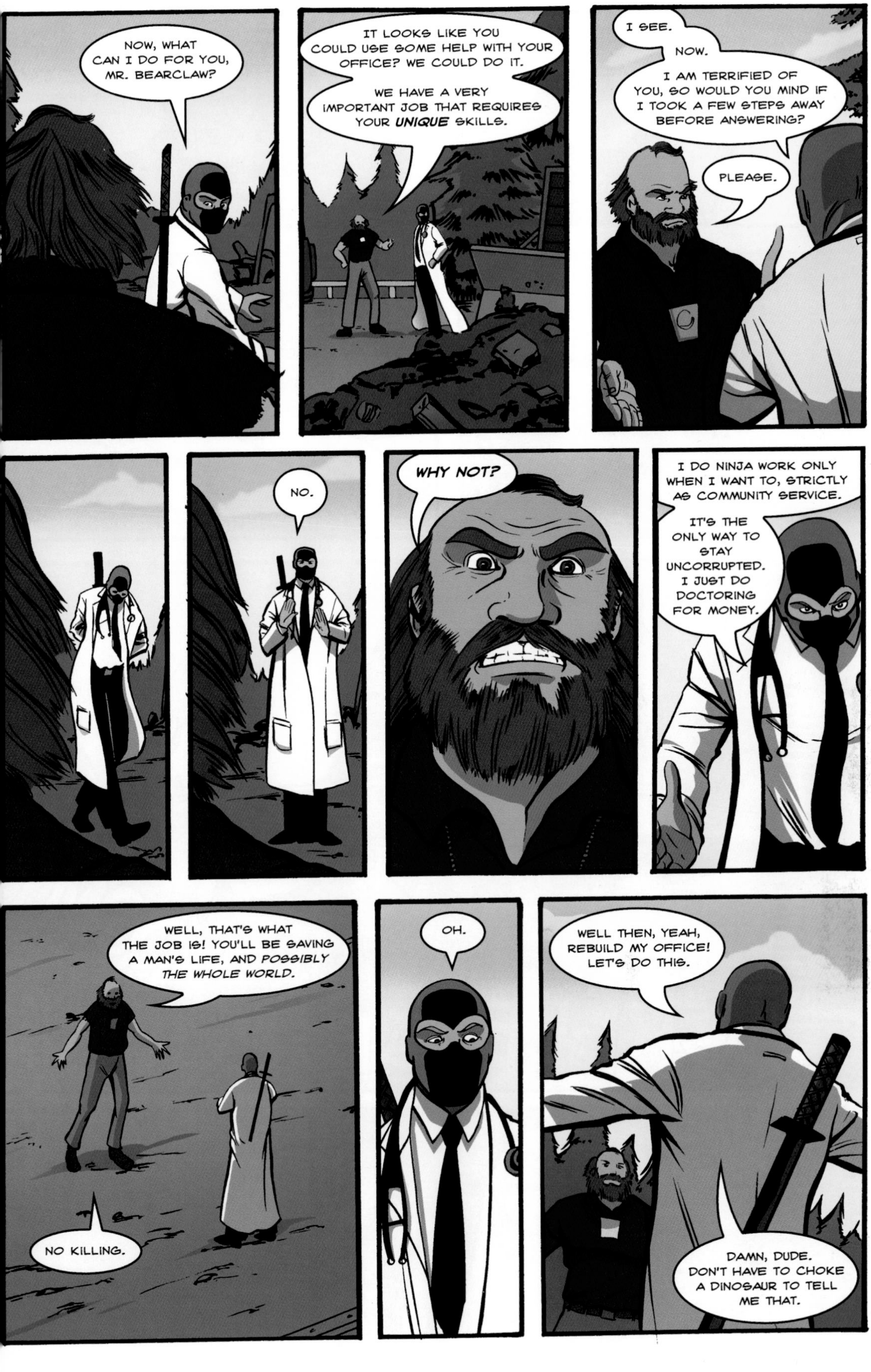
NOW, WHAT CAN I DO FOR YOU, MR. BEARCLAW?
IT LOOKS LIKE YOU COULD USE SOME HELP WITH YOUR OFFICE? WE COULD DO IT.
WE HAVE A VERY IMPORTANT JOB THAT REQUIRES YOUR *UNIQUE* SKILLS.
I SEE.
NOW.
I AM TERRIFIED OF YOU, SO WOULD YOU MIND IF I TOOK A FEW STEPS AWAY BEFORE ANSWERING?
PLEASE.
NO.
WHY NOT?
I DO NINJA WORK ONLY WHEN I WANT TO, STRICTLY AS COMMUNITY SERVICE.
IT'S THE ONLY WAY TO STAY UNCORRUPTED. I JUST DO DOCTORING FOR MONEY.
WELL, THAT'S WHAT THE JOB IS! YOU'LL BE SAVING A MAN'S LIFE, AND *POSSIBLY THE WHOLE WORLD.*
NO KILLING.
OH.
WELL THEN, YEAH, REBUILD MY OFFICE! LET'S DO THIS.
DAMN, DUDE. DON'T HAVE TO CHOKE A DINOSAUR TO TELL ME THAT.

Sorry, guys. Bearclaw said no killing in this story. Might as well come back in a couple months when it's done.

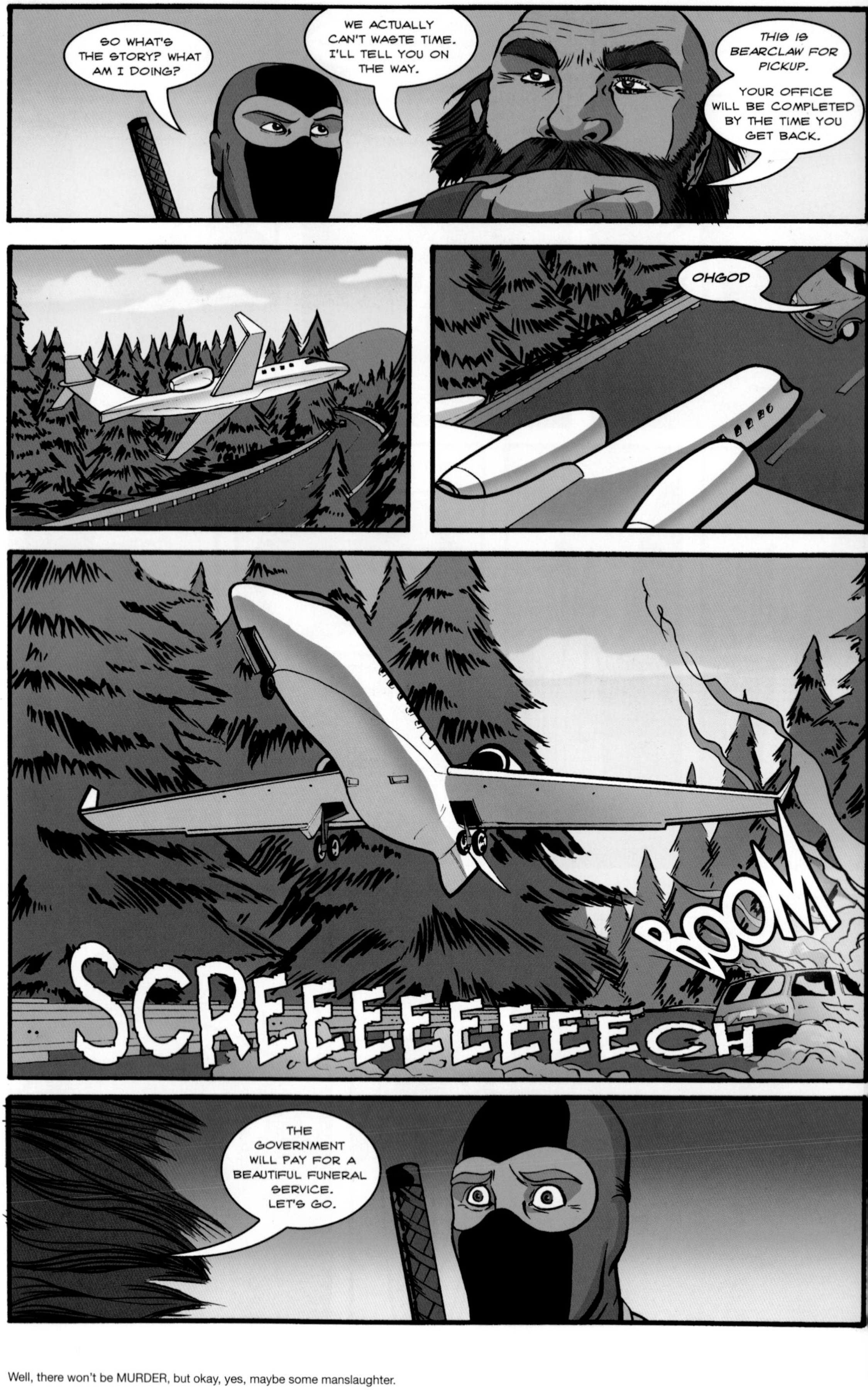
SO WHAT'S THE STORY? WHAT AM I DOING?
WE ACTUALLY CAN'T WASTE TIME. I'LL TELL YOU ON THE WAY.
THIS IS BEARCLAW FOR PICKUP.
YOUR OFFICE WILL BE COMPLETED BY THE TIME YOU GET BACK.
OHGOD
SCREEEEEEEEECH
BOOM
THE GOVERNMENT WILL PAY FOR A BEAUTIFUL FUNERAL SERVICE. LET'S GO.

Well, there won't be MURDER, but okay, yes, maybe some manslaughter.

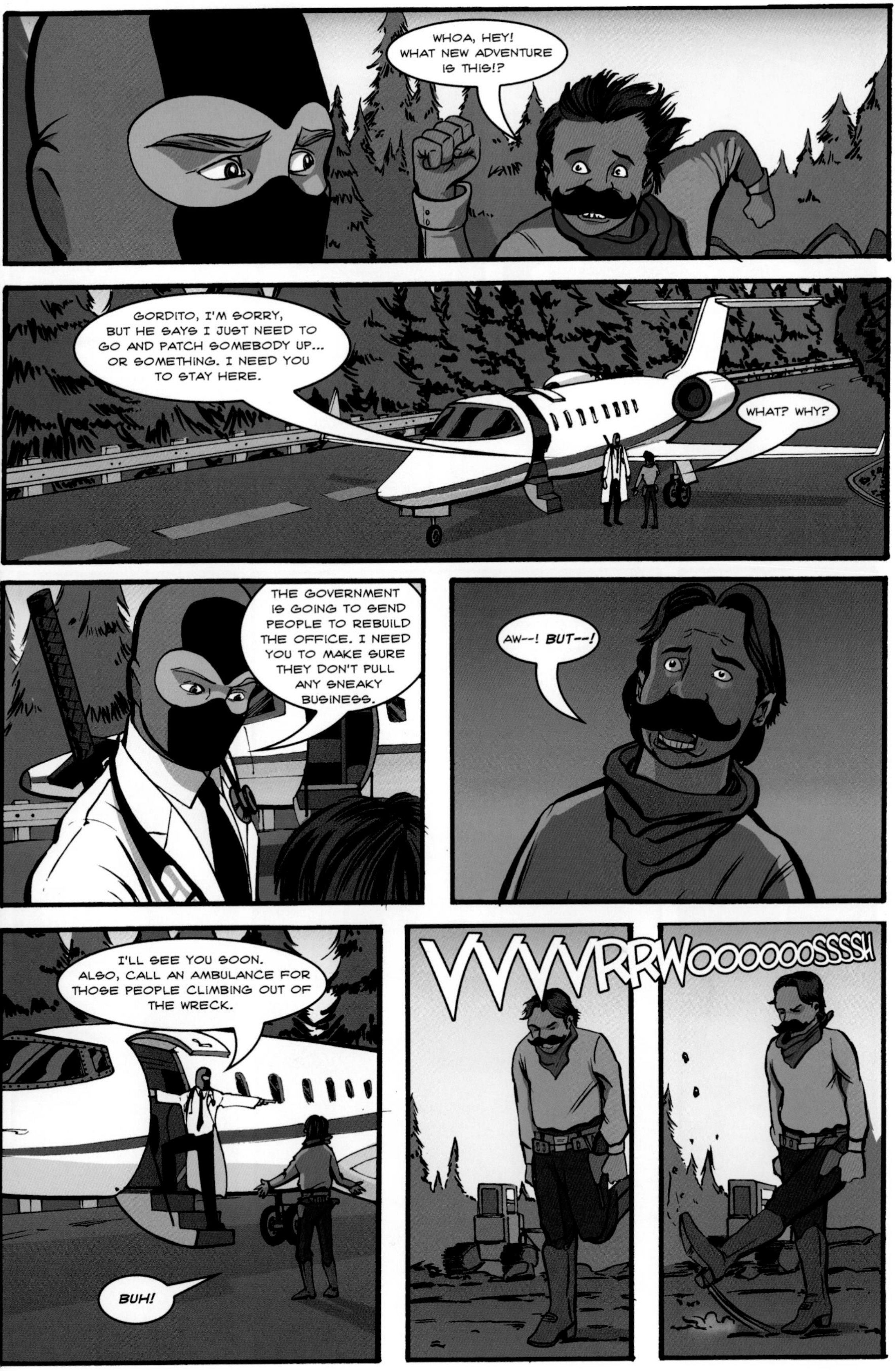
WHOA, HEY! WHAT NEW ADVENTURE IS THIS!?
GORDITO, I'M SORRY, BUT HE SAYS I JUST NEED TO GO AND PATCH SOMEBODY UP... OR SOMETHING. I NEED YOU TO STAY HERE.
WHAT? WHY?
THE GOVERNMENT IS GOING TO SEND PEOPLE TO REBUILD THE OFFICE. I NEED YOU TO MAKE SURE THEY DON'T PULL ANY SNEAKY BUSINESS.
AW--! BUT--!
I'LL SEE YOU SOON. ALSO, CALL AN AMBULANCE FOR THOSE PEOPLE CLIMBING OUT OF THE WRECK.
BUH!
VVVVRRRWOOOOOOSSSSH

Aaawwww BUTTERCUPS.

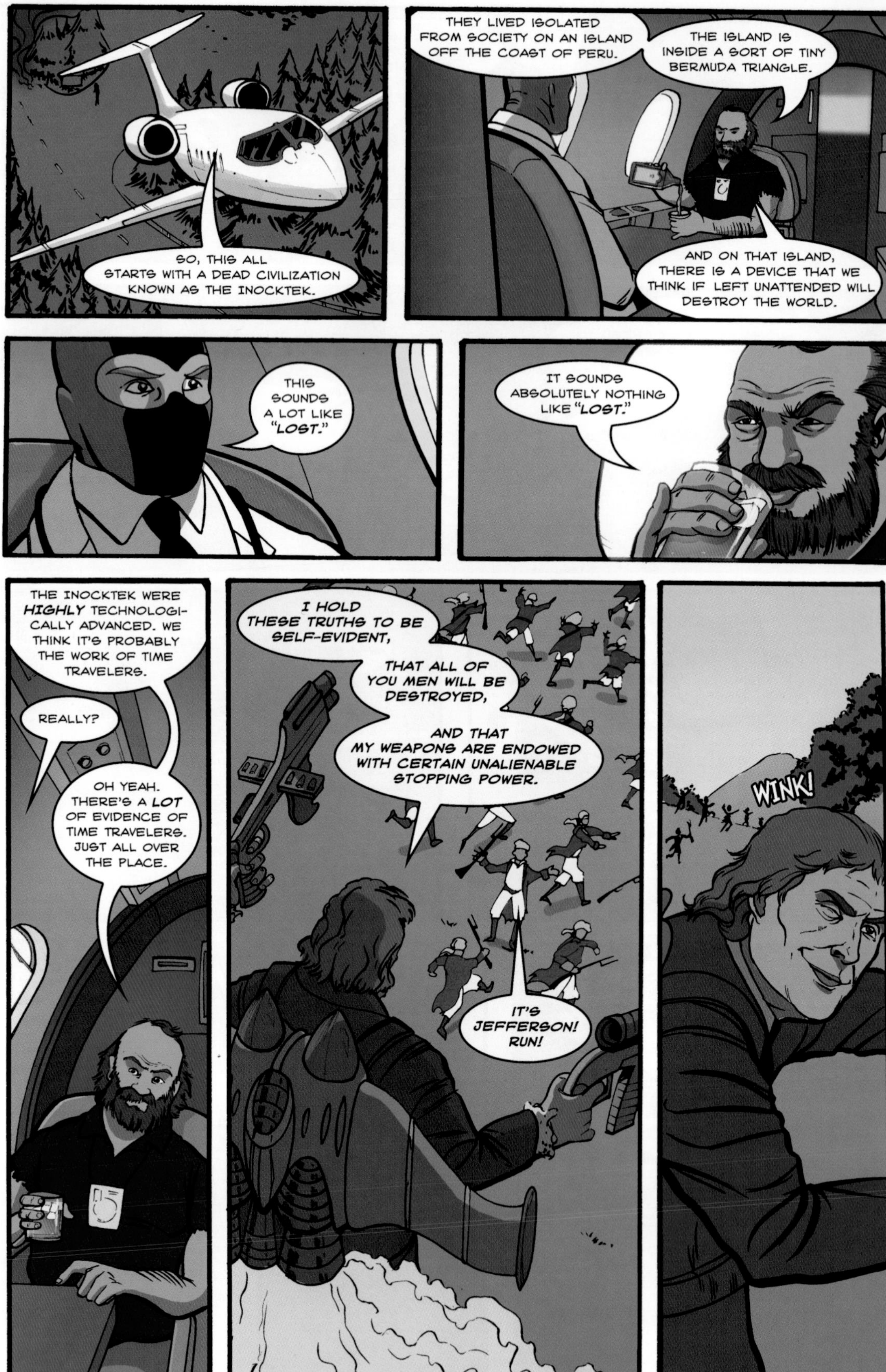
SO, THIS ALL STARTS WITH A DEAD CIVILIZATION KNOWN AS THE INOCKTEK.
THEY LIVED ISOLATED FROM SOCIETY ON AN ISLAND OFF THE COAST OF PERU.
THE ISLAND IS INSIDE A SORT OF TINY BERMUDA TRIANGLE.
AND ON THAT ISLAND, THERE IS A DEVICE THAT WE THINK IF LEFT UNATTENDED WILL DESTROY THE WORLD.
THIS SOUNDS A LOT LIKE "LOST."
IT SOUNDS ABSOLUTELY NOTHING LIKE "LOST."
THE INOCKTEK WERE HIGHLY TECHNOLOGICALLY ADVANCED. WE THINK IT'S PROBABLY THE WORK OF TIME TRAVELERS.
REALLY?
OH YEAH. THERE'S A LOT OF EVIDENCE OF TIME TRAVELERS. JUST ALL OVER THE PLACE.
I HOLD THESE TRUTHS TO BE SELF-EVIDENT,
THAT ALL OF YOU MEN WILL BE DESTROYED,
AND THAT MY WEAPONS ARE ENDOWED WITH CERTAIN UNALIENABLE STOPPING POWER.
IT'S JEFFERSON! RUN!
WINK!

HE SEES YOU.

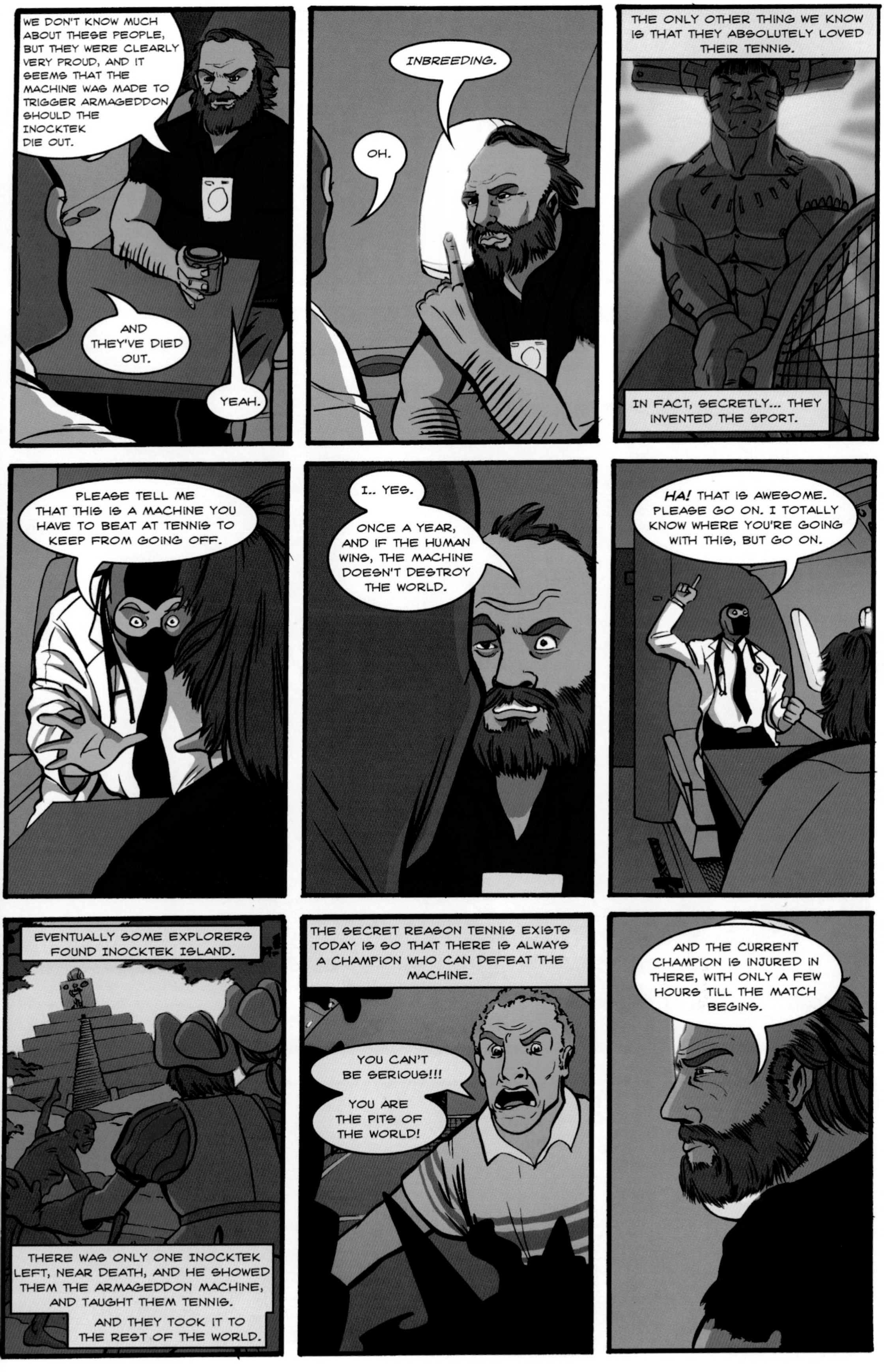
WE DON'T KNOW MUCH ABOUT THESE PEOPLE, BUT THEY WERE CLEARLY VERY PROUD, AND IT SEEMS THAT THE MACHINE WAS MADE TO TRIGGER ARMAGEDDON SHOULD THE INOCKTEK DIE OUT.
AND THEY'VE DIED OUT.
YEAH.
INBREEDING.
OH.
THE ONLY OTHER THING WE KNOW IS THAT THEY ABSOLUTELY LOVED THEIR TENNIS.
IN FACT, SECRETLY... THEY INVENTED THE SPORT.
PLEASE TELL ME THAT THIS IS A MACHINE YOU HAVE TO BEAT AT TENNIS TO KEEP FROM GOING OFF.
I.. YES.
ONCE A YEAR, AND IF THE HUMAN WINS, THE MACHINE DOESN'T DESTROY THE WORLD.
HA! THAT IS AWESOME. PLEASE GO ON. I TOTALLY KNOW WHERE YOU'RE GOING WITH THIS, BUT GO ON.
EVENTUALLY SOME EXPLORERS FOUND INOCKTEK ISLAND.
THERE WAS ONLY ONE INOCKTEK LEFT, NEAR DEATH, AND HE SHOWED THEM THE ARMAGEDDON MACHINE, AND TAUGHT THEM TENNIS.
AND THEY TOOK IT TO THE REST OF THE WORLD.
THE SECRET REASON TENNIS EXISTS TODAY IS SO THAT THERE IS ALWAYS A CHAMPION WHO CAN DEFEAT THE MACHINE.
YOU CAN'T BE SERIOUS!!!
YOU ARE THE PITS OF THE WORLD!
AND THE CURRENT CHAMPION IS INJURED IN THERE, WITH ONLY A FEW HOURS TILL THE MATCH BEGINS.

I wanted to do all this stuff about the history of tennis, but then I decided instead to forget. This happens sometimes.

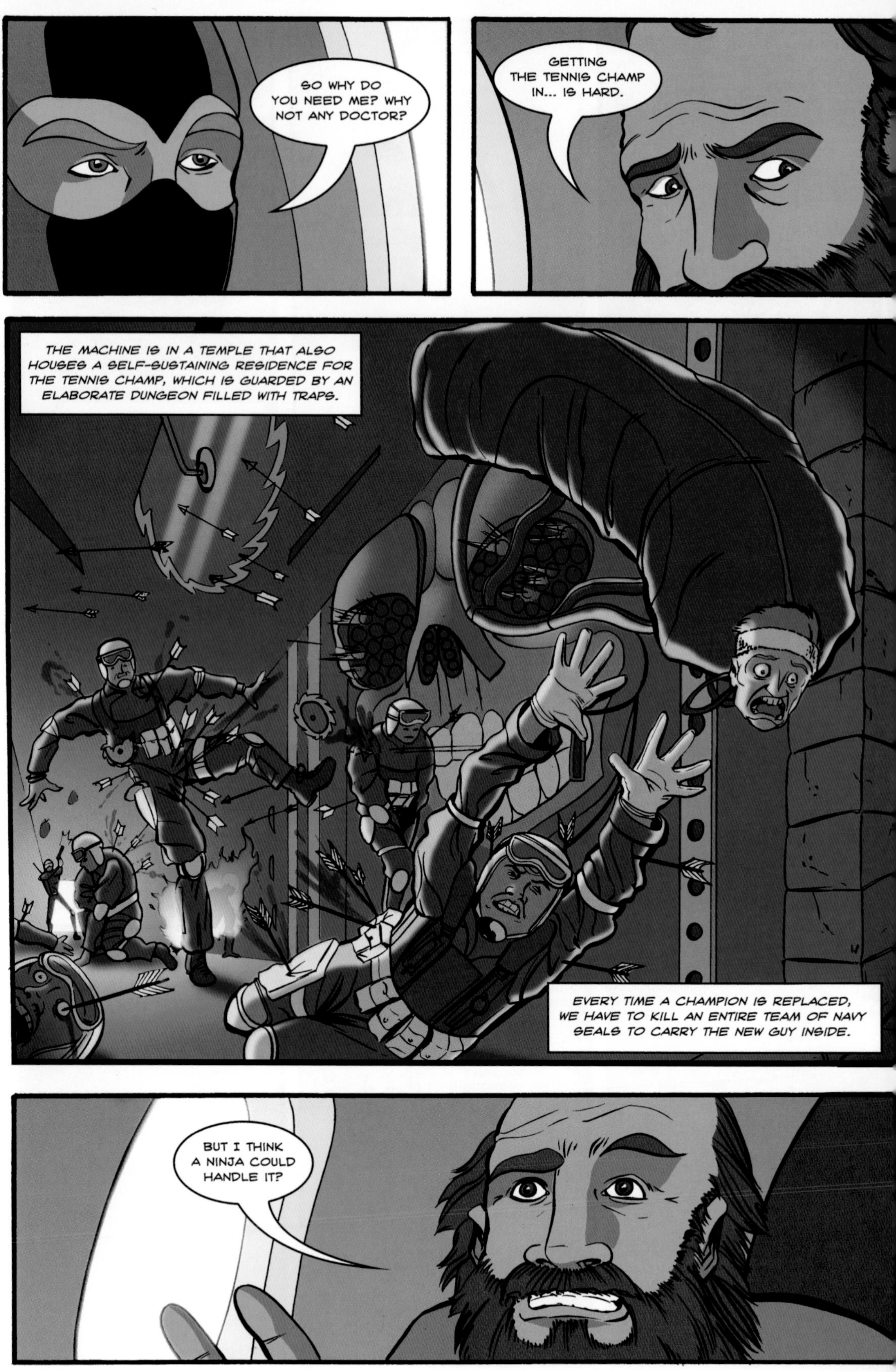
SO WHY DO YOU NEED ME? WHY NOT ANY DOCTOR?
GETTING THE TENNIS CHAMP IN... IS HARD.
THE MACHINE IS IN A TEMPLE THAT ALSO HOUSES A SELF-SUSTAINING RESIDENCE FOR THE TENNIS CHAMP, WHICH IS GUARDED BY AN ELABORATE DUNGEON FILLED WITH TRAPS.
EVERY TIME A CHAMPION IS REPLACED, WE HAVE TO KILL AN ENTIRE TEAM OF NAVY SEALS TO CARRY THE NEW GUY INSIDE.
BUT I THINK A NINJA COULD HANDLE IT?

And please don't ask me how the tennis pros get back out when they're replaced because I haven't figured that out yet. They probably die in there. I dunno.

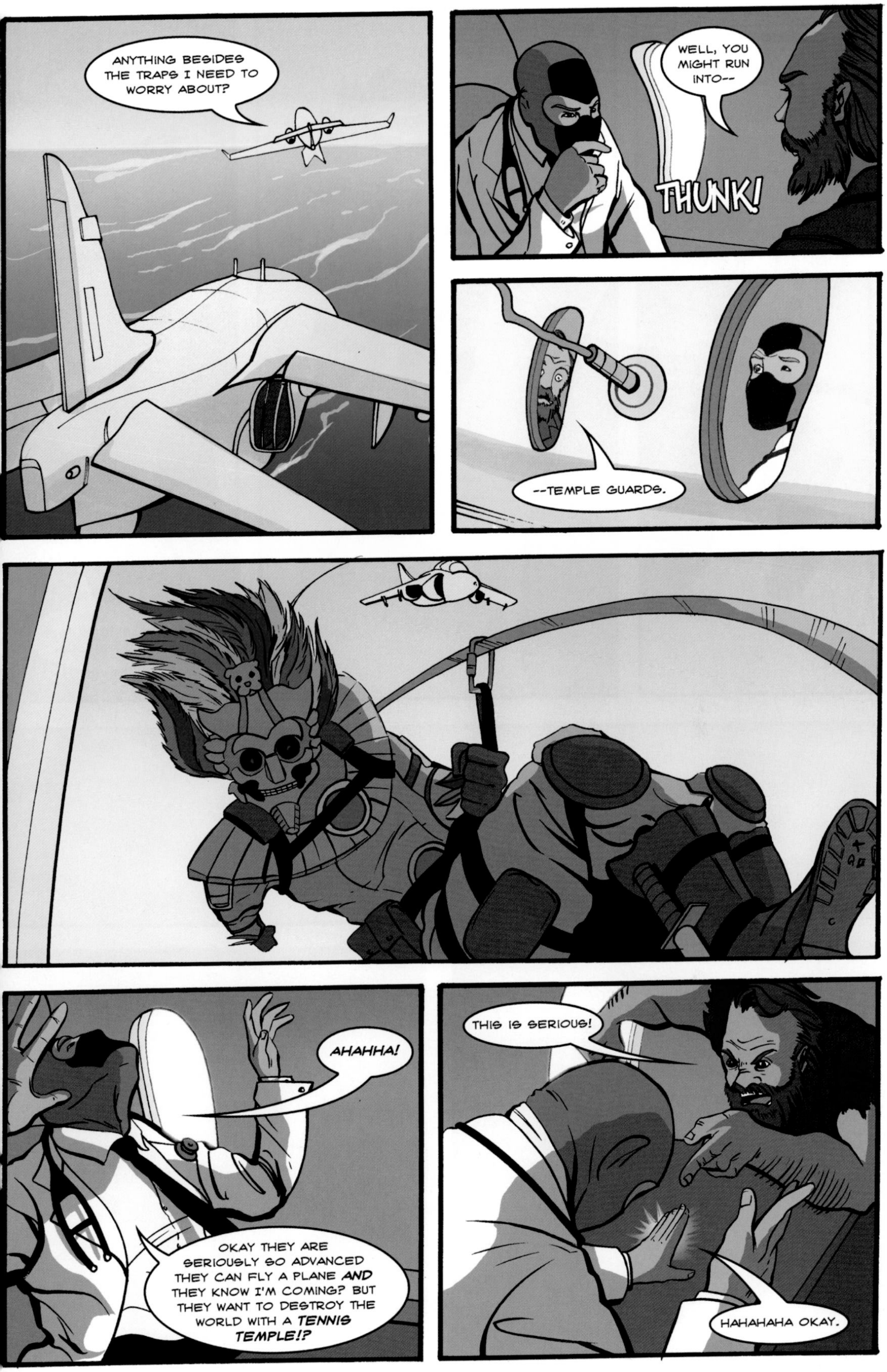
ANYTHING BESIDES THE TRAPS I NEED TO WORRY ABOUT?
WELL, YOU MIGHT RUN INTO--
THUNK!
--TEMPLE GUARDS.
AHAHHA!
OKAY THEY ARE SERIOUSLY SO ADVANCED THEY CAN FLY A PLANE *AND* THEY KNOW I'M COMING? BUT THEY WANT TO DESTROY THE WORLD WITH A *TENNIS TEMPLE!?*
THIS IS SERIOUS!
HAHAHAHA OKAY.

Those feathers look suspiciously like they came from a mall craft store.

OH GOODNESS, THIS *IS* SERIOUS.

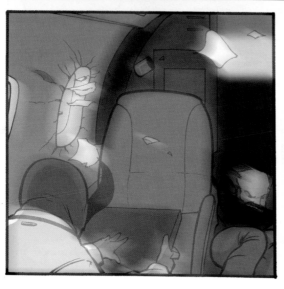

My dad used to fly a jet like this one, and I asked him about what would really happen in this situation, but in the end I still just went with what I thought would be coolest.

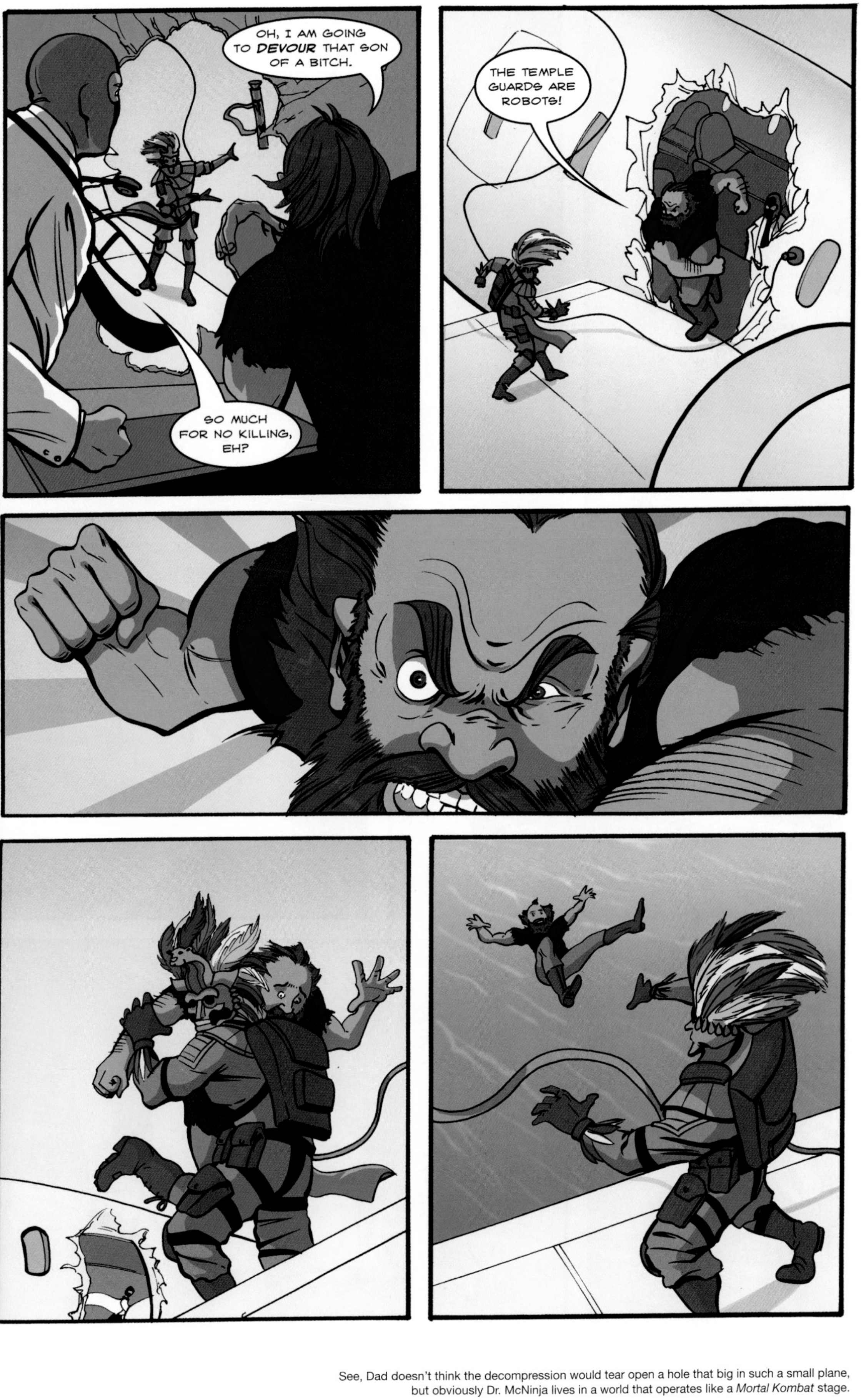
OH, I AM GOING TO ***DEVOUR*** THAT SON OF A BITCH.
SO MUCH FOR NO KILLING, EH?
THE TEMPLE GUARDS ARE ROBOTS!

See, Dad doesn't think the decompression would tear open a hole that big in such a small plane, but obviously Dr. McNinja lives in a world that operates like a *Mortal Kombat* stage.

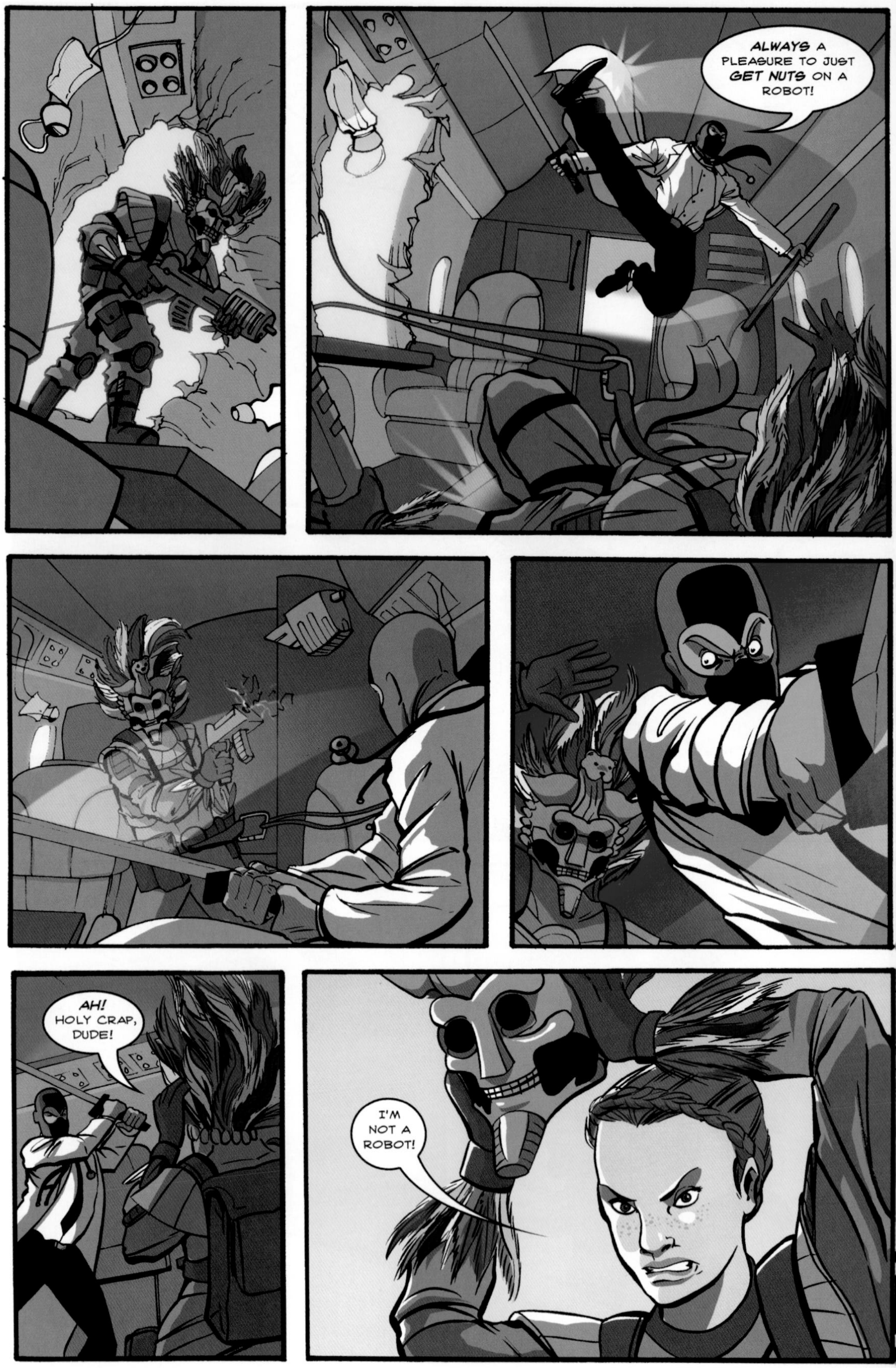
ALWAYS A PLEASURE TO JUST GET NUTS ON A ROBOT!
AH! HOLY CRAP, DUDE!
I'M NOT A ROBOT!

OR the whole plane would blow up, OR everyone would have a nasty earache. Either way, *Mortal Kombat* stage, I think, is the best route.

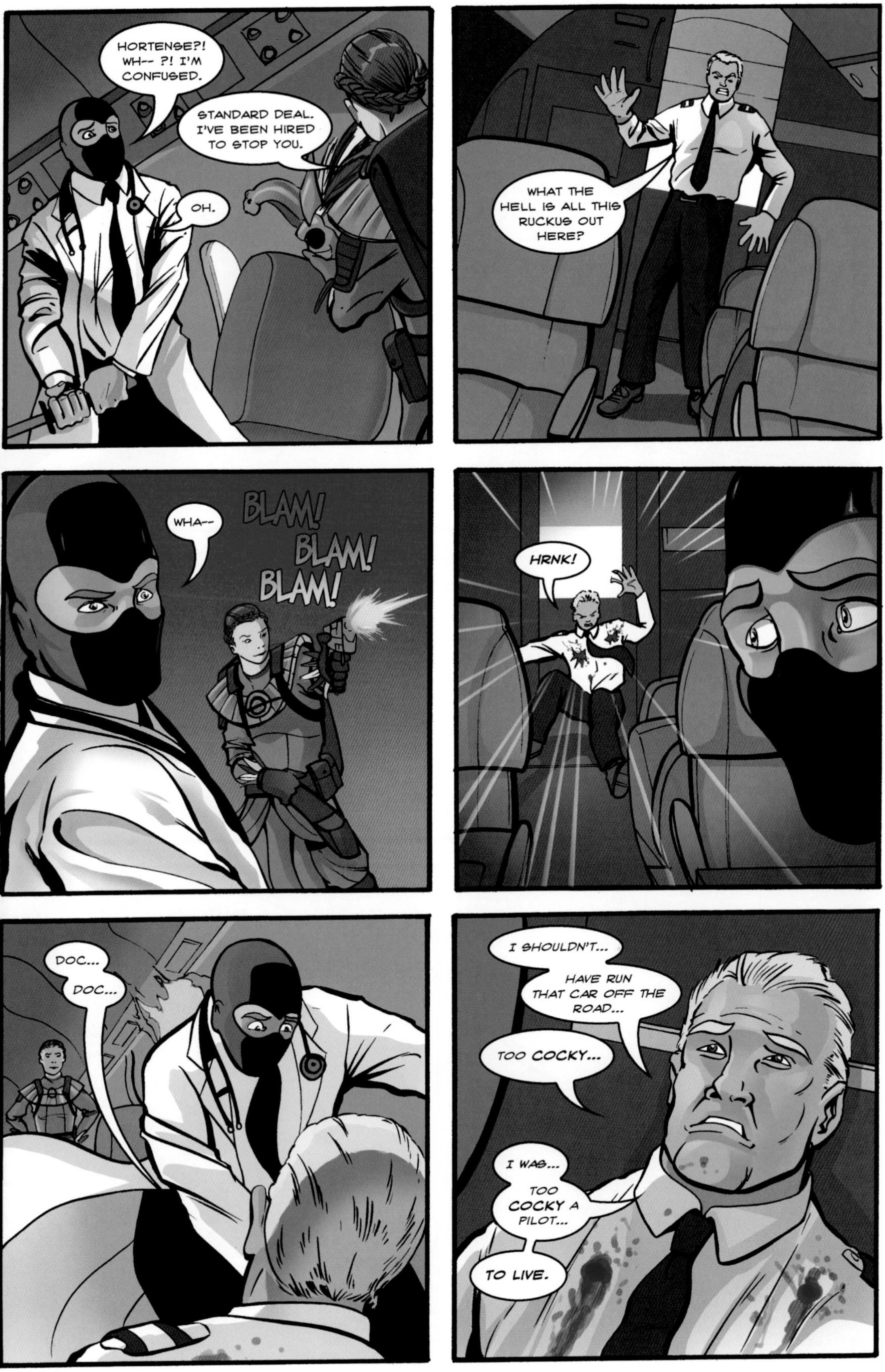
HORTENSE?! WH-- ?! I'M CONFUSED.
STANDARD DEAL. I'VE BEEN HIRED TO STOP YOU.
OH.
WHAT THE HELL IS ALL THIS RUCKUS OUT HERE?
WHA--
BLAM!
BLAM!
BLAM!
HRNK!
DOC...
DOC...
I SHOULDN'T...
HAVE RUN THAT CAR OFF THE ROAD...
TOO COCKY...
I WAS...
TOO COCKY A PILOT...
TO LIVE.

You may have an awkward time running into an ex, but at least she doesn't have a GUN YOU WHINY BABY.

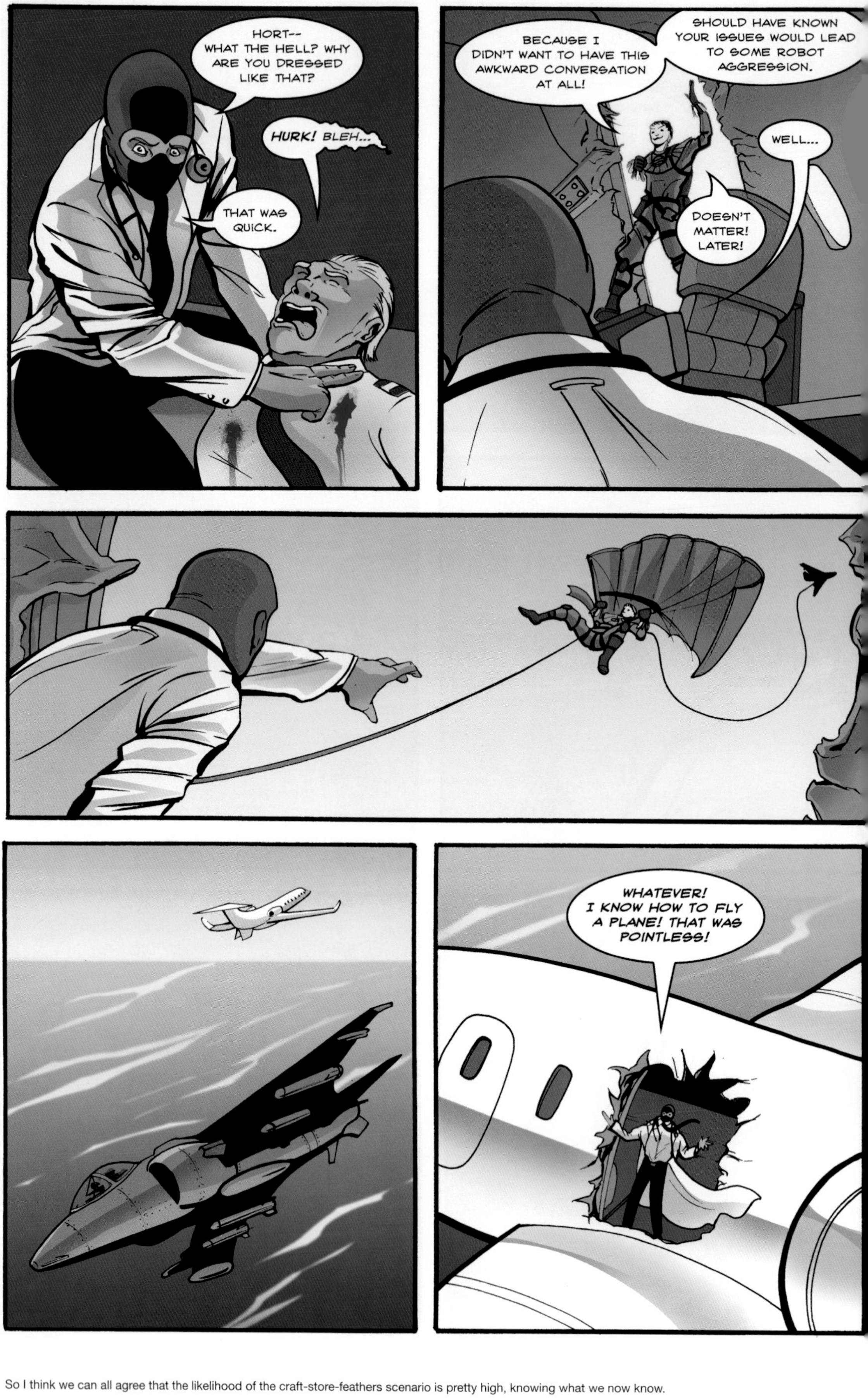
HORT-- WHAT THE HELL? WHY ARE YOU DRESSED LIKE THAT?
HURK! BLEH...
THAT WAS QUICK.
BECAUSE I DIDN'T WANT TO HAVE THIS AWKWARD CONVERSATION AT ALL!
SHOULD HAVE KNOWN YOUR ISSUES WOULD LEAD TO SOME ROBOT AGGRESSION.
WELL...
DOESN'T MATTER! LATER!
WHATEVER! I KNOW HOW TO FLY A PLANE! THAT WAS POINTLESS!

So I think we can all agree that the likelihood of the craft-store-feathers scenario is pretty high, knowing what we now know.

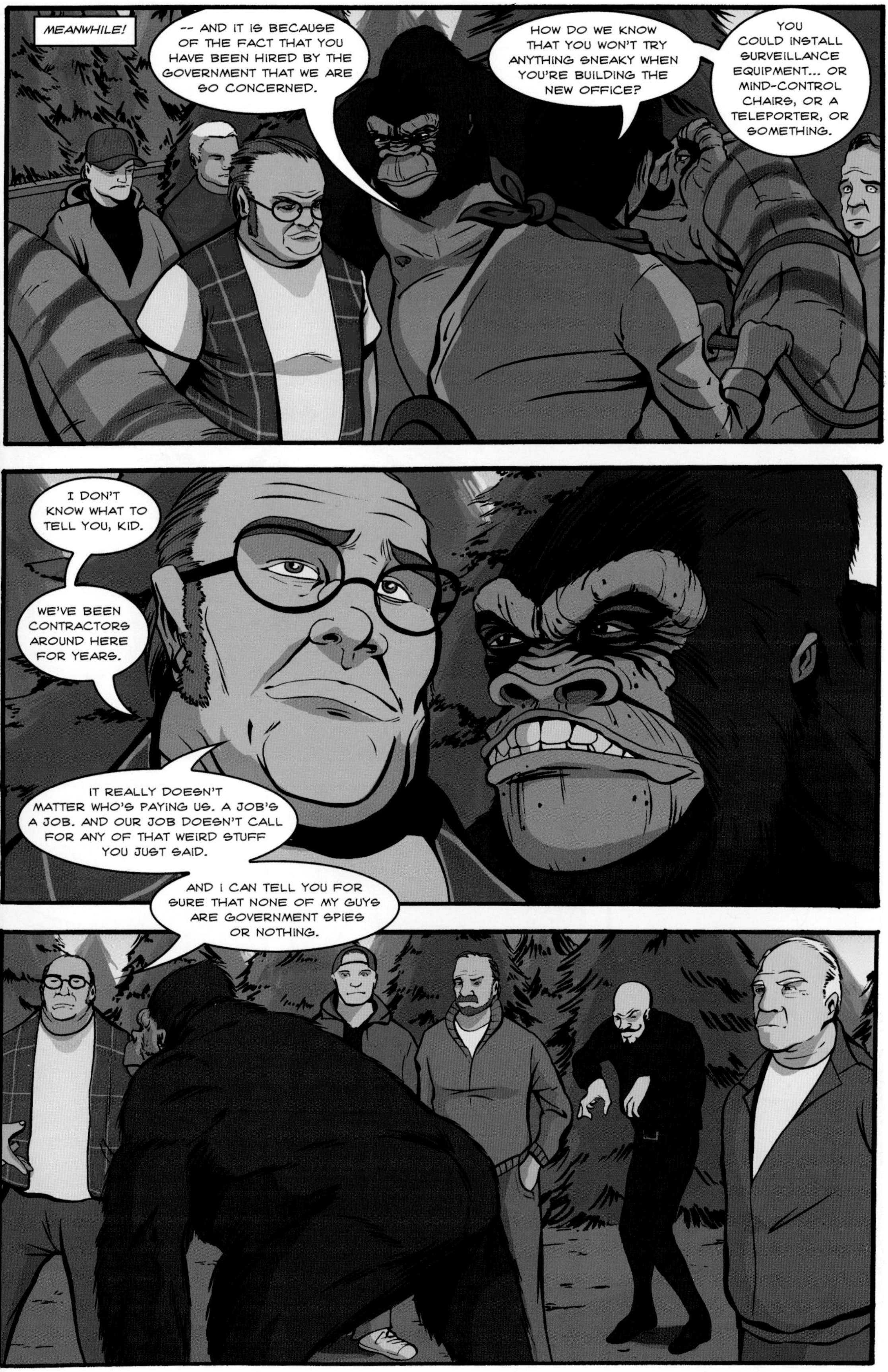
MEANWHILE!
-- AND IT IS BECAUSE OF THE FACT THAT YOU HAVE BEEN HIRED BY THE GOVERNMENT THAT WE ARE SO CONCERNED.
HOW DO WE KNOW THAT YOU WON'T TRY ANYTHING SNEAKY WHEN YOU'RE BUILDING THE NEW OFFICE?
YOU COULD INSTALL SURVEILLANCE EQUIPMENT... OR MIND-CONTROL CHAIRS, OR A TELEPORTER, OR SOMETHING.
I DON'T KNOW WHAT TO TELL YOU, KID.
WE'VE BEEN CONTRACTORS AROUND HERE FOR YEARS.
IT REALLY DOESN'T MATTER WHO'S PAYING US. A JOB'S A JOB. AND OUR JOB DOESN'T CALL FOR ANY OF THAT WEIRD STUFF YOU JUST SAID.
AND I CAN TELL YOU FOR SURE THAT NONE OF MY GUYS ARE GOVERNMENT SPIES OR NOTHING.

Nobody ever stops talking after they say, "I don't know what to tell you, kid."

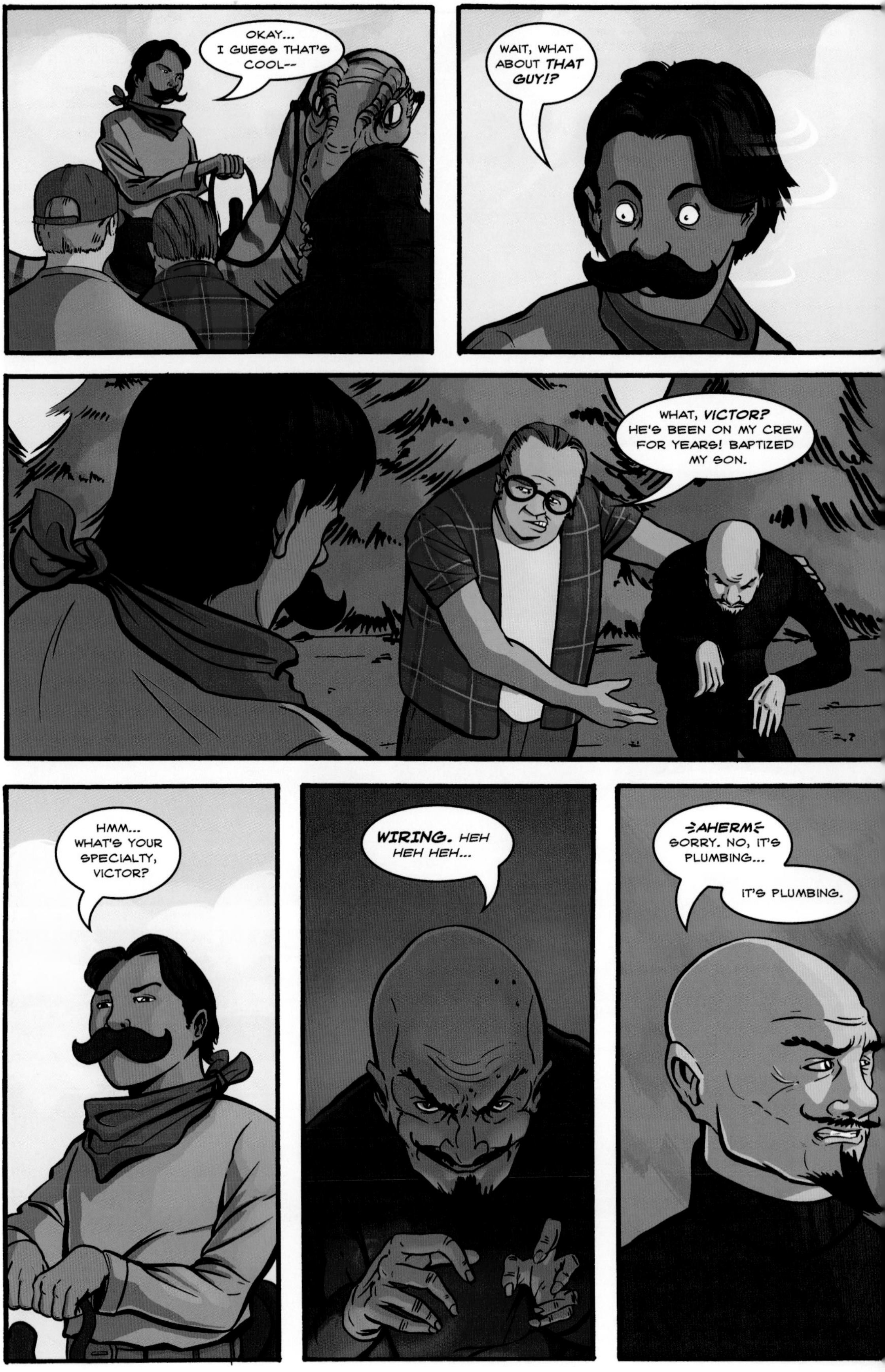
OKAY... I GUESS THAT'S COOL--
WAIT, WHAT ABOUT THAT GUY!?
WHAT, VICTOR? HE'S BEEN ON MY CREW FOR YEARS! BAPTIZED MY SON.
HMM... WHAT'S YOUR SPECIALTY, VICTOR?
WIRING. HEH HEH HEH...
AHERM SORRY. NO, IT'S PLUMBING...
IT'S PLUMBING.

This is based off of this one really creepy plumber I met. Okay, no, that is a lie.

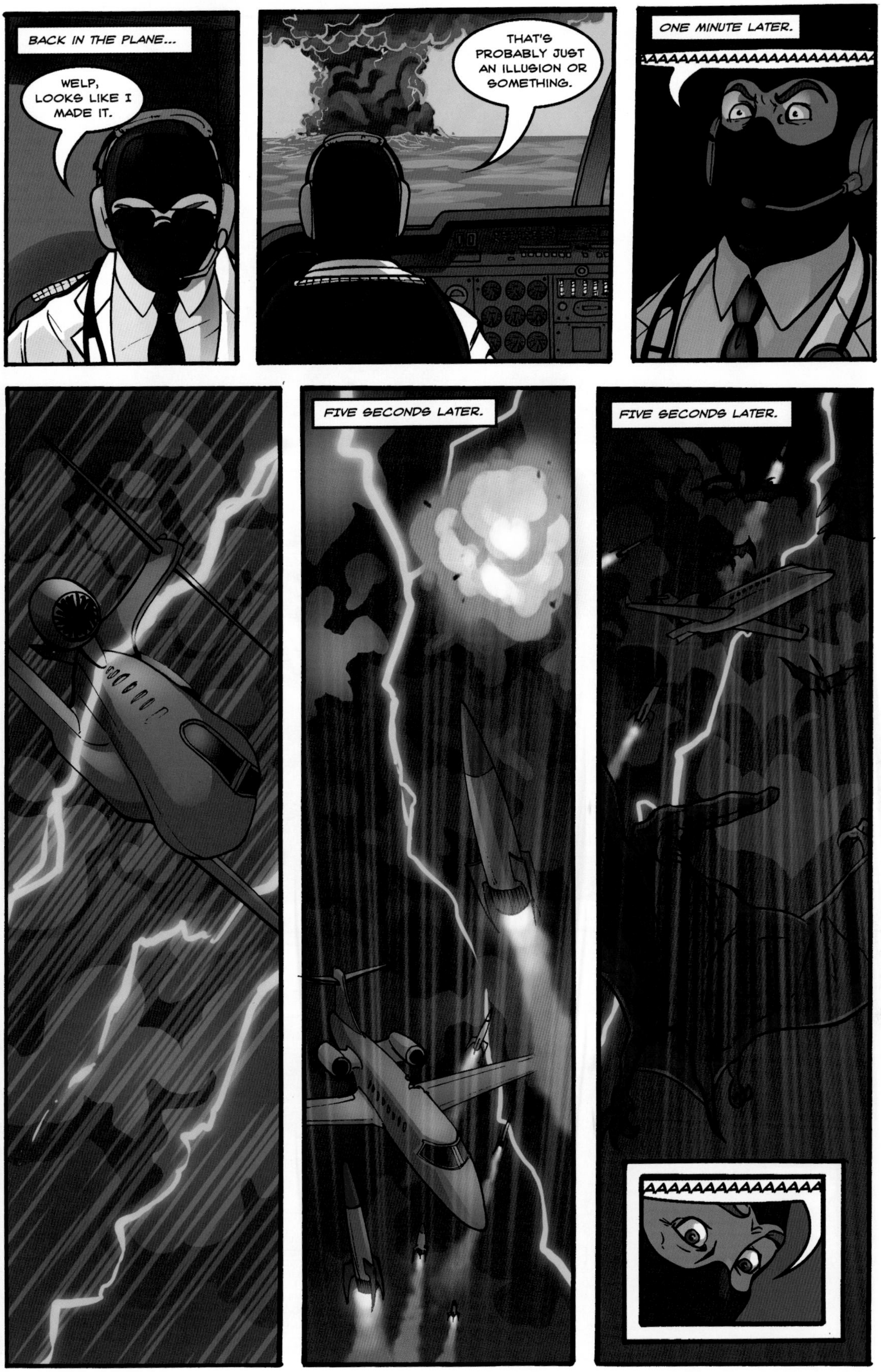
BACK IN THE PLANE...
WELP, LOOKS LIKE I MADE IT.
THAT'S PROBABLY JUST AN ILLUSION OR SOMETHING.
ONE MINUTE LATER.
AAAAAAAAAAAAAAAAAAAAAAAAAA
FIVE SECONDS LATER.
FIVE SECONDS LATER.
AAAAAAAAAAAAAAAA

Whoever determined the spelling for "pterodactyl" is kind of a jerk.

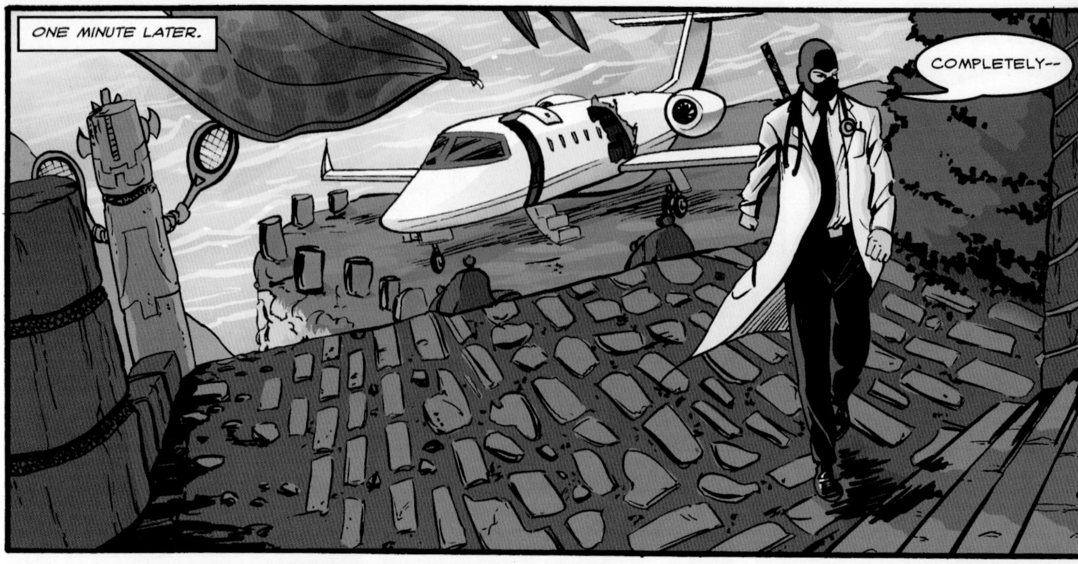
ONE MINUTE LATER.
COMPLETELY--

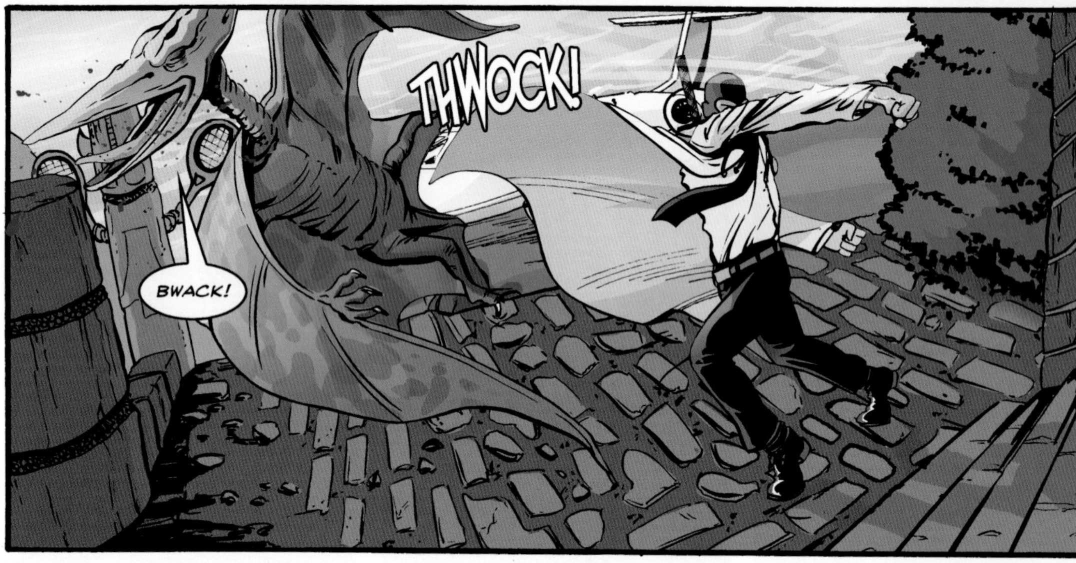
THWOCK!
BWACK!

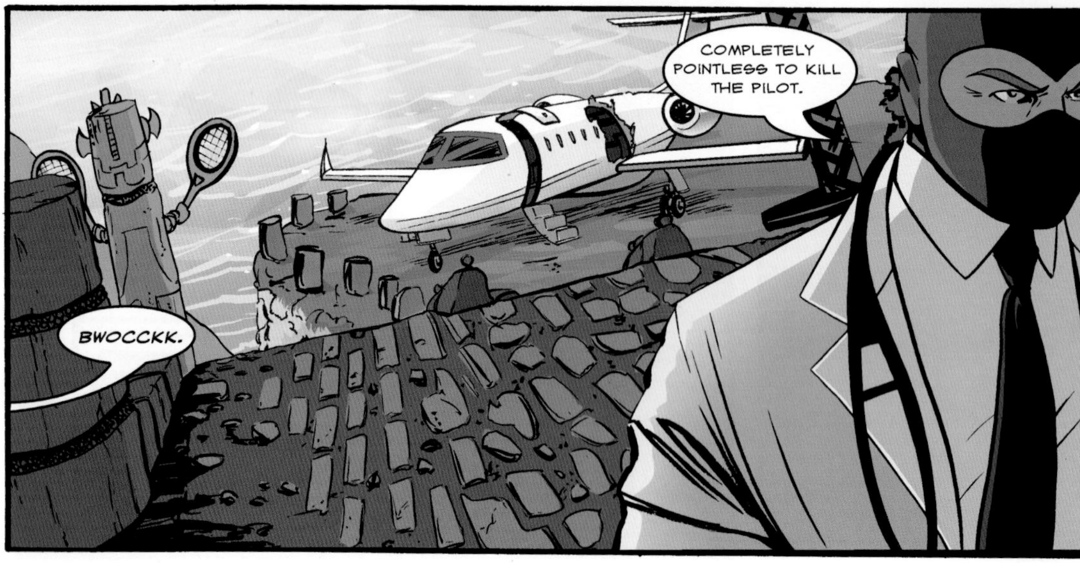
COMPLETELY POINTLESS TO KILL THE PILOT.
BWOCCKK.

Punching dinosaurs can quickly become an addiction.

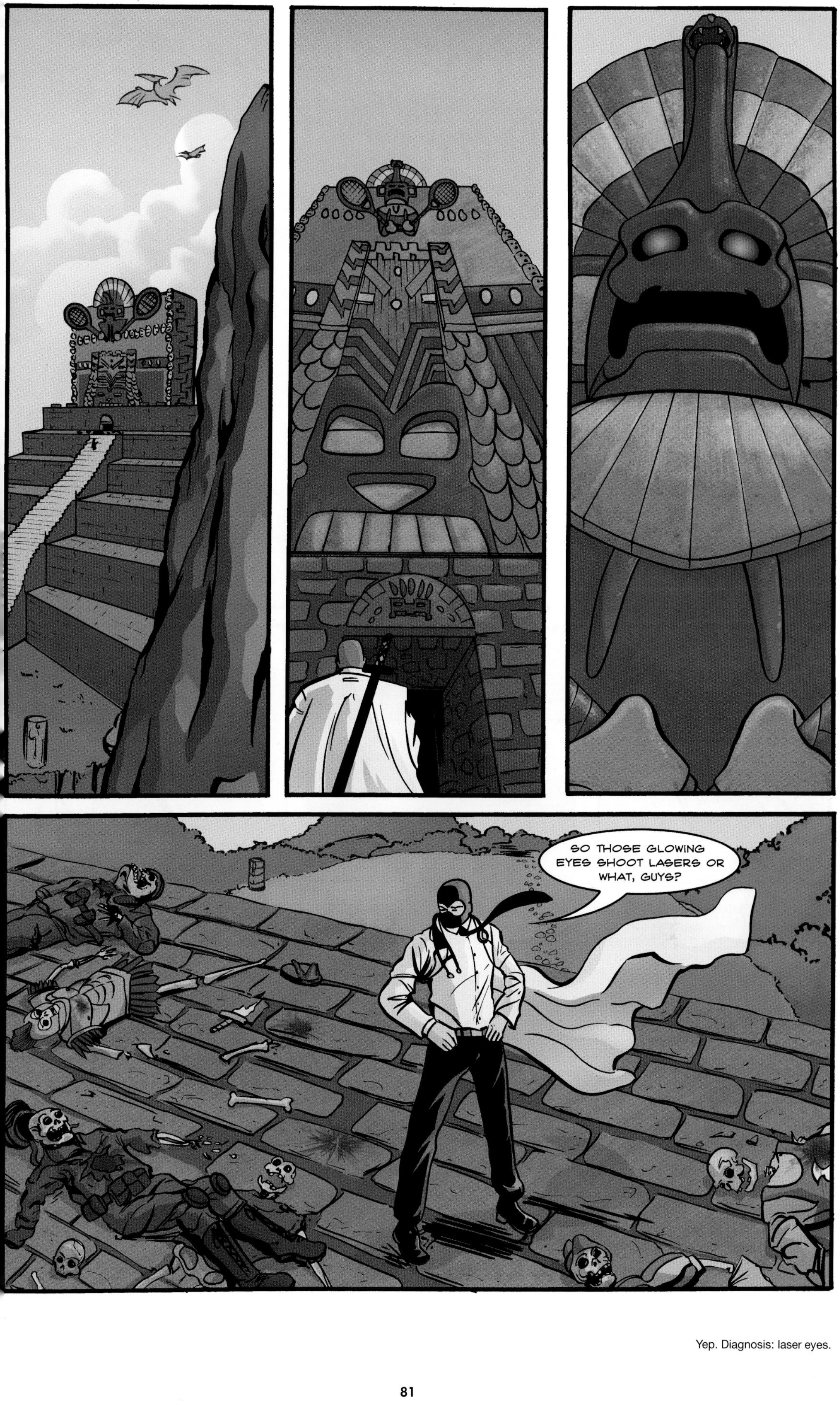
SO THOSE GLOWING EYES SHOOT LASERS OR WHAT, GUYS?

Yep. Diagnosis: laser eyes.

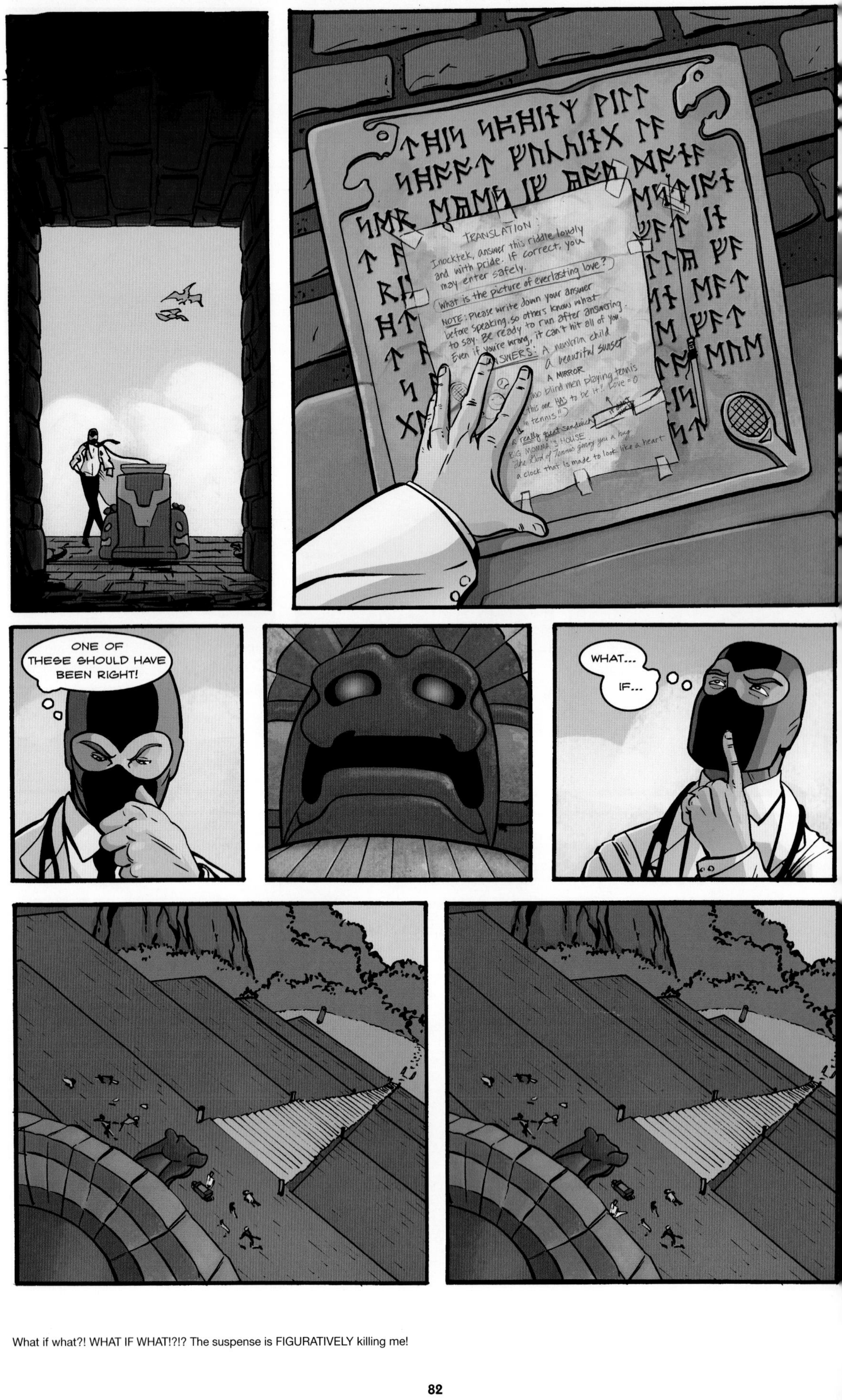
TRANSLATION:
Inocktek, answer this riddle loudly and with pride. If correct, you may enter safely.
What is the picture of everlasting love?
NOTE: Please write down your answer before speaking, so others know what to say. Be ready to run after answering. Even if you're wrong, it can't hit all of you.
SWERS: A newborn child
a beautiful sunset
A MIRROR
wo blind men playing tennis
this one HAS to be it!! Love = 0
in tennis!!)
a really great sandwich
BIG MOMMA'S HOUSE
The God of Tennis giving you a hug
a clock that is made to look like a heart
ONE OF THESE SHOULD HAVE BEEN RIGHT!
WHAT...
IF...

What if what?! WHAT IF WHAT!?!? The suspense is FIGURATIVELY killing me!

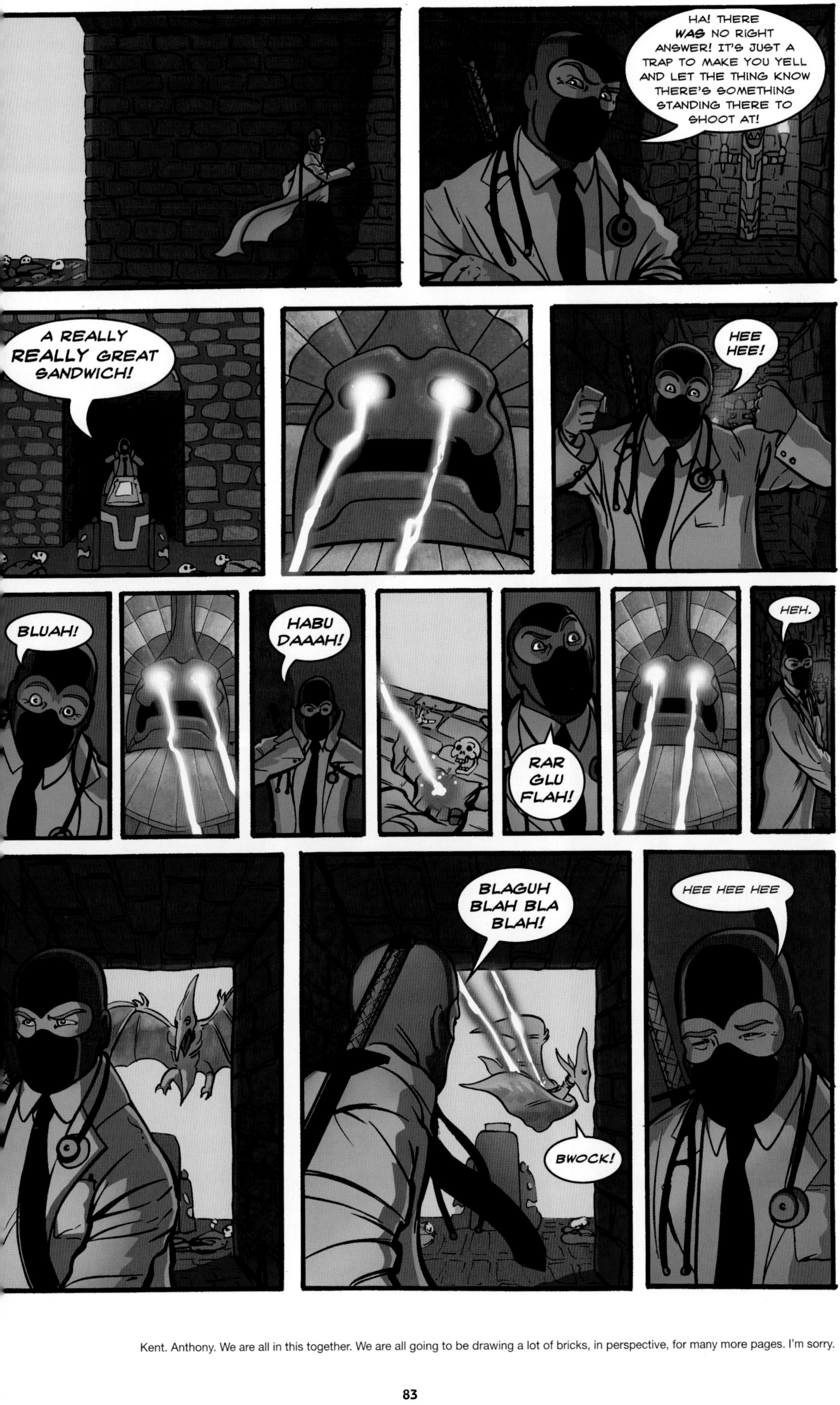
HA! THERE WAS NO RIGHT ANSWER! IT'S JUST A TRAP TO MAKE YOU YELL AND LET THE THING KNOW THERE'S SOMETHING STANDING THERE TO SHOOT AT!
A REALLY REALLY GREAT SANDWICH!
HEE HEE!
BLUAH!
HABU DAAAH!
RAR GLU FLAH!
HEH.
BLAGUH BLAH BLA BLAH!
BWOCK!
HEE HEE HEE

Kent. Anthony. We are all in this together. We are all going to be drawing a lot of bricks, in perspective, for many more pages. I'm sorry.

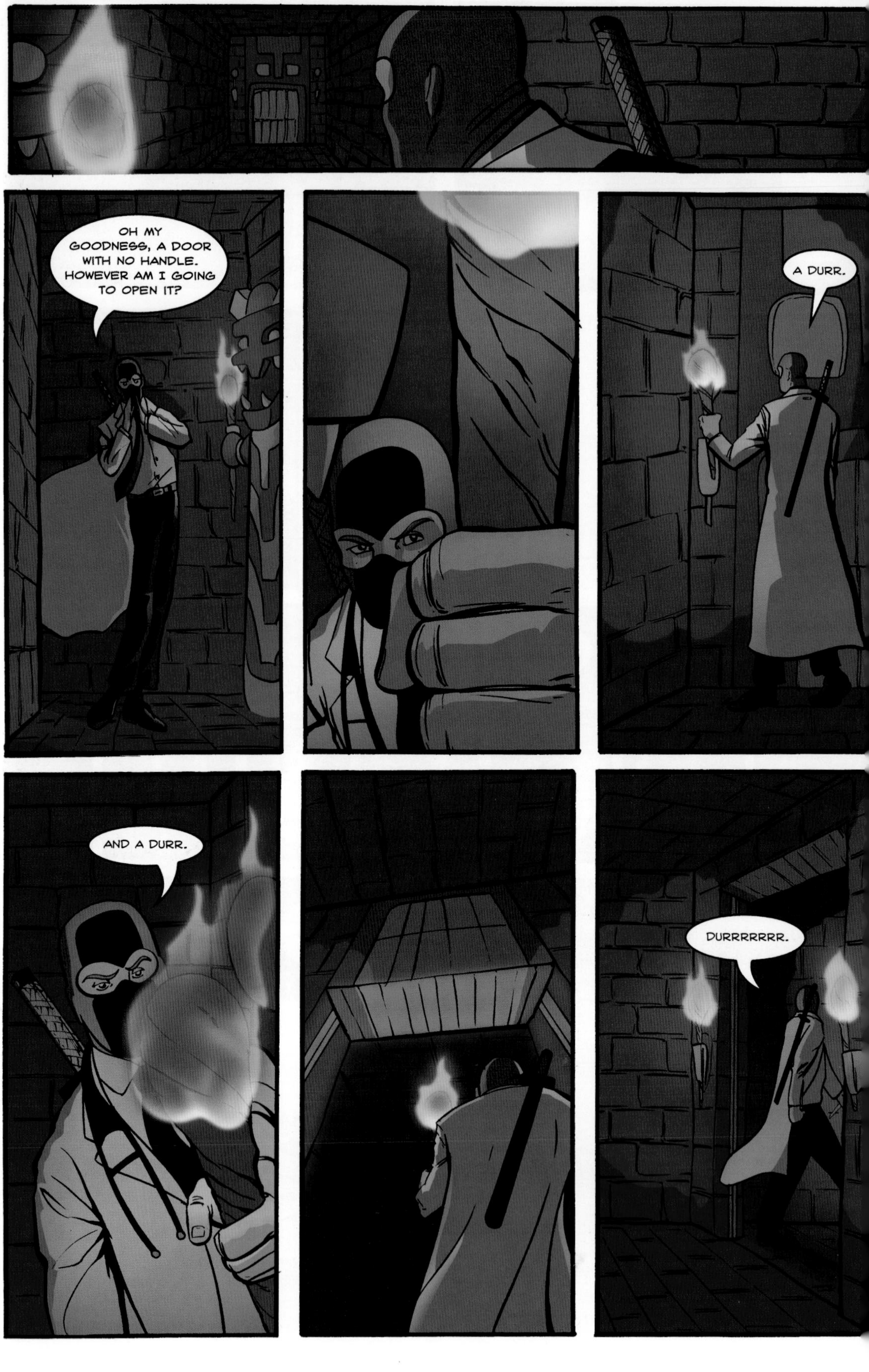

OH MY GOODNESS, A DOOR WITH NO HANDLE. HOWEVER AM I GOING TO OPEN IT?
A DURR.
AND A DURR.
DURRRRRRR.

Zelda, I dare you to make a game without this puzzle in it.

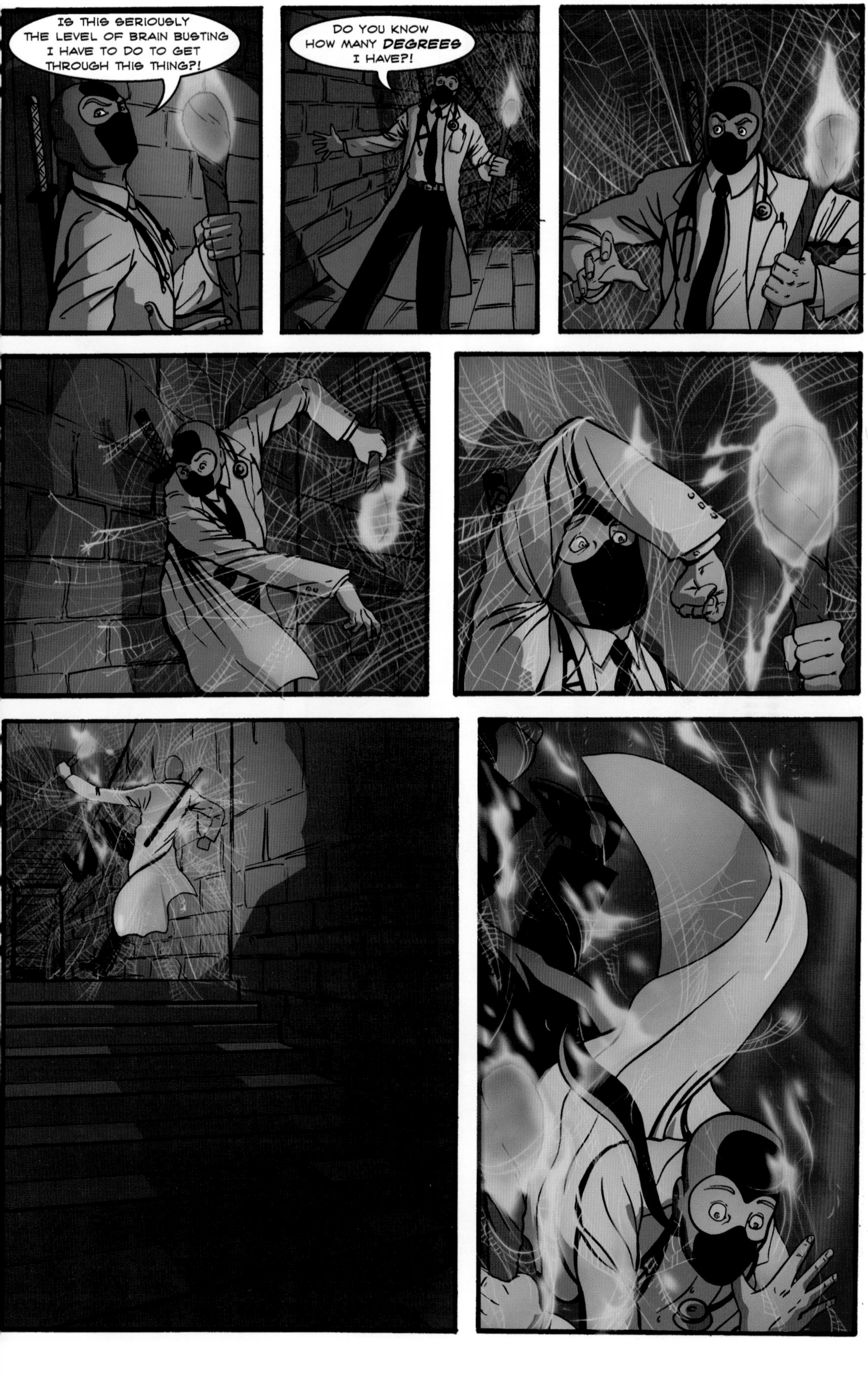
IS THIS SERIOUSLY THE LEVEL OF BRAIN BUSTING I HAVE TO DO TO GET THROUGH THIS THING?!
DO YOU KNOW HOW MANY DEGREES I HAVE?!

I don't even know if spider webs are flammable. Again, this is *Zelda* basically steering this comic.

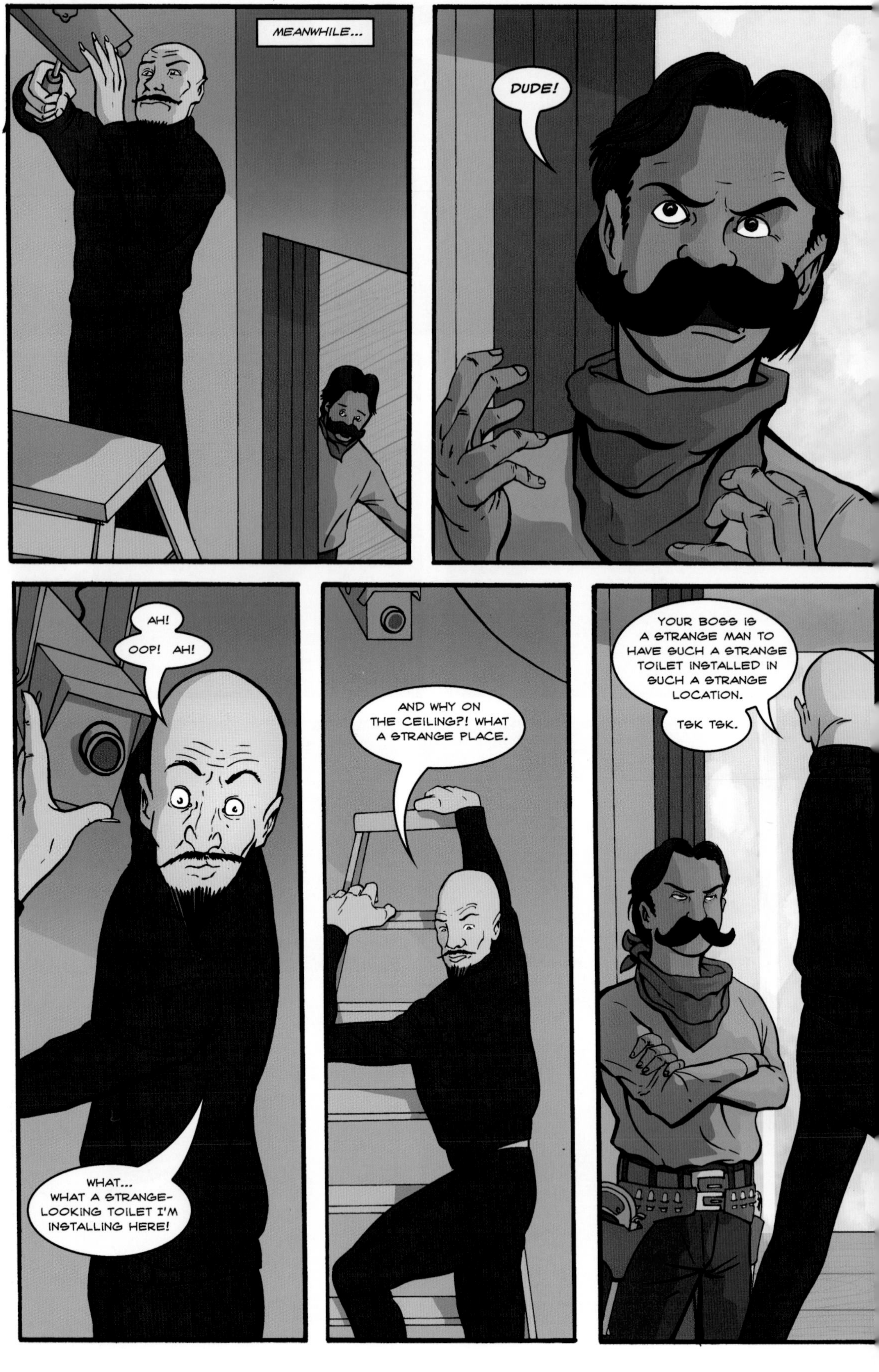
MEANWHILE...
DUDE!
AH!
OOP! AH!
WHAT... WHAT A STRANGE-LOOKING TOILET I'M INSTALLING HERE!
AND WHY ON THE CEILING?! WHAT A STRANGE PLACE.
YOUR BOSS IS A STRANGE MAN TO HAVE SUCH A STRANGE TOILET INSTALLED IN SUCH A STRANGE LOCATION.
TSK TSK.

The script for this page says, "Panel 2: Gordito is all wtf mate." It's fun to write for yourself.

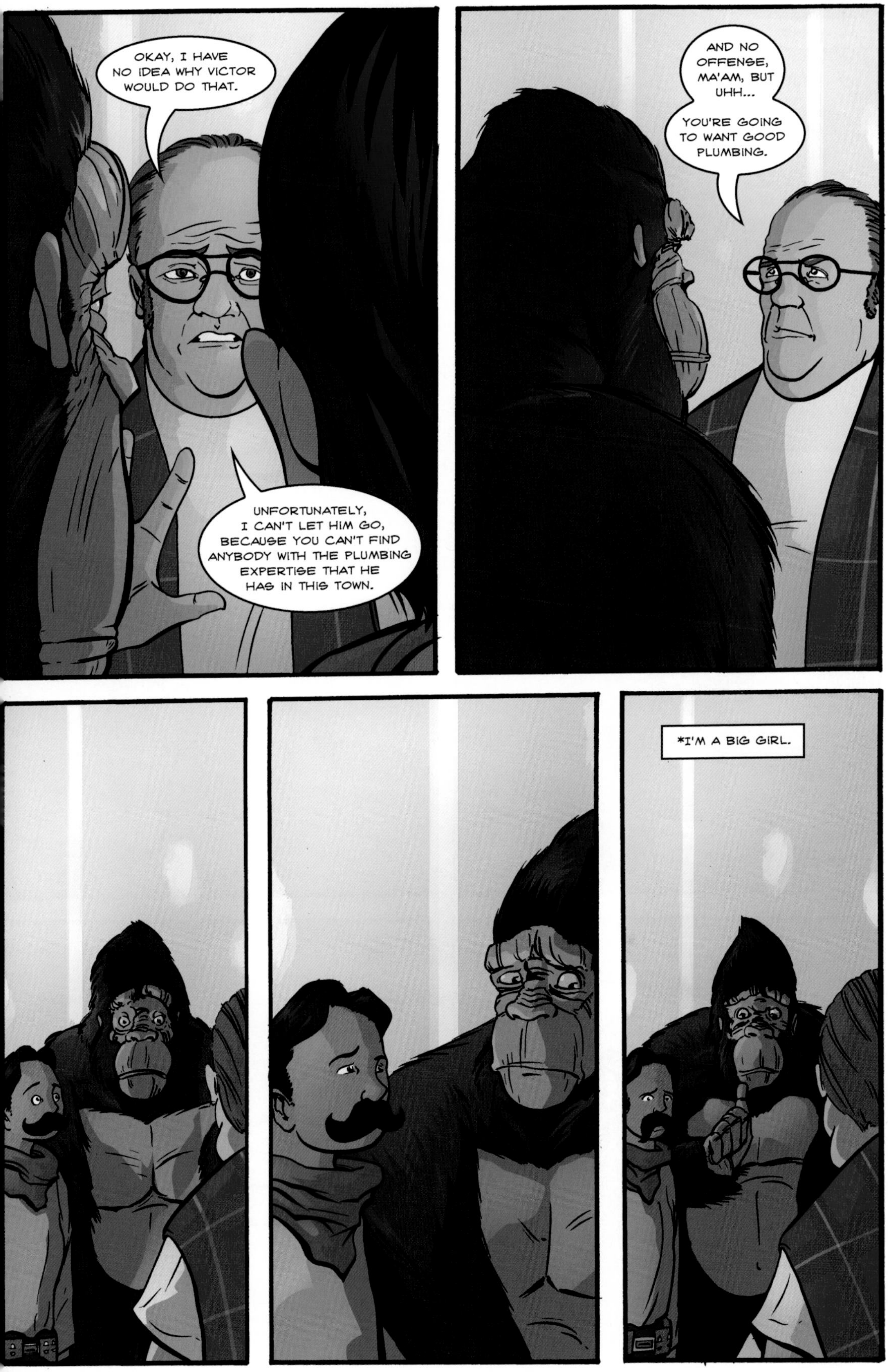
OKAY, I HAVE NO IDEA WHY VICTOR WOULD DO THAT.
UNFORTUNATELY, I CAN'T LET HIM GO, BECAUSE YOU CAN'T FIND ANYBODY WITH THE PLUMBING EXPERTISE THAT HE HAS IN THIS TOWN.
AND NO OFFENSE, MA'AM, BUT UHH...
YOU'RE GOING TO WANT GOOD PLUMBING.
*I'M A BIG GIRL.

Pounds and pounds of gorilla waste.

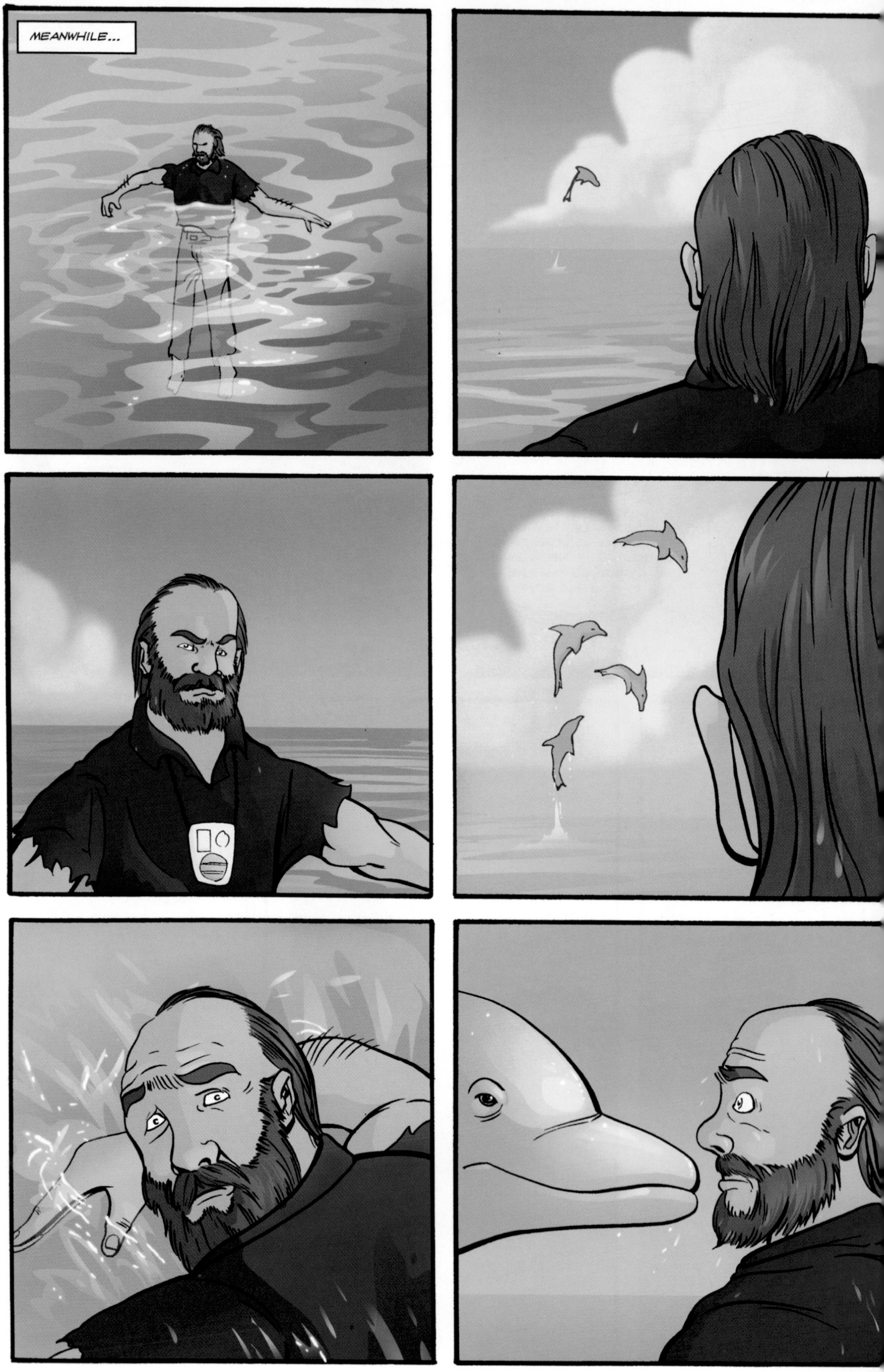
MEANWHILE...

A submarine somewhere picks up the screams.

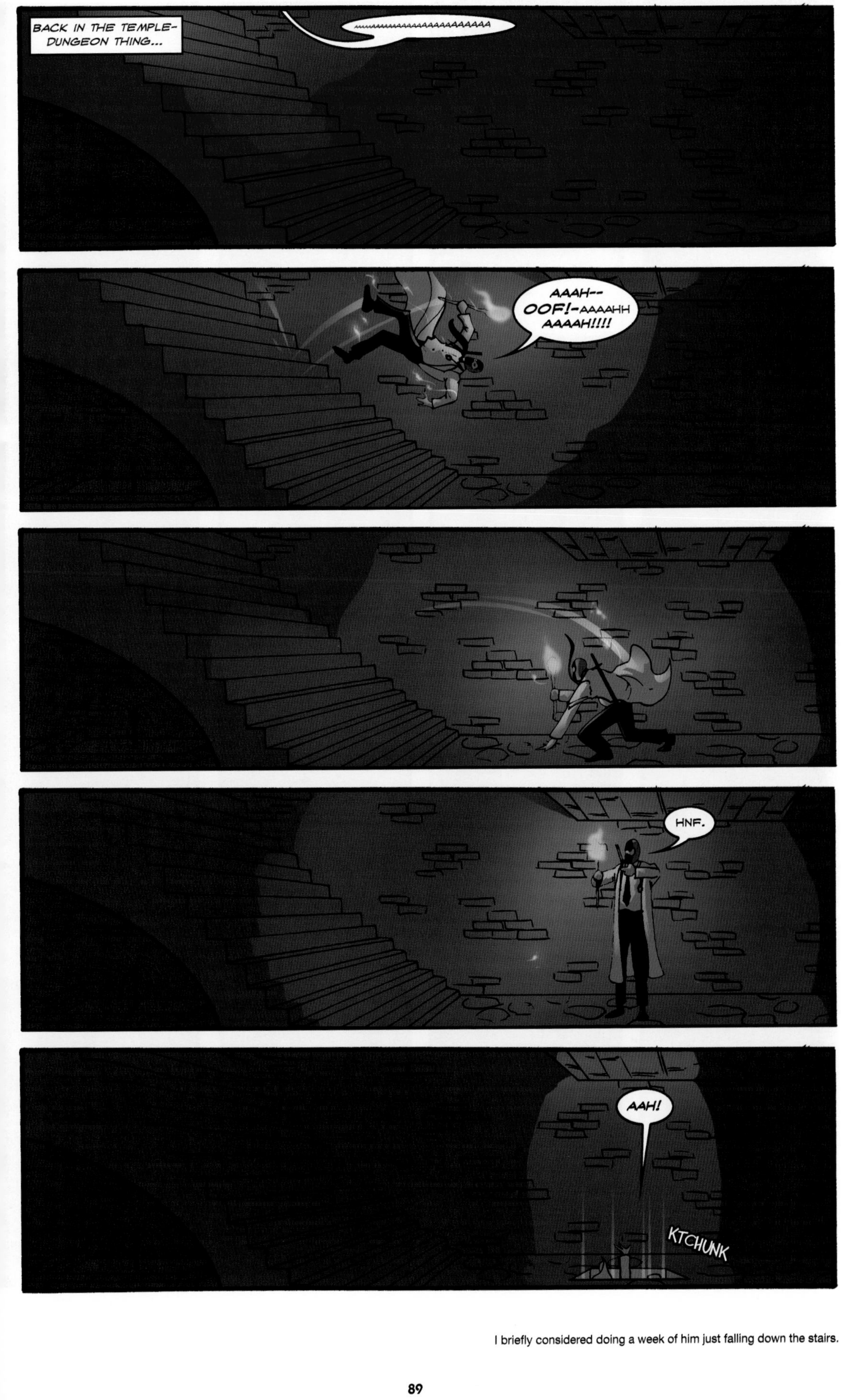

BACK IN THE TEMPLE-DUNGEON THING...
AAAAAAAAAAAAAAAAAAAAAAAAAAA
AAAH--OOF!-AAAAHH AAAAH!!!!
HNF.
AAH!
KTCHUNK

I briefly considered doing a week of him just falling down the stairs.

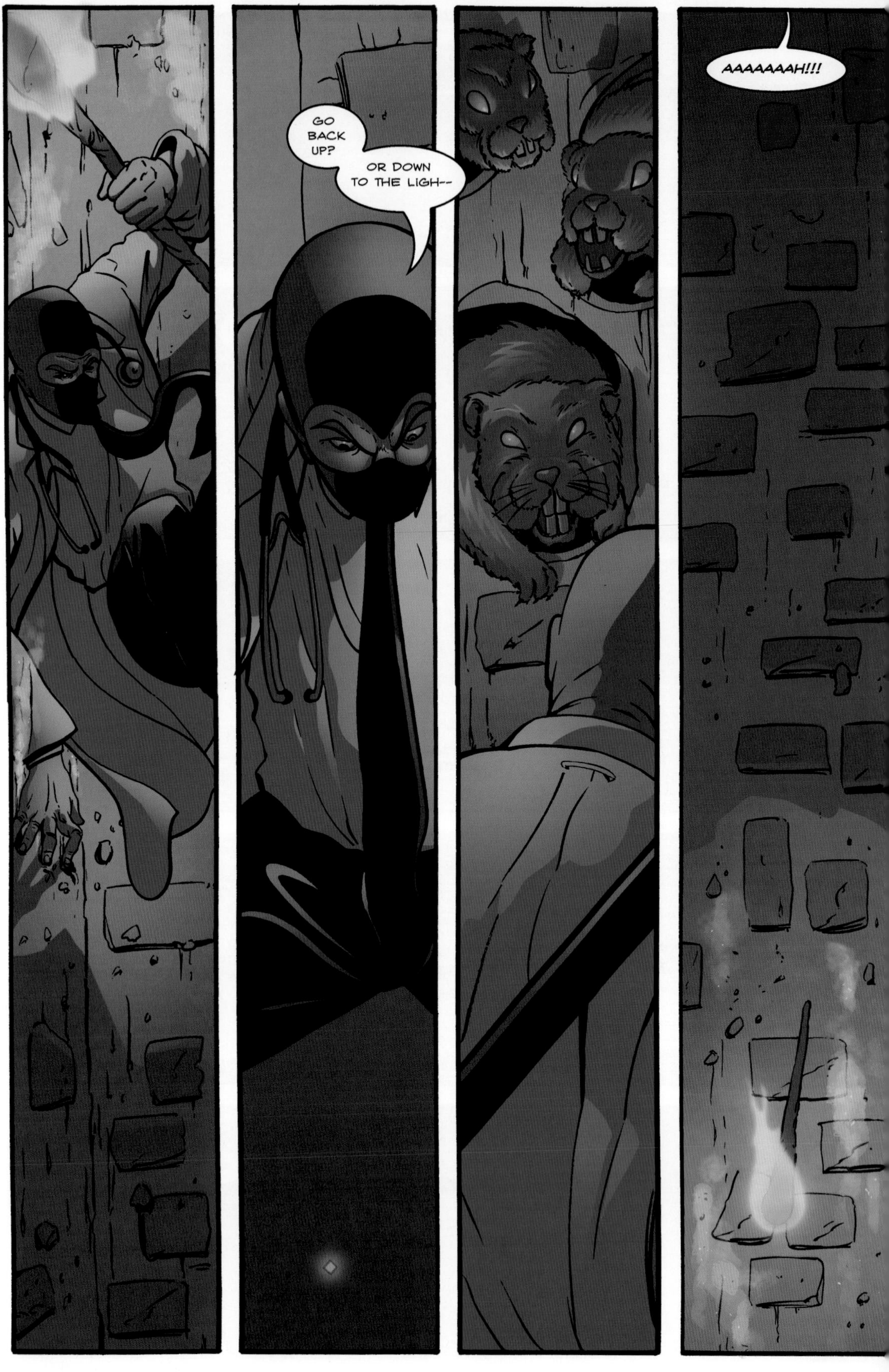
GO BACK UP?
OR DOWN TO THE LIGH--
AAAAAAAH!!!

Well, I guess the doctor is going to just continue to assume there is nobody around for him to be stealthy for.

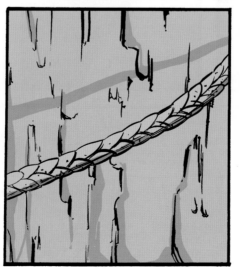

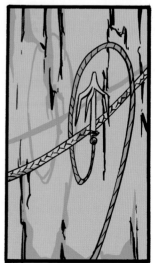

Anthony said he colored this page with a machine that harvests the regrets of children.

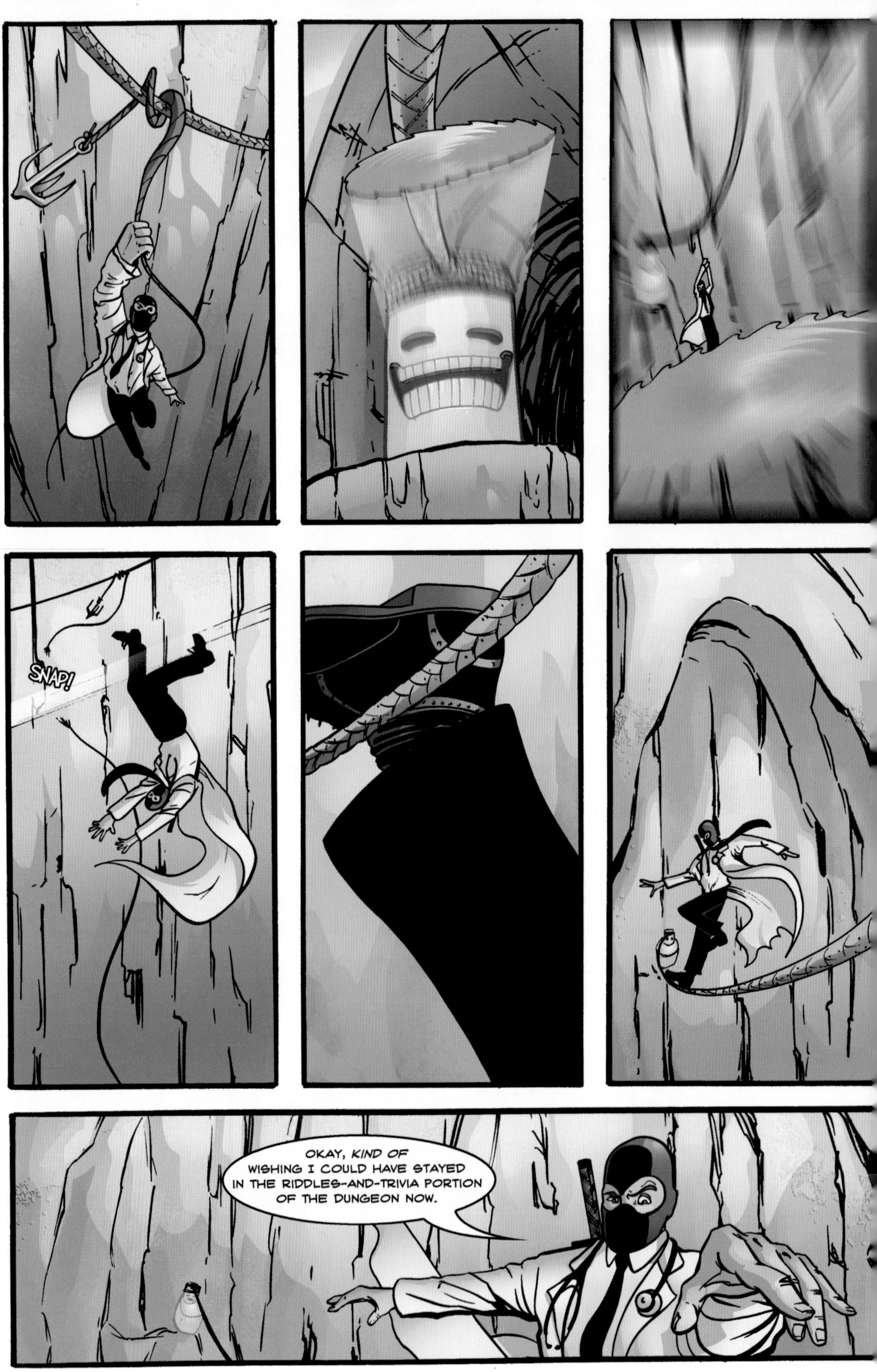
SNAP!
OKAY, KIND OF WISHING I COULD HAVE STAYED IN THE RIDDLES-AND-TRIVIA PORTION OF THE DUNGEON NOW.

WHO ARE YOU TALKING TO

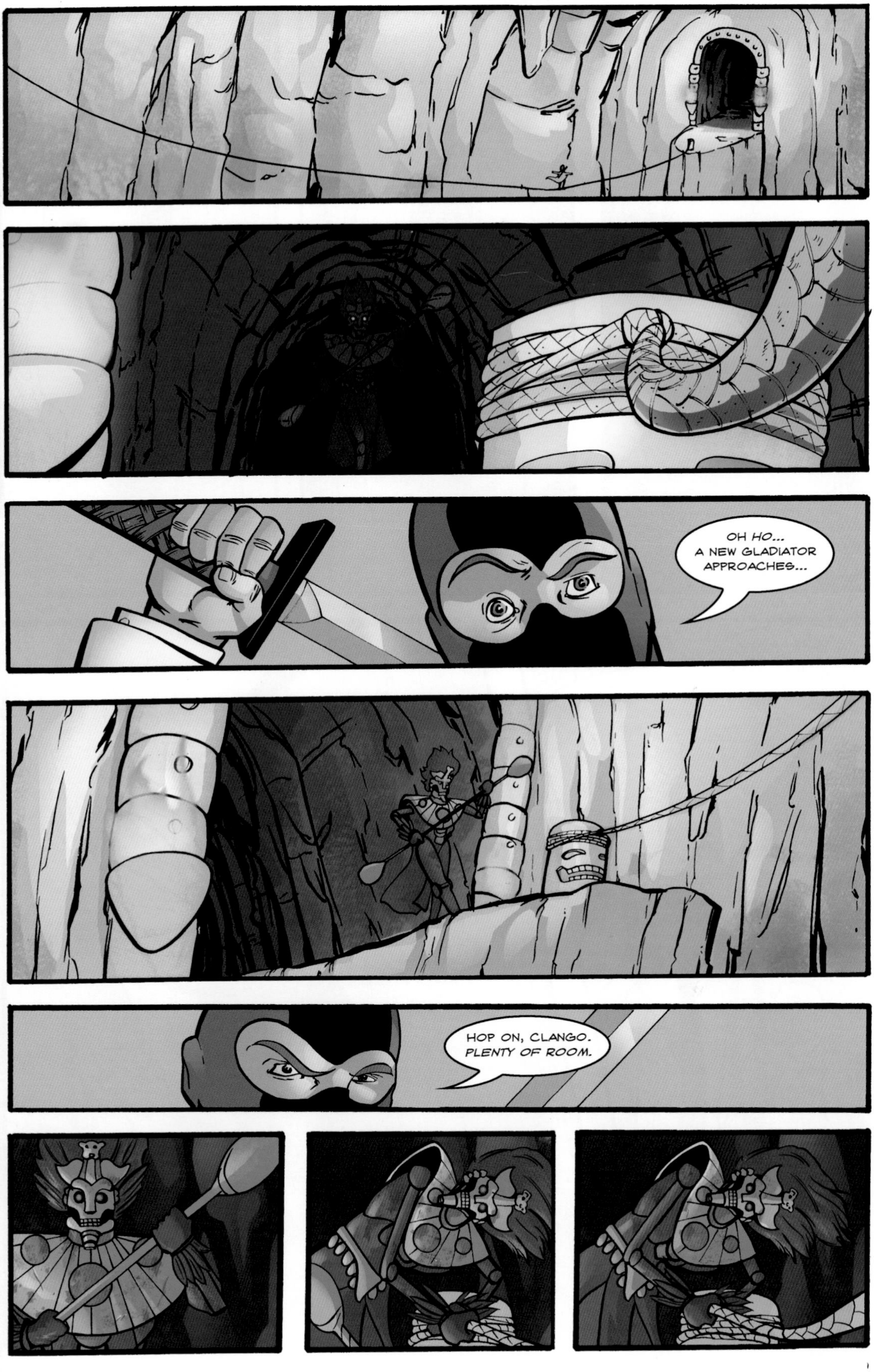
OH HO... A NEW GLADIATOR APPROACHES...
HOP ON, CLANGO. PLENTY OF ROOM.

What a little turd. What a turd of a robot.

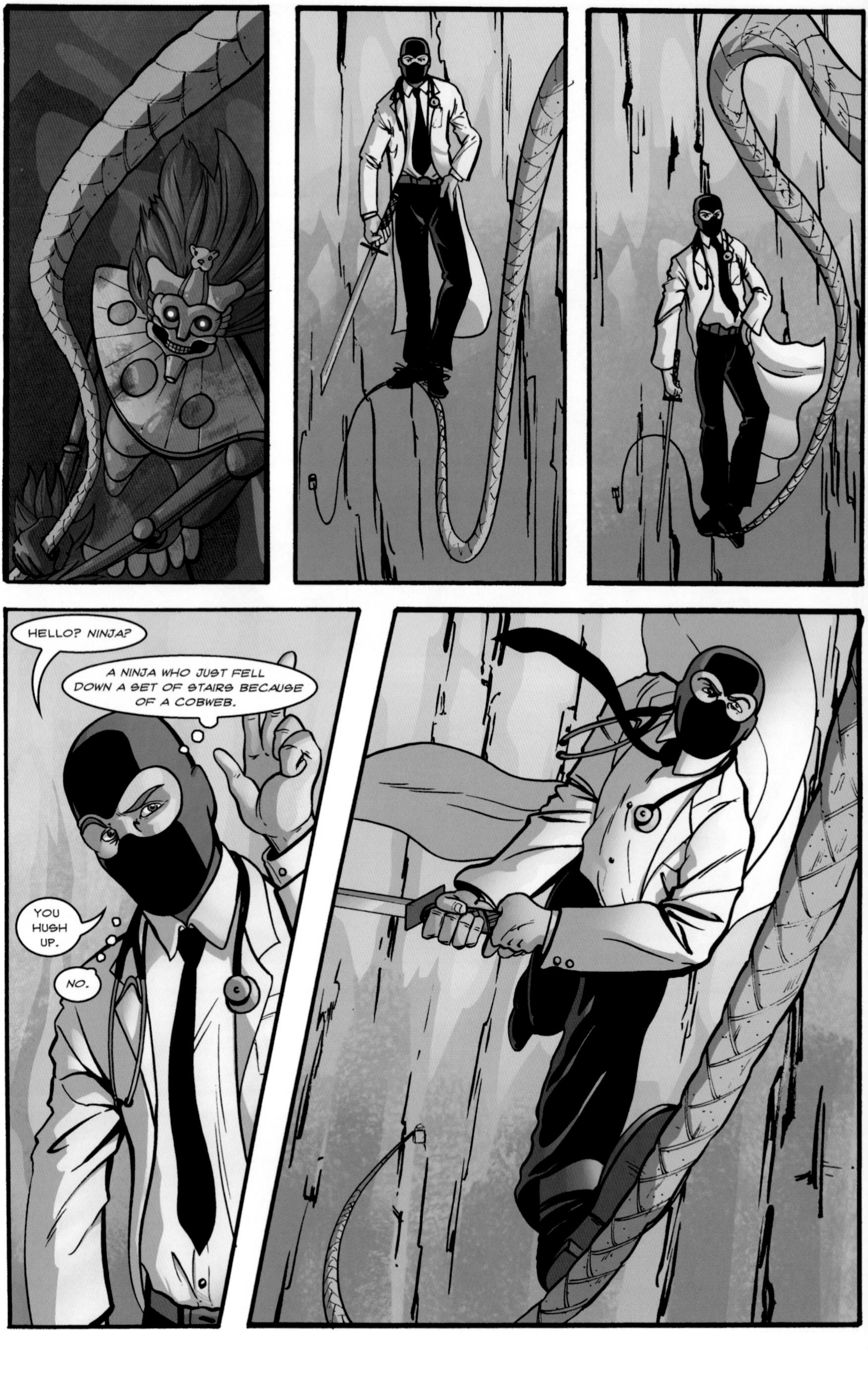
HELLO? NINJA?
A NINJA WHO JUST FELL DOWN A SET OF STAIRS BECAUSE OF A COBWEB.
YOU HUSH UP.
NO.

Don't forget! Dr. McNinja is CRAZY.

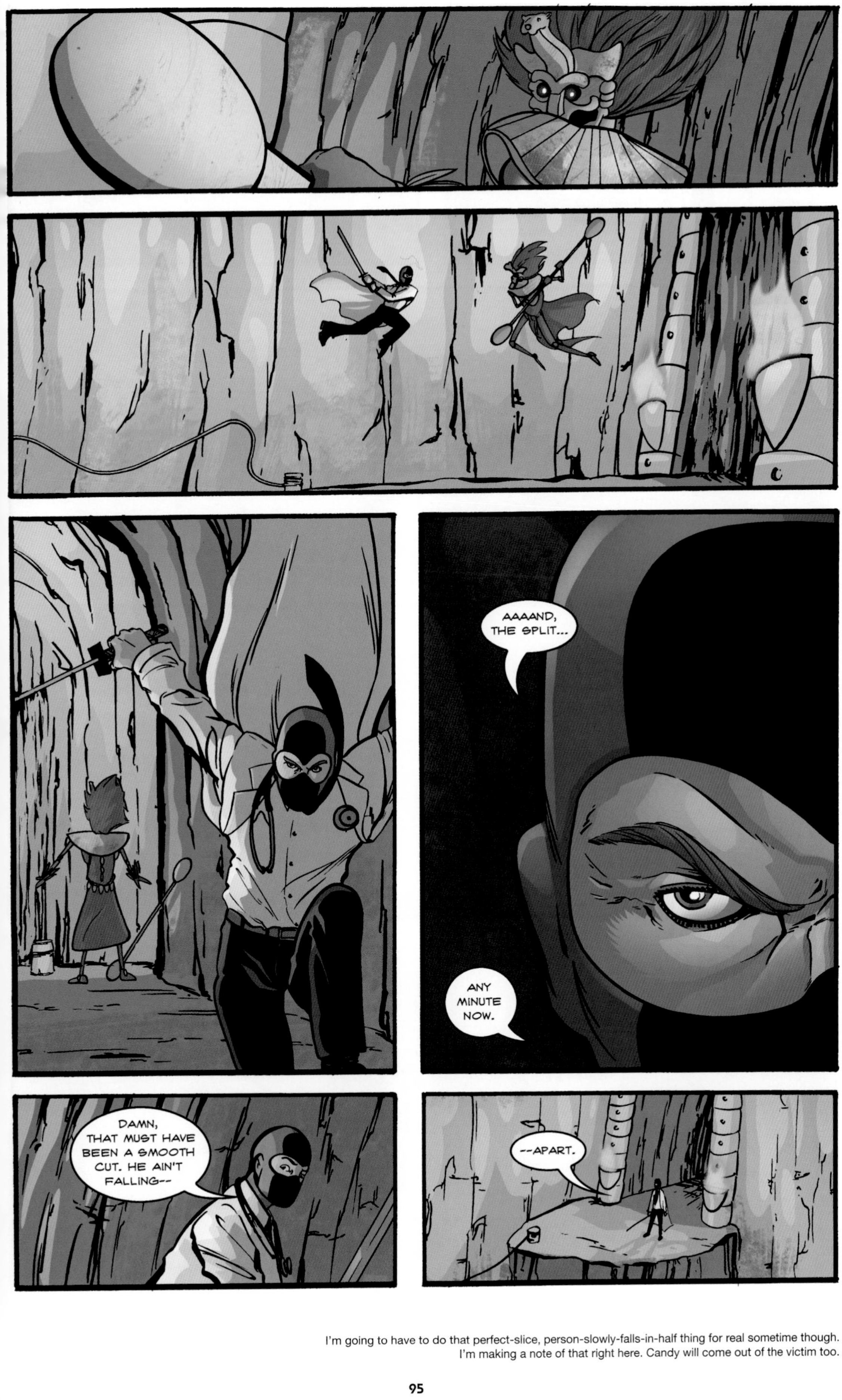
AAAAND, THE SPLIT...
ANY MINUTE NOW.
DAMN, THAT MUST HAVE BEEN A SMOOTH CUT. HE AIN'T FALLING--
--APART.

I'm going to have to do that perfect-slice, person-slowly-falls-in-half thing for real sometime though.
I'm making a note of that right here. Candy will come out of the victim too.

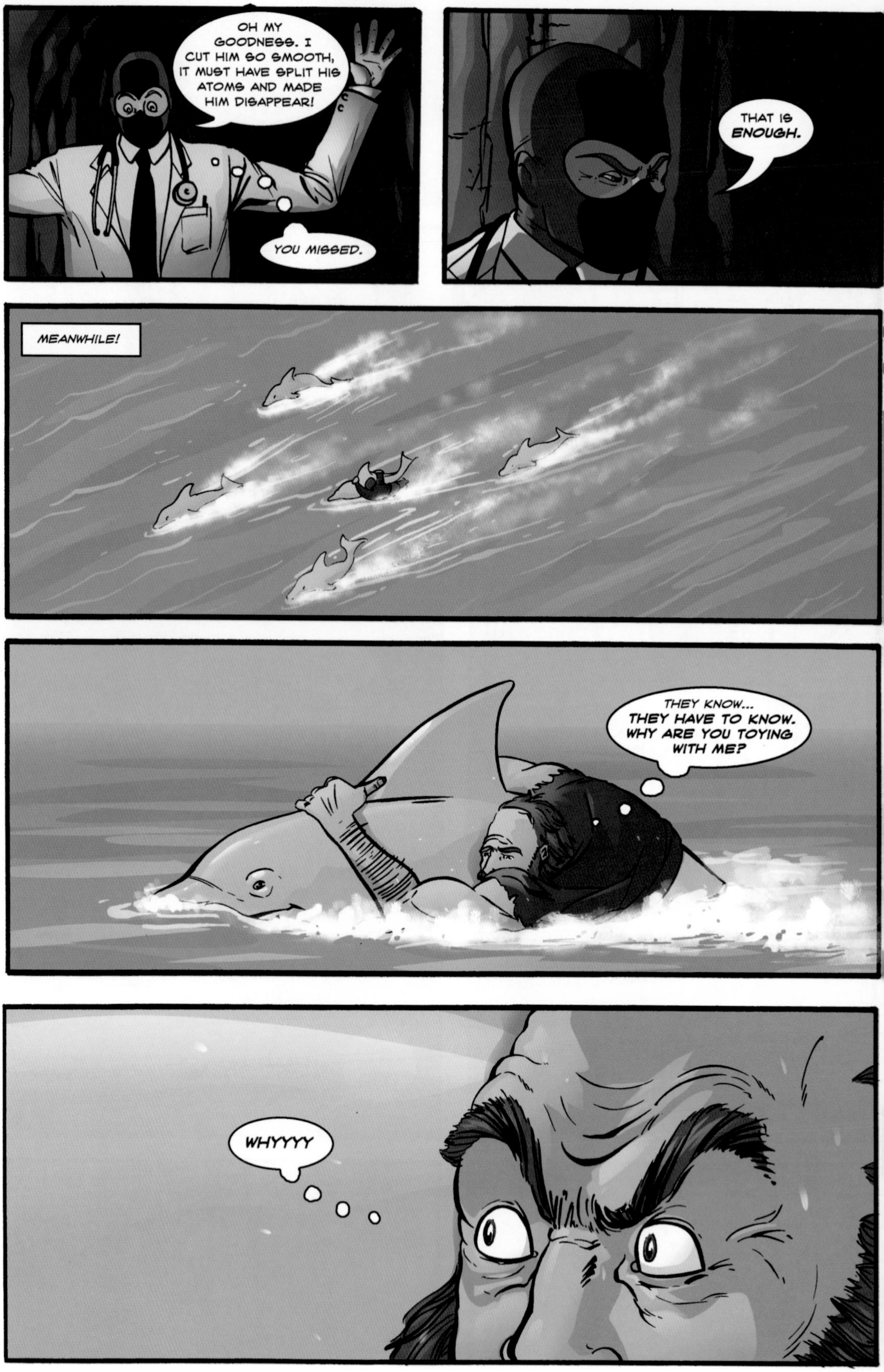
OH MY GOODNESS. I CUT HIM SO SMOOTH, IT MUST HAVE SPLIT HIS ATOMS AND MADE HIM DISAPPEAR!
YOU MISSED.
THAT IS ENOUGH.
MEANWHILE!
THEY KNOW... THEY HAVE TO KNOW. WHY ARE YOU TOYING WITH ME?
WHYYYY

You ever sort of screamed at someone with your mind? You ever sort of screamed at a DOLPHIN with your mind?

AND YET MEANWHILE!

SMACK!

STOP IT.

WHAT!? OH! LITTLE GORDITO! I MUST HAVE BEEN SLEEP-WALKING!

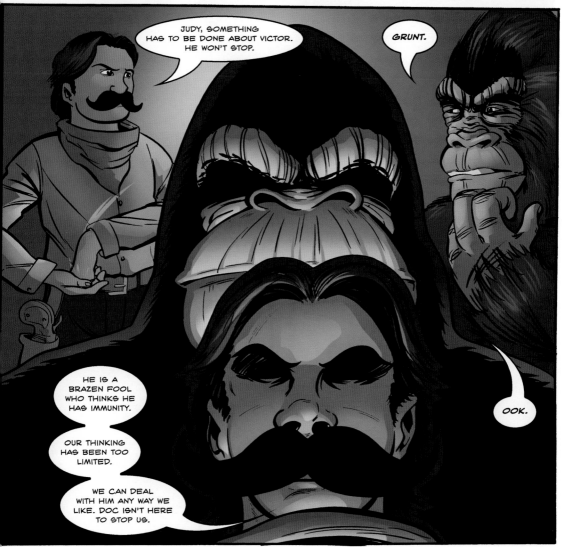

JUDY, SOMETHING HAS TO BE DONE ABOUT VICTOR. HE WON'T STOP.

GRUNT.

HE IS A BRAZEN FOOL WHO THINKS HE HAS IMMUNITY.

OUR THINKING HAS BEEN TOO LIMITED.

WE CAN DEAL WITH HIM ANY WAY WE LIKE. DOC ISN'T HERE TO STOP US.

OOK.

SCHEMES.

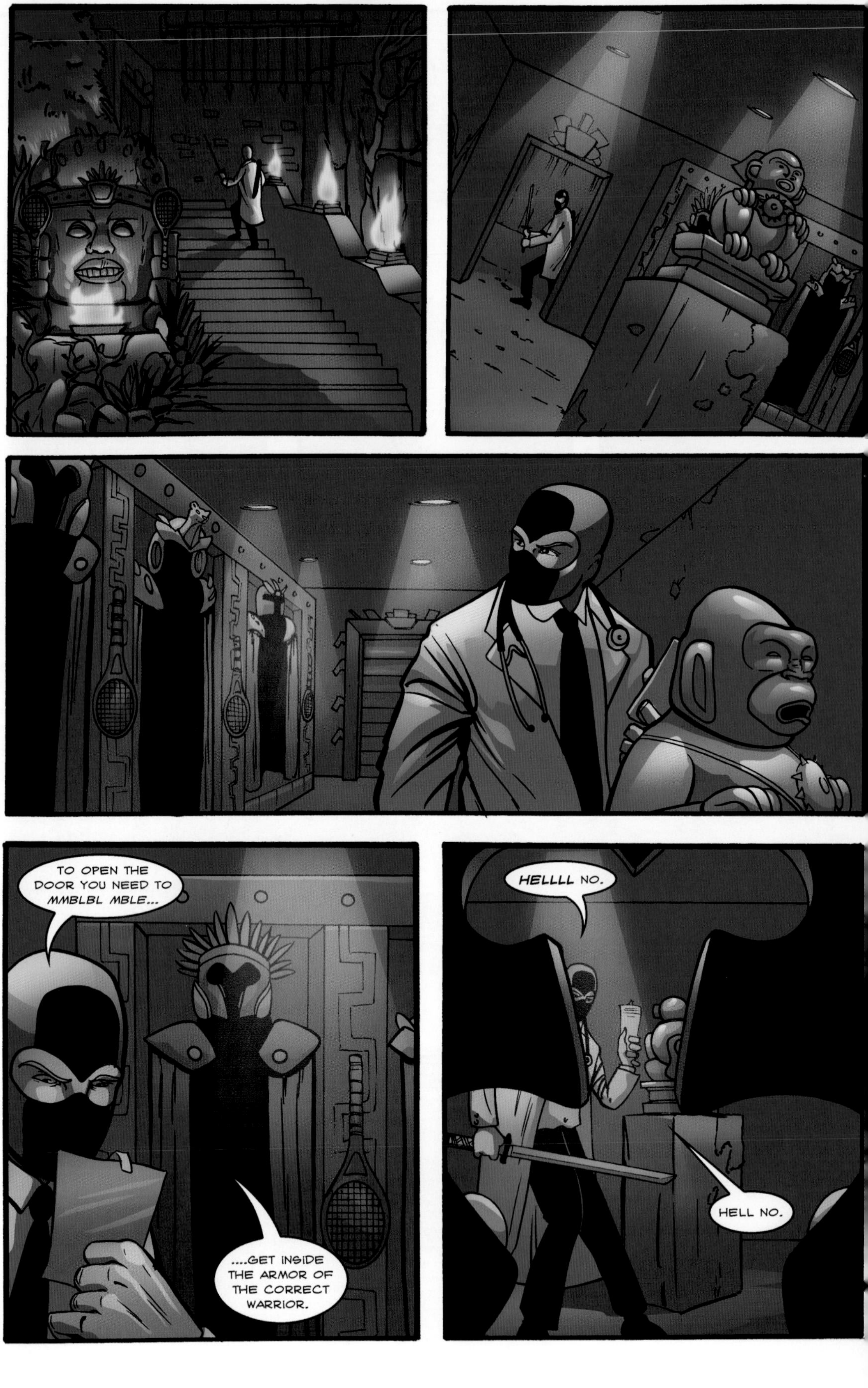
TO OPEN THE DOOR YOU NEED TO MMBLBL MBLE...
....GET INSIDE THE ARMOR OF THE CORRECT WARRIOR.
HELLLL NO.
HELL NO.

You knew this was coming. It had to happen.

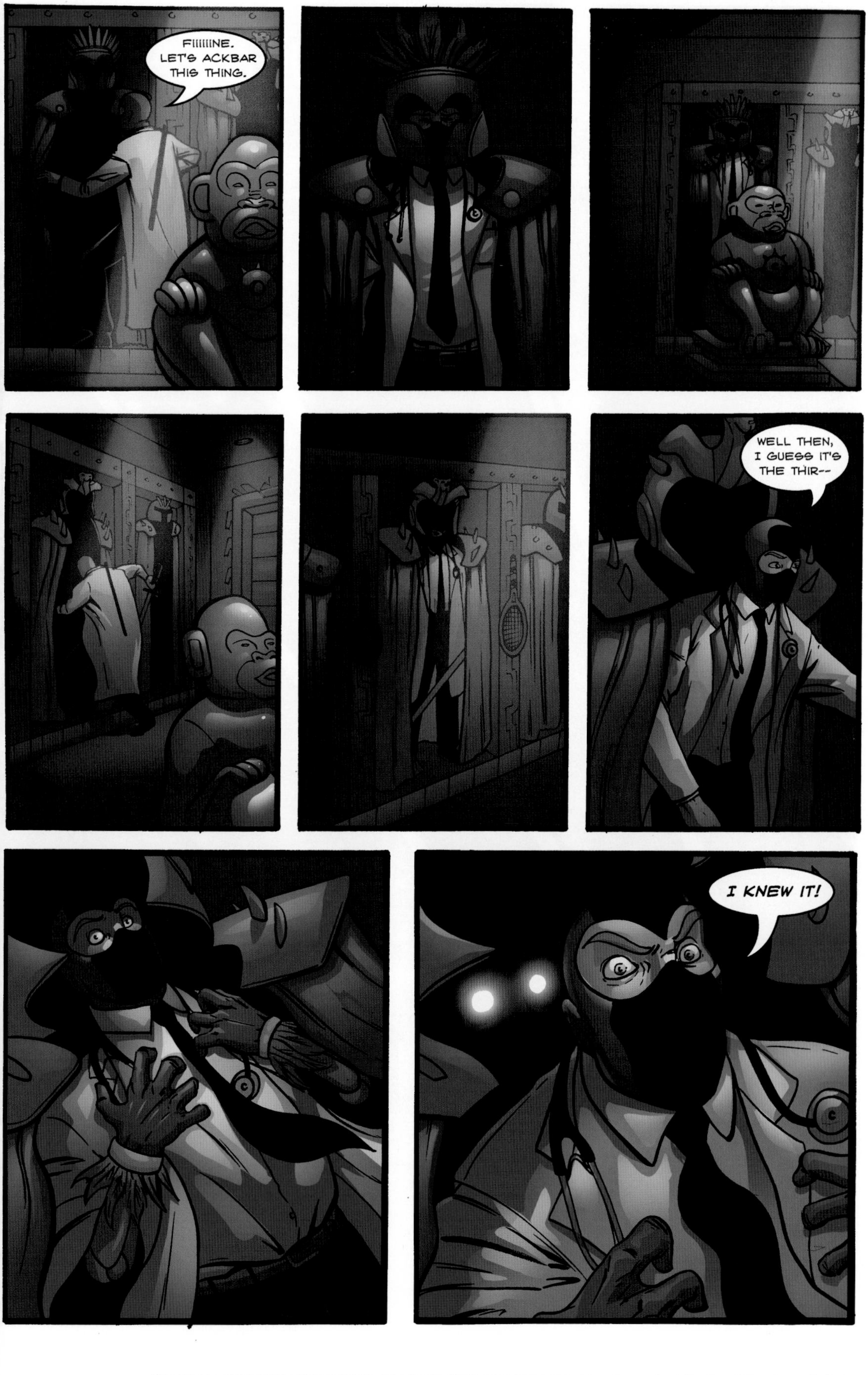
FIIIIINE. LET'S ACKBAR THIS THING.
WELL THEN, I GUESS IT'S THE THIR--
I KNEW IT!

One kid on *Legends of the Hidden Temple* actually ran off the set in terror when a temple guard got him. I would love to see that one.

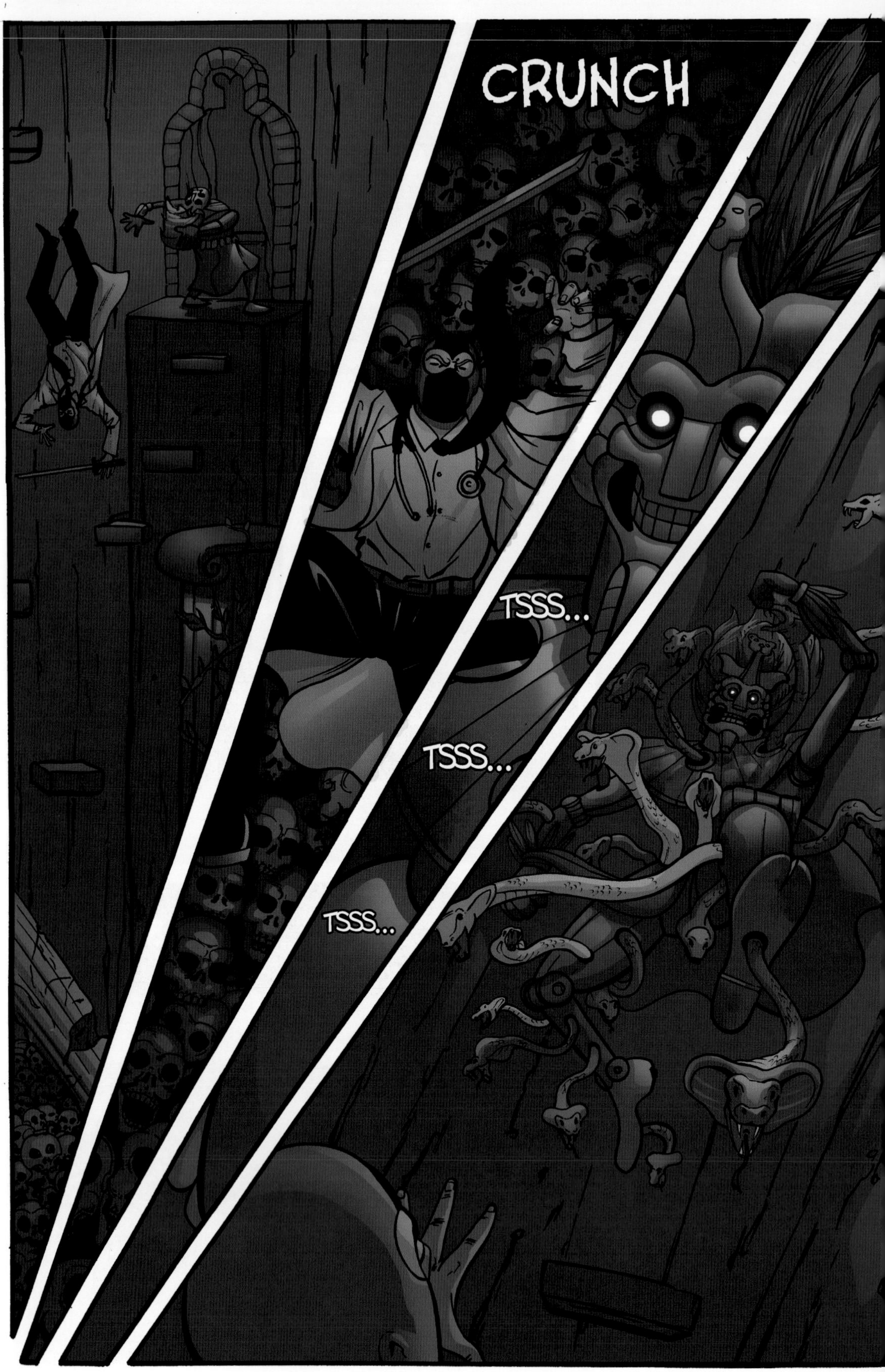
CRUNCH
TSSS...
TSSS...
TSSS...

Snakes coming out of the robot is a good example of me drastically changing the story at the last second, whimsically, while I'm drawing it.

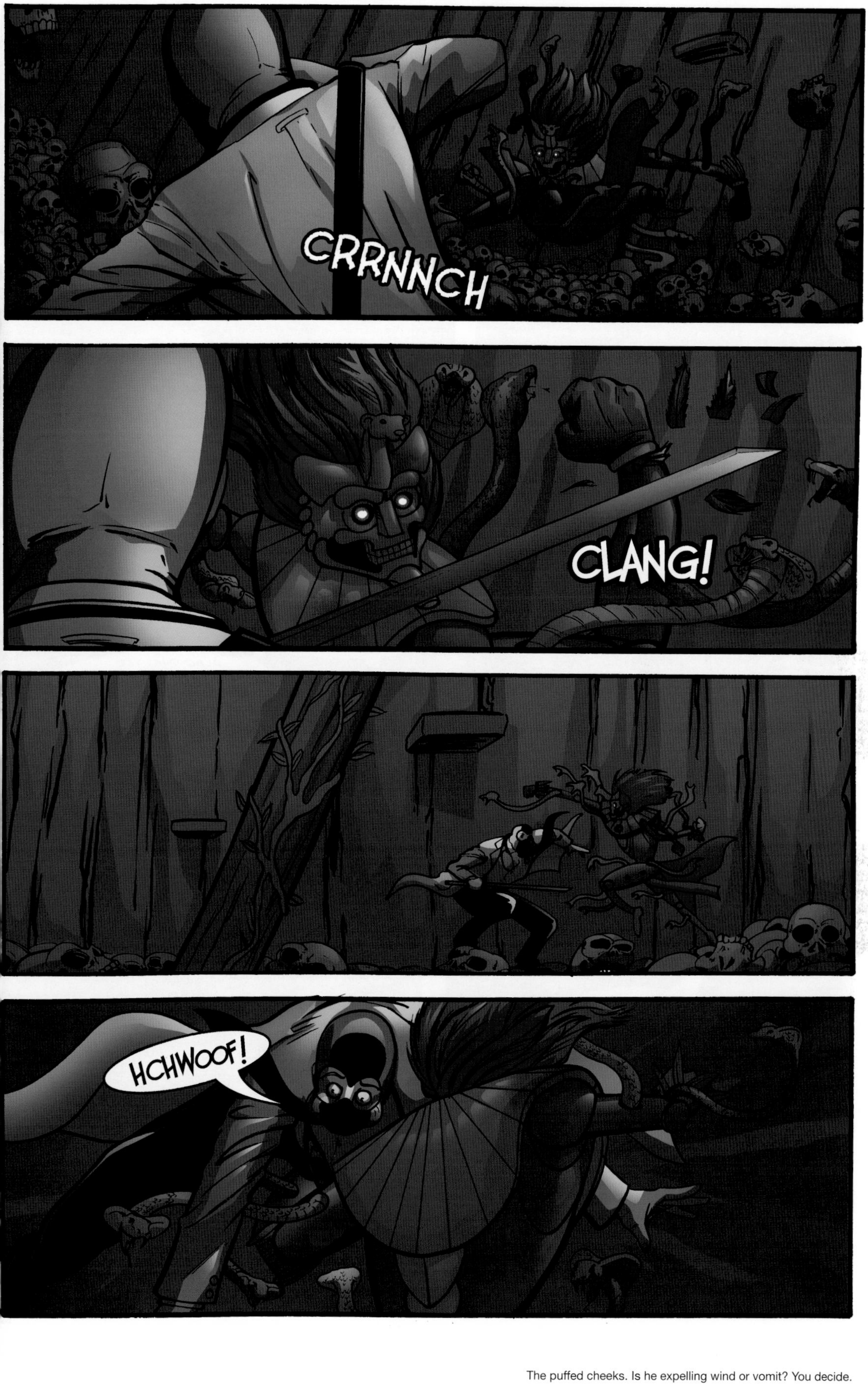
CRRNNCH
CLANG!
HCHWOOF!

The puffed cheeks. Is he expelling wind or vomit? You decide.

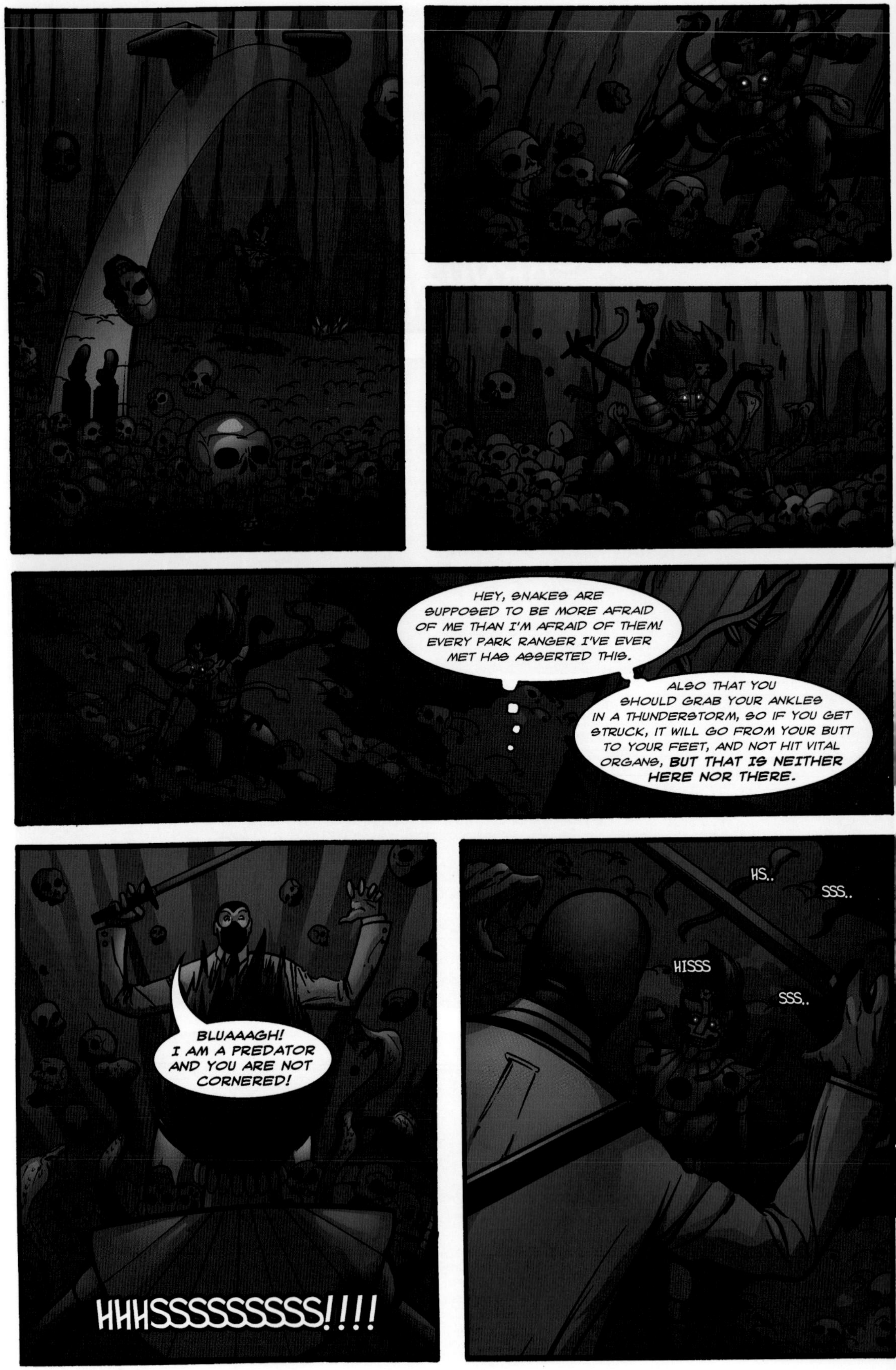
HEY, SNAKES ARE SUPPOSED TO BE MORE AFRAID OF ME THAN I'M AFRAID OF THEM! EVERY PARK RANGER I'VE EVER MET HAS ASSERTED THIS.
ALSO THAT YOU SHOULD GRAB YOUR ANKLES IN A THUNDERSTORM, SO IF YOU GET STRUCK, IT WILL GO FROM YOUR BUTT TO YOUR FEET, AND NOT HIT VITAL ORGANS, BUT THAT IS NEITHER HERE NOR THERE.
BLUAAAGH! I AM A PREDATOR AND YOU ARE NOT CORNERED!
HHHSSSSSSSSSS!!!!
HS..
SSS..
HISSS
SSS..

Well, the snakes find that perfectly reasonable. Good day.

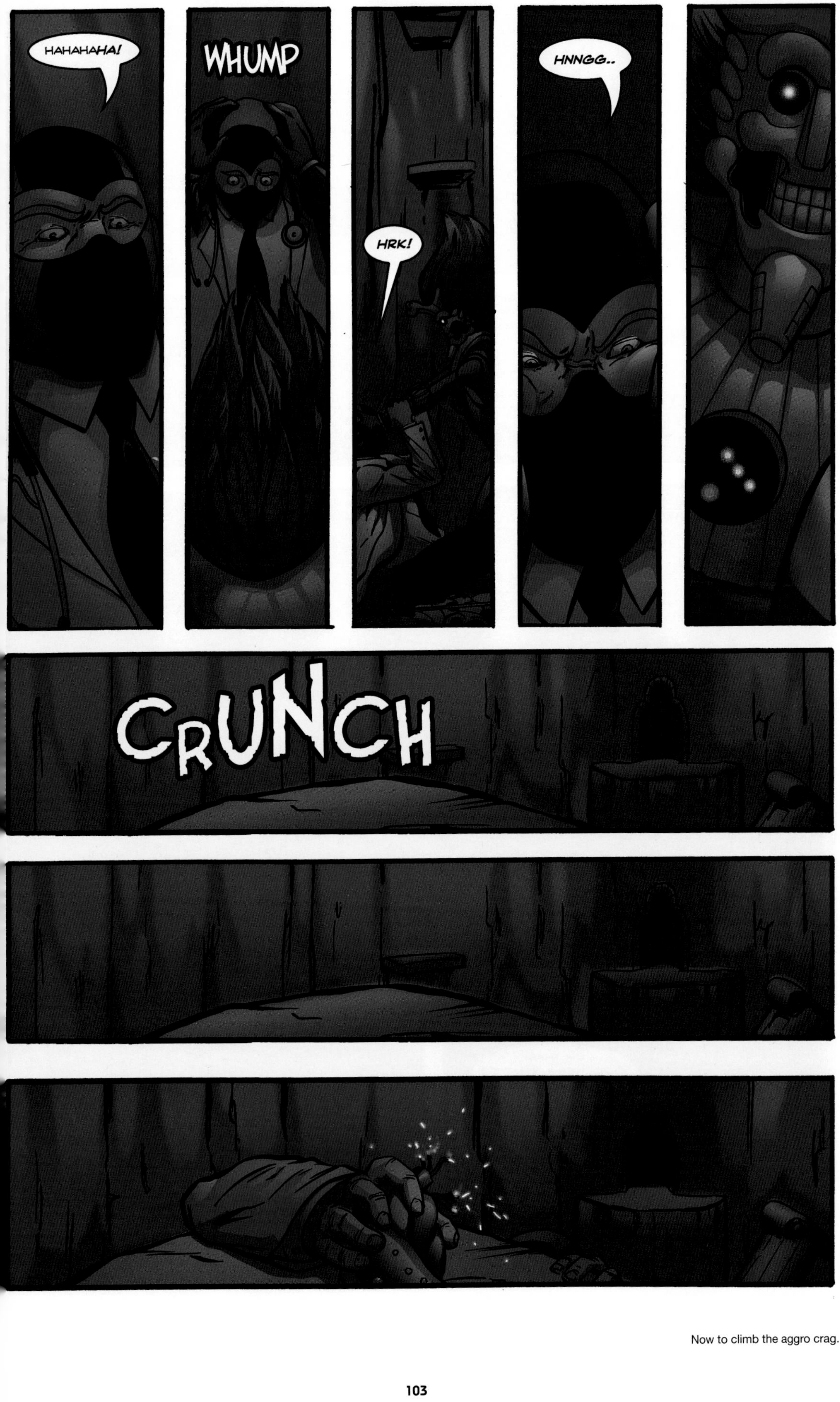
HAHAHAHA!
WHUMP
HRK!
HNNGG..
CRUNCH

Now to climb the aggro crag.

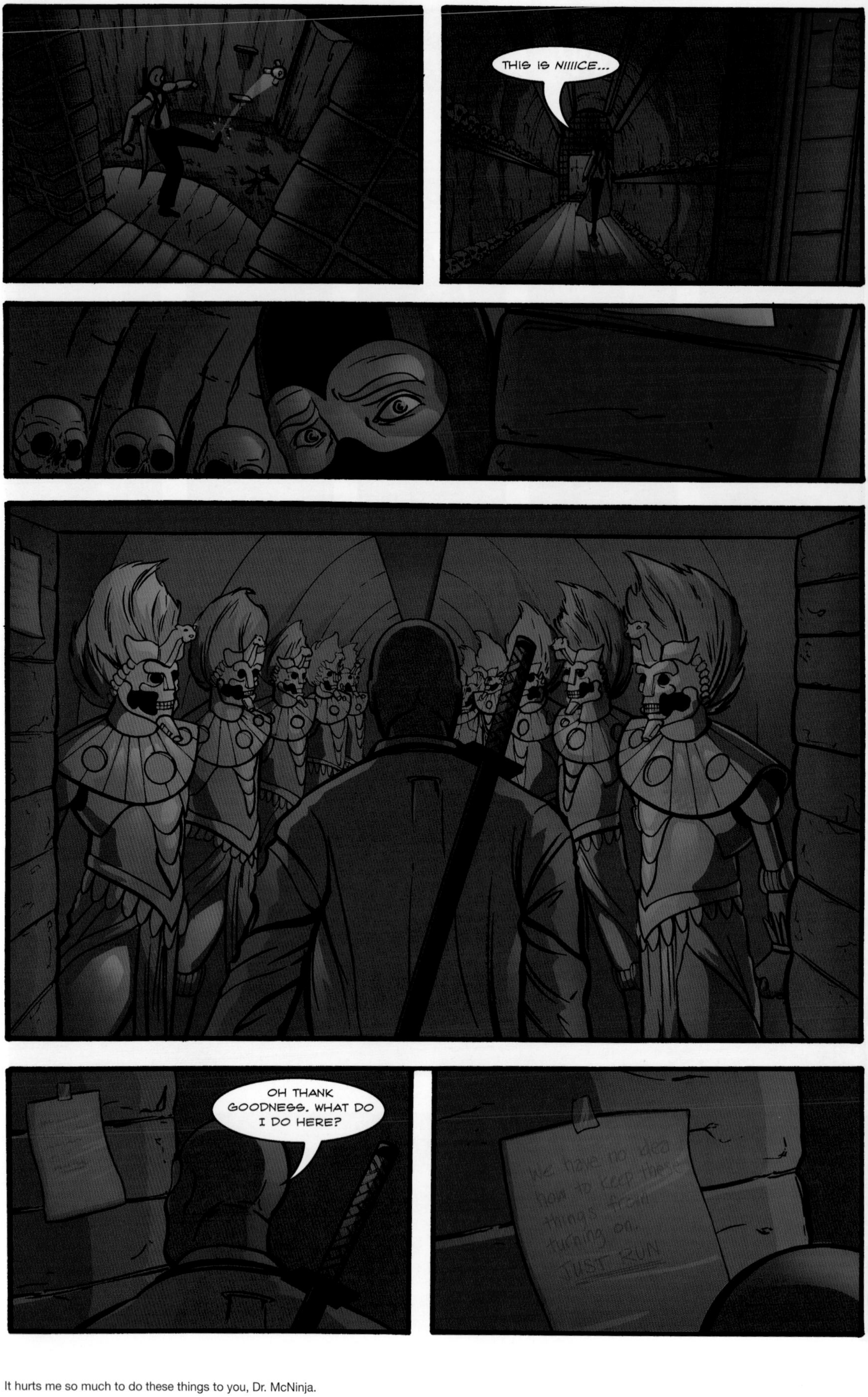
THIS IS NIIIICE...
OH THANK GOODNESS. WHAT DO I DO HERE?
We have no idea how to keep these things from turning on. JUST RUN

It hurts me so much to do these things to you, Dr. McNinja.

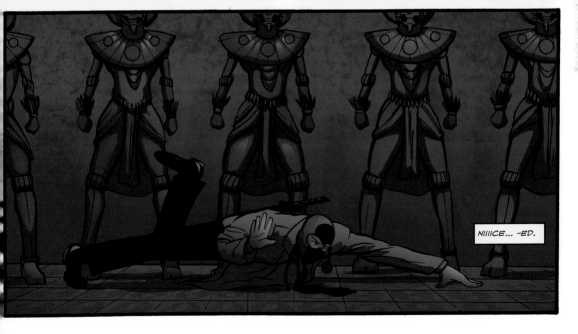

NIIICE... -ED.

Want to see how many pages I can go that are mostly silent except someone saying, "Niiice..."? PS: Yes, there is a difference in the tiles.

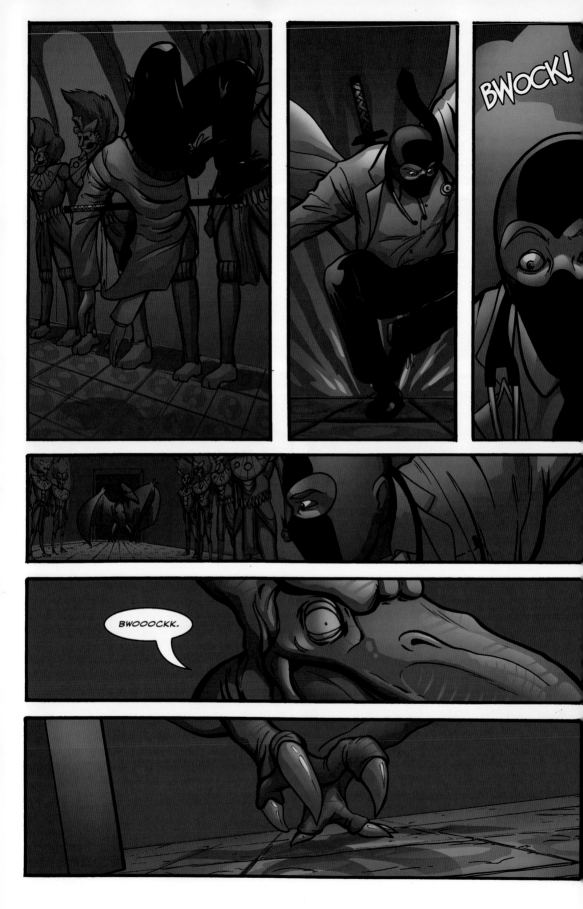

I think I'll have that thing stalk Doc forever now.

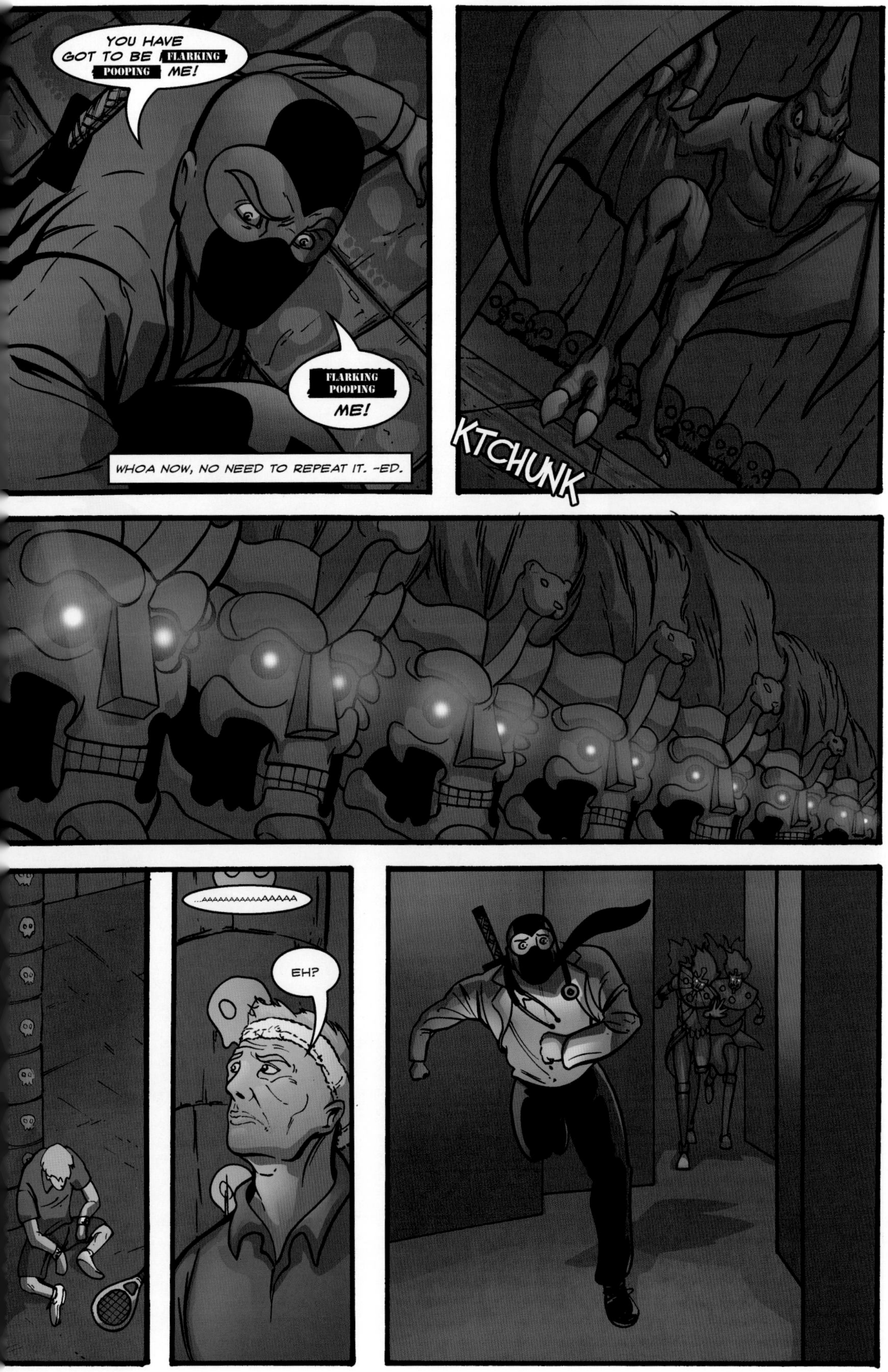

YOU HAVE GOT TO BE FLARKING POOPING ME!
FLARKING POOPING ME!
WHOA NOW, NO NEED TO REPEAT IT. -ED.
KTCHUNK
...AAAAAAAAAAAAAAAAA
EH?

I hope my completely made-up-out-of-my-mind-with-no-reference-whatsoever way of drawing the birdosaurus doesn't upset any of you junior paleontologists.

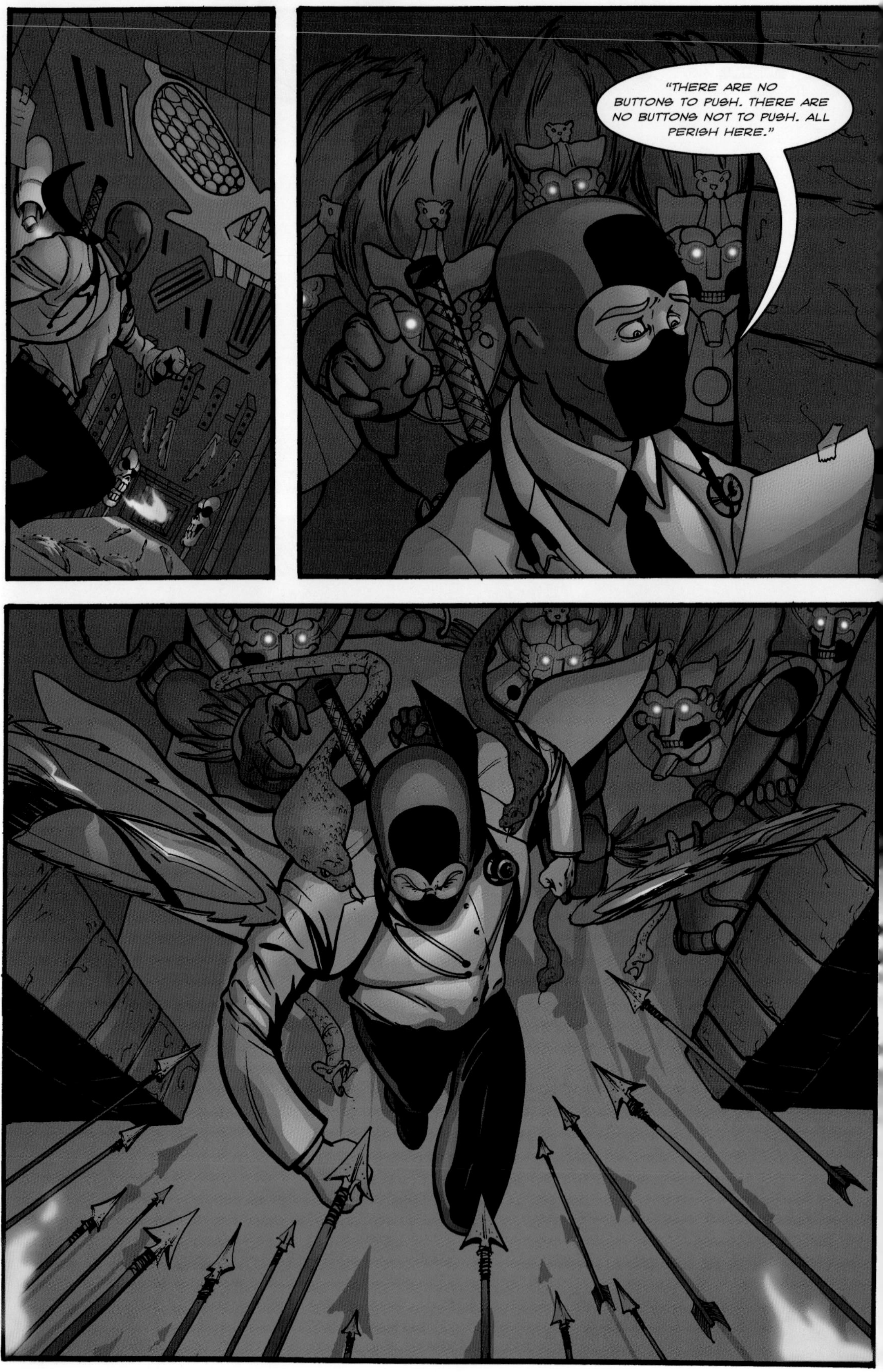
"THERE ARE NO BUTTONS TO PUSH. THERE ARE NO BUTTONS NOT TO PUSH. ALL PERISH HERE."

Obviously he dies on the next page.

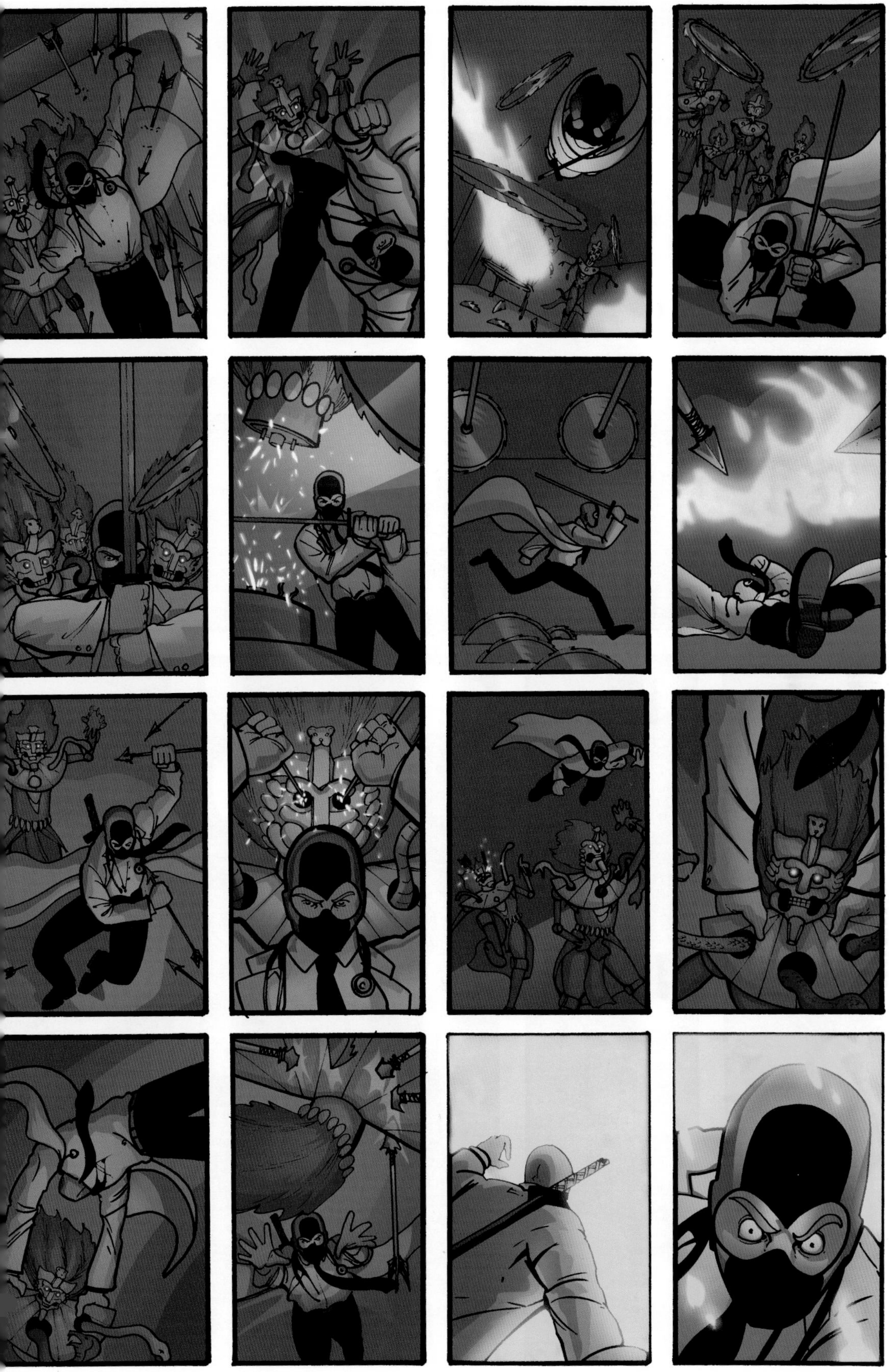

I caught myself making sound effects with my mouth when I drew this.

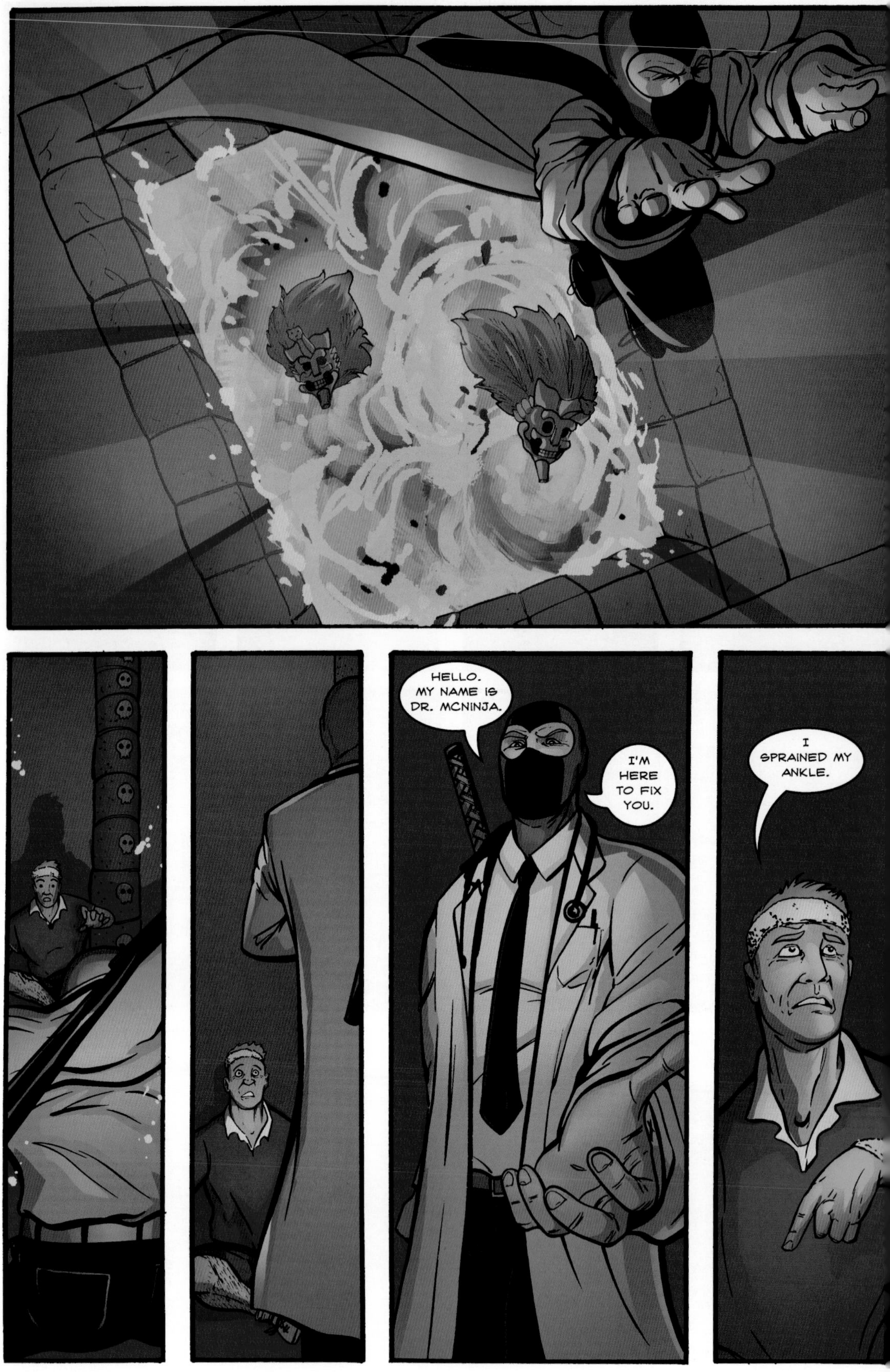
HELLO. MY NAME IS DR. MCNINJA.
I'M HERE TO FIX YOU.
I SPRAINED MY ANKLE.

Yes! ROBOT HEADS ON FIRE! More of this in my entertainment, please.

I'M PERRY. PERRY WINCHESTER. NICE WORK GETTING THROUGH THE TEMPLE!

A SPRAINED ANKLE.

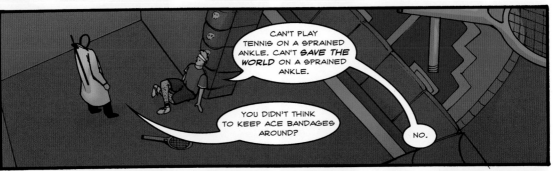

CAN'T PLAY TENNIS ON A SPRAINED ANKLE. CAN'T *SAVE THE WORLD* ON A SPRAINED ANKLE.

YOU DIDN'T THINK TO KEEP ACE BANDAGES AROUND?

NO.

BLAM!

Hortense ruined Dr. McNinja's magic trick.

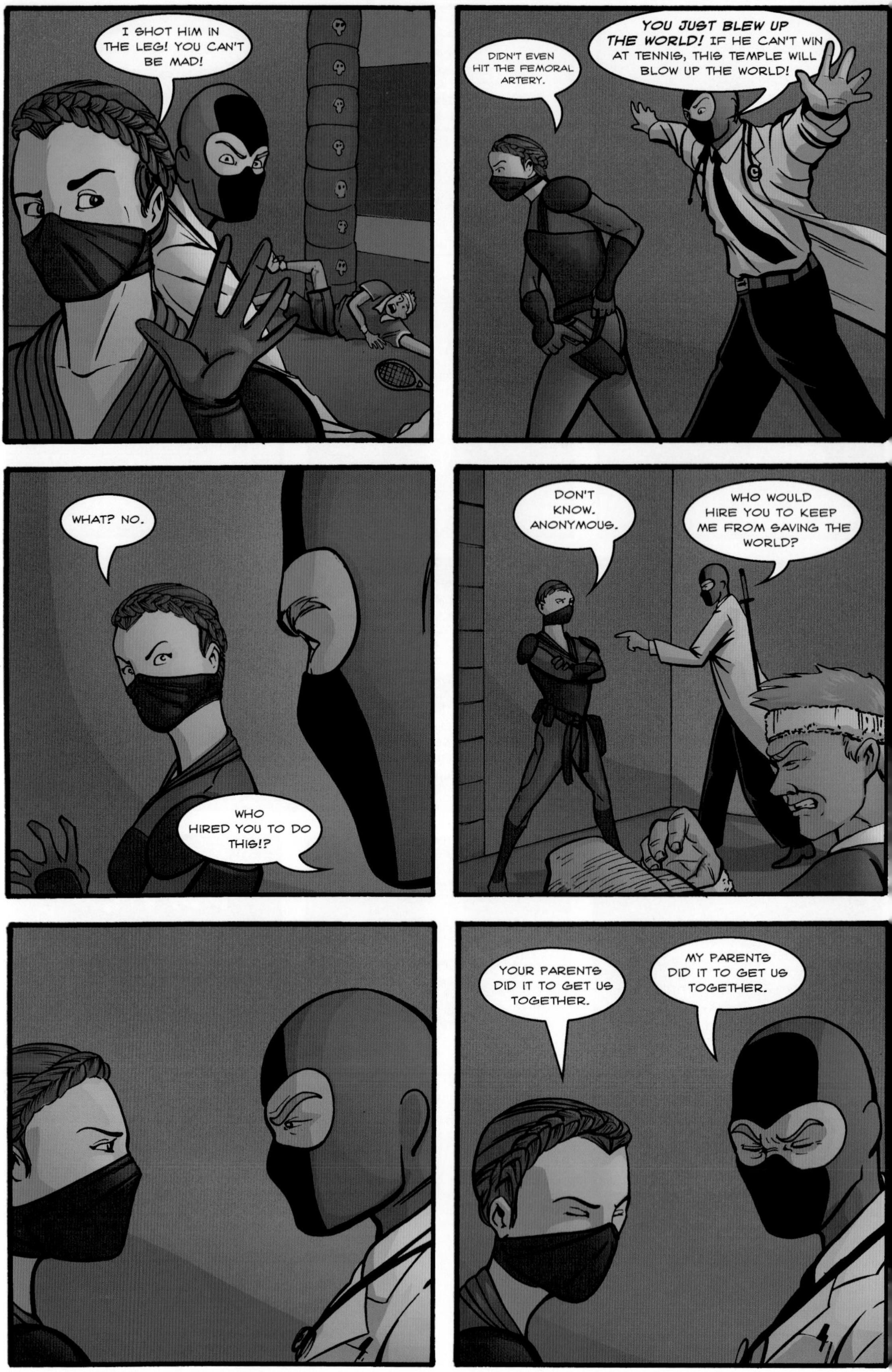
I SHOT HIM IN THE LEG! YOU CAN'T BE MAD!
DIDN'T EVEN HIT THE FEMORAL ARTERY.
YOU JUST BLEW UP THE WORLD! IF HE CAN'T WIN AT TENNIS, THIS TEMPLE WILL BLOW UP THE WORLD!
WHAT? NO.
WHO HIRED YOU TO DO THIS!?
WHO WOULD HIRE YOU TO KEEP ME FROM SAVING THE WORLD?
DON'T KNOW. ANONYMOUS.
MY PARENTS DID IT TO GET US TOGETHER.
YOUR PARENTS DID IT TO GET US TOGETHER.

Imagine Mr. and Mrs. McNinja giggling over encrypted e-mails sent to Hortense. They're a cute couple.

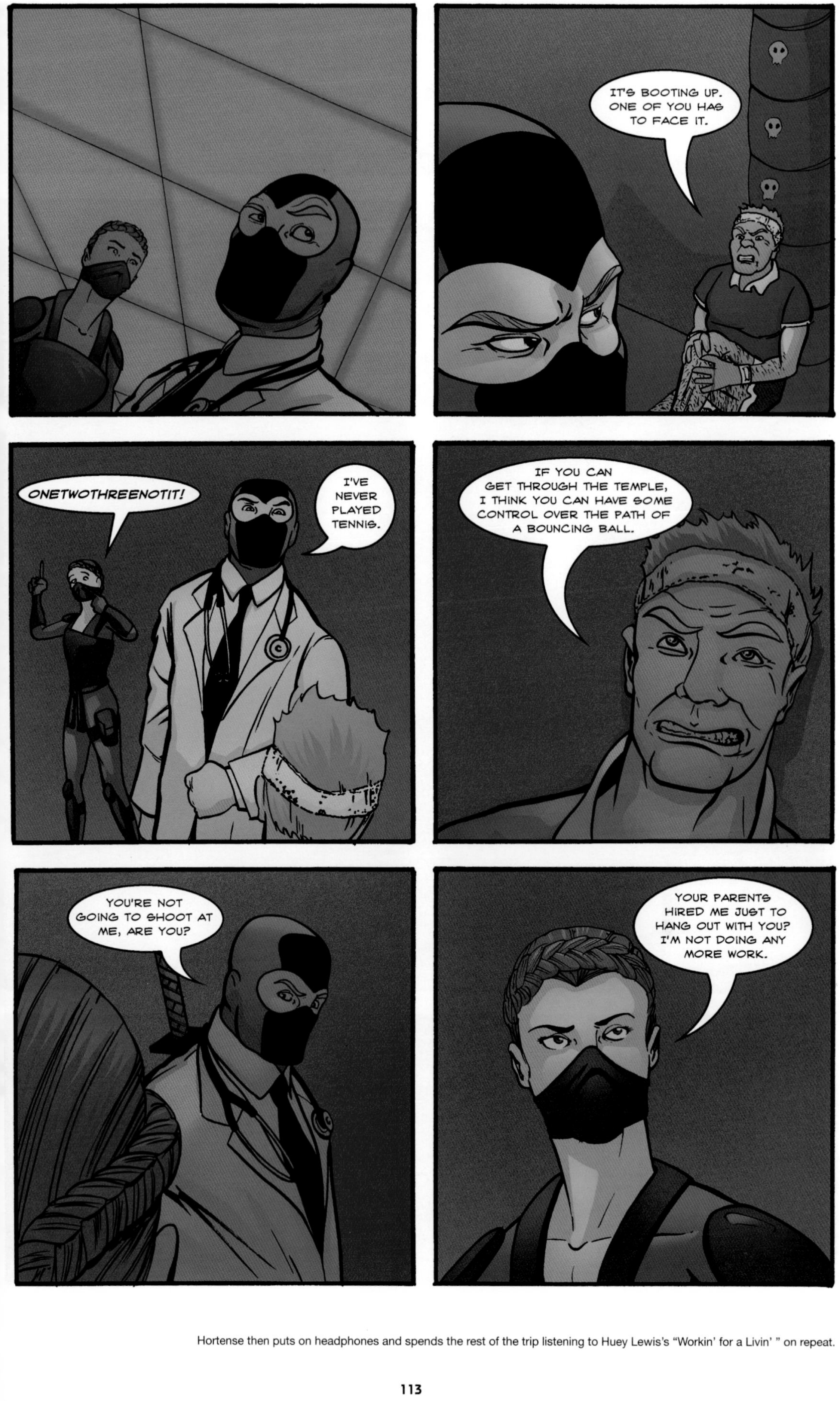
IT'S BOOTING UP. ONE OF YOU HAS TO FACE IT.
ONETWOTHREENOTIT!
I'VE NEVER PLAYED TENNIS.
IF YOU CAN GET THROUGH THE TEMPLE, I THINK YOU CAN HAVE SOME CONTROL OVER THE PATH OF A BOUNCING BALL.
YOU'RE NOT GOING TO SHOOT AT ME, ARE YOU?
YOUR PARENTS HIRED ME JUST TO HANG OUT WITH YOU? I'M NOT DOING ANY MORE WORK.

Hortense then puts on headphones and spends the rest of the trip listening to Huey Lewis's "Workin' for a Livin' " on repeat.

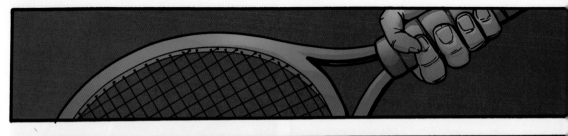

OH MY GOODNESS, WAS I SERIOUSLY JUST SO PREOCCUPIED WITH MY EX THAT I FORGOT TO ATTEND TO A BLEEDING MAN?

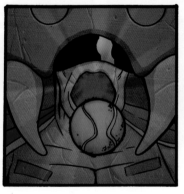

The real challenge is getting a clean vector off those cobblestones.

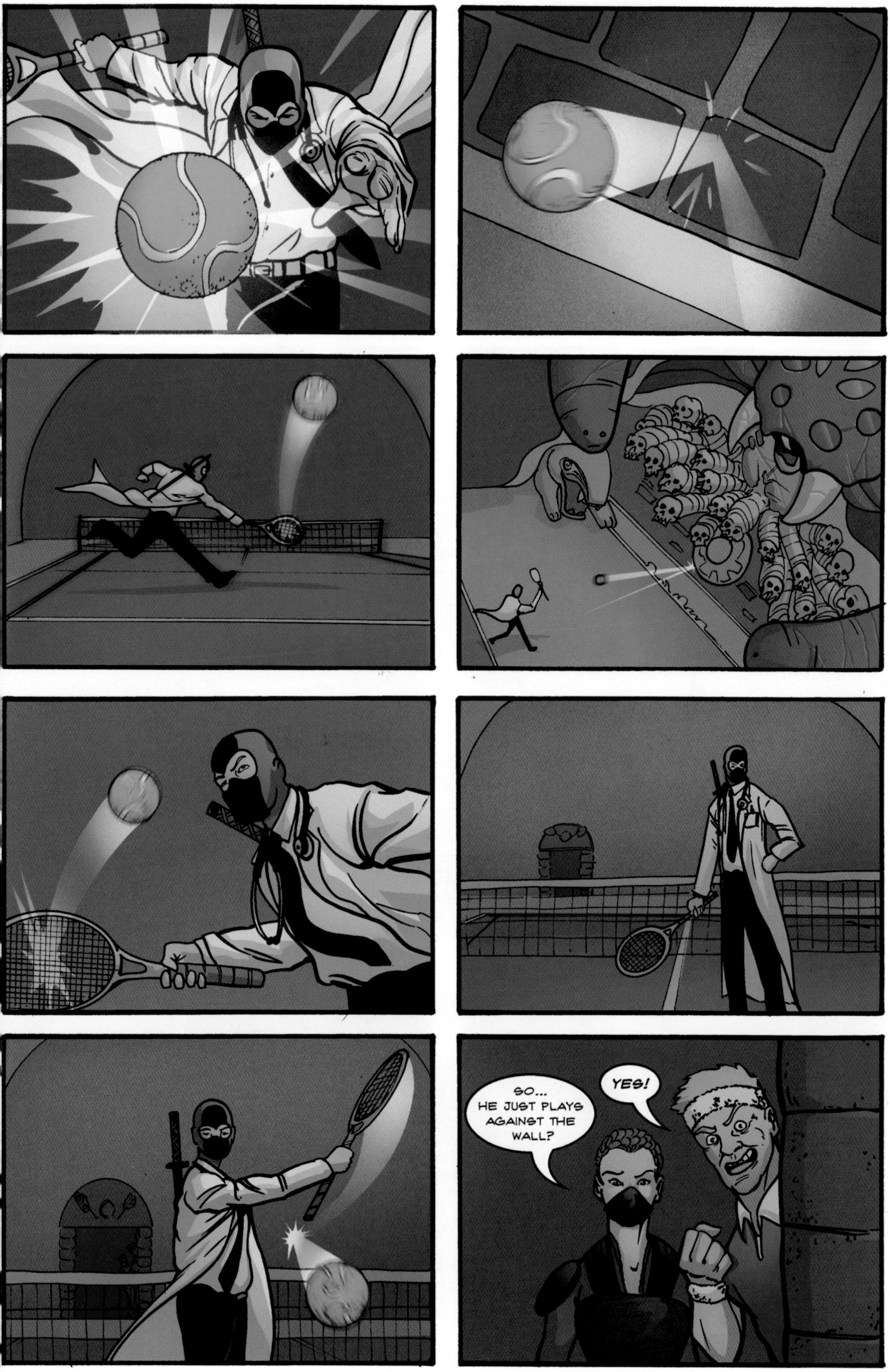
SO...
HE JUST PLAYS
AGAINST THE
WALL?
YES!

He has to keep it above the line too!!!

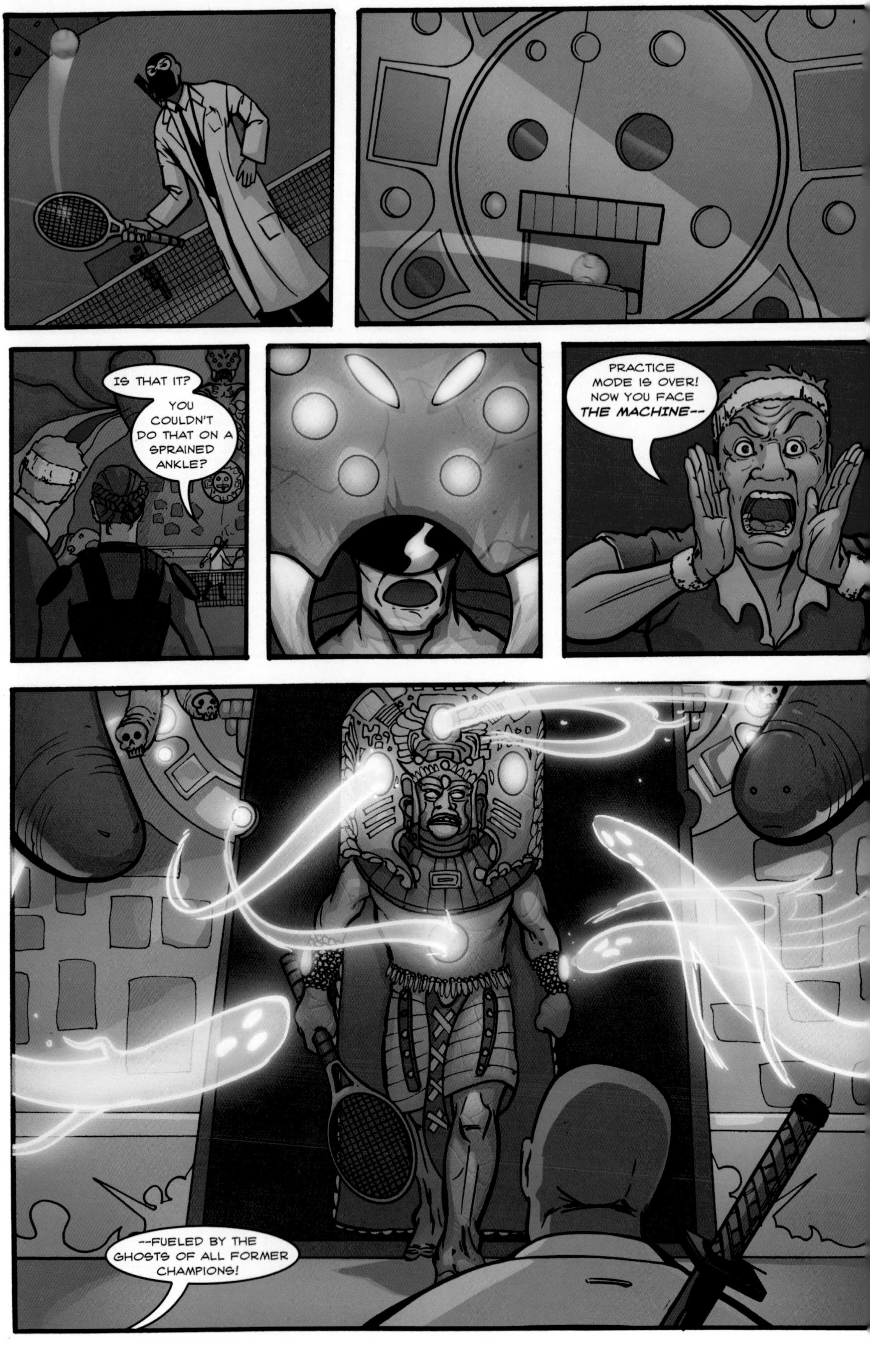
IS THAT IT?
YOU COULDN'T DO THAT ON A SPRAINED ANKLE?
PRACTICE MODE IS OVER! NOW YOU FACE *THE MACHINE--*
--FUELED BY THE GHOSTS OF ALL FORMER CHAMPIONS!

What, and you can't face the ghost-driven giant golem on a sprained ankle either? Or a shot-up leg?

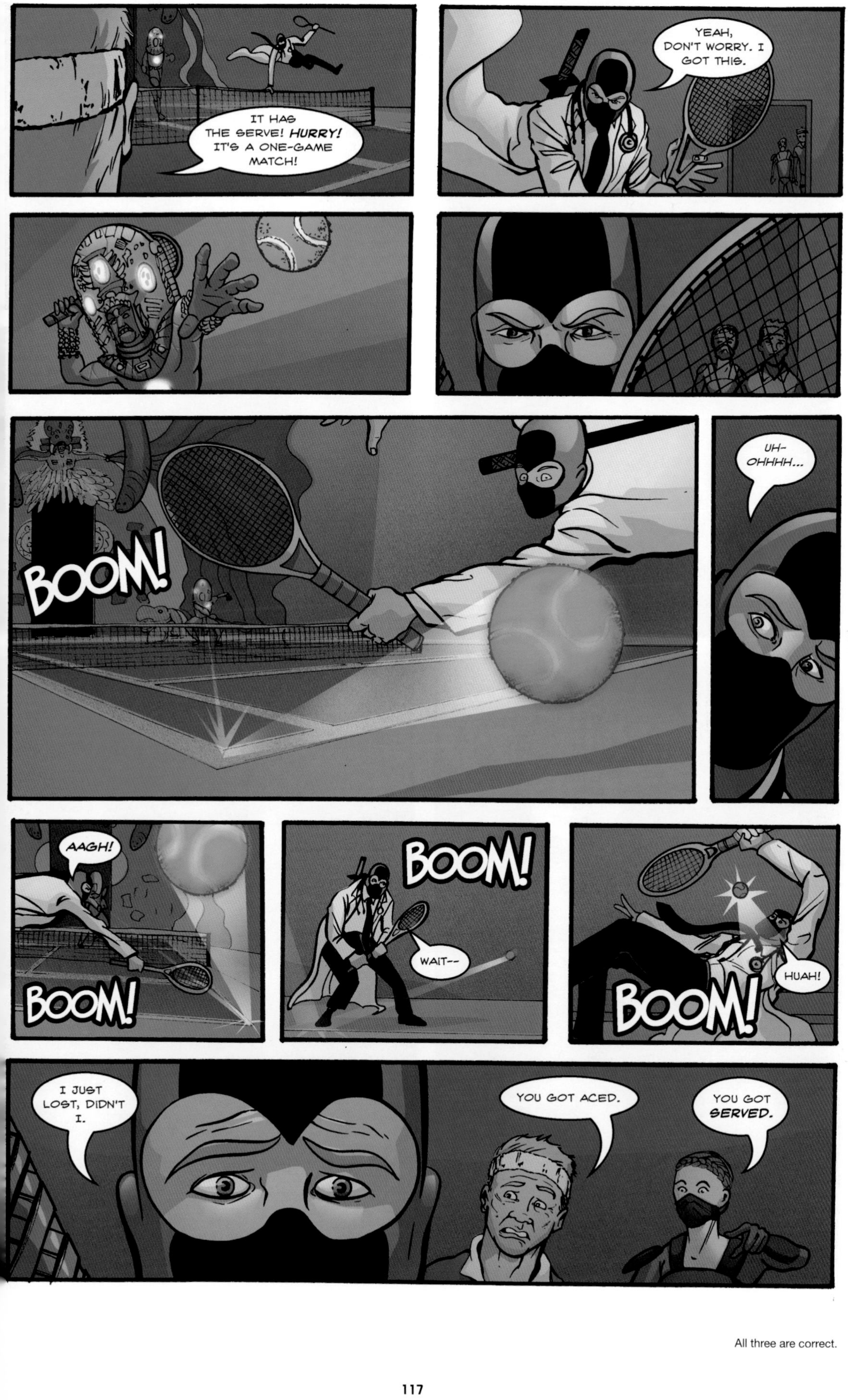
IT HAS THE SERVE! *HURRY!* IT'S A ONE-GAME MATCH!
YEAH, DON'T WORRY. I GOT THIS.
BOOM!
UH-OHHHH...
AAGH!
BOOM!
BOOM!
WAIT--
BOOM!
HUAH!
I JUST LOST, DIDN'T I.
YOU GOT ACED.
YOU GOT *SERVED.*

All three are correct.

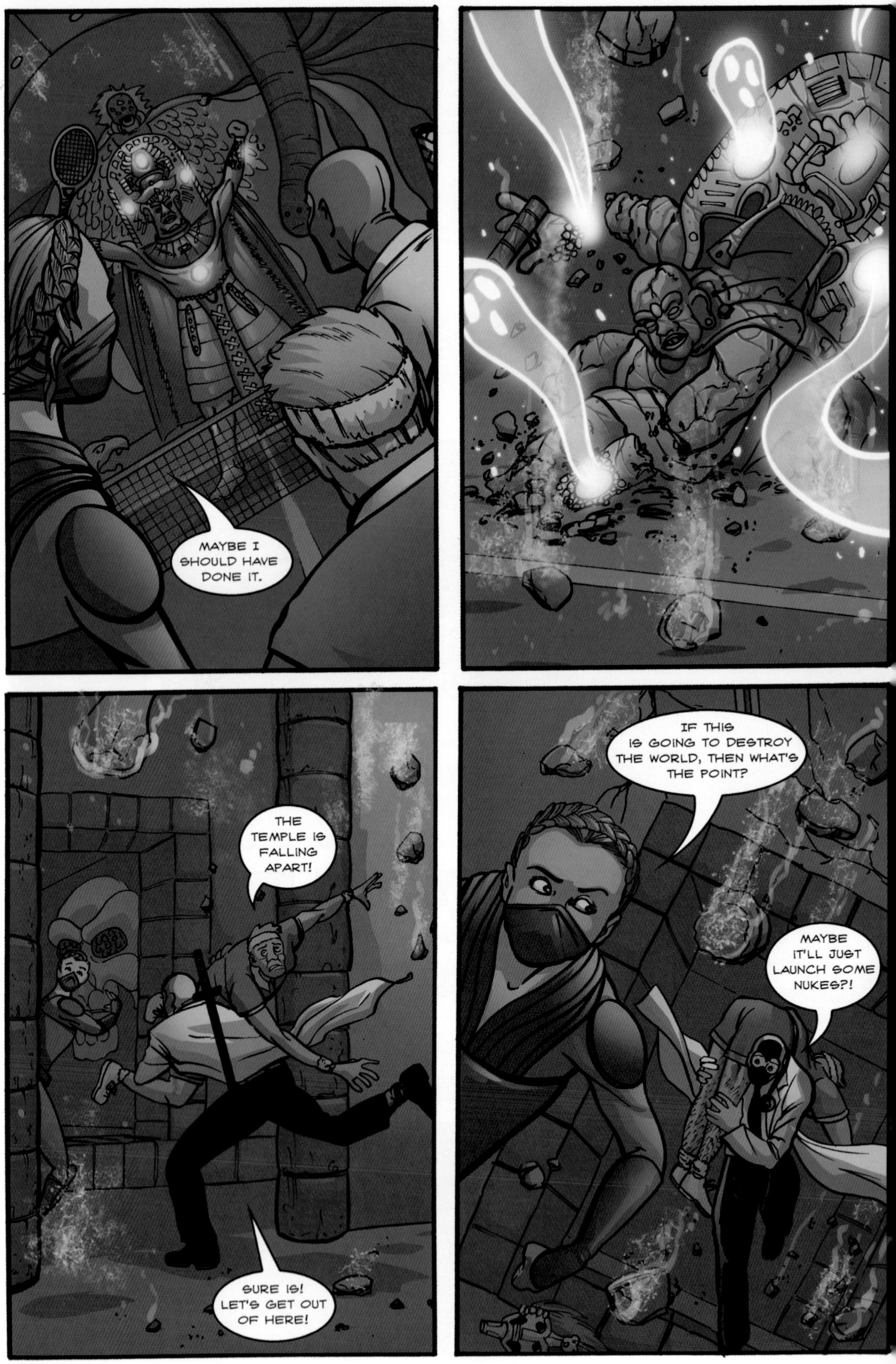

MAYBE I SHOULD HAVE DONE IT.
THE TEMPLE IS FALLING APART!
SURE IS! LET'S GET OUT OF HERE!
IF THIS IS GOING TO DESTROY THE WORLD, THEN WHAT'S THE POINT?
MAYBE IT'LL JUST LAUNCH SOME NUKES?!

Don't forget to grab Mr. and Mrs. Rockadoodle!

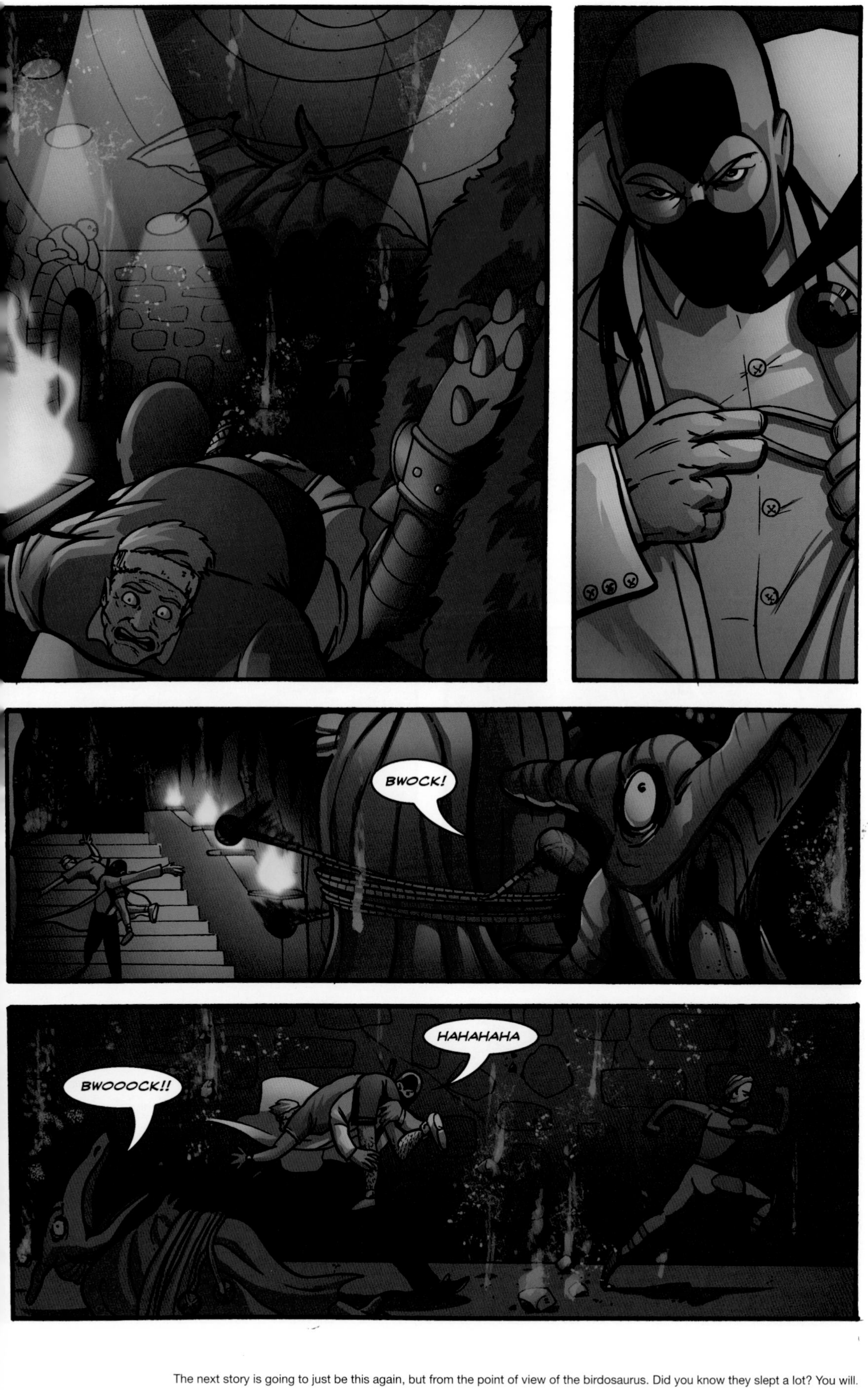
BWOCK!
BWOOOCK!!
HAHAHAHA

The next story is going to just be this again, but from the point of view of the birdosaurus. Did you know they slept a lot? You will.

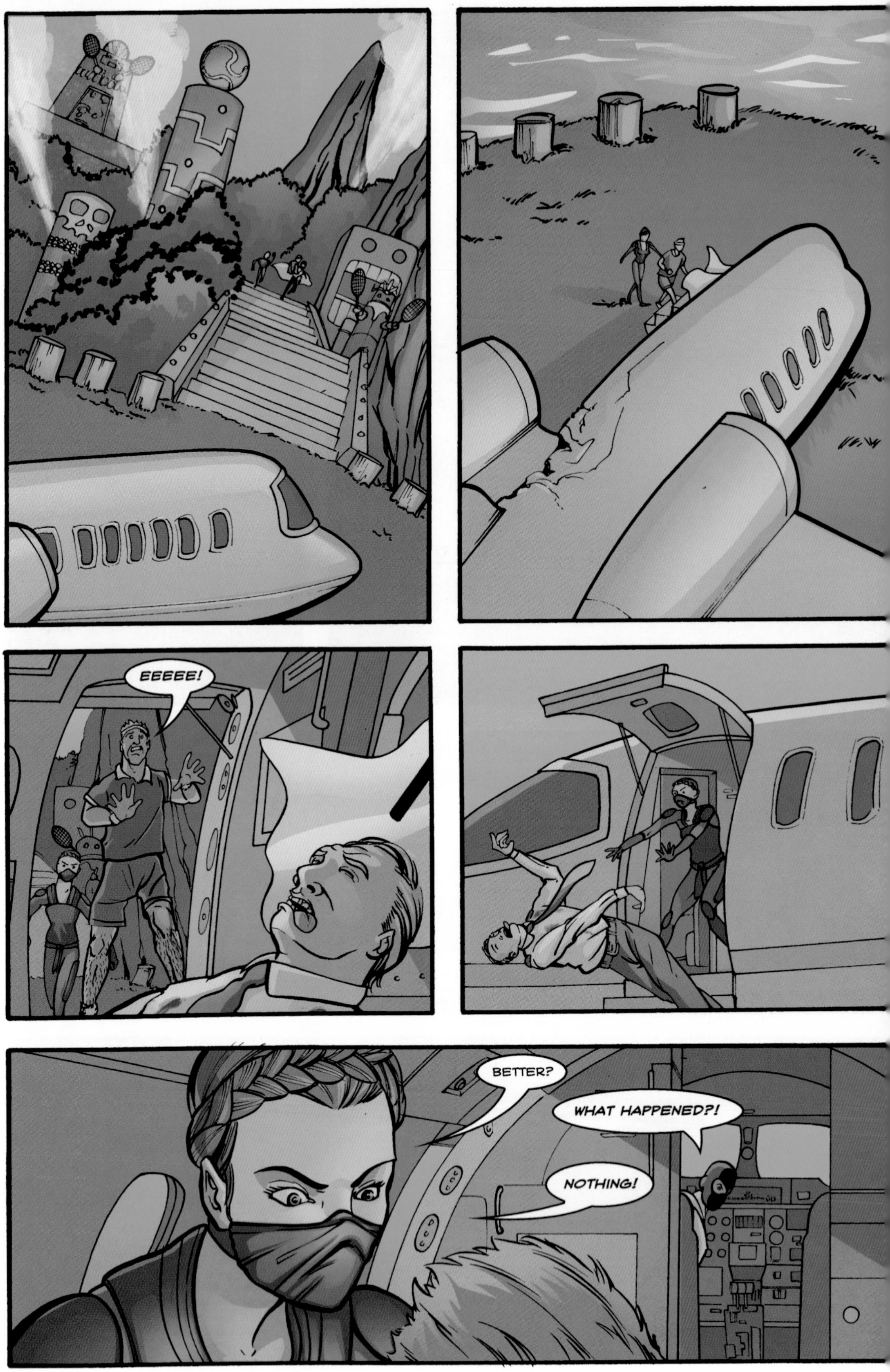
EEEEEE!
BETTER?
WHAT HAPPENED?!
NOTHING!

Okay, so I guess it's become clear that Perry didn't get shot THAT bad.

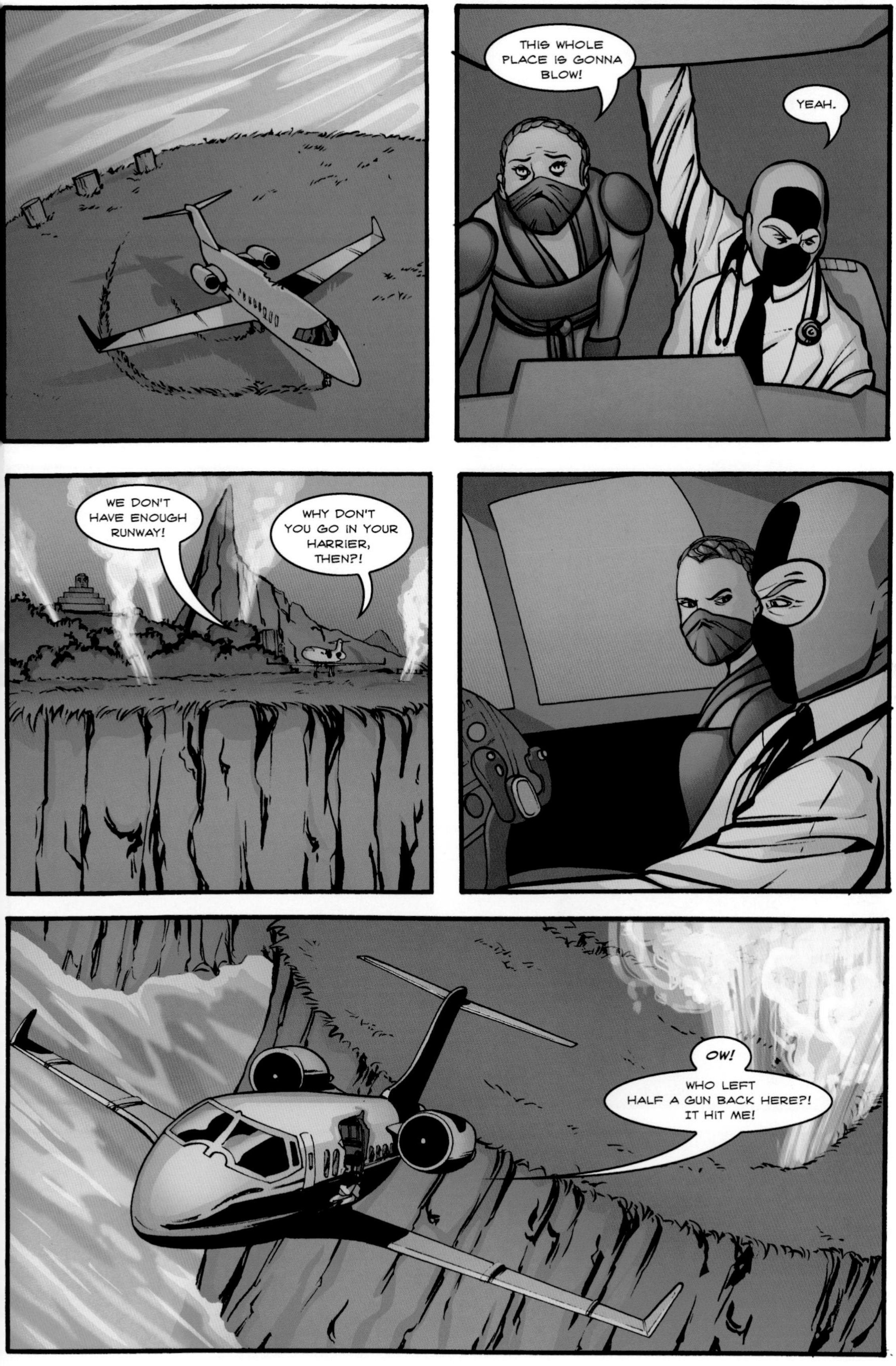

THIS WHOLE PLACE IS GONNA BLOW!
YEAH.
WE DON'T HAVE ENOUGH RUNWAY!
WHY DON'T YOU GO IN YOUR HARRIER, THEN?!
OW!
WHO LEFT HALF A GUN BACK HERE?! IT HIT ME!

The birdosauruses took down Hortense's jet.

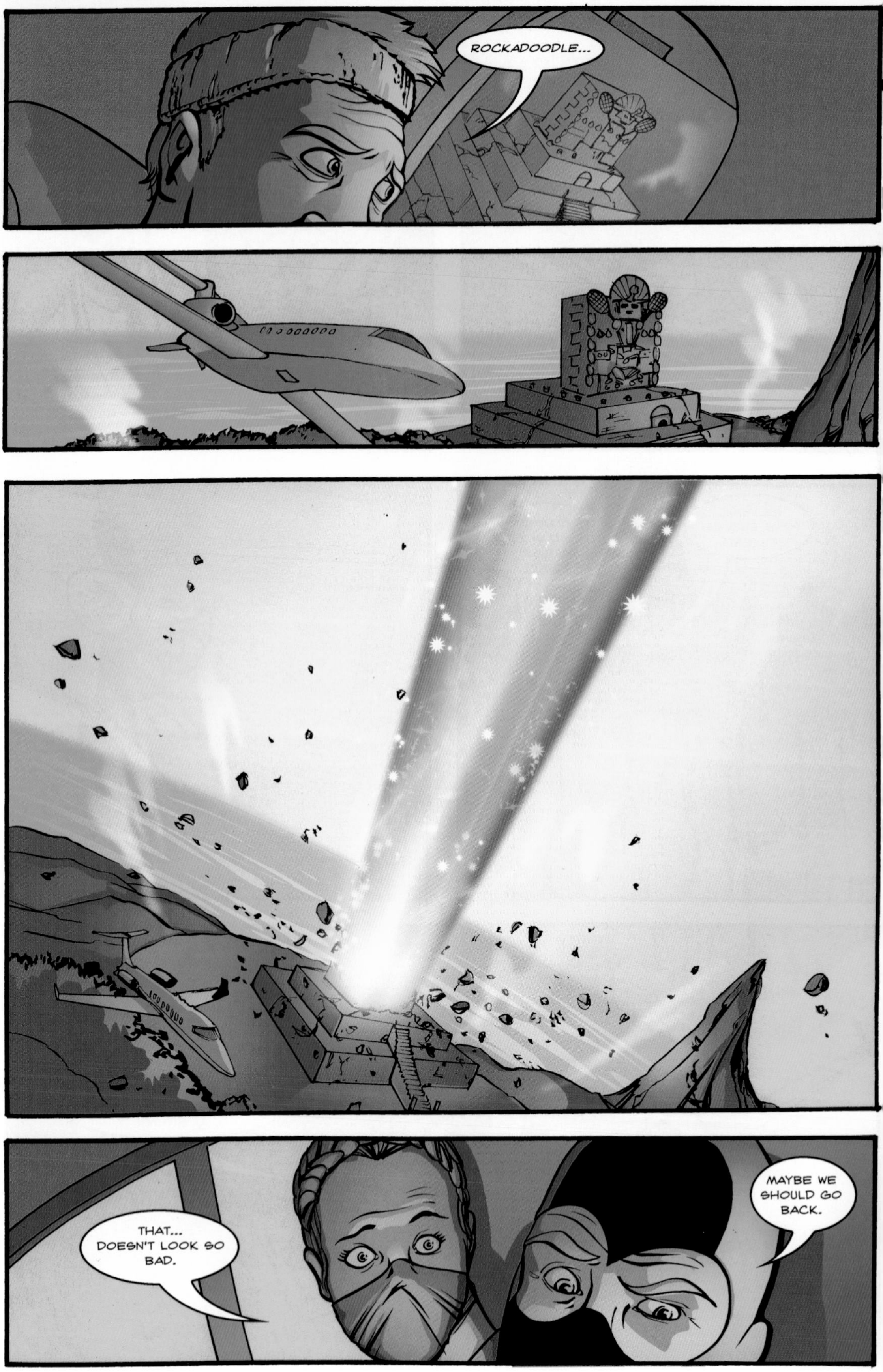
ROCKADOODLE...
THAT... DOESN'T LOOK SO BAD.
MAYBE WE SHOULD GO BACK.

So magical.

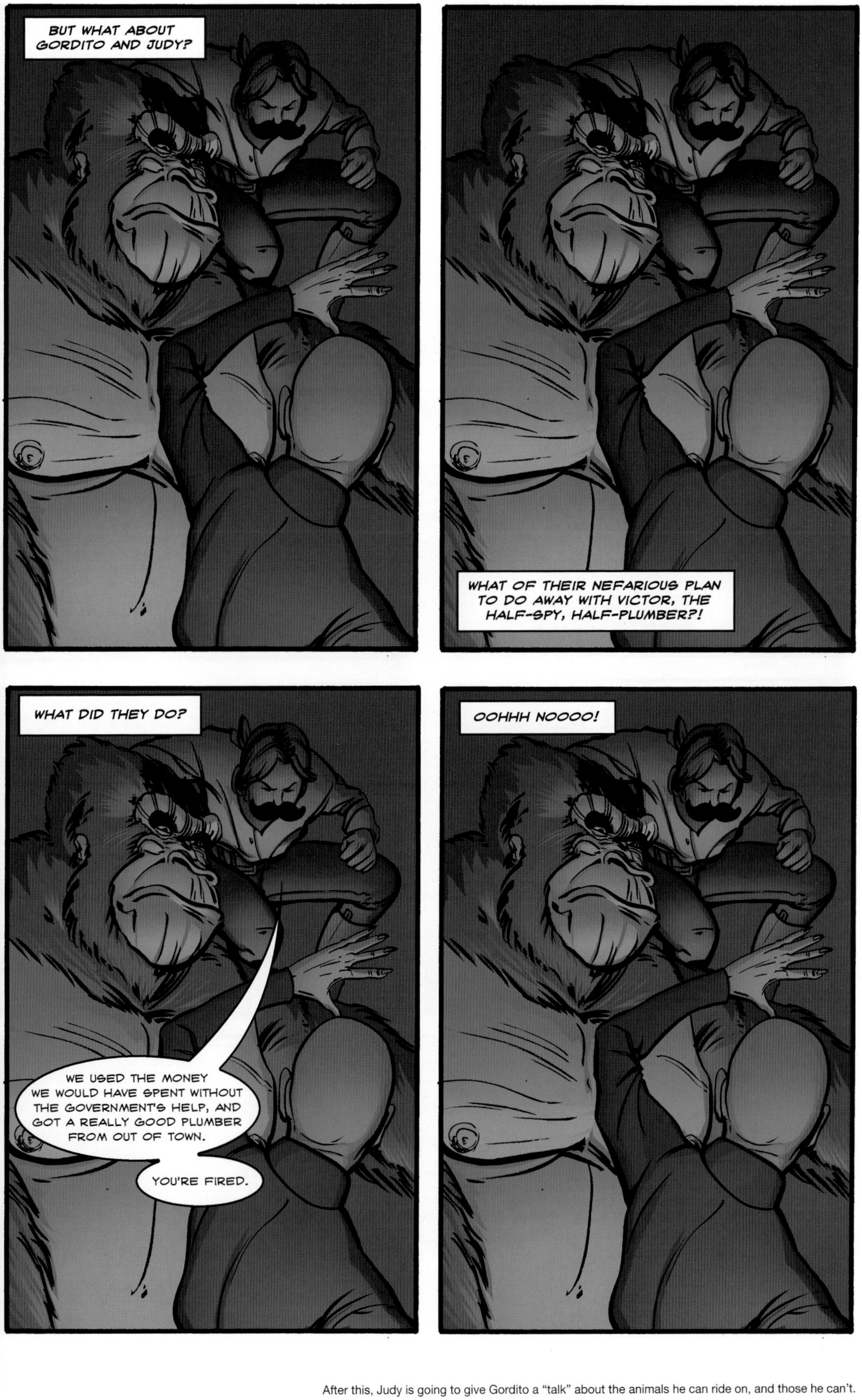
BUT WHAT ABOUT GORDITO AND JUDY?
WHAT OF THEIR NEFARIOUS PLAN TO DO AWAY WITH VICTOR, THE HALF-SPY, HALF-PLUMBER?!
WHAT DID THEY DO?
WE USED THE MONEY WE WOULD HAVE SPENT WITHOUT THE GOVERNMENT'S HELP, AND GOT A REALLY GOOD PLUMBER FROM OUT OF TOWN.
YOU'RE FIRED.
OOHHH NOOOO!

After this, Judy is going to give Gordito a "talk" about the animals he can ride on, and those he can't.

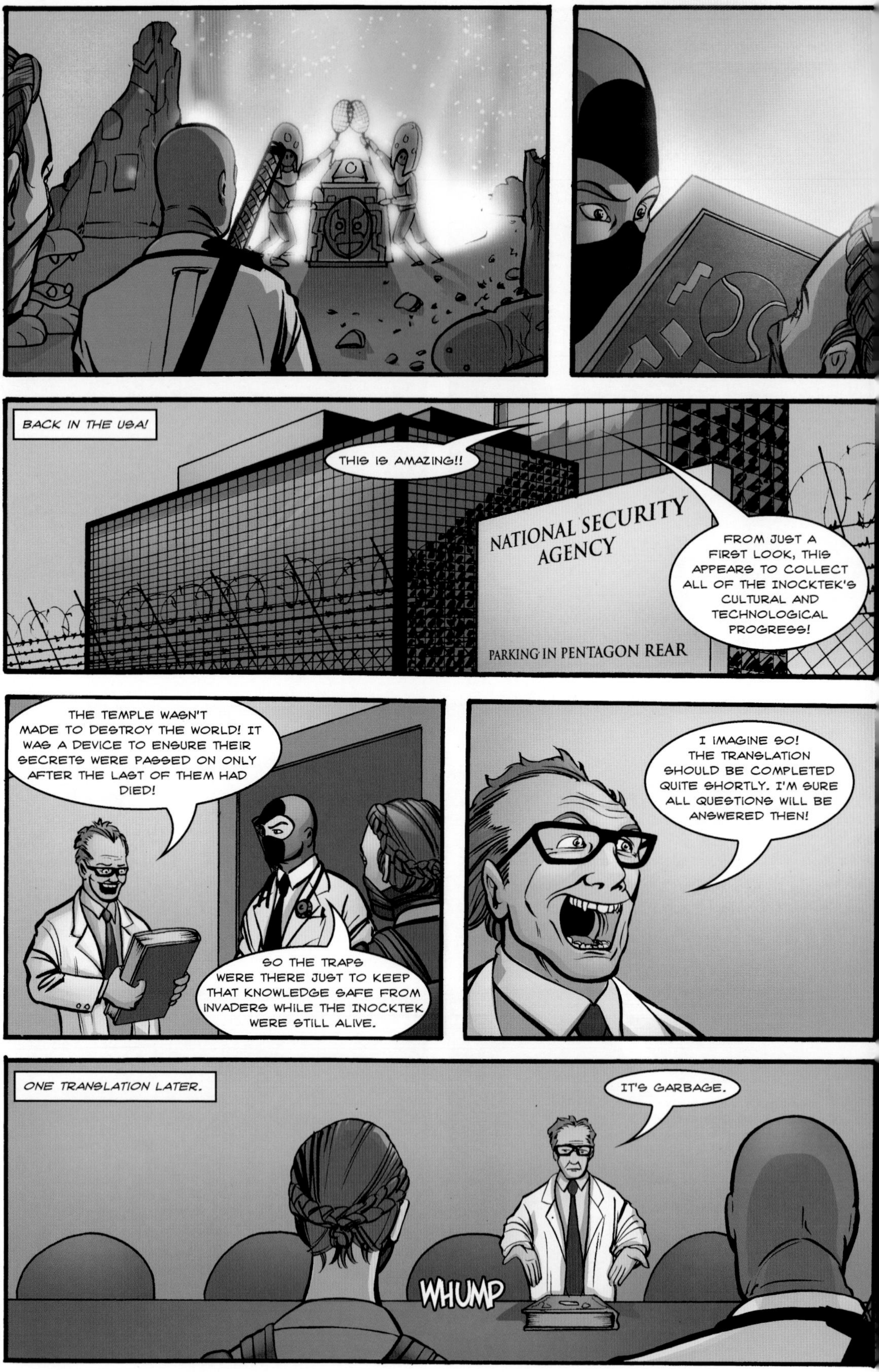
BACK IN THE USA!
THIS IS AMAZING!!
NATIONAL SECURITY AGENCY
PARKING IN PENTAGON REAR
FROM JUST A FIRST LOOK, THIS APPEARS TO COLLECT ALL OF THE INOCKTEK'S CULTURAL AND TECHNOLOGICAL PROGRESS!
THE TEMPLE WASN'T MADE TO DESTROY THE WORLD! IT WAS A DEVICE TO ENSURE THEIR SECRETS WERE PASSED ON ONLY AFTER THE LAST OF THEM HAD DIED!
SO THE TRAPS WERE THERE JUST TO KEEP THAT KNOWLEDGE SAFE FROM INVADERS WHILE THE INOCKTEK WERE STILL ALIVE.
I IMAGINE SO! THE TRANSLATION SHOULD BE COMPLETED QUITE SHORTLY. I'M SURE ALL QUESTIONS WILL BE ANSWERED THEN!
ONE TRANSLATION LATER.
IT'S GARBAGE.
WHUMP

I have no idea why Hortense is allowed in this meeting.

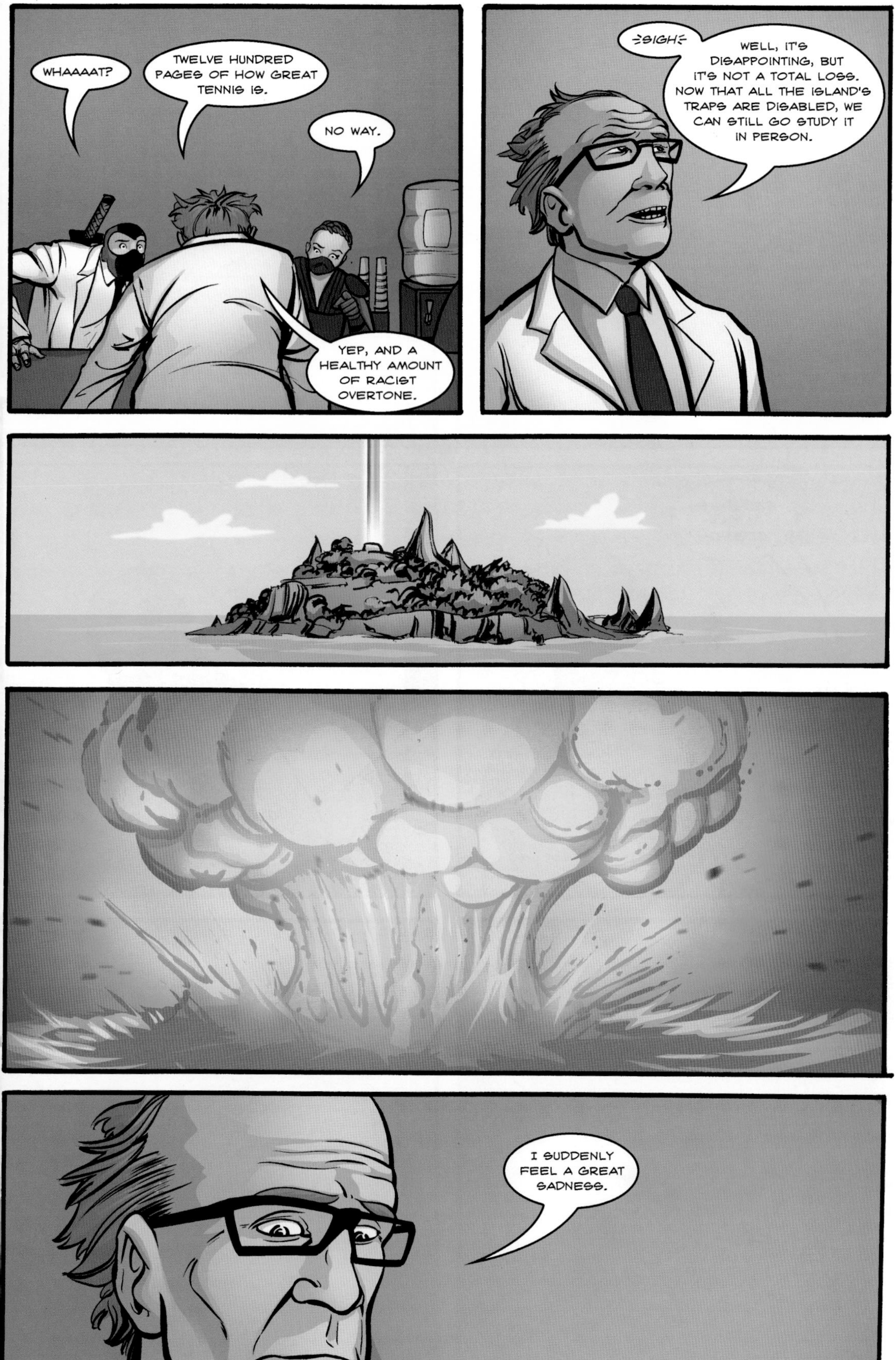
WHAAAAT?
TWELVE HUNDRED PAGES OF HOW GREAT TENNIS IS.
NO WAY.
YEP, AND A HEALTHY AMOUNT OF RACIST OVERTONE.
SIGH
WELL, IT'S DISAPPOINTING, BUT IT'S NOT A TOTAL LOSS. NOW THAT ALL THE ISLAND'S TRAPS ARE DISABLED, WE CAN STILL GO STUDY IT IN PERSON.
I SUDDENLY FEEL A GREAT SADNESS.

It sometimes feels quite powerful to write comics.

EPILOGUE

MEANWHILE! AT ANOTHER, STILL INTACT ISLAND!

I... I CAN'T BELIEVE IT. THANK YOU SO MUCH. I THINK I'LL BE FINE FROM HERE.

EEEEHH-- CLICK-- EEEECH

EH?

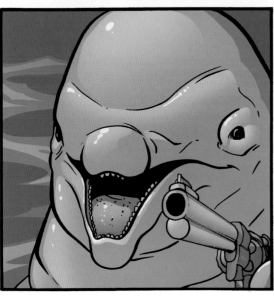

THE END

BLAM!

Stupid dolphin noise is hard to type.

SO MY NEW OFFICE IS ALMOST DONE! AND TECHNICALLY I FAILED THE MISSION SPECTACULARLY, BUT THE GOVERNMENT'S GONNA PAY FOR IT ANYWAY! PRETTY SW--

...

EXCUSE ME FOR A MOMENT.

JUDY! DID ALL THE CONTRACTORS GO HOME?

BECAUSE I NEED TO TELL THEM THAT A BUST OF SHAKESPEARE WITH A CAMERA IN THE EYE IS REALLY OBVIOUS!

MARYLAND'S BEST DOCTORS.

DR. MCNINJA.
WE HAVE NO IDEA WHAT HIS SPECIALTY IS, BUT COME ON, WHAT A COVER!

WE ALSO HAVE SOME OTHER DOCTORS, BUT BE HONEST, DOES ANYBODY SUBSCRIBE TO THIS MAGAZINE? IT'S REALLY ONLY IN WAITING ROOMS. FRAMED SO YOU CAN FEEL BETTER ABOUT WHAT YOU'RE WAITING FOR.

OCTOBER 2005

RS.

AND ALSO I NEED THEM TO PUT IN A NEW WINDOW!

UGH

BECAUSE I THREW THE SHAKESPEARE WITH THE CAMERA IN THE EYE THROUGH ONE!

UGGH

SECRET EPILOGUE

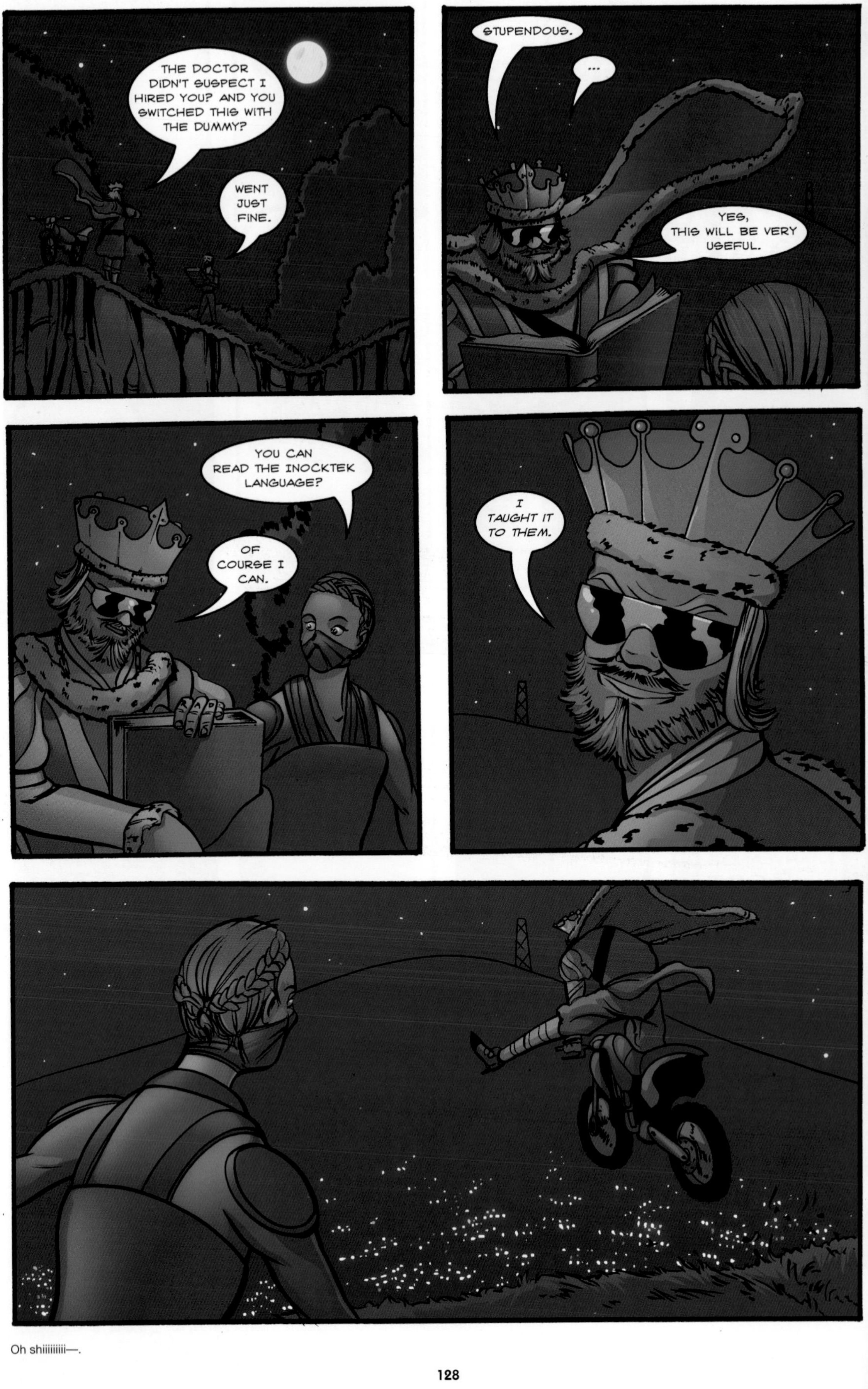

THE DOCTOR DIDN'T SUSPECT I HIRED YOU? AND YOU SWITCHED THIS WITH THE DUMMY?
WENT JUST FINE.
STUPENDOUS.
...
YES, THIS WILL BE VERY USEFUL.
YOU CAN READ THE INOCKTEK LANGUAGE?
OF COURSE I CAN.
I TAUGHT IT TO THEM.

Oh shiiiiiiii—.

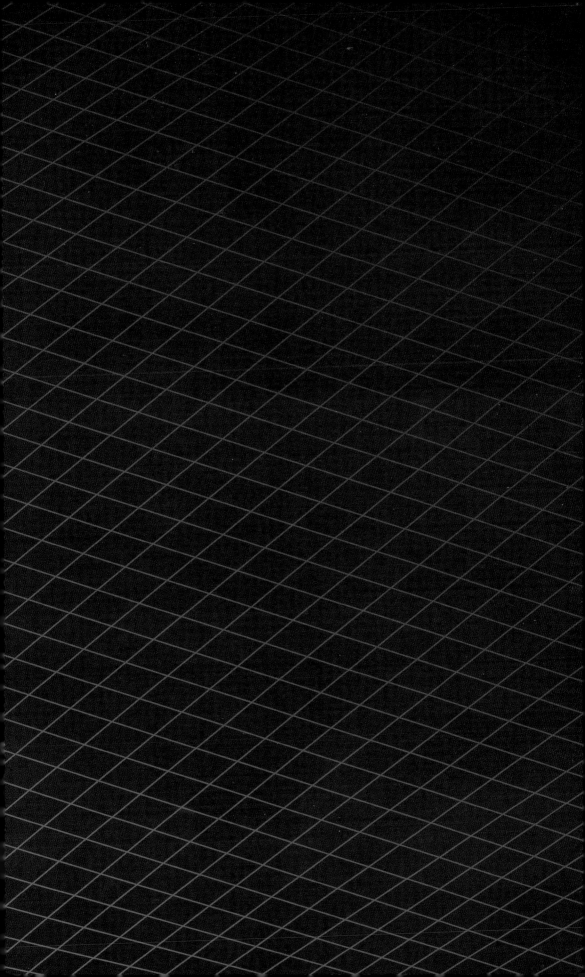

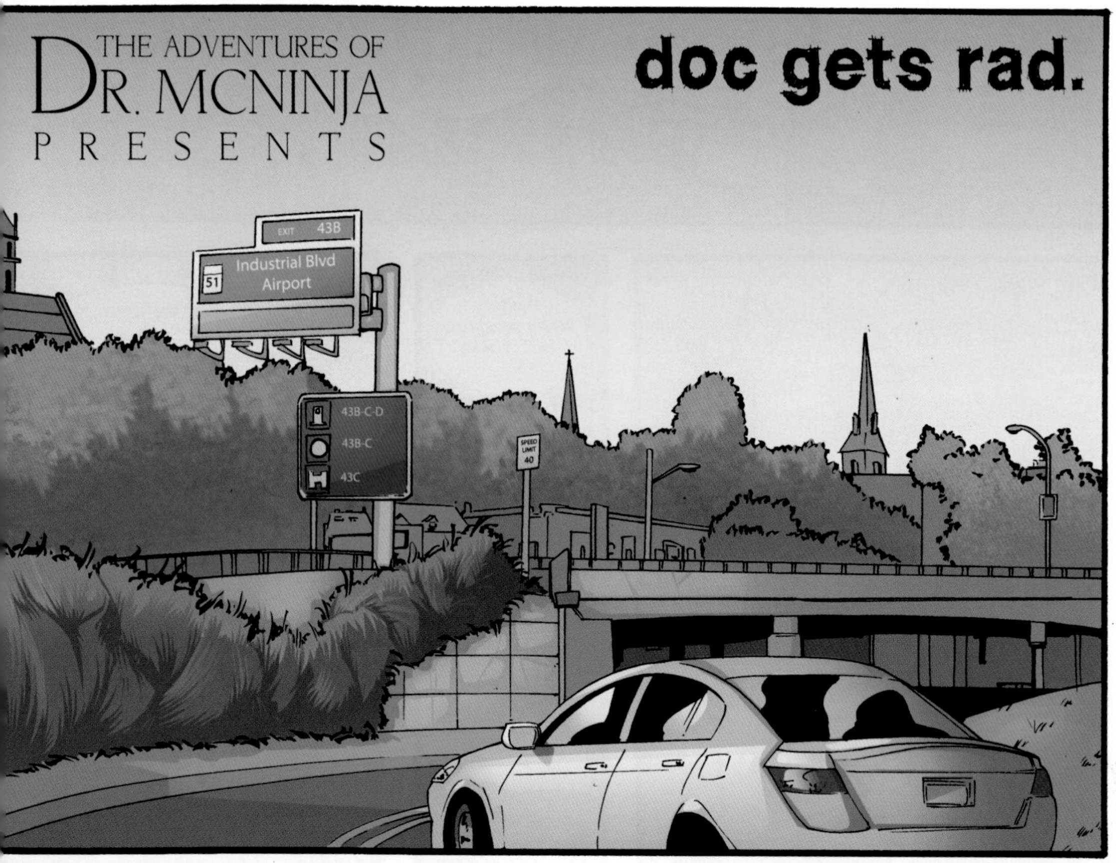
THE ADVENTURES OF DR. MCNINJA PRESENTS
doc gets rad.
EXIT 43B
51 Industrial Blvd Airport
43B-C-D
43B-C
43C
SPEED LIMIT 40

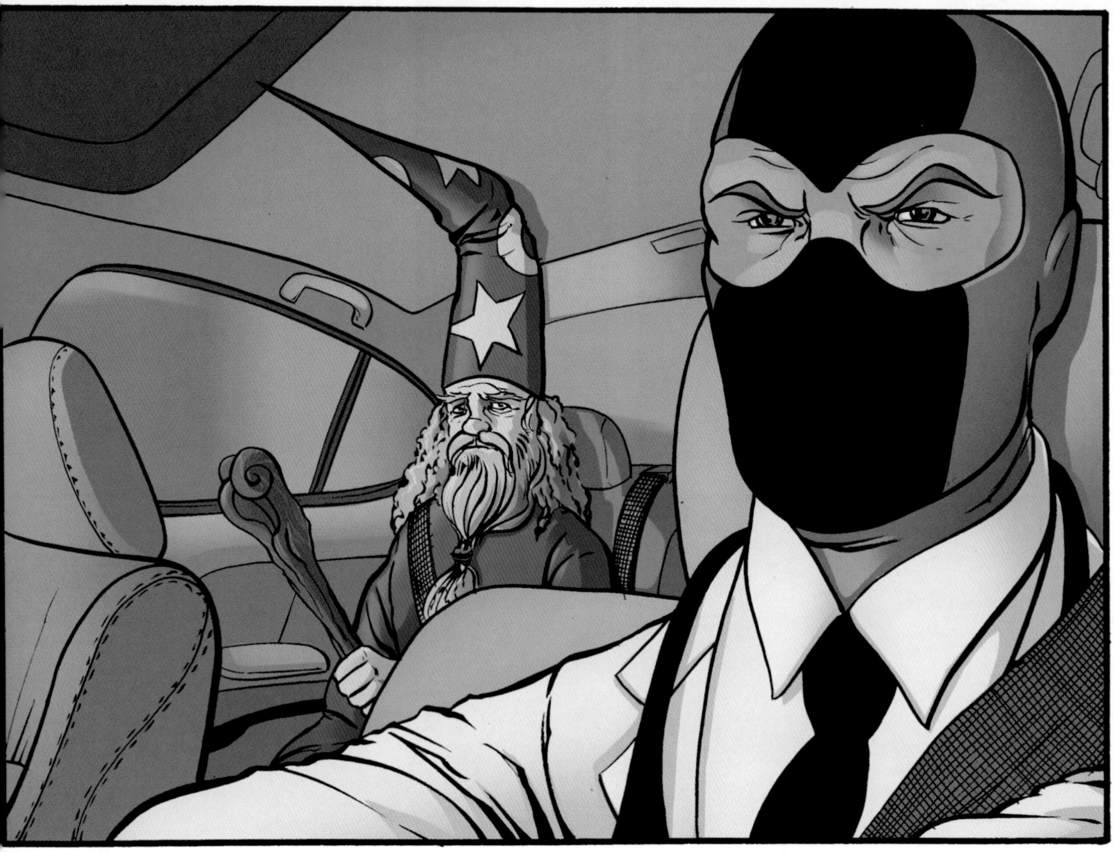

Who dat wizard.

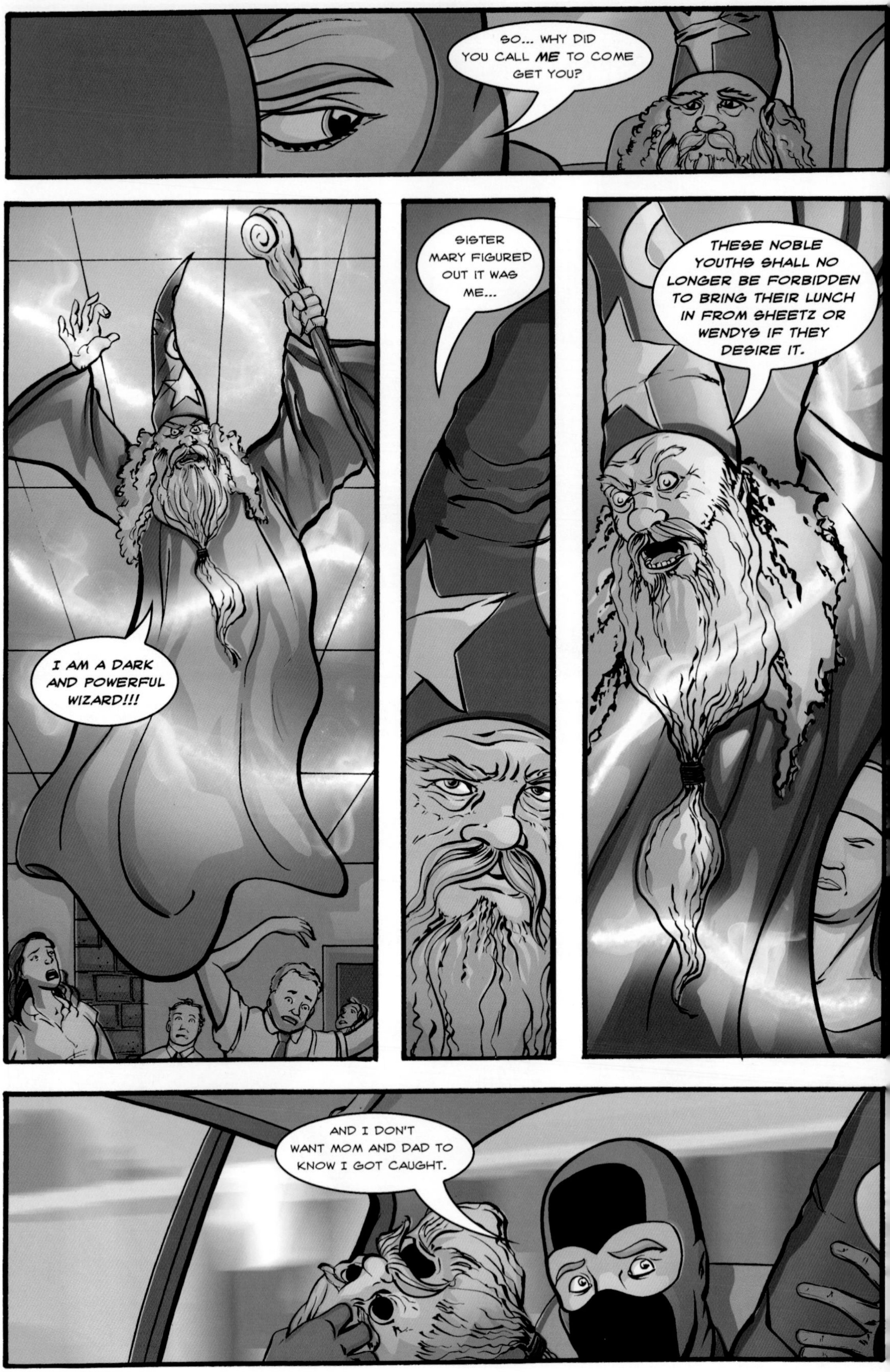
SO... WHY DID YOU CALL ME TO COME GET YOU?
I AM A DARK AND POWERFUL WIZARD!!!
SISTER MARY FIGURED OUT IT WAS ME...
THESE NOBLE YOUTHS SHALL NO LONGER BE FORBIDDEN TO BRING THEIR LUNCH IN FROM SHEETZ OR WENDYS IF THEY DESIRE IT.
AND I DON'T WANT MOM AND DAD TO KNOW I GOT CAUGHT.

You should be allowed to bring your lunch in from wherever. IT'S A STUPID RULE. >:(

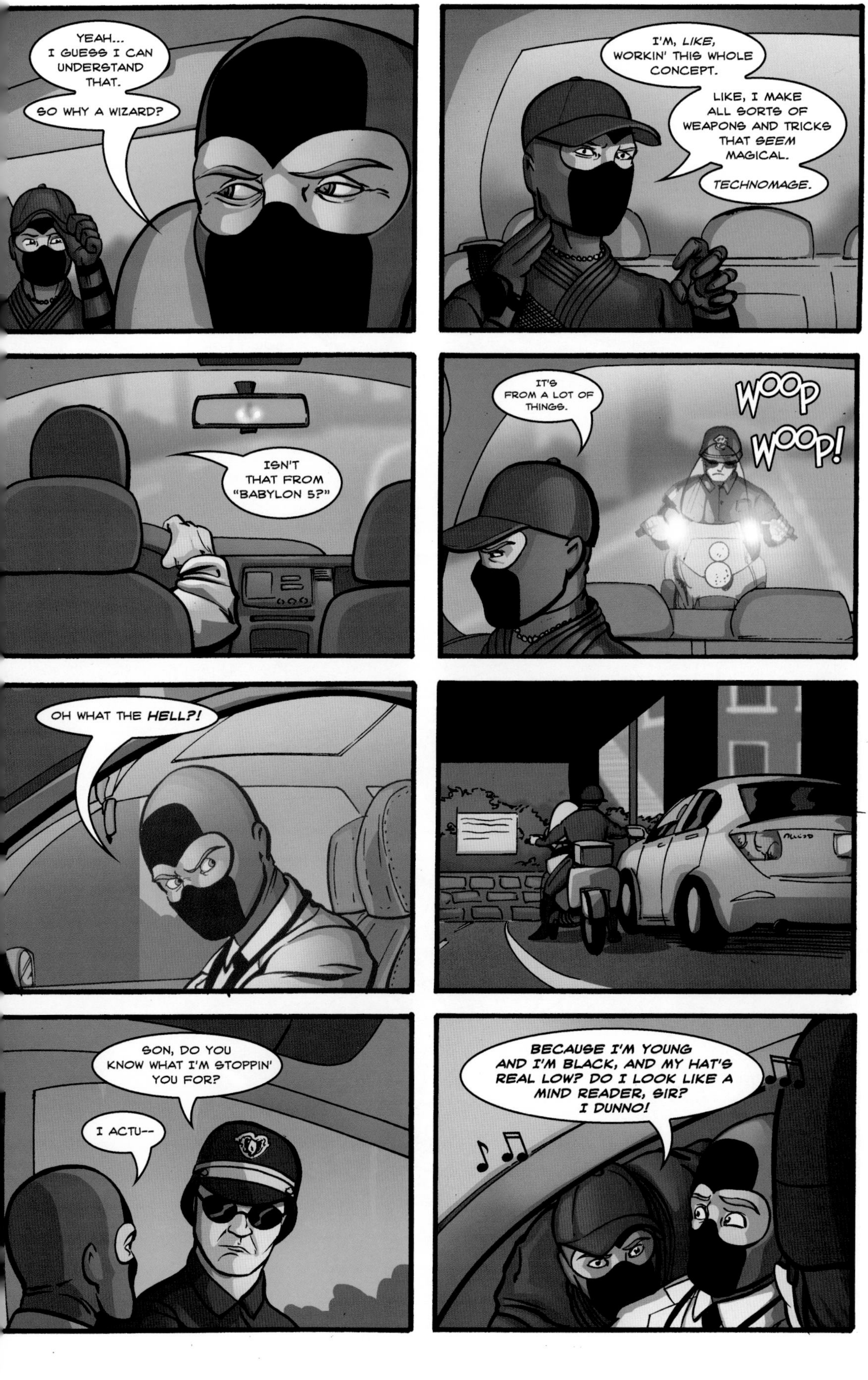
YEAH... I GUESS I CAN UNDERSTAND THAT.
SO WHY A WIZARD?
I'M, LIKE, WORKIN' THIS WHOLE CONCEPT.
LIKE, I MAKE ALL SORTS OF WEAPONS AND TRICKS THAT SEEM MAGICAL.
TECHNOMAGE.
ISN'T THAT FROM "BABYLON 5?"
IT'S FROM A LOT OF THINGS.
WOOP WOOP!
OH WHAT THE HELL?!
SON, DO YOU KNOW WHAT I'M STOPPIN' YOU FOR?
I ACTU--
BECAUSE I'M YOUNG AND I'M BLACK, AND MY HAT'S REAL LOW? DO I LOOK LIKE A MIND READER, SIR? I DUNNO!

It's like Roger Rabbit and "Shave and a Haircut."

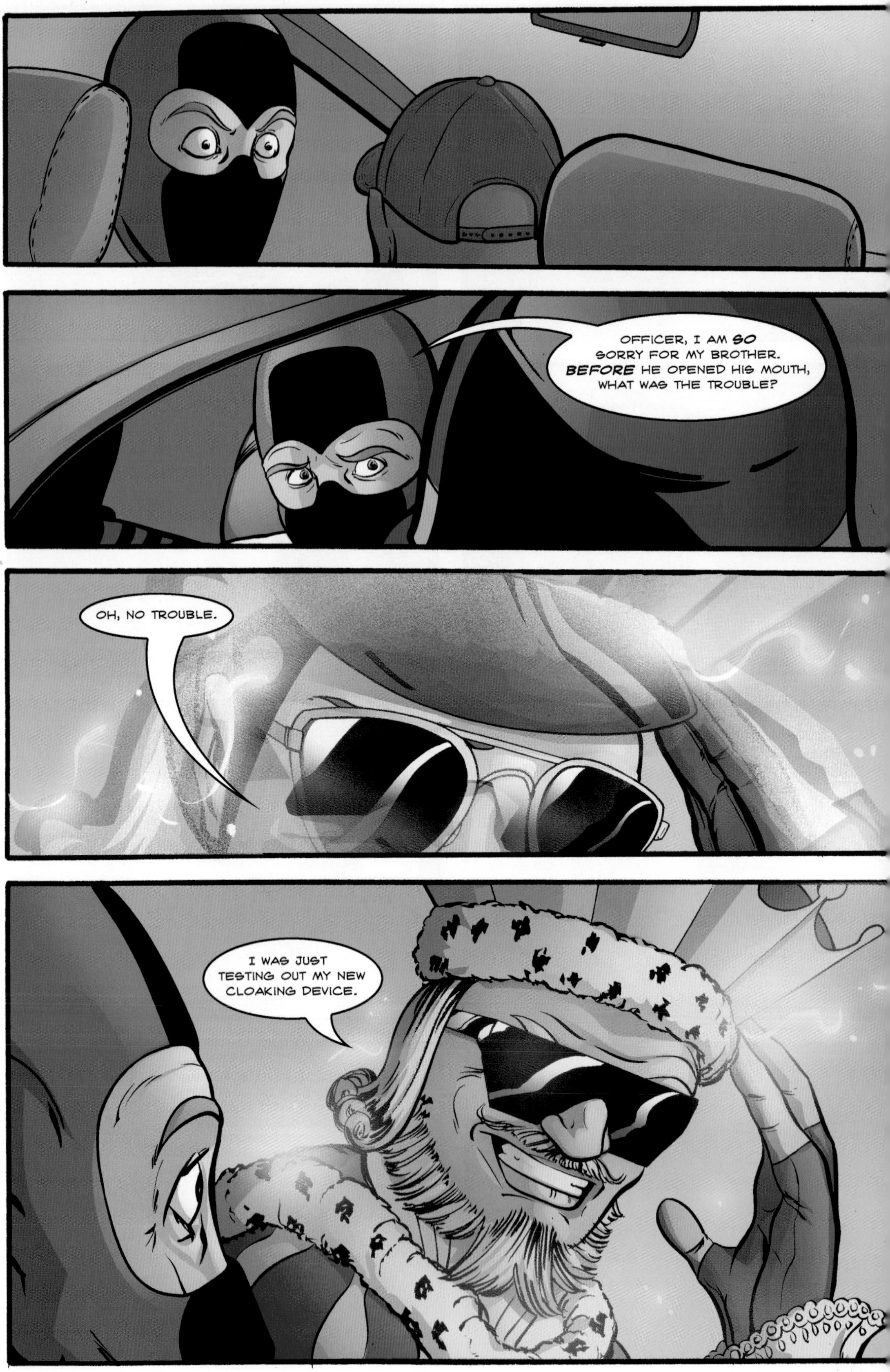
OFFICER, I AM SO SORRY FOR MY BROTHER. BEFORE HE OPENED HIS MOUTH, WHAT WAS THE TROUBLE?
OH, NO TROUBLE.
I WAS JUST TESTING OUT MY NEW CLOAKING DEVICE.

More like King Rascal.

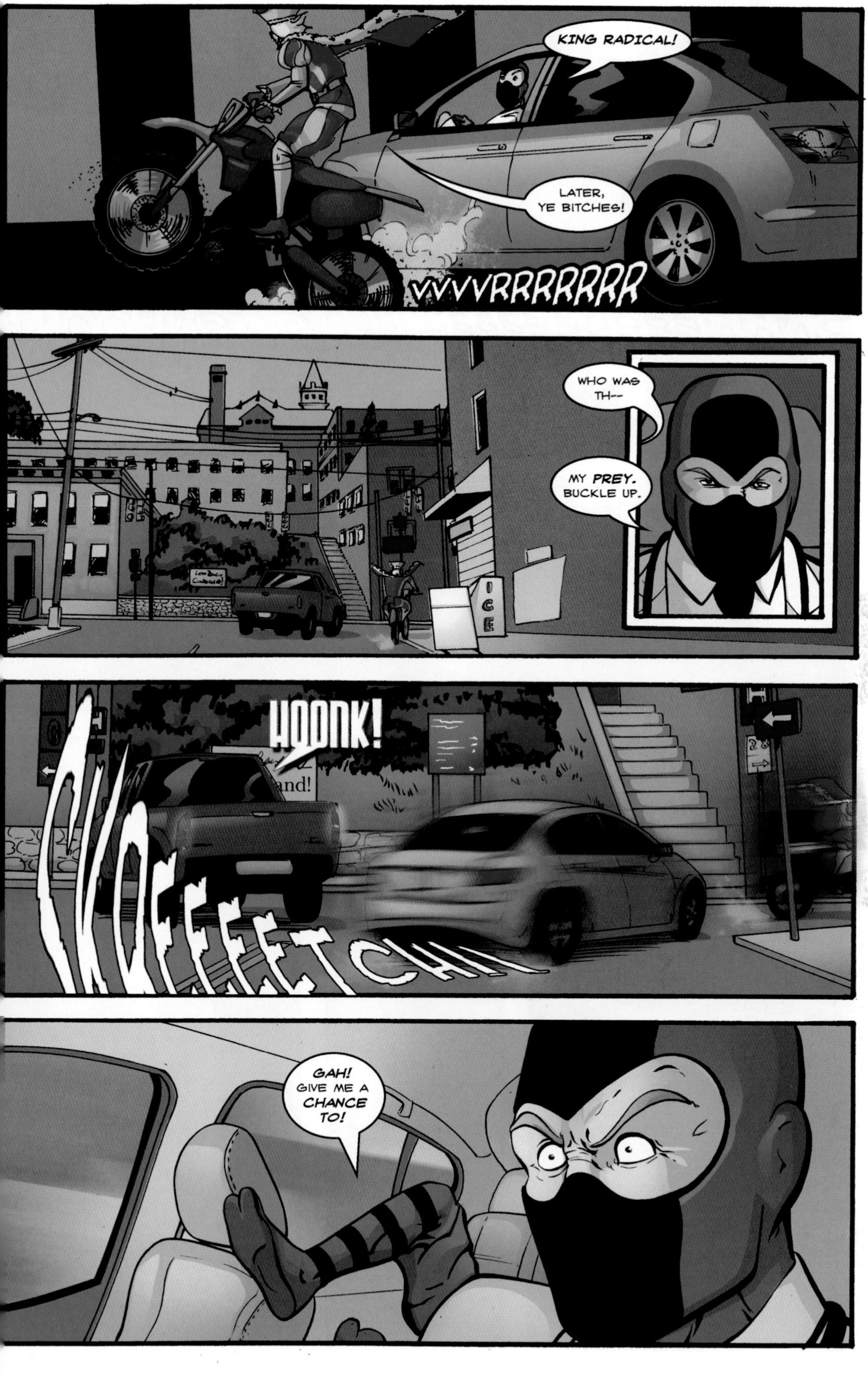
KING RADICAL!
LATER, YE BITCHES!
VVVVRRRRRRR
WHO WAS TH--
MY PREY. BUCKLE UP.
ICE
HOONK!
SKREEEETCH!
GAH! GIVE ME A CHANCE TO!

Do your pupils get smaller when you get crazy angry? Mine do. Mine almost DISAPPEAR.

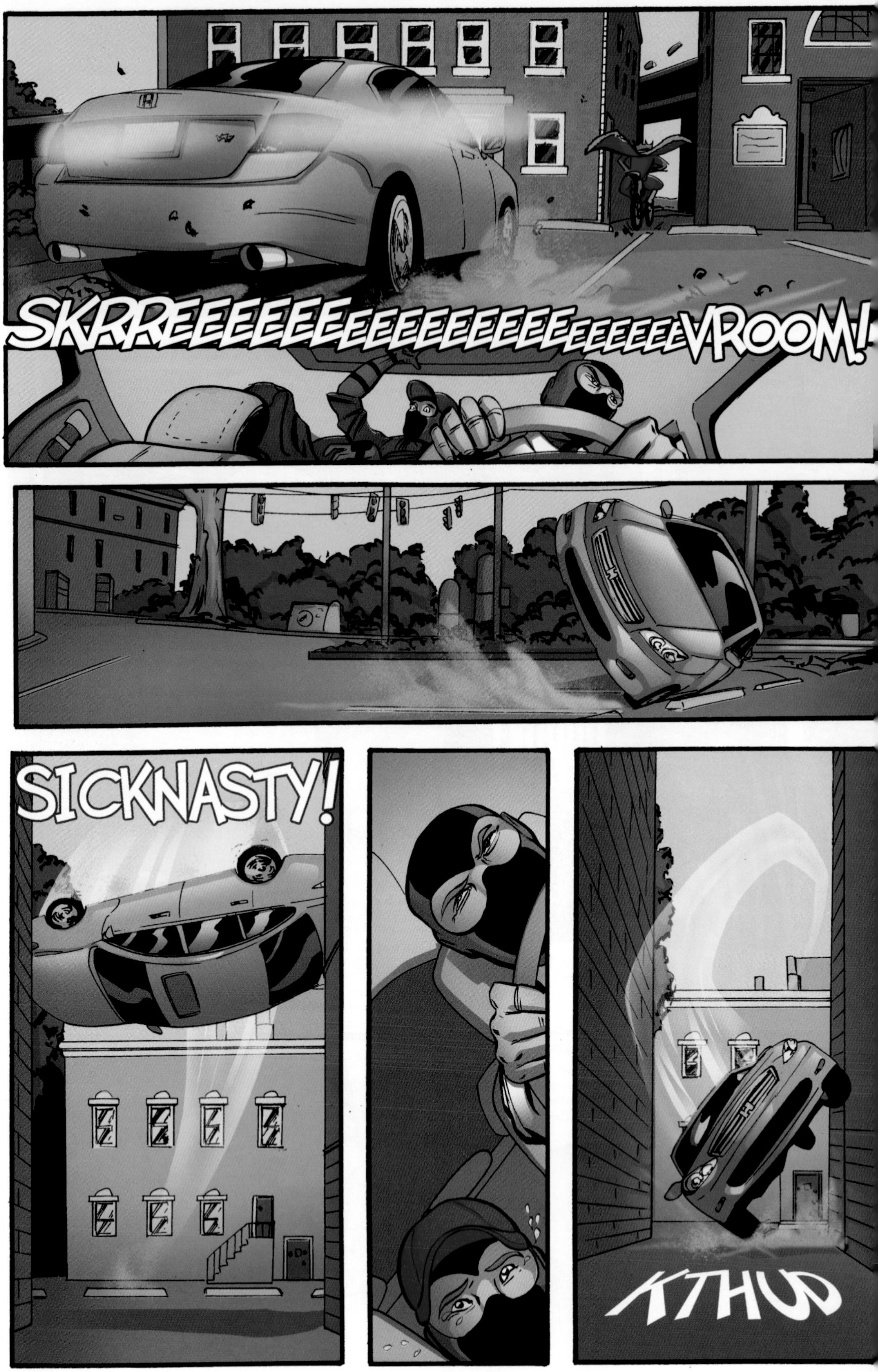
SKRREEEEEEEEEEEEEEEEEEEEEEEEVROOM!
SICKNASTY!
KTHUD

I want to see SICKNASTY! as a sound effect more often. The snowboarding-adventure genre might have to be invented to support it, but that's fine.

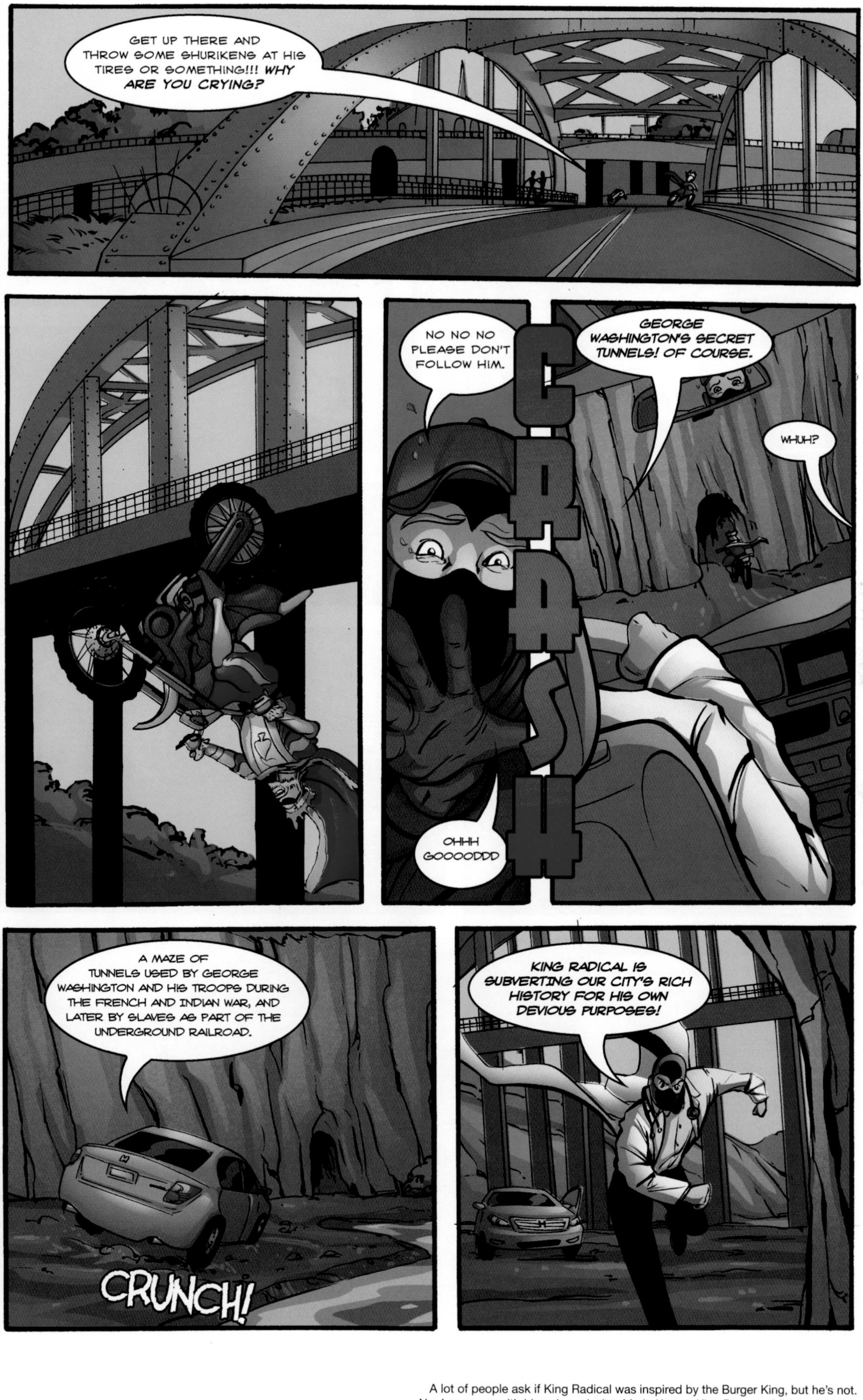
GET UP THERE AND THROW SOME SHURIKENS AT HIS TIRES OR SOMETHING!!! WHY ARE YOU CRYING?
NO NO NO PLEASE DON'T FOLLOW HIM.
CRASH
GEORGE WASHINGTON'S SECRET TUNNELS! OF COURSE.
WHUH?
OHHH GOOOODDD
A MAZE OF TUNNELS USED BY GEORGE WASHINGTON AND HIS TROOPS DURING THE FRENCH AND INDIAN WAR, AND LATER BY SLAVES AS PART OF THE UNDERGROUND RAILROAD.
CRUNCH!
KING RADICAL IS SUBVERTING OUR CITY'S RICH HISTORY FOR HIS OWN DEVIOUS PURPOSES!

A lot of people ask if King Radical was inspired by the Burger King, but he's not. No, I came up with him when playing *Mario Kart* as King Boo . . . riding a dirt bike.

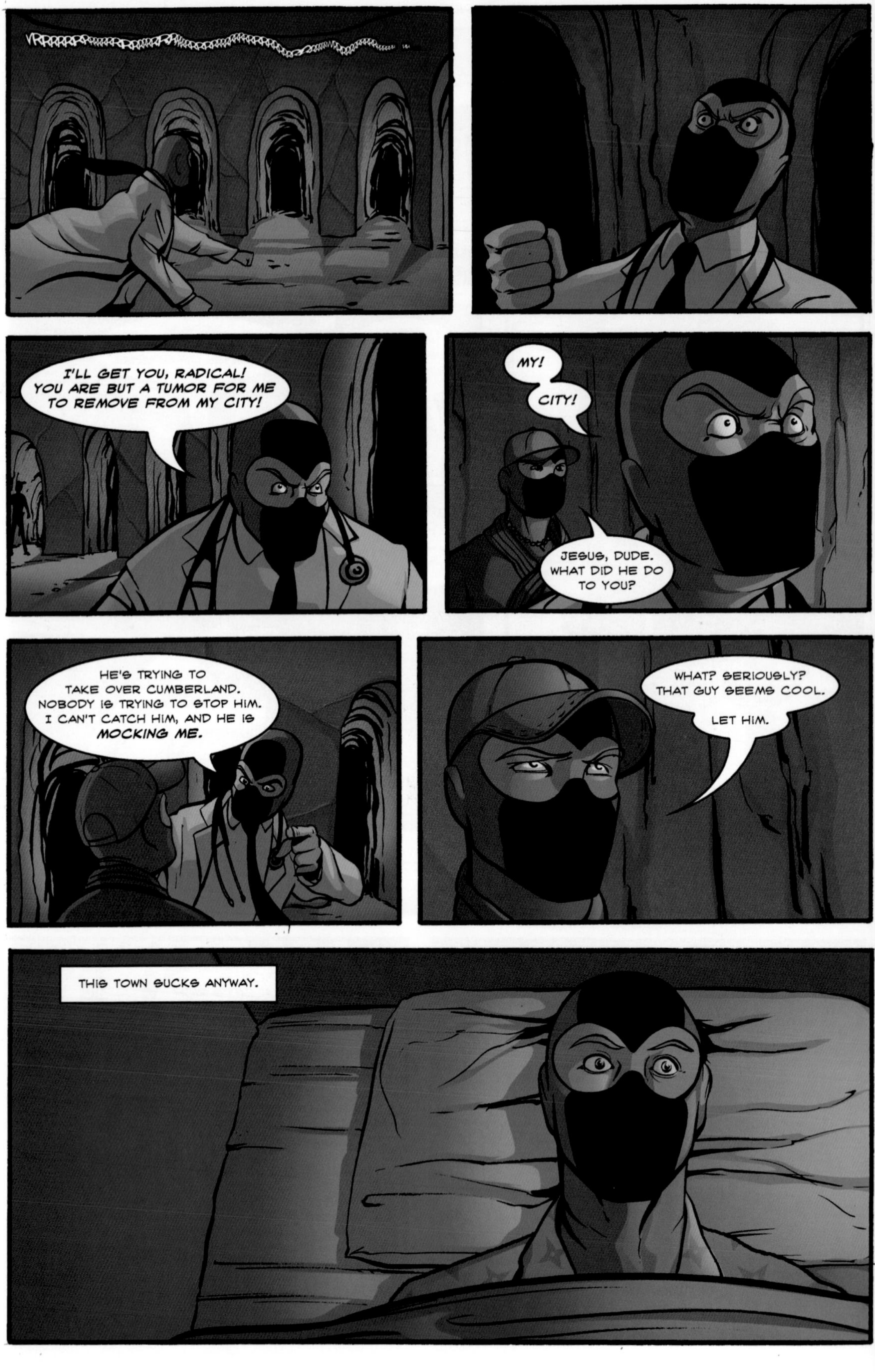
VRRRRRRRRRRRRRRRRRR
I'LL GET YOU, RADICAL! YOU ARE BUT A TUMOR FOR ME TO REMOVE FROM MY CITY!
MY!
CITY!
JESUS, DUDE. WHAT DID HE DO TO YOU?
HE'S TRYING TO TAKE OVER CUMBERLAND. NOBODY IS TRYING TO STOP HIM. I CAN'T CATCH HIM, AND HE IS MOCKING ME.
WHAT? SERIOUSLY? THAT GUY SEEMS COOL.
LET HIM.
THIS TOWN SUCKS ANYWAY.

My brother got me a Crayola Color Explosion variety pack for my birthday. It has forty sheets of Color Explosion paper. So . . . please enjoy the next forty pages of Color Explosion McNinja!

I NEED A MOTORCYCLE.
BABOOM
SCREEEEETCH

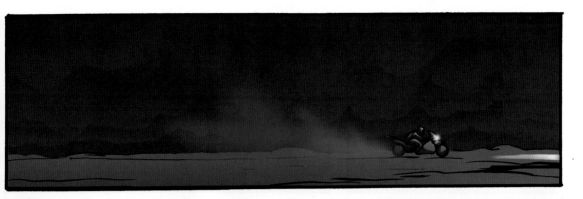

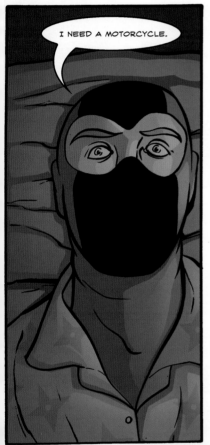

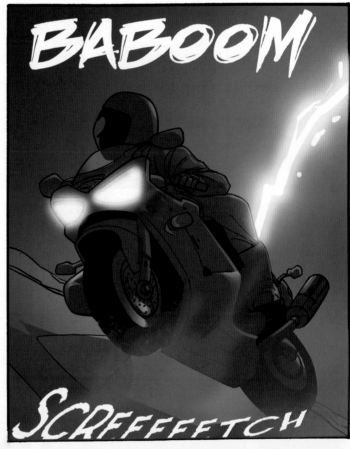

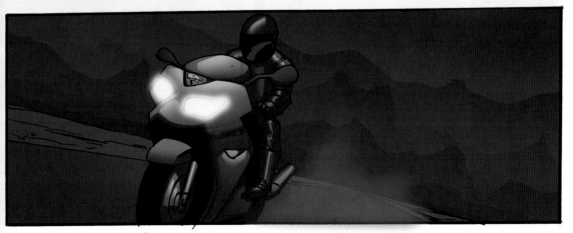

vroom vroom vroom

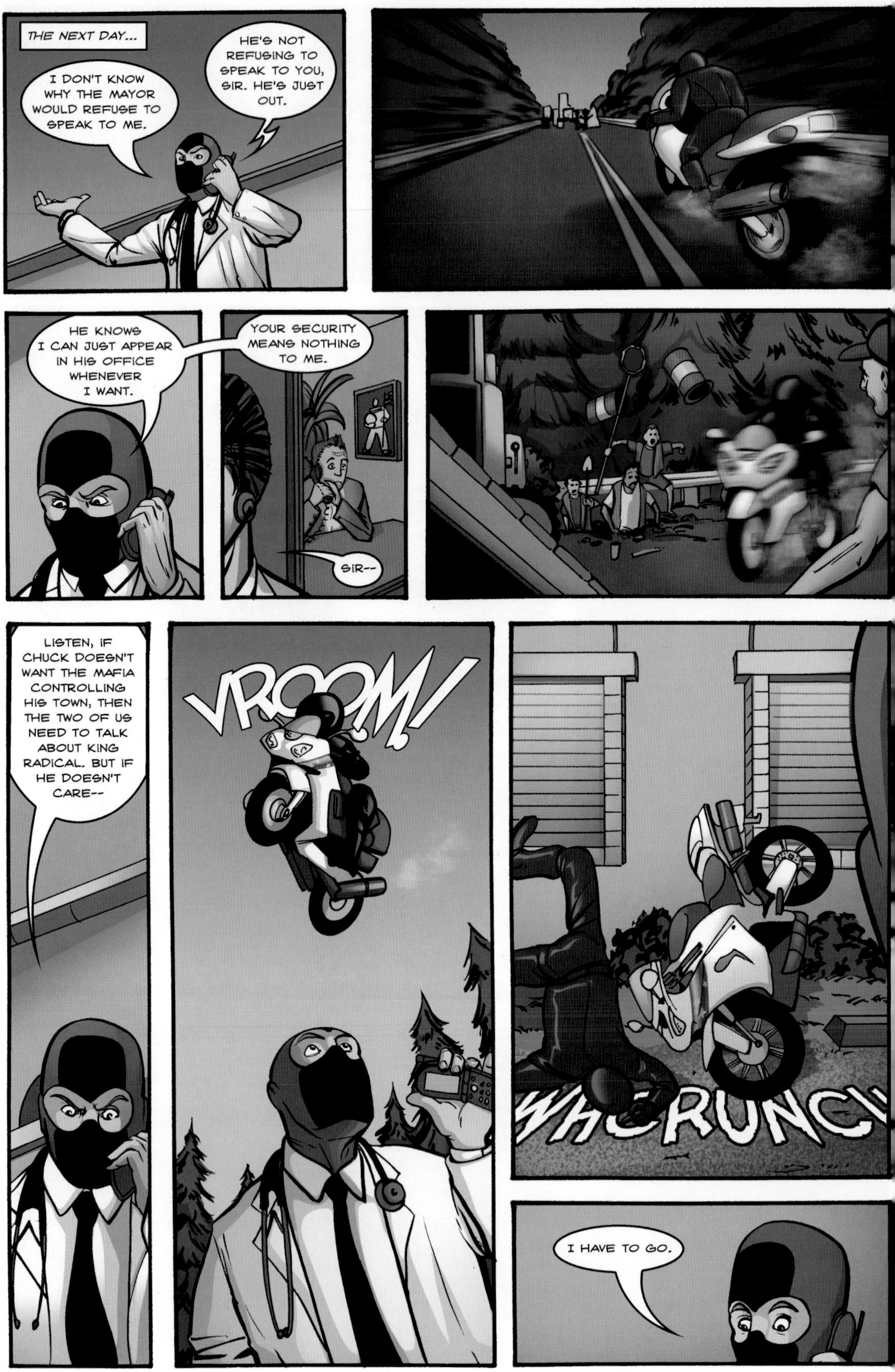
THE NEXT DAY...
I DON'T KNOW WHY THE MAYOR WOULD REFUSE TO SPEAK TO ME.
HE'S NOT REFUSING TO SPEAK TO YOU, SIR. HE'S JUST OUT.
HE KNOWS I CAN JUST APPEAR IN HIS OFFICE WHENEVER I WANT.
YOUR SECURITY MEANS NOTHING TO ME.
SIR--
LISTEN, IF CHUCK DOESN'T WANT THE MAFIA CONTROLLING HIS TOWN, THEN THE TWO OF US NEED TO TALK ABOUT KING RADICAL. BUT IF HE DOESN'T CARE--
VROOM!
WHCRUNCH
I HAVE TO GO.

Weird that the motorcycle guy landed right where Doc had painted "WHCRUNCH" in his parking lot. Because that's probably exactly what it sounded like.

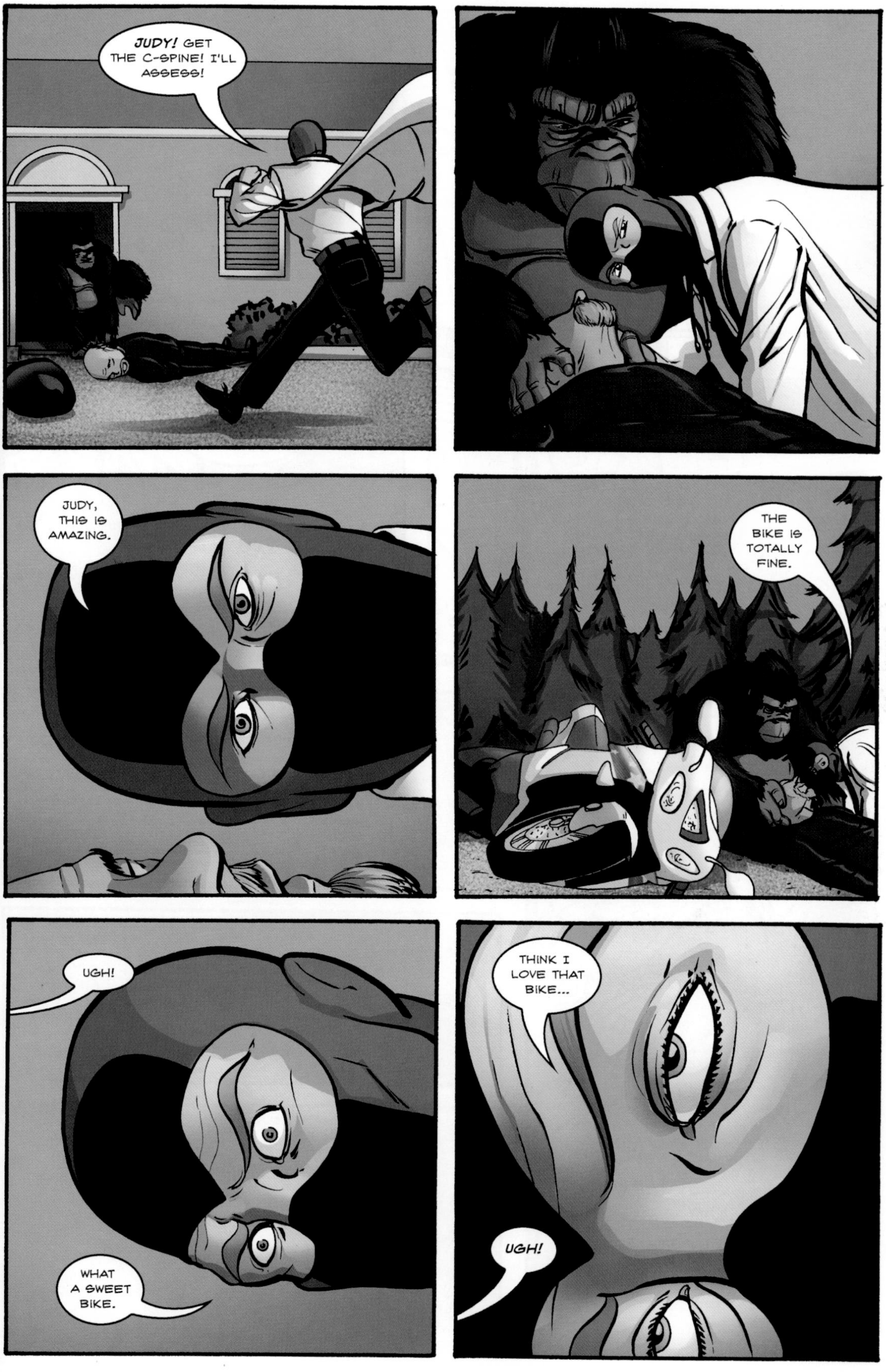
JUDY! GET THE C-SPINE! I'LL ASSESS!
JUDY, THIS IS AMAZING.
THE BIKE IS TOTALLY FINE.
UGH!
WHAT A SWEET BIKE.
THINK I LOVE THAT BIKE...
UGH!

Wanna meet that bike.

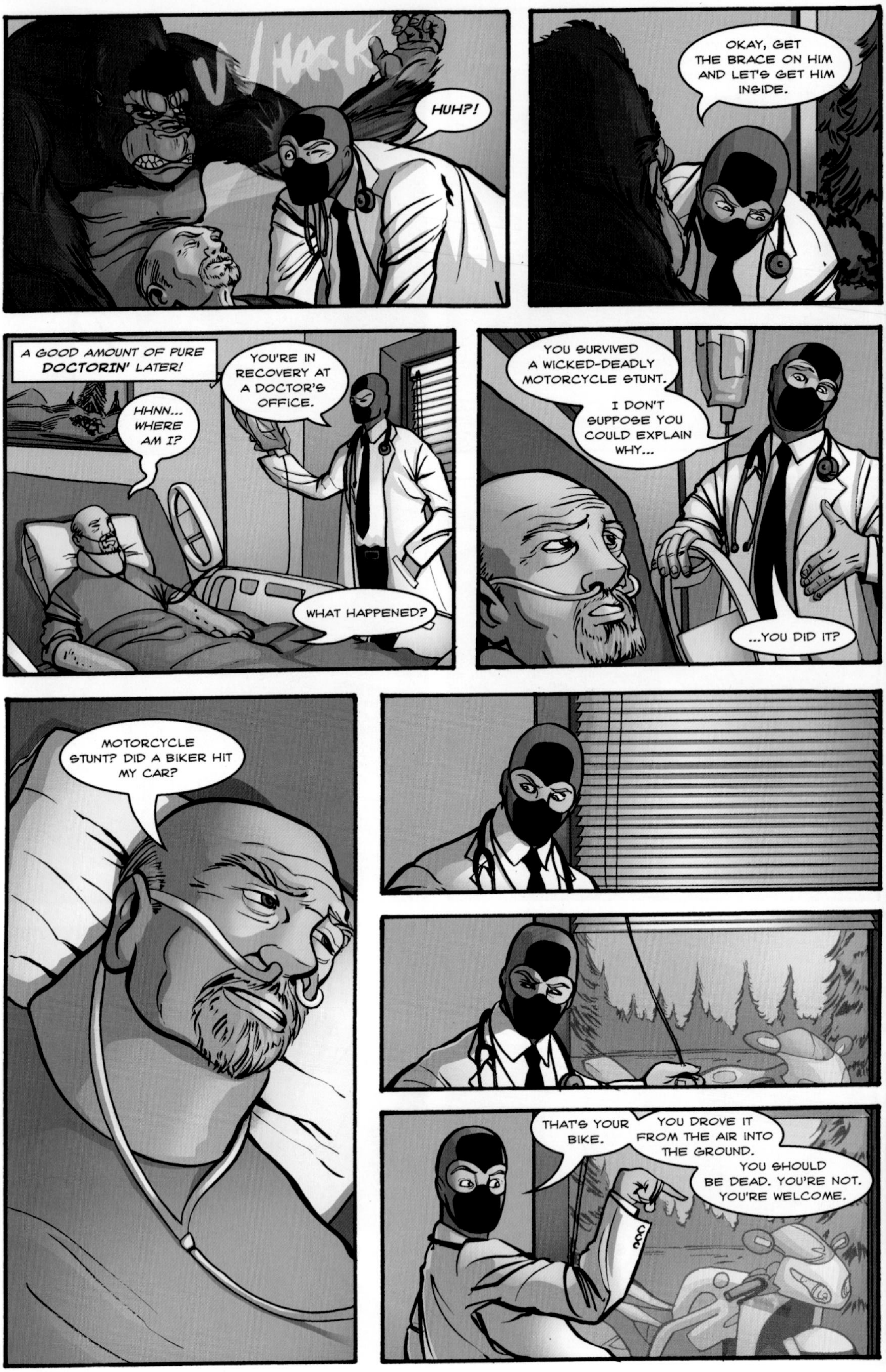
WHACK
HUH?!
OKAY, GET THE BRACE ON HIM AND LET'S GET HIM INSIDE.
A GOOD AMOUNT OF PURE DOCTORIN' LATER!
HHNN... WHERE AM I?
YOU'RE IN RECOVERY AT A DOCTOR'S OFFICE.
WHAT HAPPENED?
YOU SURVIVED A WICKED-DEADLY MOTORCYCLE STUNT.
I DON'T SUPPOSE YOU COULD EXPLAIN WHY...
...YOU DID IT?
MOTORCYCLE STUNT? DID A BIKER HIT MY CAR?
THAT'S YOUR BIKE.
YOU DROVE IT FROM THE AIR INTO THE GROUND.
YOU SHOULD BE DEAD. YOU'RE NOT. YOU'RE WELCOME.

Doc's office is filled with Thomas Kinkade/shopping-mall-type artwork, except he had a guy go and paint ninjas in all of them. Exquisite work, unfortunately to the point where you can't really tell the difference.

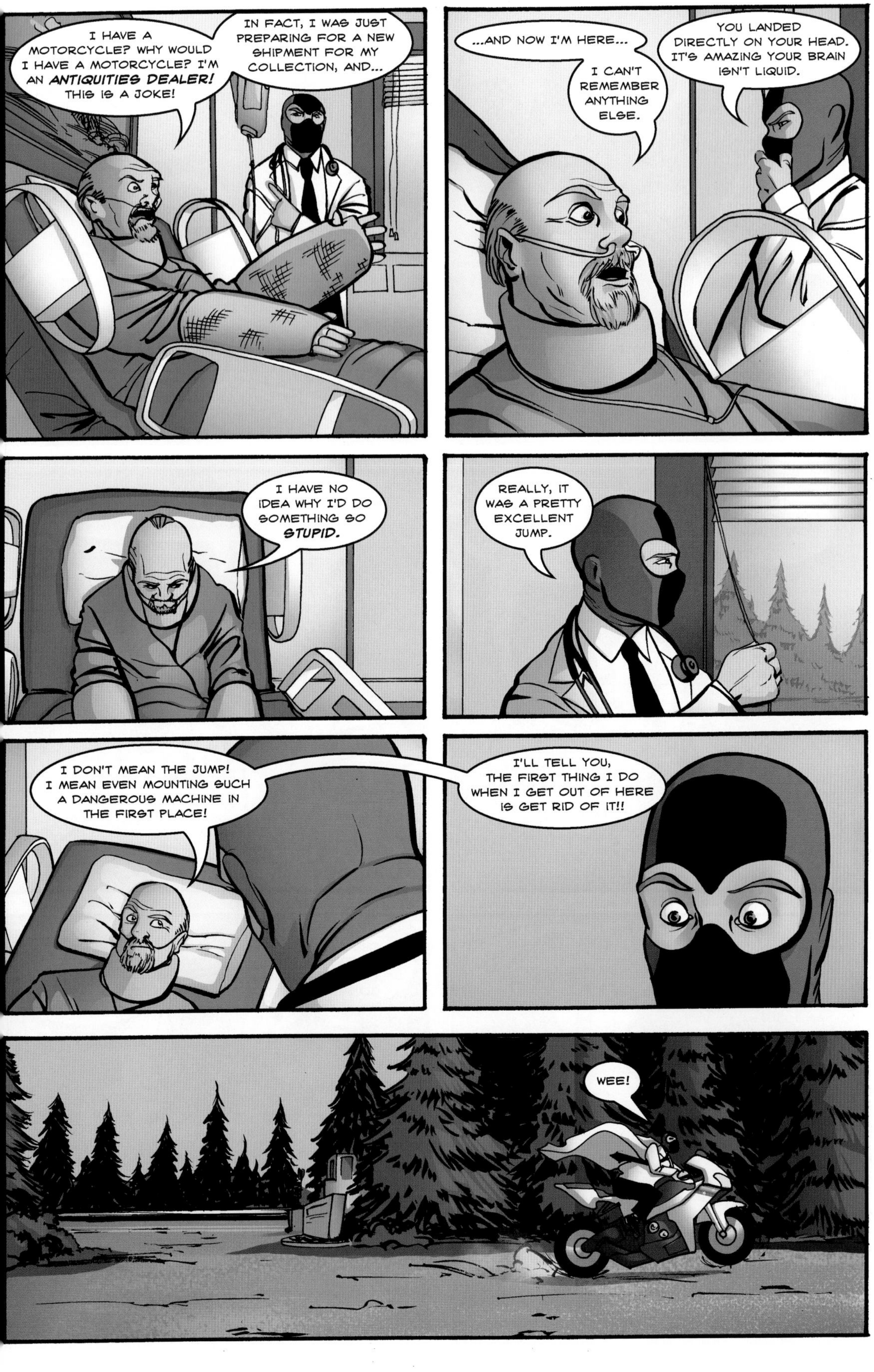
I HAVE A MOTORCYCLE? WHY WOULD I HAVE A MOTORCYCLE? I'M AN ANTIQUITIES DEALER! THIS IS A JOKE!
IN FACT, I WAS JUST PREPARING FOR A NEW SHIPMENT FOR MY COLLECTION, AND...
...AND NOW I'M HERE...
I CAN'T REMEMBER ANYTHING ELSE.
YOU LANDED DIRECTLY ON YOUR HEAD. IT'S AMAZING YOUR BRAIN ISN'T LIQUID.
I HAVE NO IDEA WHY I'D DO SOMETHING SO STUPID.
REALLY, IT WAS A PRETTY EXCELLENT JUMP.
I DON'T MEAN THE JUMP! I MEAN EVEN MOUNTING SUCH A DANGEROUS MACHINE IN THE FIRST PLACE!
I'LL TELL YOU, THE FIRST THING I DO WHEN I GET OUT OF HERE IS GET RID OF IT!!
WEE!

I thought about buying a motorcycle my senior year of high school, but my friends convinced me that people would make fun of me for it. WHAT KIND OF MIXED-UP HIGH SCHOOL DID I GO TO??

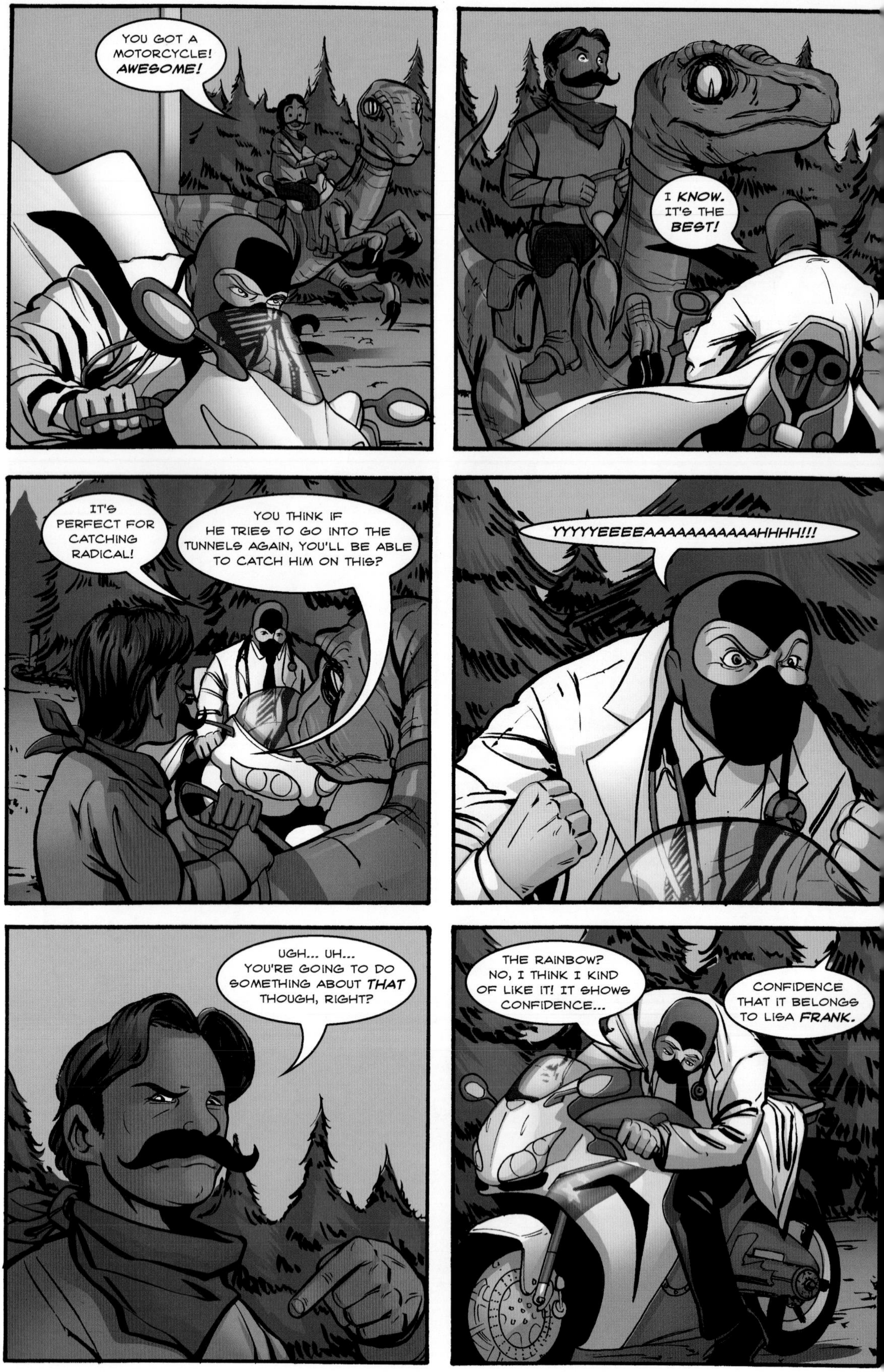
YOU GOT A MOTORCYCLE! AWESOME!
I KNOW. IT'S THE BEST!
IT'S PERFECT FOR CATCHING RADICAL!
YOU THINK IF HE TRIES TO GO INTO THE TUNNELS AGAIN, YOU'LL BE ABLE TO CATCH HIM ON THIS?
YYYYYEEEEAAAAAAAAAAAHHHH!!!
UGH... UH... YOU'RE GOING TO DO SOMETHING ABOUT THAT THOUGH, RIGHT?
THE RAINBOW? NO, I THINK I KIND OF LIKE IT! IT SHOWS CONFIDENCE...
CONFIDENCE THAT IT BELONGS TO LISA FRANK.

If you were not a child in the early nineties, go ahead and do an image search for Lisa Frank, and you'll immediately see what Gordito is talking about.

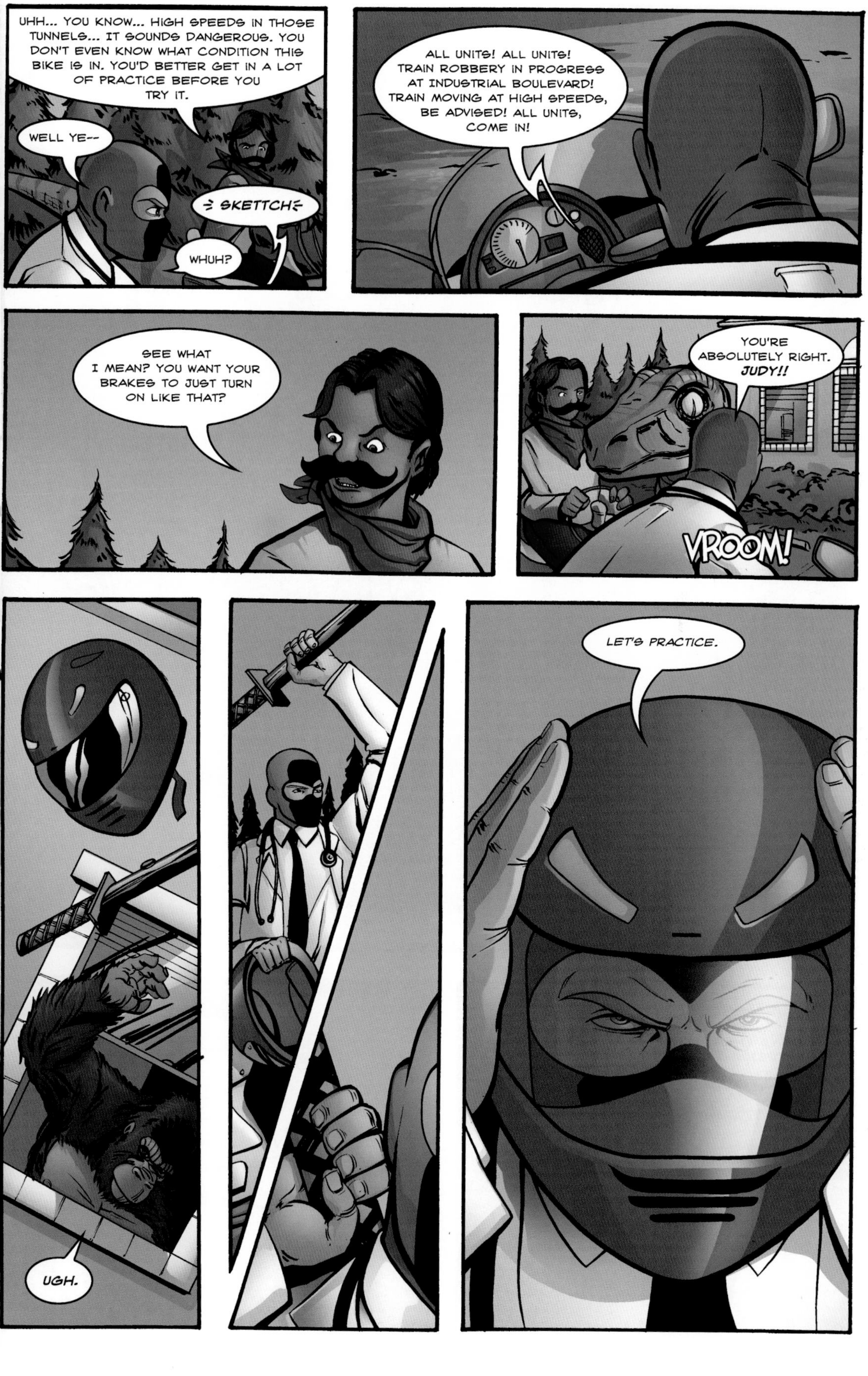
UHH... YOU KNOW... HIGH SPEEDS IN THOSE TUNNELS... IT SOUNDS DANGEROUS. YOU DON'T EVEN KNOW WHAT CONDITION THIS BIKE IS IN. YOU'D BETTER GET IN A LOT OF PRACTICE BEFORE YOU TRY IT.
WELL YE--
SKETTCH
WHUH?
ALL UNITS! ALL UNITS! TRAIN ROBBERY IN PROGRESS AT INDUSTRIAL BOULEVARD! TRAIN MOVING AT HIGH SPEEDS, BE ADVISED! ALL UNITS, COME IN!
SEE WHAT I MEAN? YOU WANT YOUR BRAKES TO JUST TURN ON LIKE THAT?
YOU'RE ABSOLUTELY RIGHT. JUDY!!
VROOM!
UGH.
LET'S PRACTICE.

Then Horatio jumps out of the bushes and puts on his sunglasses.

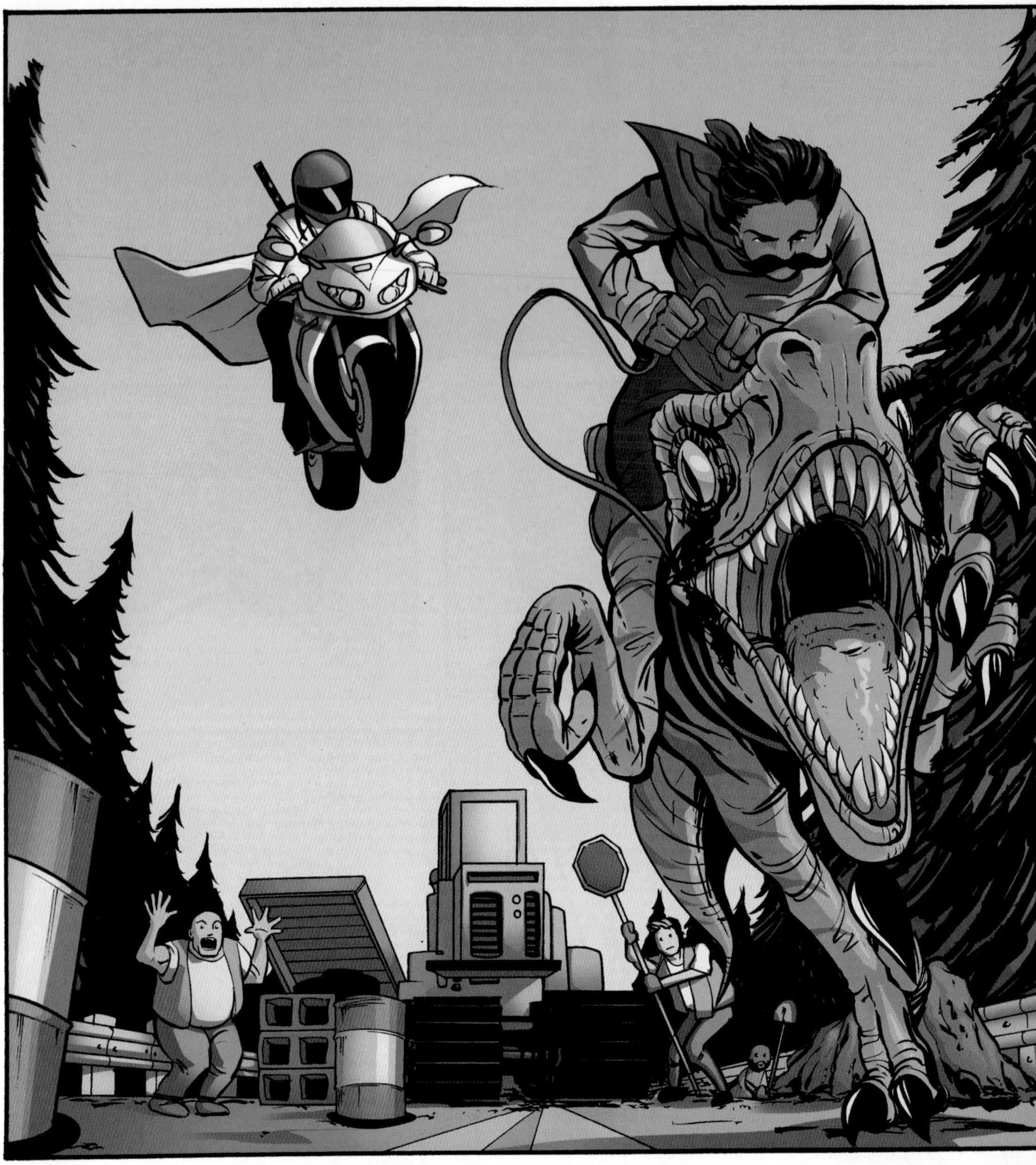

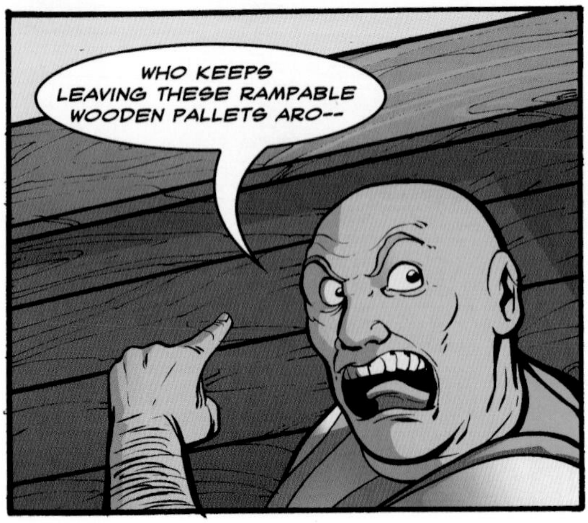
WHO KEEPS
LEAVING THESE RAMPABLE
WOODEN PALLETS ARO--

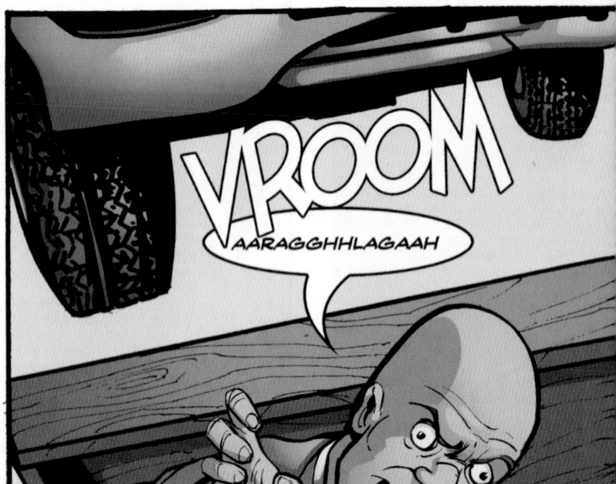
VROOM
AARAGGHHLAGAAH

I wish this foreman guy could have been a bad guy in the Tony Hawk or GTA games. He'd chase you around, so mad.

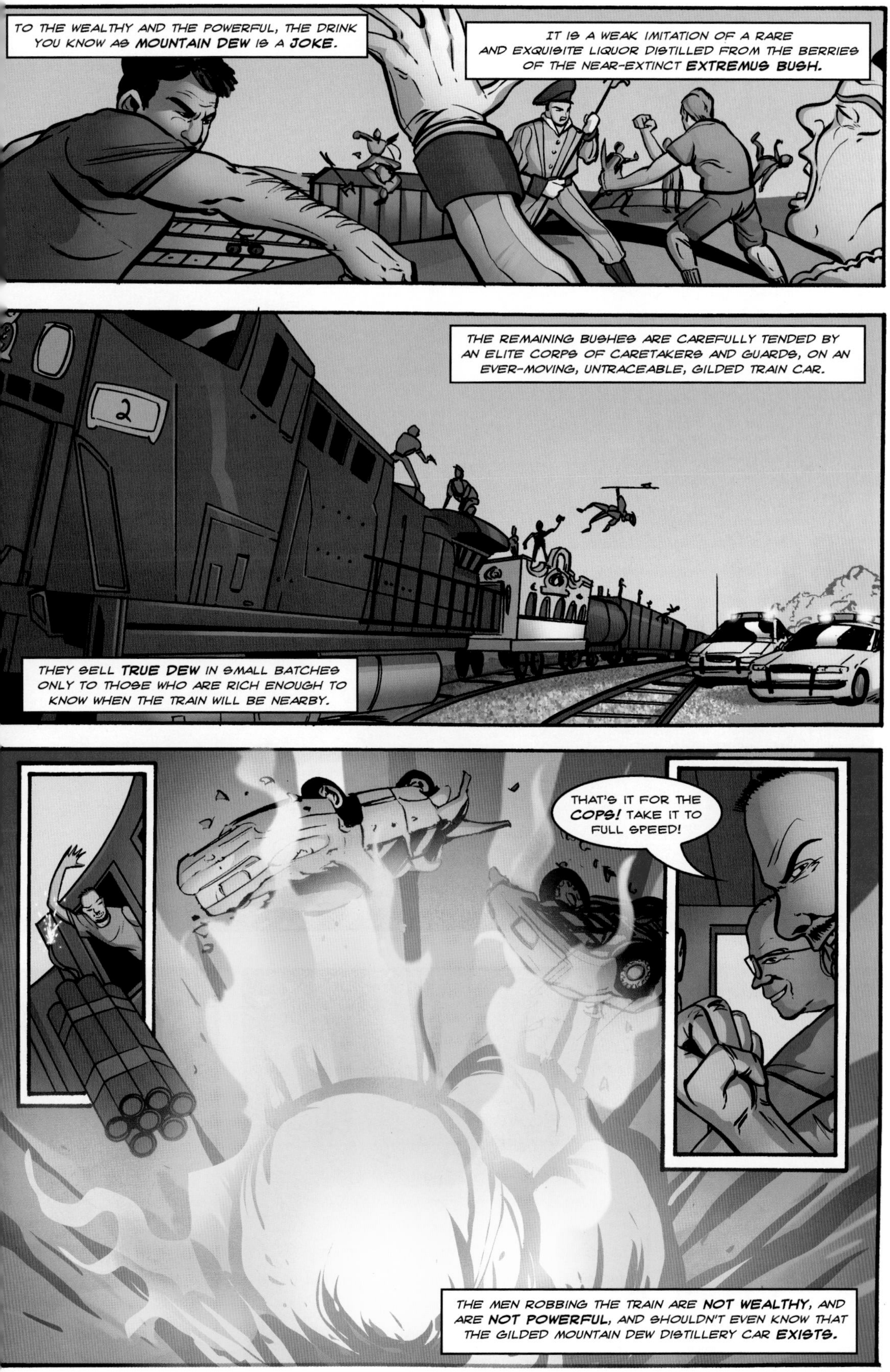
TO THE WEALTHY AND THE POWERFUL, THE DRINK YOU KNOW AS MOUNTAIN DEW IS A JOKE.
IT IS A WEAK IMITATION OF A RARE AND EXQUISITE LIQUOR DISTILLED FROM THE BERRIES OF THE NEAR-EXTINCT EXTREMUS BUSH.
THE REMAINING BUSHES ARE CAREFULLY TENDED BY AN ELITE CORPS OF CARETAKERS AND GUARDS, ON AN EVER-MOVING, UNTRACEABLE, GILDED TRAIN CAR.
2
THEY SELL TRUE DEW IN SMALL BATCHES ONLY TO THOSE WHO ARE RICH ENOUGH TO KNOW WHEN THE TRAIN WILL BE NEARBY.
THAT'S IT FOR THE COPS! TAKE IT TO FULL SPEED!
THE MEN ROBBING THE TRAIN ARE NOT WEALTHY, AND ARE NOT POWERFUL, AND SHOULDN'T EVEN KNOW THAT THE GILDED MOUNTAIN DEW DISTILLERY CAR EXISTS.

All of this is 100 percent true.

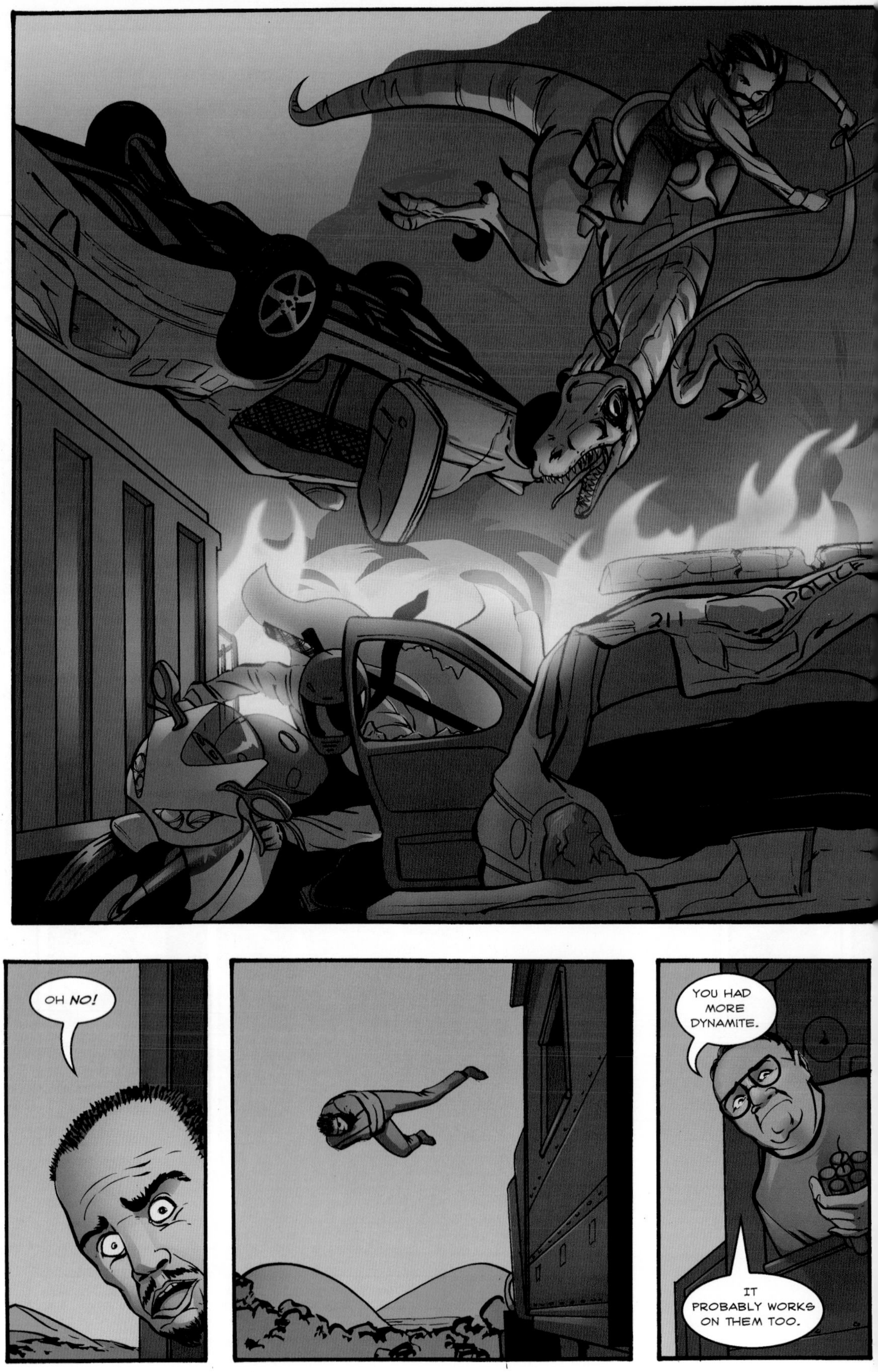
211
POLICE
OH NO!
YOU HAD MORE DYNAMITE.
IT PROBABLY WORKS ON THEM TOO.

I really wish that window could have been closed so that he would have broken it when he jumped out.

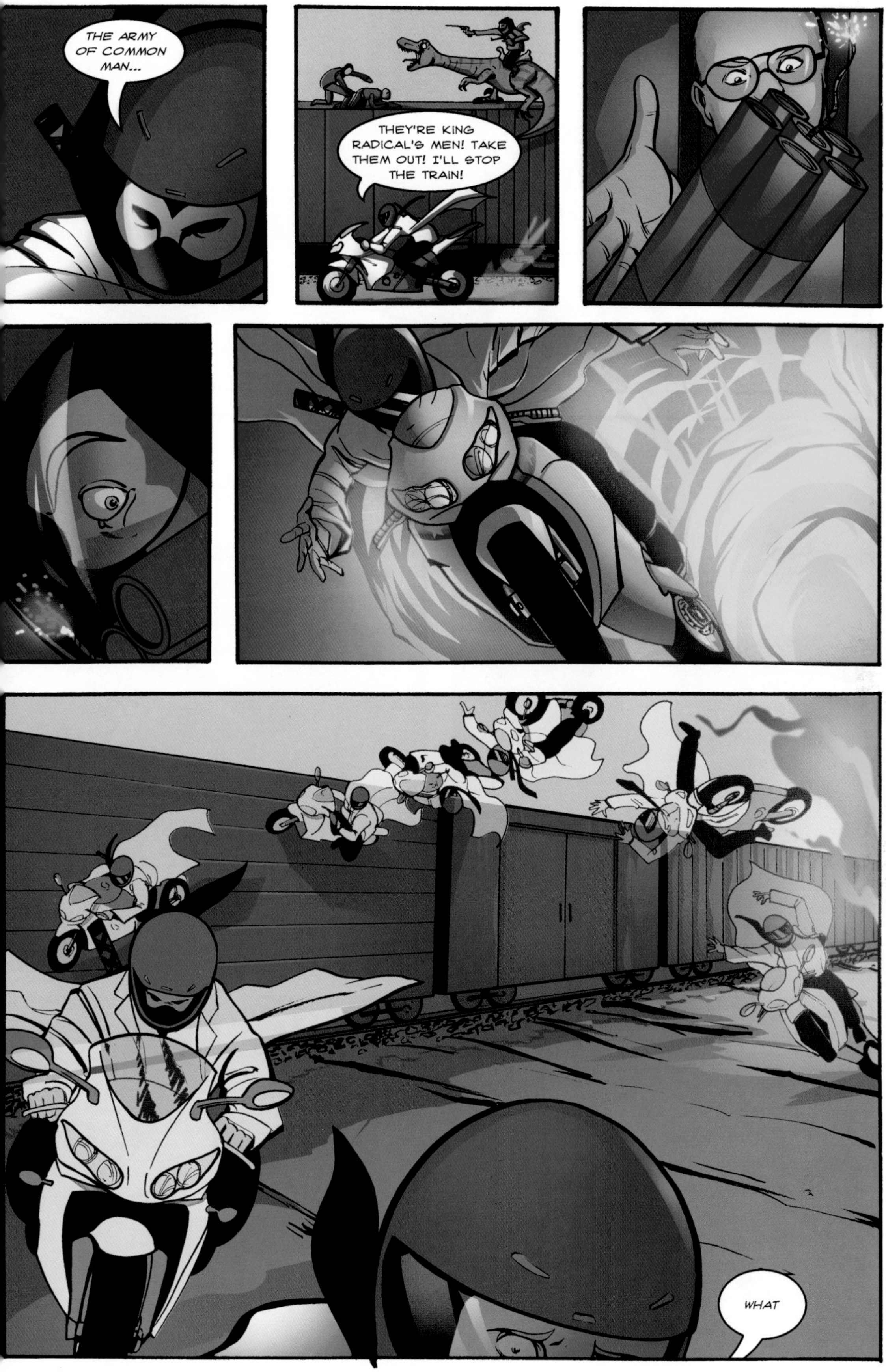
THE ARMY OF COMMON MAN...
THEY'RE KING RADICAL'S MEN! TAKE THEM OUT! I'LL STOP THE TRAIN!
WHAT

just happened

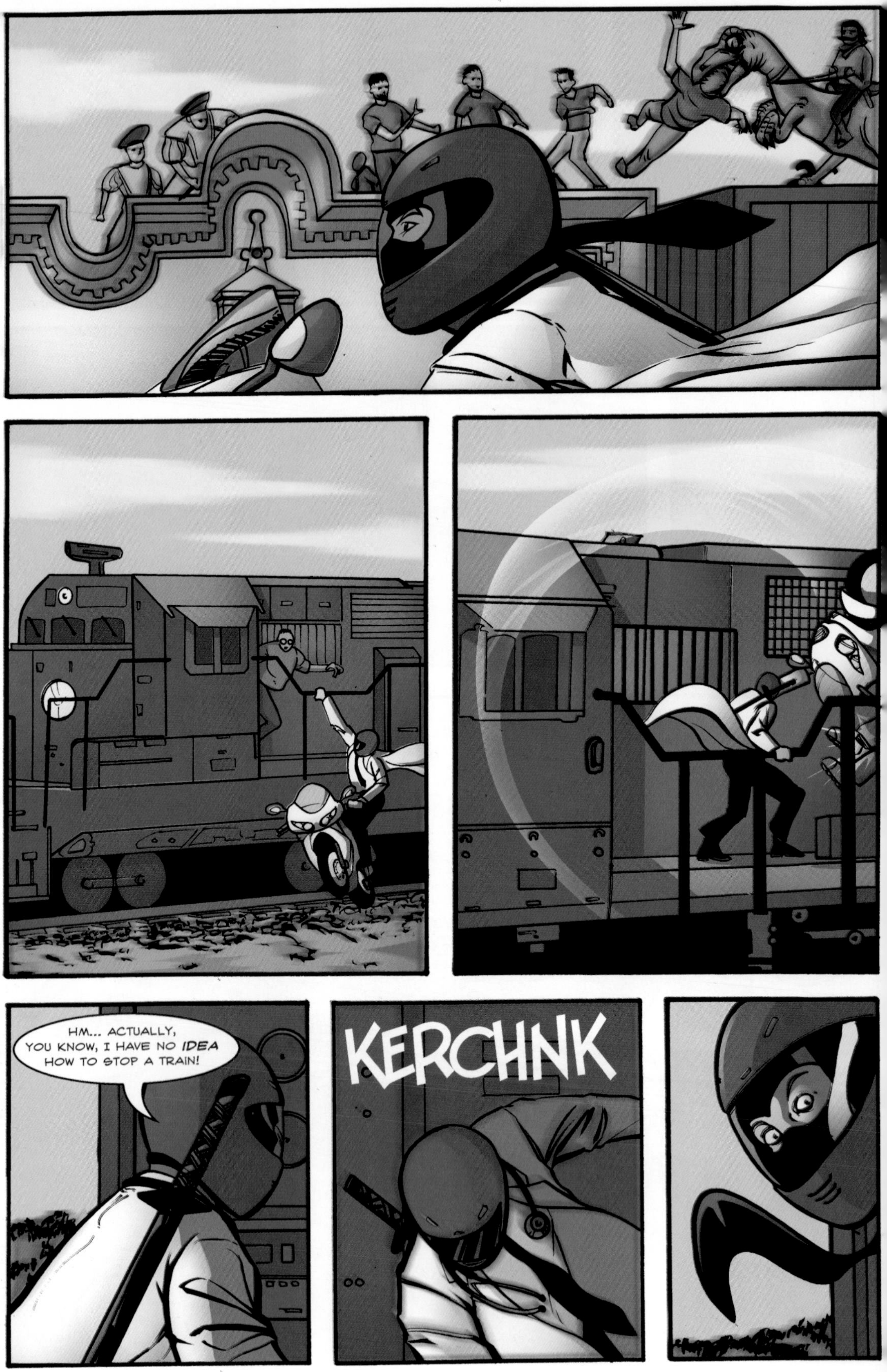
HM... ACTUALLY, YOU KNOW, I HAVE NO *IDEA* HOW TO STOP A TRAIN!
KERCHNK

Back when we were black and white, we'd just have little squiggles all over this page, but now we have BLURRING!

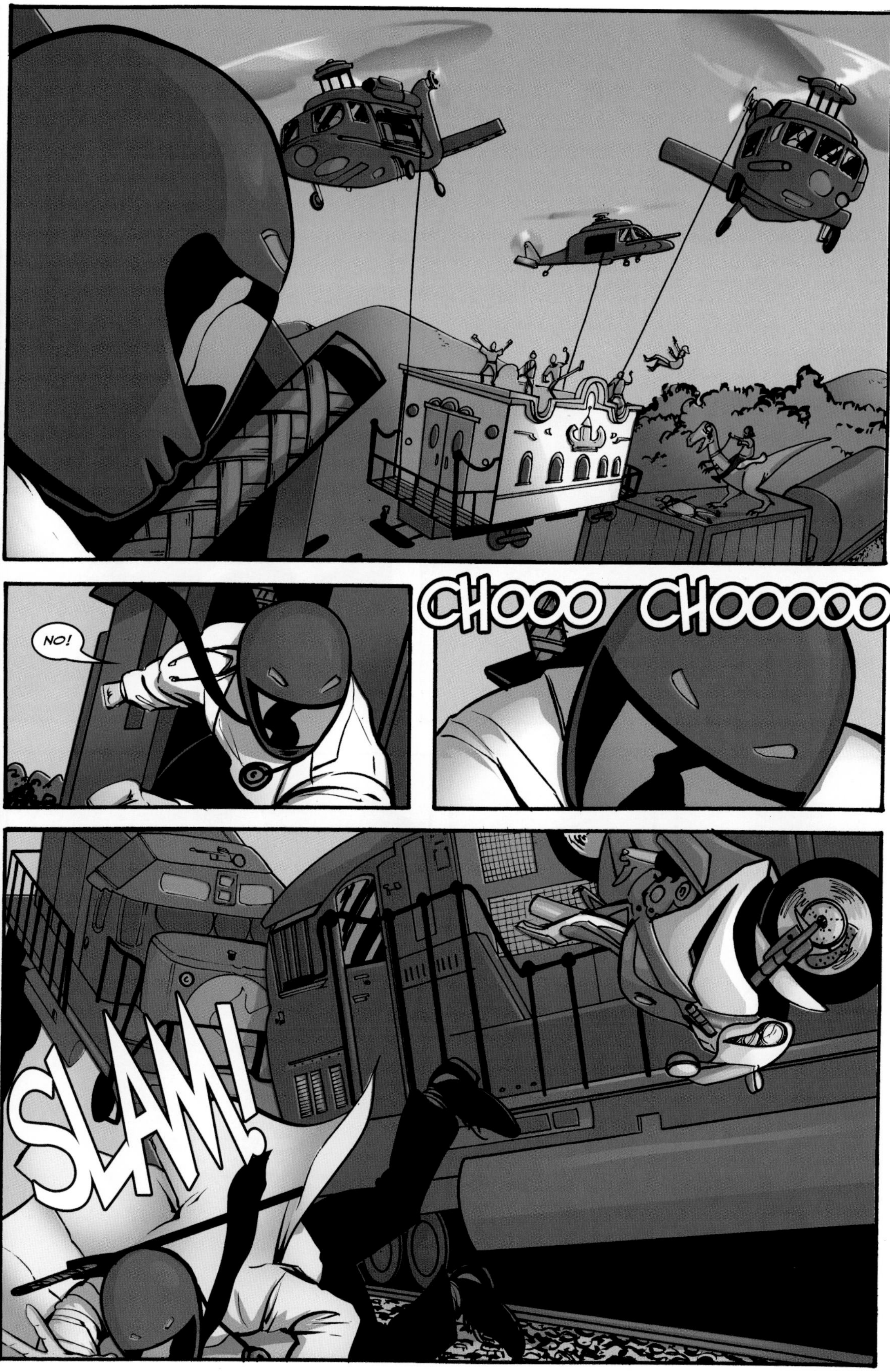
NO!
CHOOO CHOOOOO
SLAM!

Here is another image for you to use if your forum discussions get off topic.

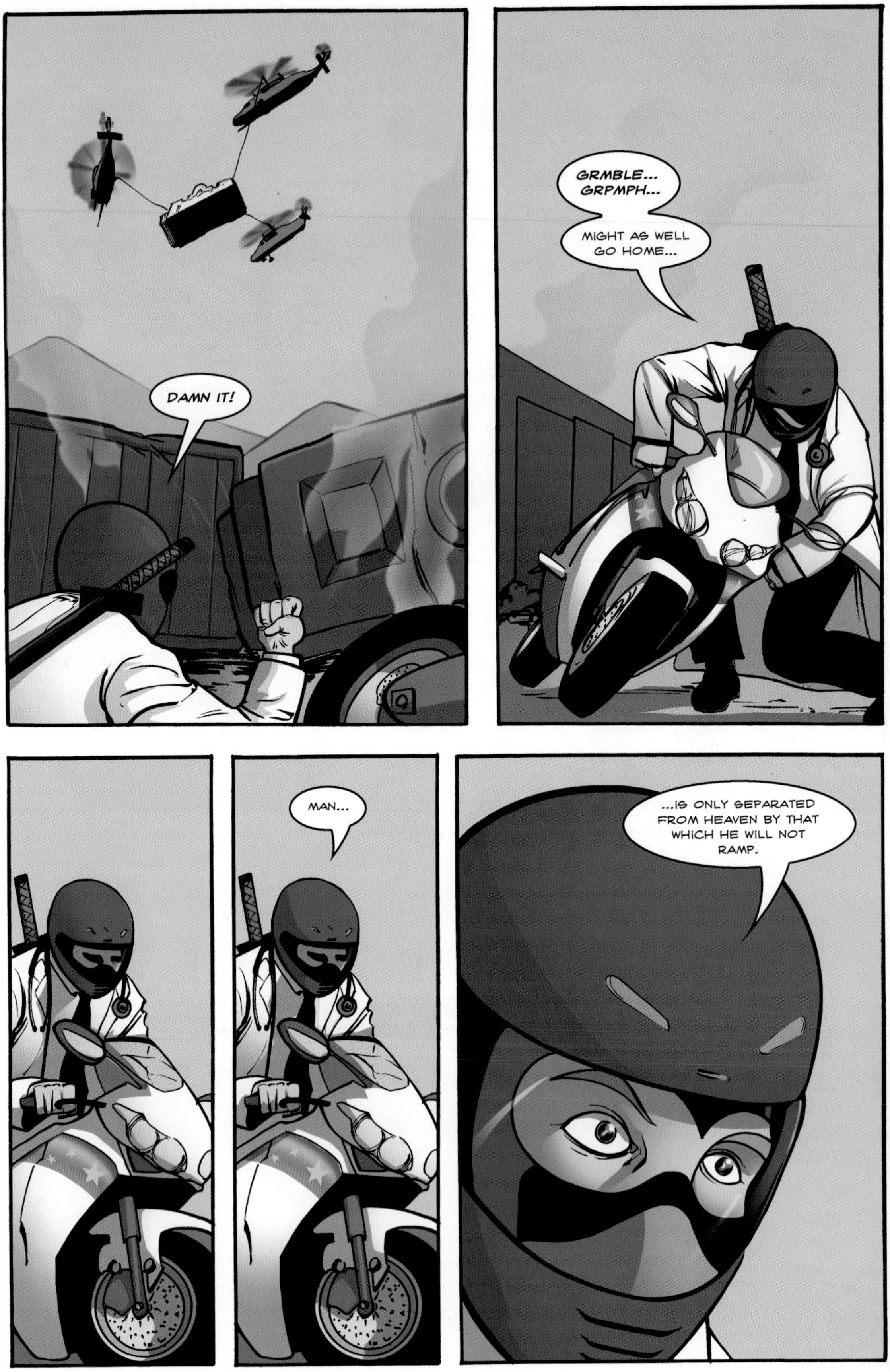
DAMN IT!
GRMBLE... GRPMPH...
MIGHT AS WELL GO HOME...
MAN...
...IS ONLY SEPARATED FROM HEAVEN BY THAT WHICH HE WILL NOT RAMP.

BELIEVE IN YOURSELF.

WHERE ARE YOU GOING?

I CAN STOP THEM. I'LL HEAD THEM OFF IN THE NARROWS.

WHAT? MAN, THEY ARE GONE. THEY ARE LITERALLY *FLYING AWAY.*

I CAN STOP THEM IN THE NARROWS.

THERE ARE INJURED PEOPLE HERE!!

DAMN. YOU'RE RIGHT.

UH... OKAY, HERE IS WHAT YOU NEED TO DO.

FIRST THING, YOU'RE GOING TO NEED TO STABILIZE THE CERVICAL SPINE. SEE IF THERE IS SOMEONE ELSE HERE OKAY ENOUGH TO HELP WITH THAT. NEXT, YOU'LL NEED TO DO A RAPID TRAUMA ASSESSMENT. STARTING FROM THE HEAD, LOOK, LISTEN, FEEL FOR MAJOR INJURIES AND LIFE THREATS.
MAKE SURE THERE'S AN OPEN AIRWAY, THE PATIENT IS BREATHING, CHECK THE LEVEL OF CONSCIOUSNESS. "WIGGLE YOUR TOES," STUFF LIKE THAT. AFTER ALL THAT, LOGROLL THE PATIENT TO ONE SIDE, CHECKING FOR POOLED BLOOD, OR BACK INJURIES. GIVE A QUICK LISTEN TO THE LUNGS, AND THEN ROLL THEM ONTO A LONG BOARD. OH, YOU SHOULD HAVE GOTTEN SOME DEBRIS AT THIS ... MAKE A LONG ... SECURE ... LONG BO... KEEP ... AND ST...

What do you mean, "Chris Hastings, did you just copy that from an e-mail from an EMT?" I have no idea what you are talking about.

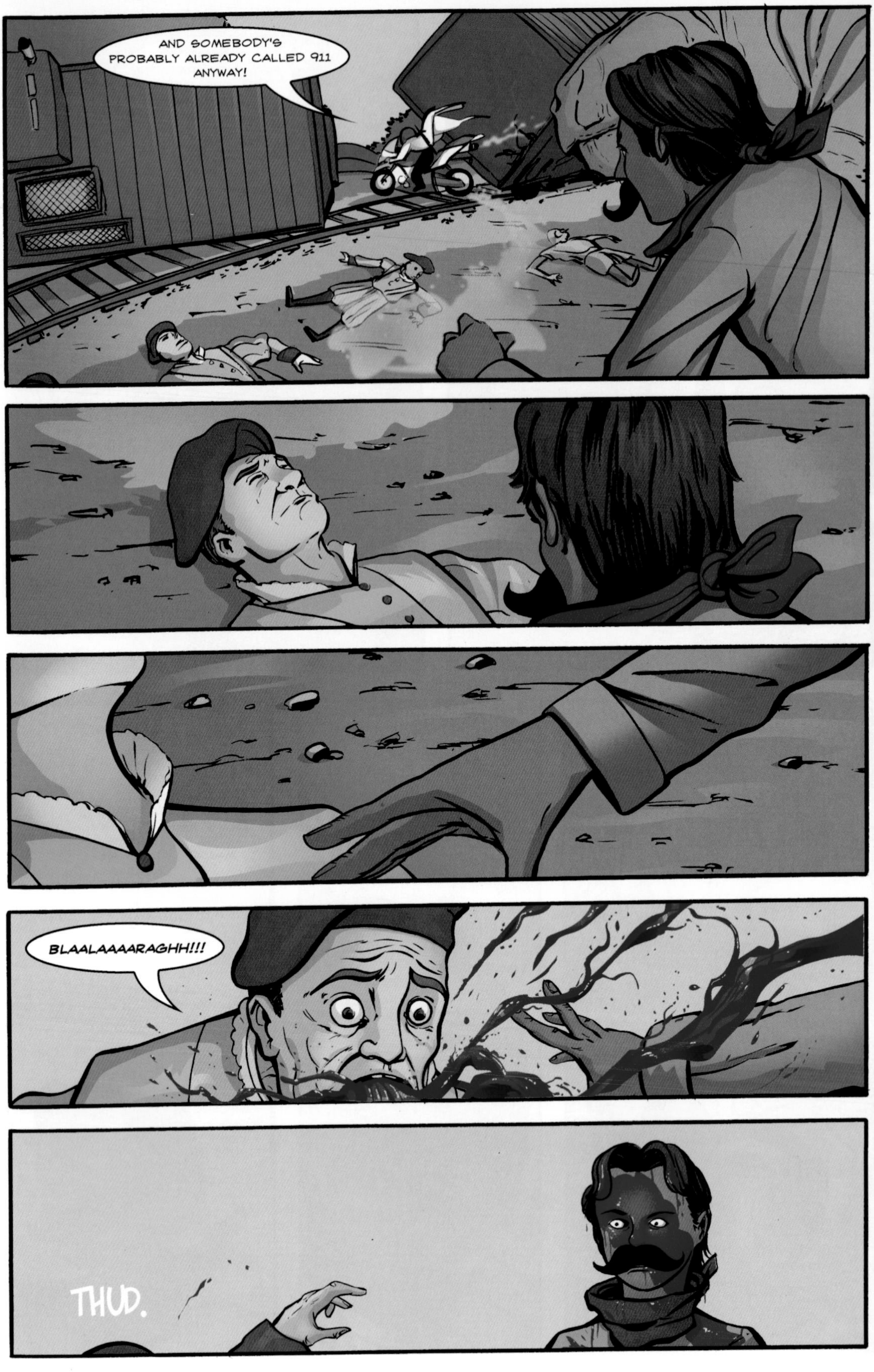
AND SOMEBODY'S PROBABLY ALREADY CALLED 911 ANYWAY!
BLAALAAAARAGHH!!!
THUD.

Gordito failed his skill check.

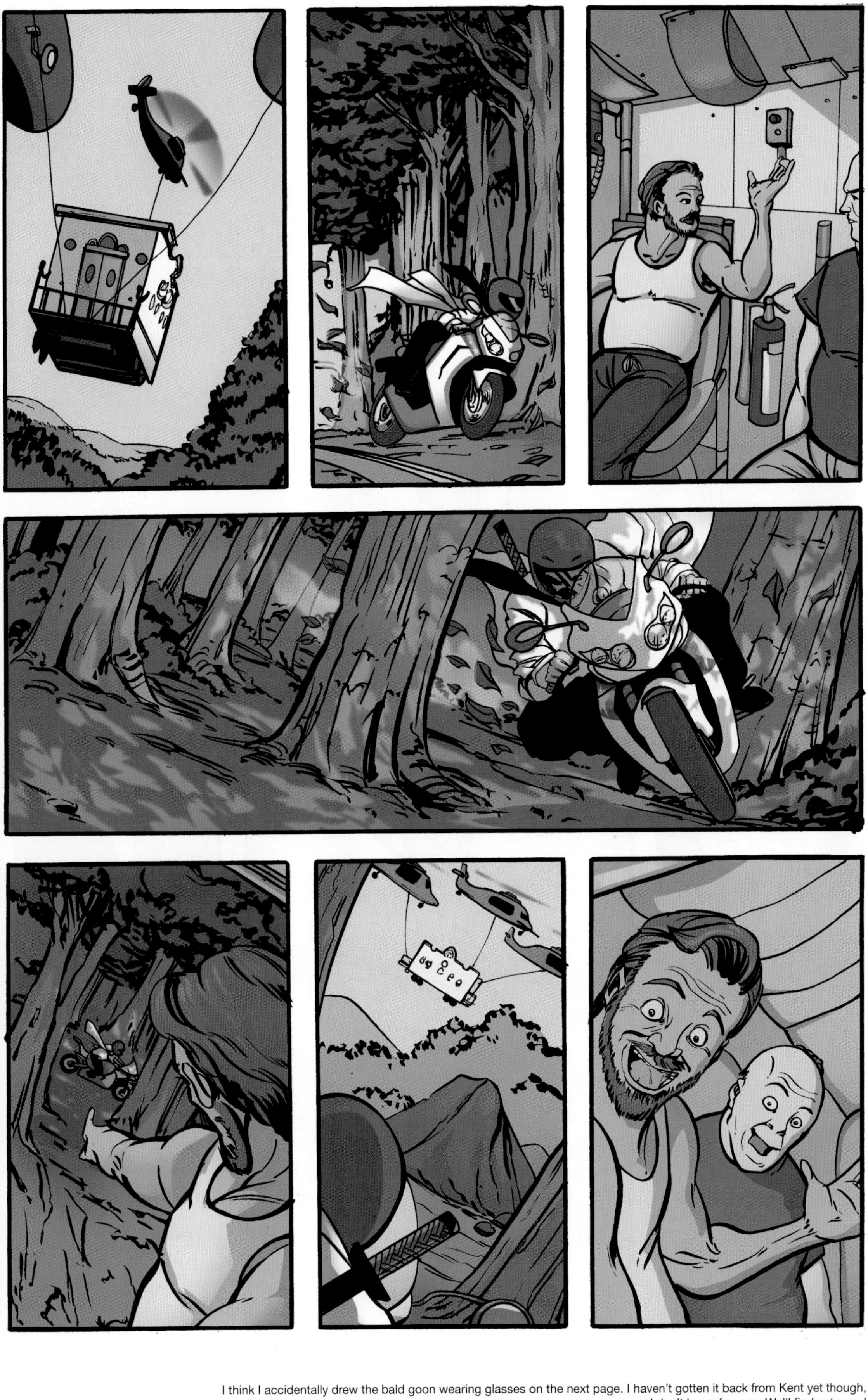

I think I accidentally drew the bald goon wearing glasses on the next page. I haven't gotten it back from Kent yet though, so I don't know for sure. We'll find out soon!

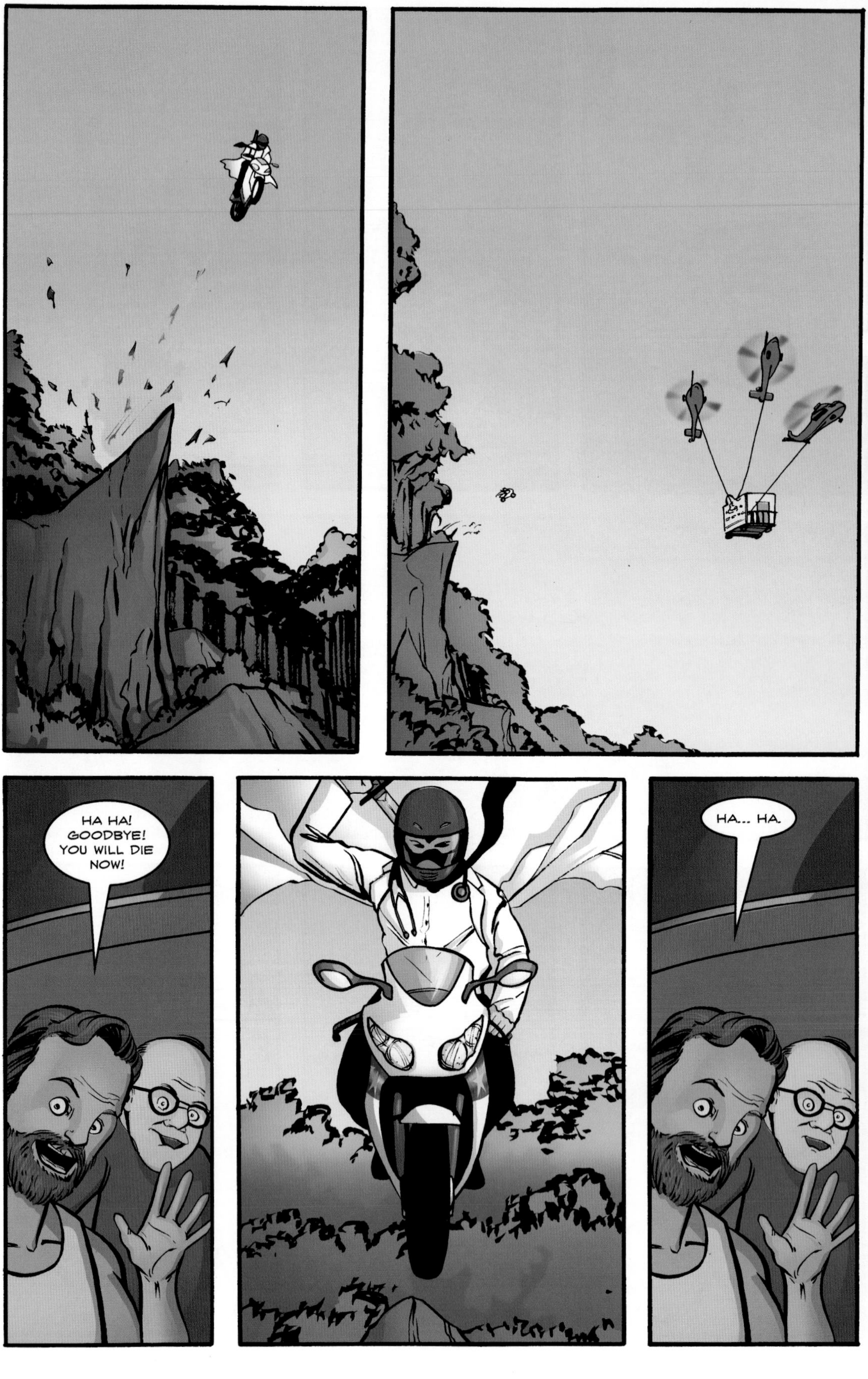
HA HA! GOODBYE! YOU WILL DIE NOW!
HA... HA.

Yup! Put on glasses!

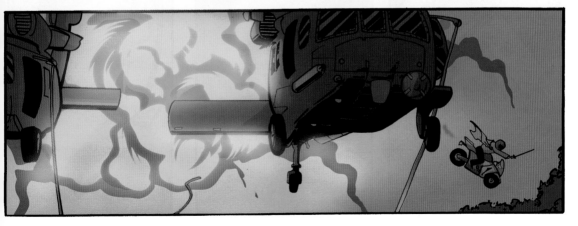

Oh, you know what? The other guy's beard changed to— OOP NOW HE DEAD.

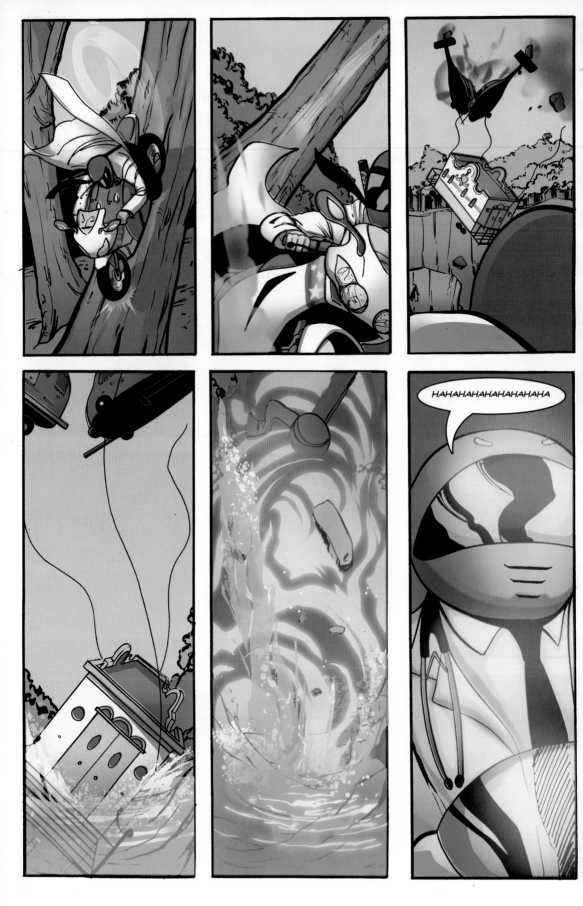

Doc just remembered a *Garfield* he'd read earlier that day.

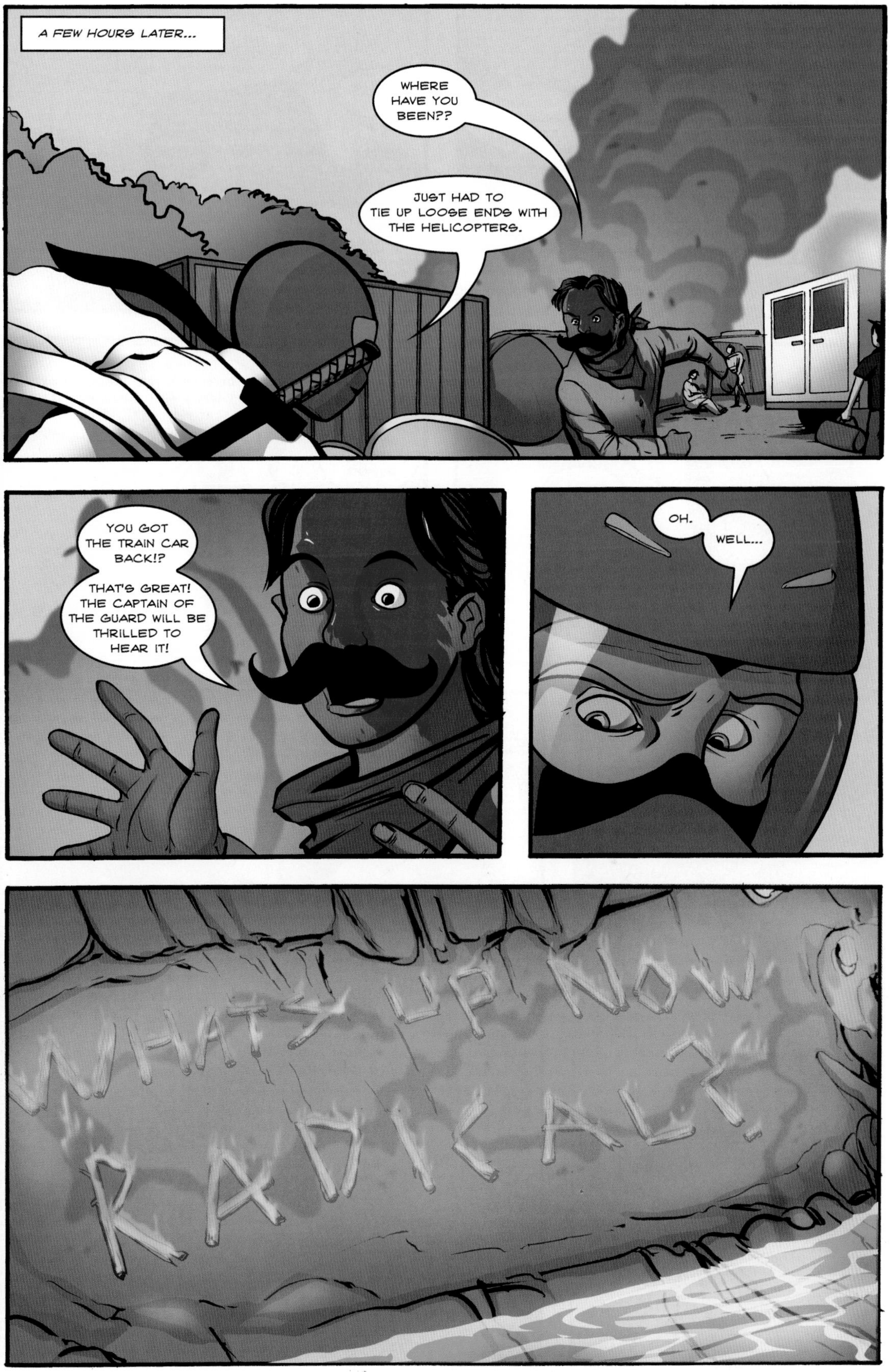
A FEW HOURS LATER...
WHERE HAVE YOU BEEN??
JUST HAD TO TIE UP LOOSE ENDS WITH THE HELICOPTERS.
YOU GOT THE TRAIN CAR BACK!?
THAT'S GREAT! THE CAPTAIN OF THE GUARD WILL BE THRILLED TO HEAR IT!
OH.
WELL...
WHAT'S UP NOW RADICAL?

Does he just assume that ALL of his enemies have moon bases now?

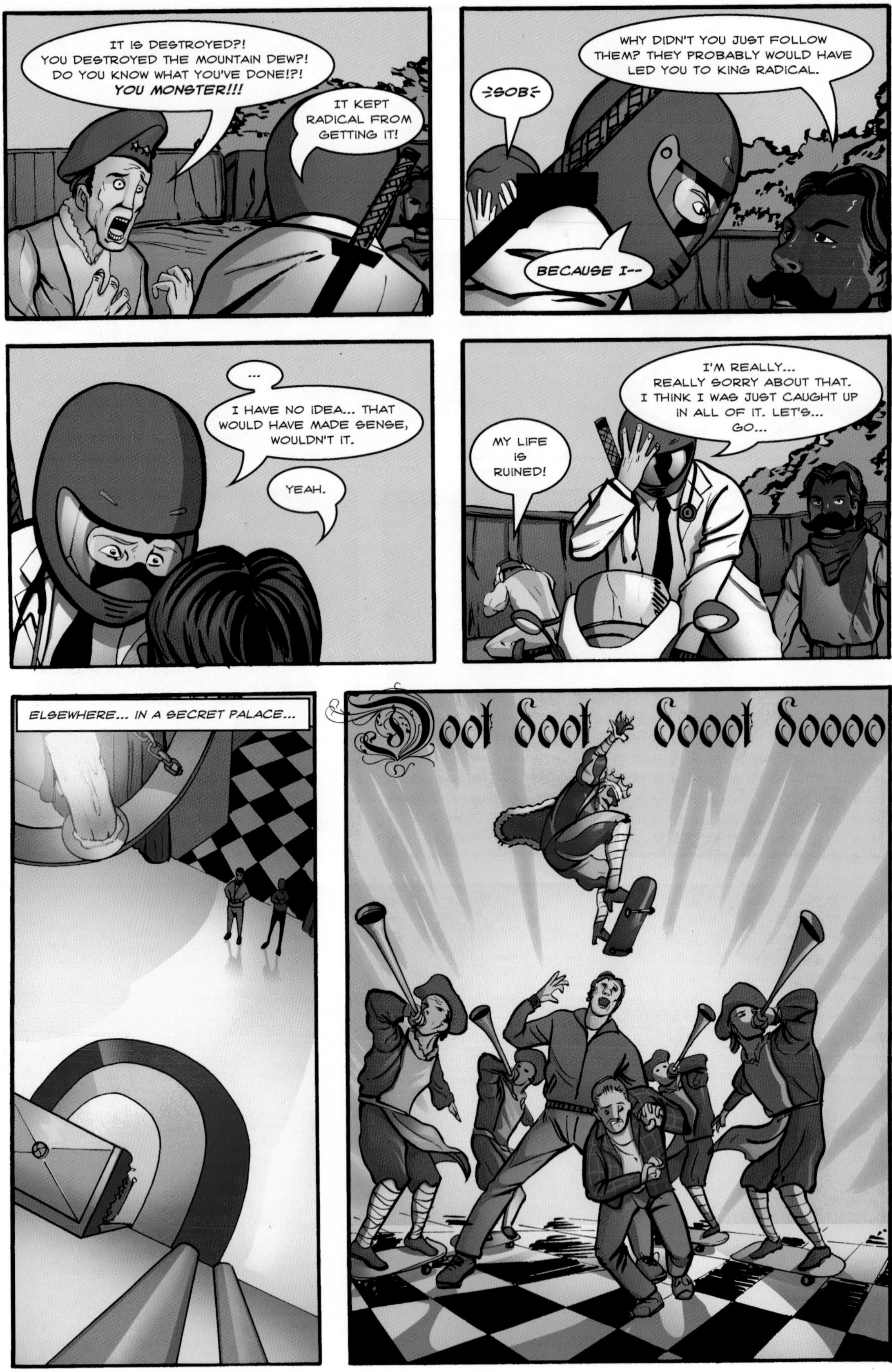
IT IS DESTROYED?! YOU DESTROYED THE MOUNTAIN DEW?! DO YOU KNOW WHAT YOU'VE DONE!?! *YOU MONSTER!!!*
IT KEPT RADICAL FROM GETTING IT!
WHY DIDN'T YOU JUST FOLLOW THEM? THEY PROBABLY WOULD HAVE LED YOU TO KING RADICAL.
SOB
BECAUSE I--
...
I HAVE NO IDEA... THAT WOULD HAVE MADE SENSE, WOULDN'T IT.
YEAH.
I'M REALLY... REALLY SORRY ABOUT THAT. I THINK I WAS JUST CAUGHT UP IN ALL OF IT. LET'S... GO...
MY LIFE IS RUINED!
ELSEWHERE... IN A SECRET PALACE...
Doot Doot Dooot Doooo

The trumpeters are probably very funny to watch when they are just starting out their profession.

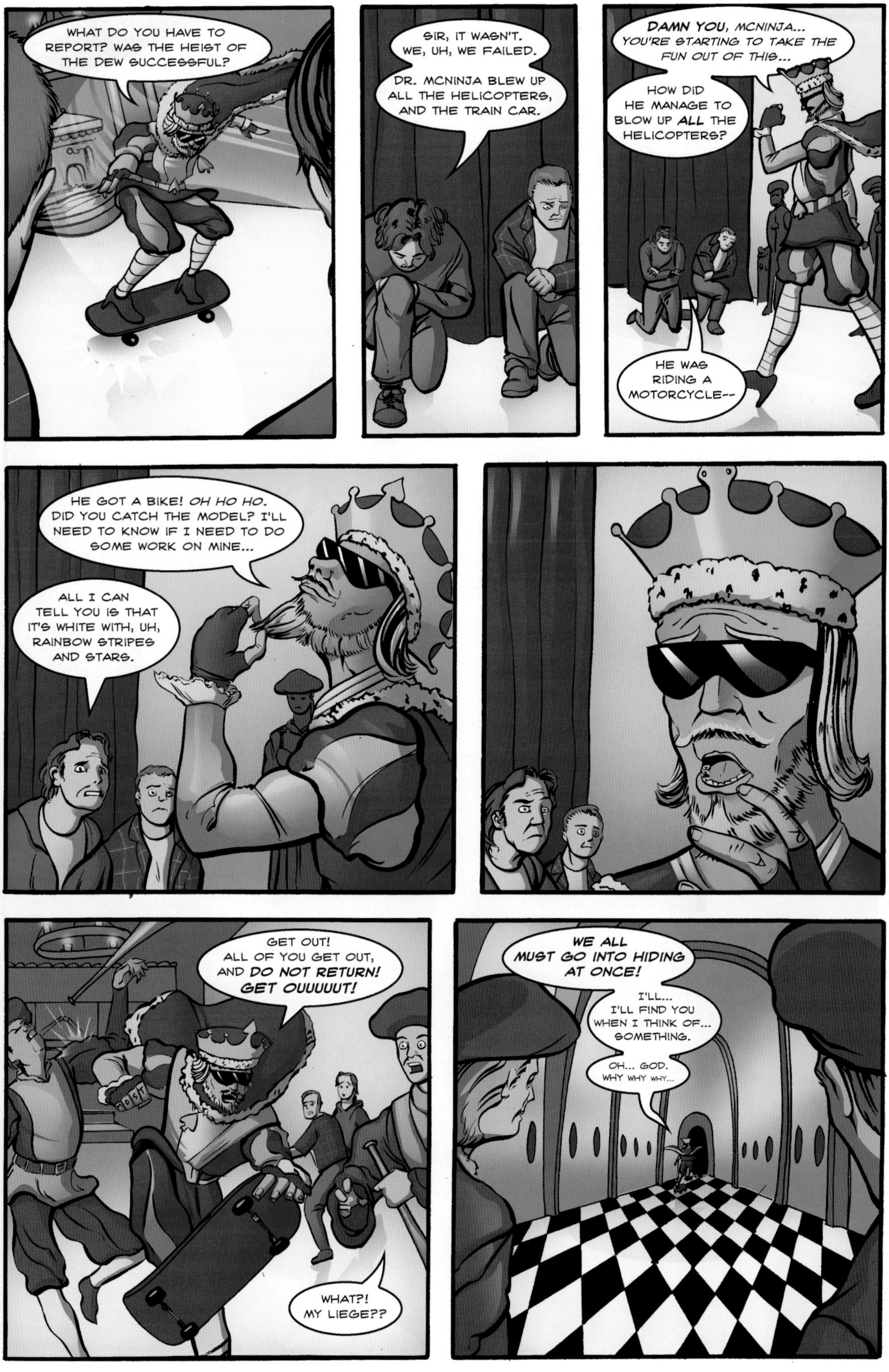

WHAT DO YOU HAVE TO REPORT? WAS THE HEIST OF THE DEW SUCCESSFUL?
SIR, IT WASN'T. WE, UH, WE FAILED.
DR. MCNINJA BLEW UP ALL THE HELICOPTERS, AND THE TRAIN CAR.
DAMN YOU, MCNINJA... YOU'RE STARTING TO TAKE THE FUN OUT OF THIS...
HOW DID HE MANAGE TO BLOW UP ALL THE HELICOPTERS?
HE WAS RIDING A MOTORCYCLE--
HE GOT A BIKE! OH HO HO. DID YOU CATCH THE MODEL? I'LL NEED TO KNOW IF I NEED TO DO SOME WORK ON MINE...
ALL I CAN TELL YOU IS THAT IT'S WHITE WITH, UH, RAINBOW STRIPES AND STARS.
GET OUT! ALL OF YOU GET OUT, AND DO NOT RETURN! GET OUUUUUT!
WHAT?! MY LIEGE??
WE ALL MUST GO INTO HIDING AT ONCE!
I'LL... I'LL FIND YOU WHEN I THINK OF... SOMETHING.
OH... GOD. WHY WHY WHY...

SIR, THE PALACE IS, UH . . . HIDDEN ALREADY.

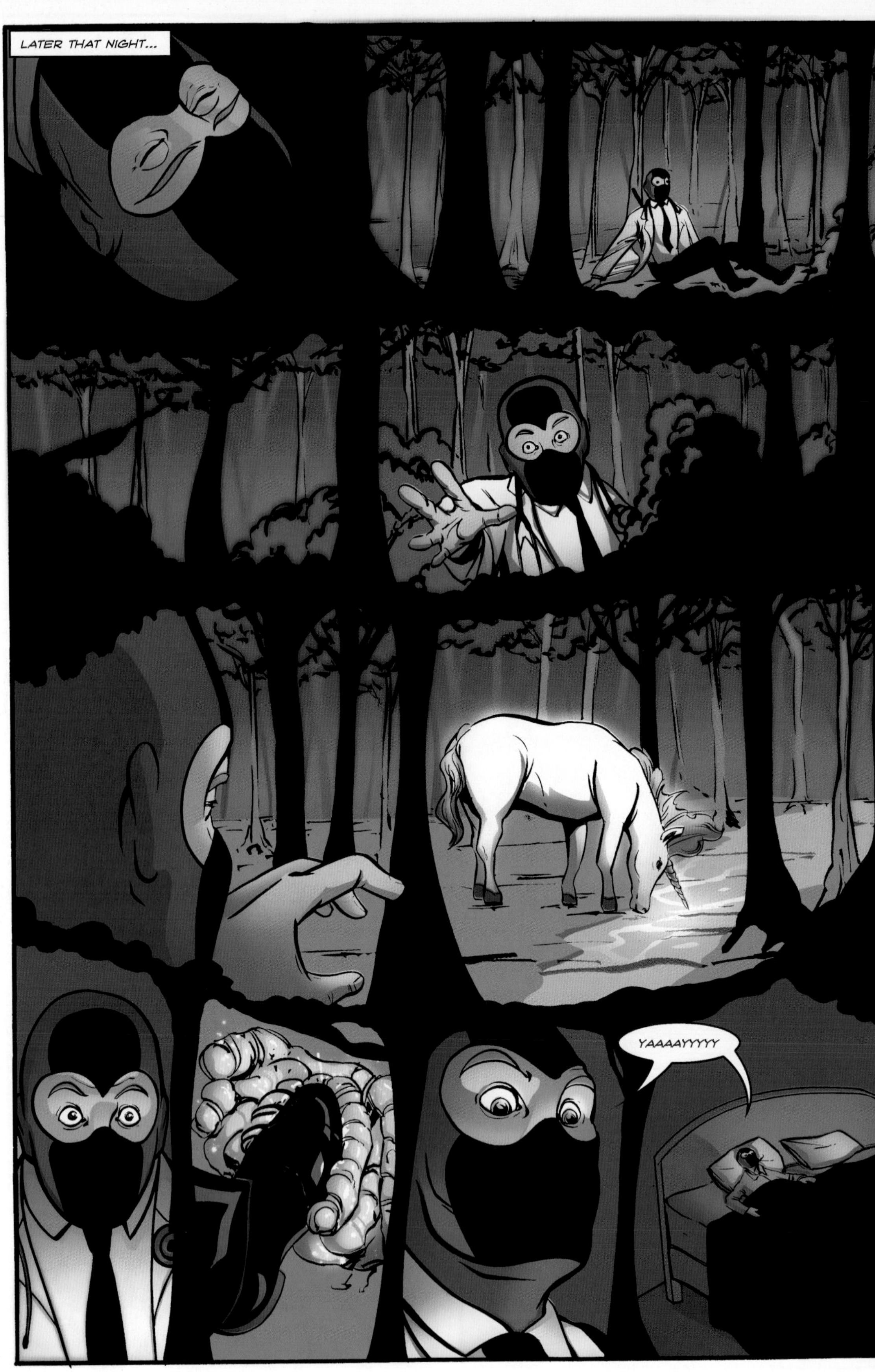
LATER THAT NIGHT...
YAAAAYYYYY

It's surprisingly hard to draw unicorn droppings.

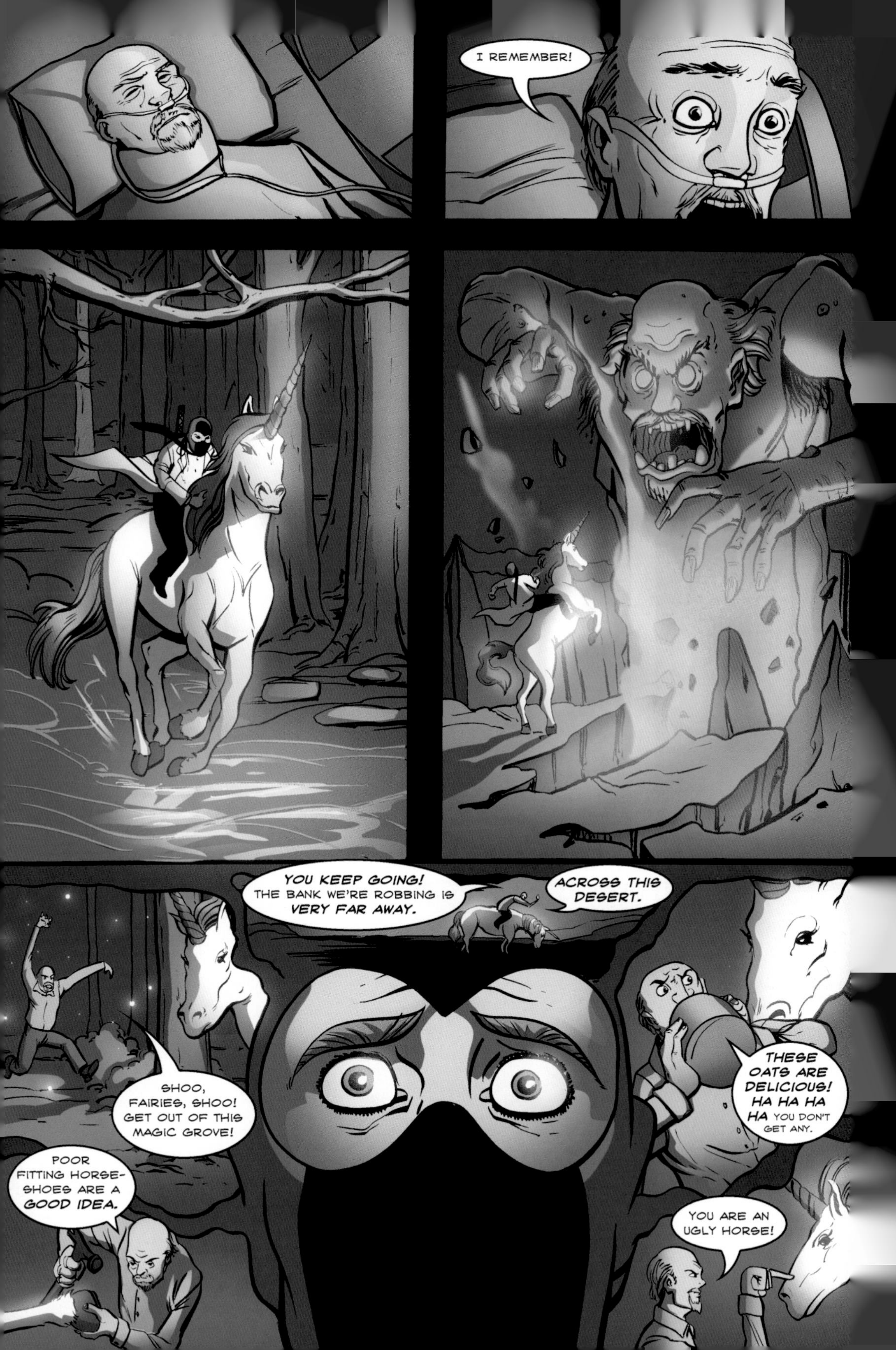
I REMEMBER!
YOU KEEP GOING! THE BANK WE'RE ROBBING IS VERY FAR AWAY.
ACROSS THIS DESERT.
SHOO, FAIRIES, SHOO! GET OUT OF THIS MAGIC GROVE!
POOR FITTING HORSE-SHOES ARE A GOOD IDEA.
THESE OATS ARE DELICIOUS! HA HA HA HA YOU DON'T GET ANY.
YOU ARE AN UGLY HORSE!

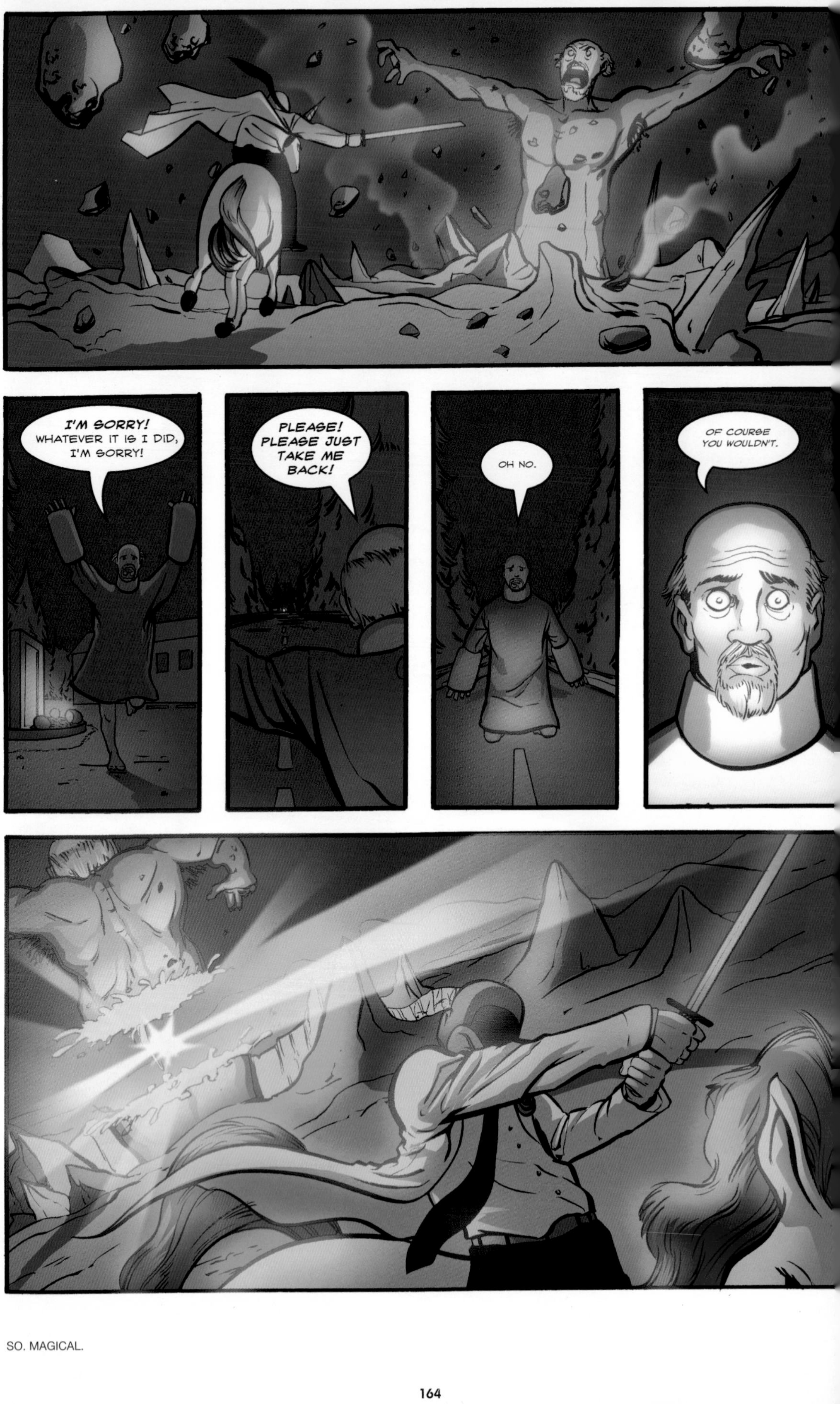
I'M SORRY! WHATEVER IT IS I DID, I'M SORRY!
PLEASE! PLEASE JUST TAKE ME BACK!
OH NO.
OF COURSE YOU WOULDN'T.

SO. MAGICAL.

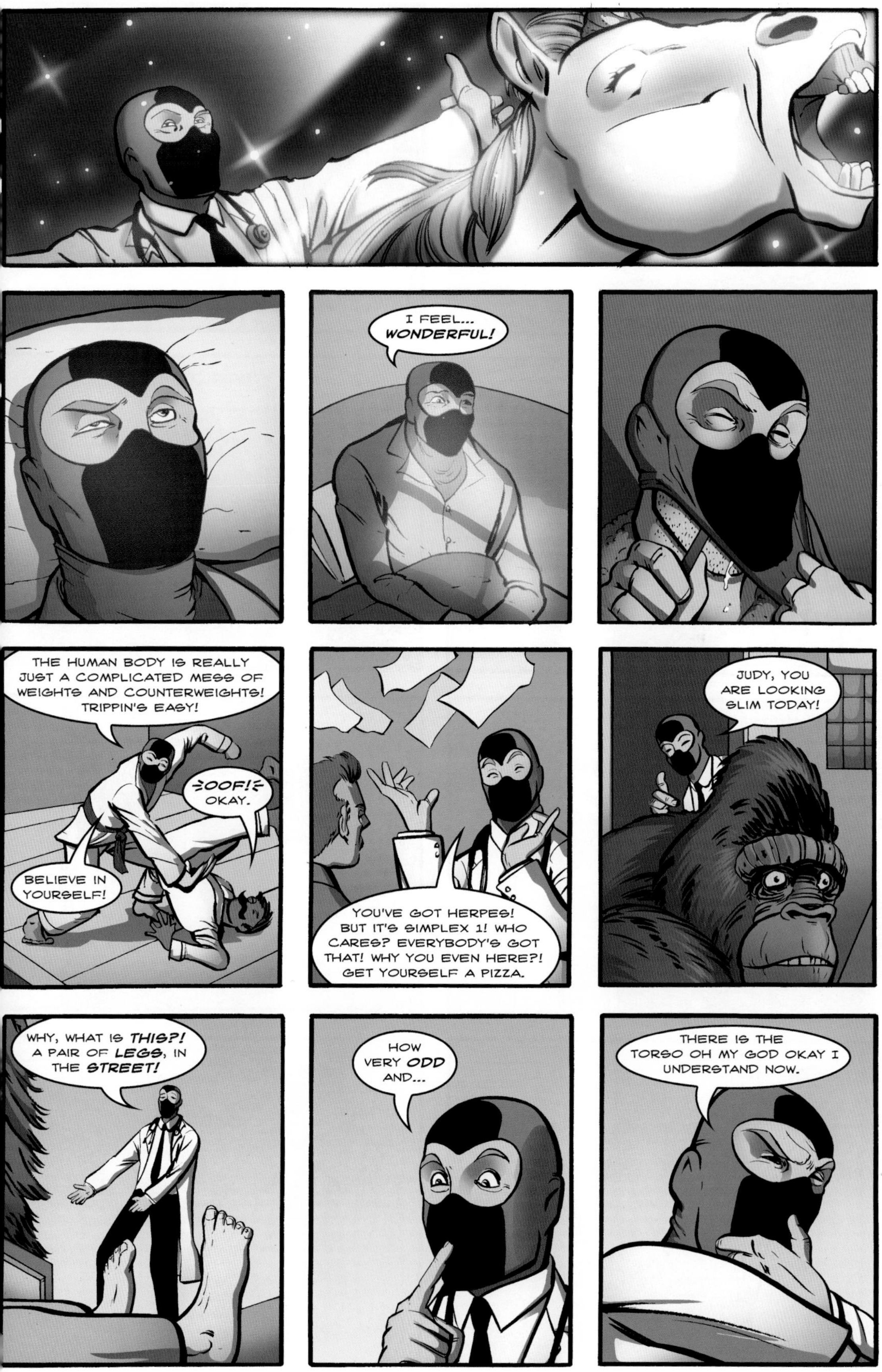
I FEEL... WONDERFUL!
THE HUMAN BODY IS REALLY JUST A COMPLICATED MESS OF WEIGHTS AND COUNTERWEIGHTS! TRIPPIN'S EASY!
OOF! OKAY.
BELIEVE IN YOURSELF!
YOU'VE GOT HERPES! BUT IT'S SIMPLEX 1! WHO CARES? EVERYBODY'S GOT THAT! WHY YOU EVEN HERE?! GET YOURSELF A PIZZA.
JUDY, YOU ARE LOOKING SLIM TODAY!
WHY, WHAT IS THIS?! A PAIR OF LEGS, IN THE STREET!
HOW VERY ODD AND...
THERE IS THE TORSO OH MY GOD OKAY I UNDERSTAND NOW.

HSV1 can spread to the brain and be fatal though . . . So be careful of that.

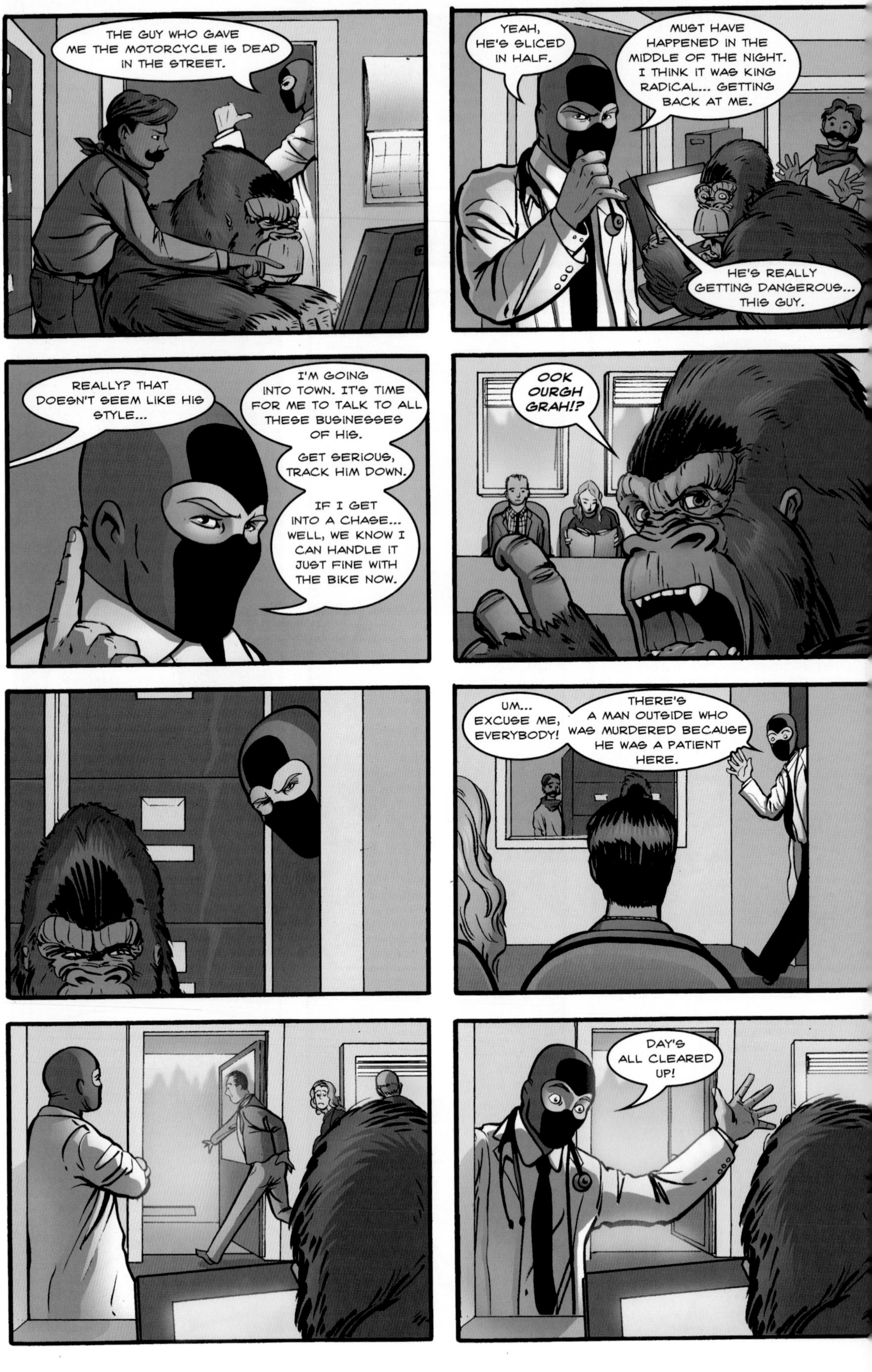
THE GUY WHO GAVE ME THE MOTORCYCLE IS DEAD IN THE STREET.
YEAH, HE'S SLICED IN HALF.
MUST HAVE HAPPENED IN THE MIDDLE OF THE NIGHT. I THINK IT WAS KING RADICAL... GETTING BACK AT ME.
HE'S REALLY GETTING DANGEROUS... THIS GUY.
REALLY? THAT DOESN'T SEEM LIKE HIS STYLE...
I'M GOING INTO TOWN. IT'S TIME FOR ME TO TALK TO ALL THESE BUSINESSES OF HIS.
GET SERIOUS, TRACK HIM DOWN.
IF I GET INTO A CHASE... WELL, WE KNOW I CAN HANDLE IT JUST FINE WITH THE BIKE NOW.
OOK OURGH GRAH!?
UM... EXCUSE ME, EVERYBODY!
THERE'S A MAN OUTSIDE WHO WAS MURDERED BECAUSE HE WAS A PATIENT HERE.
DAY'S ALL CLEARED UP!

Gordito is showing Judy that Weird Al has a Twitter page.

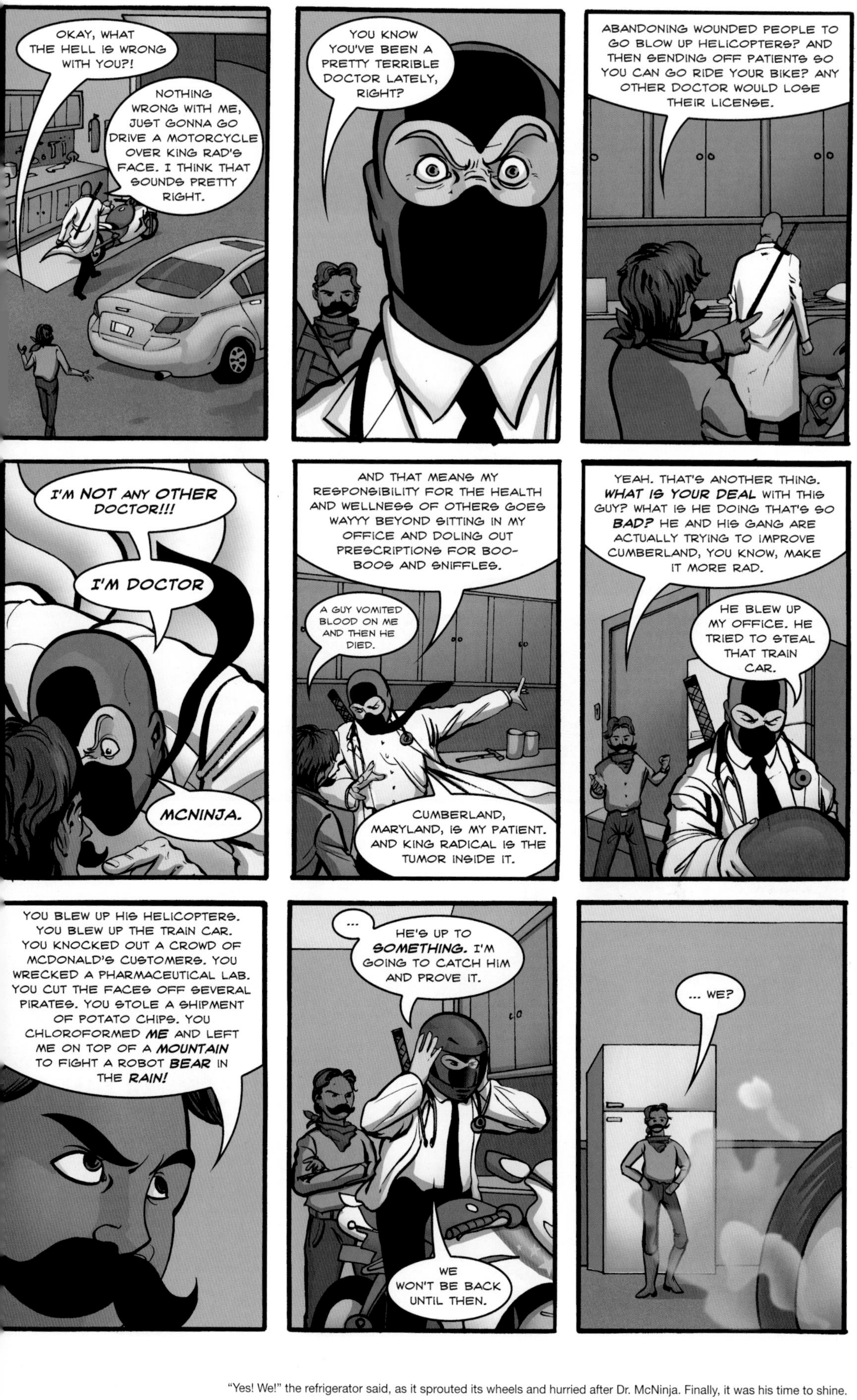
OKAY, WHAT THE HELL IS WRONG WITH YOU?!
NOTHING WRONG WITH ME, JUST GONNA GO DRIVE A MOTORCYCLE OVER KING RAD'S FACE. I THINK THAT SOUNDS PRETTY RIGHT.
YOU KNOW YOU'VE BEEN A PRETTY TERRIBLE DOCTOR LATELY, RIGHT?
ABANDONING WOUNDED PEOPLE TO GO BLOW UP HELICOPTERS? AND THEN SENDING OFF PATIENTS SO YOU CAN GO RIDE YOUR BIKE? ANY OTHER DOCTOR WOULD LOSE THEIR LICENSE.
I'M NOT ANY OTHER DOCTOR!!!
I'M DOCTOR
MCNINJA.
AND THAT MEANS MY RESPONSIBILITY FOR THE HEALTH AND WELLNESS OF OTHERS GOES WAYYY BEYOND SITTING IN MY OFFICE AND DOLING OUT PRESCRIPTIONS FOR BOO-BOOS AND SNIFFLES.
A GUY VOMITED BLOOD ON ME AND THEN HE DIED.
CUMBERLAND, MARYLAND, IS MY PATIENT. AND KING RADICAL IS THE TUMOR INSIDE IT.
YEAH. THAT'S ANOTHER THING. WHAT IS YOUR DEAL WITH THIS GUY? WHAT IS HE DOING THAT'S SO BAD? HE AND HIS GANG ARE ACTUALLY TRYING TO IMPROVE CUMBERLAND, YOU KNOW, MAKE IT MORE RAD.
HE BLEW UP MY OFFICE. HE TRIED TO STEAL THAT TRAIN CAR.
YOU BLEW UP HIS HELICOPTERS. YOU BLEW UP THE TRAIN CAR. YOU KNOCKED OUT A CROWD OF MCDONALD'S CUSTOMERS. YOU WRECKED A PHARMACEUTICAL LAB. YOU CUT THE FACES OFF SEVERAL PIRATES. YOU STOLE A SHIPMENT OF POTATO CHIPS. YOU CHLOROFORMED ME AND LEFT ME ON TOP OF A MOUNTAIN TO FIGHT A ROBOT BEAR IN THE RAIN!
...
HE'S UP TO SOMETHING. I'M GOING TO CATCH HIM AND PROVE IT.
WE WON'T BE BACK UNTIL THEN.
... WE?

"Yes! We!" the refrigerator said, as it sprouted its wheels and hurried after Dr. McNinja. Finally, it was his time to shine.

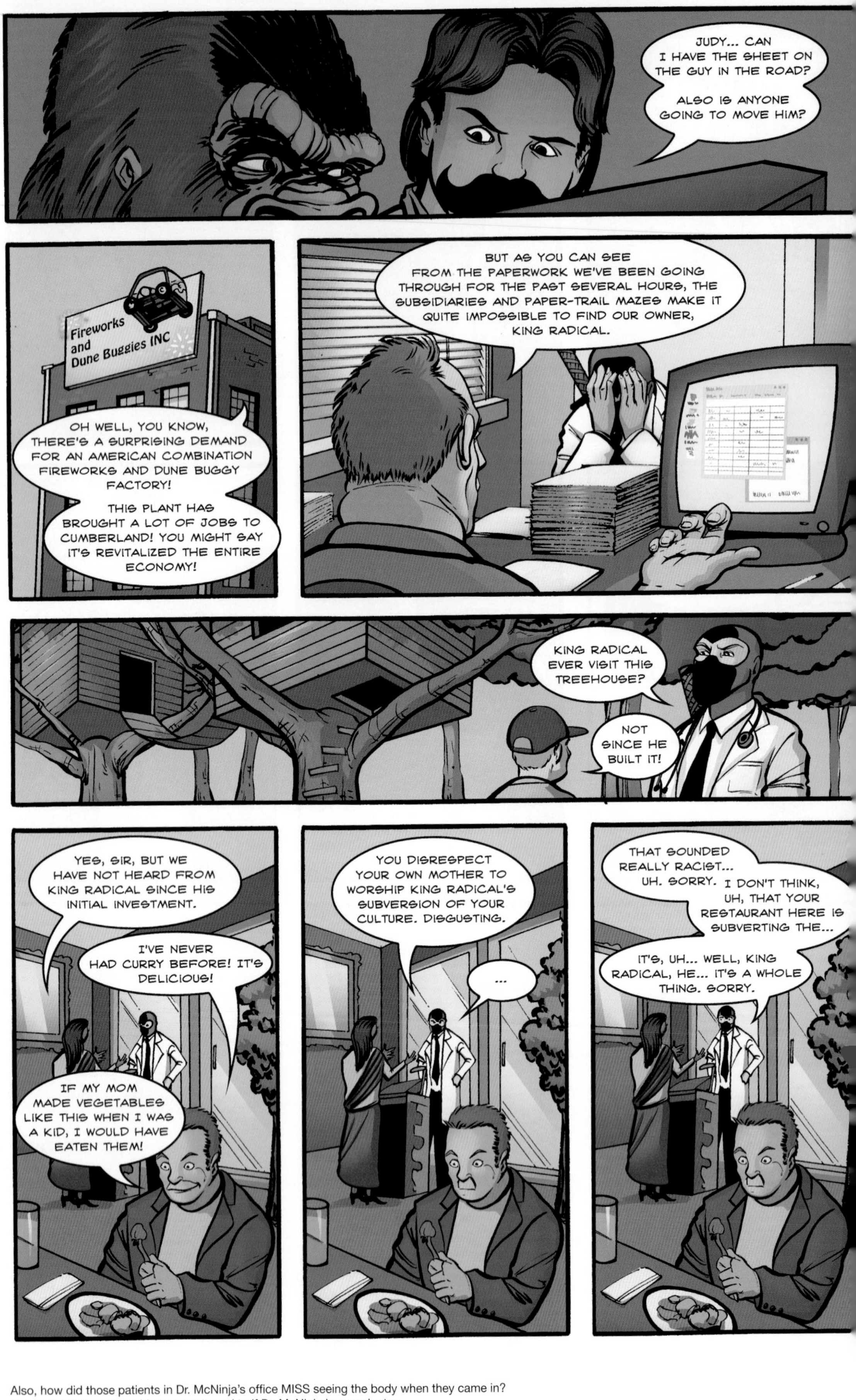
JUDY... CAN I HAVE THE SHEET ON THE GUY IN THE ROAD?
ALSO IS ANYONE GOING TO MOVE HIM?
Fireworks and Dune Buggies INC
OH WELL, YOU KNOW, THERE'S A SURPRISING DEMAND FOR AN AMERICAN COMBINATION FIREWORKS AND DUNE BUGGY FACTORY!
THIS PLANT HAS BROUGHT A LOT OF JOBS TO CUMBERLAND! YOU MIGHT SAY IT'S REVITALIZED THE ENTIRE ECONOMY!
BUT AS YOU CAN SEE FROM THE PAPERWORK WE'VE BEEN GOING THROUGH FOR THE PAST SEVERAL HOURS, THE SUBSIDIARIES AND PAPER-TRAIL MAZES MAKE IT QUITE IMPOSSIBLE TO FIND OUR OWNER, KING RADICAL.
KING RADICAL EVER VISIT THIS TREEHOUSE?
NOT SINCE HE BUILT IT!
YES, SIR, BUT WE HAVE NOT HEARD FROM KING RADICAL SINCE HIS INITIAL INVESTMENT.
I'VE NEVER HAD CURRY BEFORE! IT'S DELICIOUS!
IF MY MOM MADE VEGETABLES LIKE THIS WHEN I WAS A KID, I WOULD HAVE EATEN THEM!
YOU DISRESPECT YOUR OWN MOTHER TO WORSHIP KING RADICAL'S SUBVERSION OF YOUR CULTURE. DISGUSTING.
...
THAT SOUNDED REALLY RACIST... UH. SORRY.
I DON'T THINK, UH, THAT YOUR RESTAURANT HERE IS SUBVERTING THE...
IT'S, UH... WELL, KING RADICAL, HE... IT'S A WHOLE THING. SORRY.

Also, how did those patients in Dr. McNinja's office MISS seeing the body when they came in? Maybe that is just something you get used to if Dr. McNinja is your doctor.

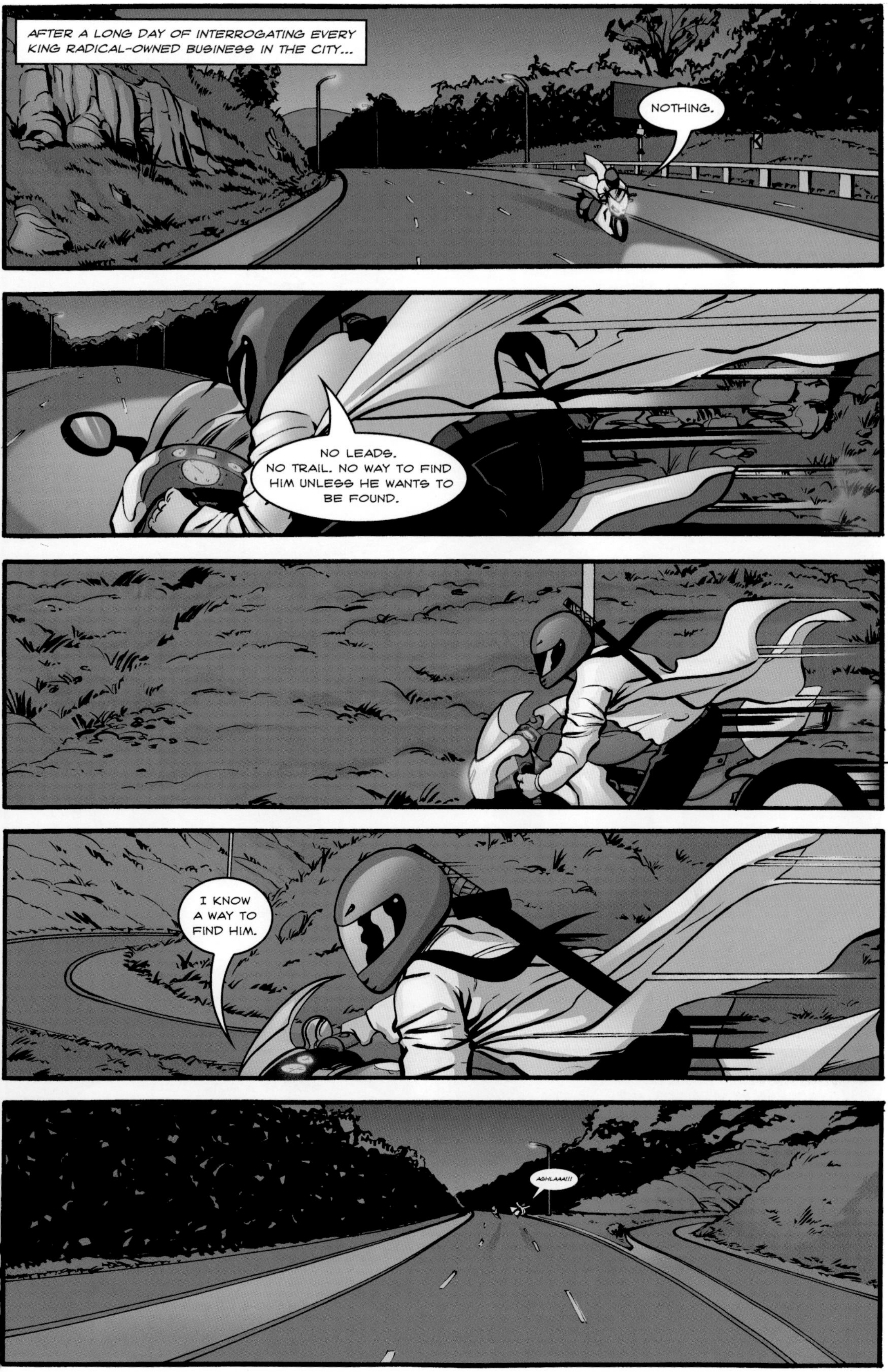
AFTER A LONG DAY OF INTERROGATING EVERY KING RADICAL-OWNED BUSINESS IN THE CITY...
NOTHING.
NO LEADS. NO TRAIL. NO WAY TO FIND HIM UNLESS HE WANTS TO BE FOUND.
I KNOW A WAY TO FIND HIM.
AGHLAAA!!!

"WHUH HUHHHH-WHUHHH-WAIT!! WHUHHH-WAIT," the refrigerator choked out between gasps for air. "YOU'RE GUH-HUH-HUH-GOING TOO FAST!"

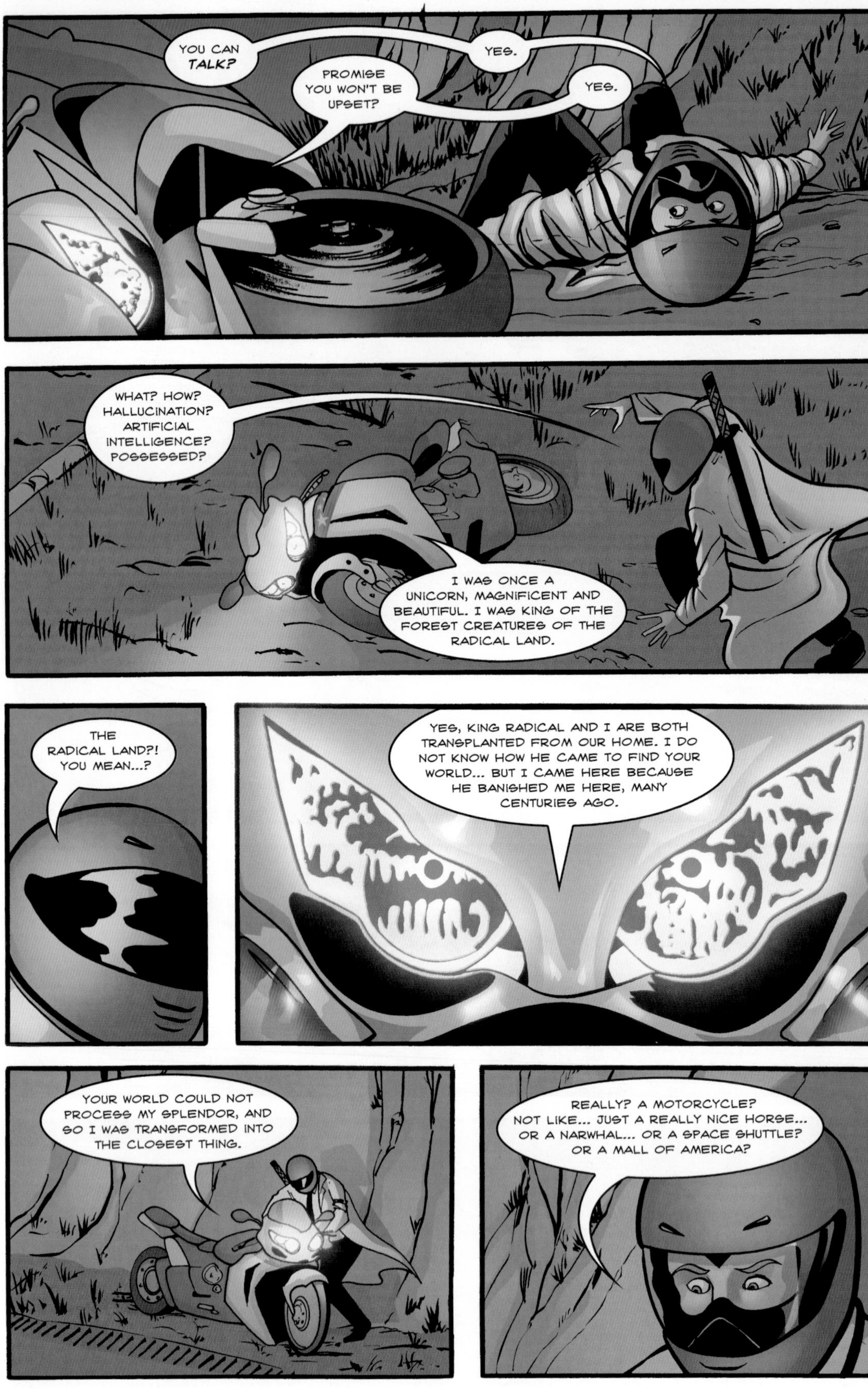
YOU CAN *TALK?*
YES.
PROMISE YOU WON'T BE UPSET?
YES.
WHAT? HOW? HALLUCINATION? ARTIFICIAL INTELLIGENCE? POSSESSED?
I WAS ONCE A UNICORN, MAGNIFICENT AND BEAUTIFUL. I WAS KING OF THE FOREST CREATURES OF THE RADICAL LAND.
THE RADICAL LAND?! YOU MEAN...?
YES, KING RADICAL AND I ARE BOTH TRANSPLANTED FROM OUR HOME. I DO NOT KNOW HOW HE CAME TO FIND YOUR WORLD... BUT I CAME HERE BECAUSE HE BANISHED ME HERE, MANY CENTURIES AGO.
YOUR WORLD COULD NOT PROCESS MY SPLENDOR, AND SO I WAS TRANSFORMED INTO THE CLOSEST THING.
REALLY? A MOTORCYCLE? NOT LIKE... JUST A REALLY NICE HORSE... OR A NARWHAL... OR A SPACE SHUTTLE? OR A MALL OF AMERICA?

Or a FLYING Mall of America?!

SO YOU'VE BEEN HERE FOR CENTURIES! THAT WOULD EXPLAIN HOW YOU'D END UP WITH AN ANTIQUITIES DEALER.

PLEASE DO NOT SPEAK OF HIM! HE WAS AN EVIL MAN. I WAS SO GRATEFUL THAT YOU CALLED OUT TO ME AND FREED ME FROM HIM.

I CALLED OUT TO YOU?

YES. YOU NEEDED A MOTORCYCLE TO DEFEAT KING RADICAL, AND THAT IS WHAT I AM.

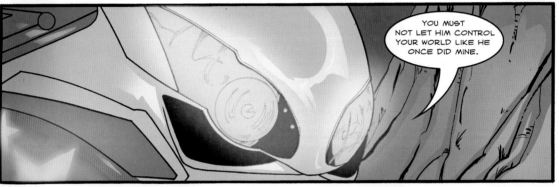

YOU MUST NOT LET HIM CONTROL YOUR WORLD LIKE HE ONCE DID MINE.

OKAY, YES. MAGICAL, TALKING MOTORCYCLE, YOU AND I ARE ON THE SAME PAGE. WHAT DO I NEED TO DO?

I HAVE PROVEN MY POWER TO YOU. ALONE, YOUR METHODS ARE WEAK AND YOU WILL FAIL. IF YOU WISH TO CAPTURE KING RADICAL, YOU MUST TRUST IN ME.

YOU MUST THREATEN WHAT HE CHERISHES MOST...

...WITHOUT ALERTING HIM TO MY PRESENCE. HE IS SCARED OF ME. BUT KING RADICAL HAS **MANY** LESSER FOES.

OH... NO...

For a second, I was going to make a joke in the alt text like, "My mom friend requested me on Facebook!" but then I remembered that Gordito's parents are dead, LOL.

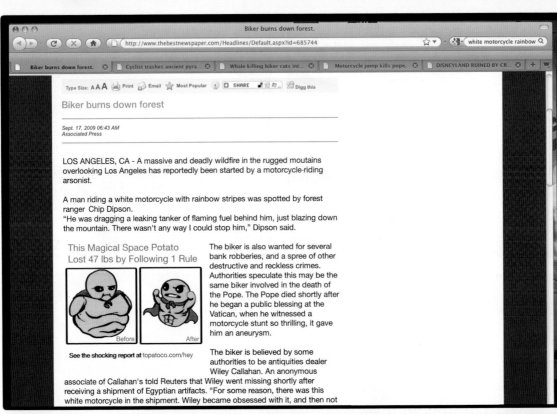

Biker burns down forest.

http://www.thebestnewspaper.com/Headlines/Default.aspx?id=685744

white motorcycle rainbow

Biker burns down forest. | Cyclist trashes ancient pyra... | Whale killing biker cuts int... | Motorcycle jump kills pope. | DISNEYLAND RUINED BY CR...

Type Size: A A A Print Email Most Popular 1 SHARE Digg this

Biker burns down forest

Sept. 17, 2009 06:43 AM
Associated Press

LOS ANGELES, CA - A massive and deadly wildfire in the rugged moutains overlooking Los Angeles has reportedly been started by a motorcycle-riding arsonist.

A man riding a white motorcycle with rainbow stripes was spotted by forest ranger Chip Dipson.
"He was dragging a leaking tanker of flaming fuel behind him, just blazing down the mountain. There wasn't any way I could stop him," Dipson said.

This Magical Space Potato Lost 47 lbs by Following 1 Rule

Before   After

See the shocking report at topatoco.com/hey

The biker is also wanted for several bank robberies, and a spree of other destructive and reckless crimes. Authorities speculate this may be the same biker involved in the death of the Pope. The Pope died shortly after he began a public blessing at the Vatican, when he witnessed a motorcycle stunt so thrilling, it gave him an aneurysm.

The biker is believed by some authorities to be antiquities dealer Wiley Callahan. An anonymous associate of Callahan's told Reuters that Wiley went missing shortly after receiving a shipment of Egyptian artifacts. "For some reason, there was this white motorcycle in the shipment. Wiley became obsessed with it, and then not

I HAVE TO GET DOC OFF THAT BIKE!

BOOP BEEP BEEP

911. WHAT'S YOUR EMERGENCY?

COME TO DR. MCNINJA'S OFFICE AND GET THESE DAMN LEGS OUT OF THE STREET.

911 help I tripped it's an emergency

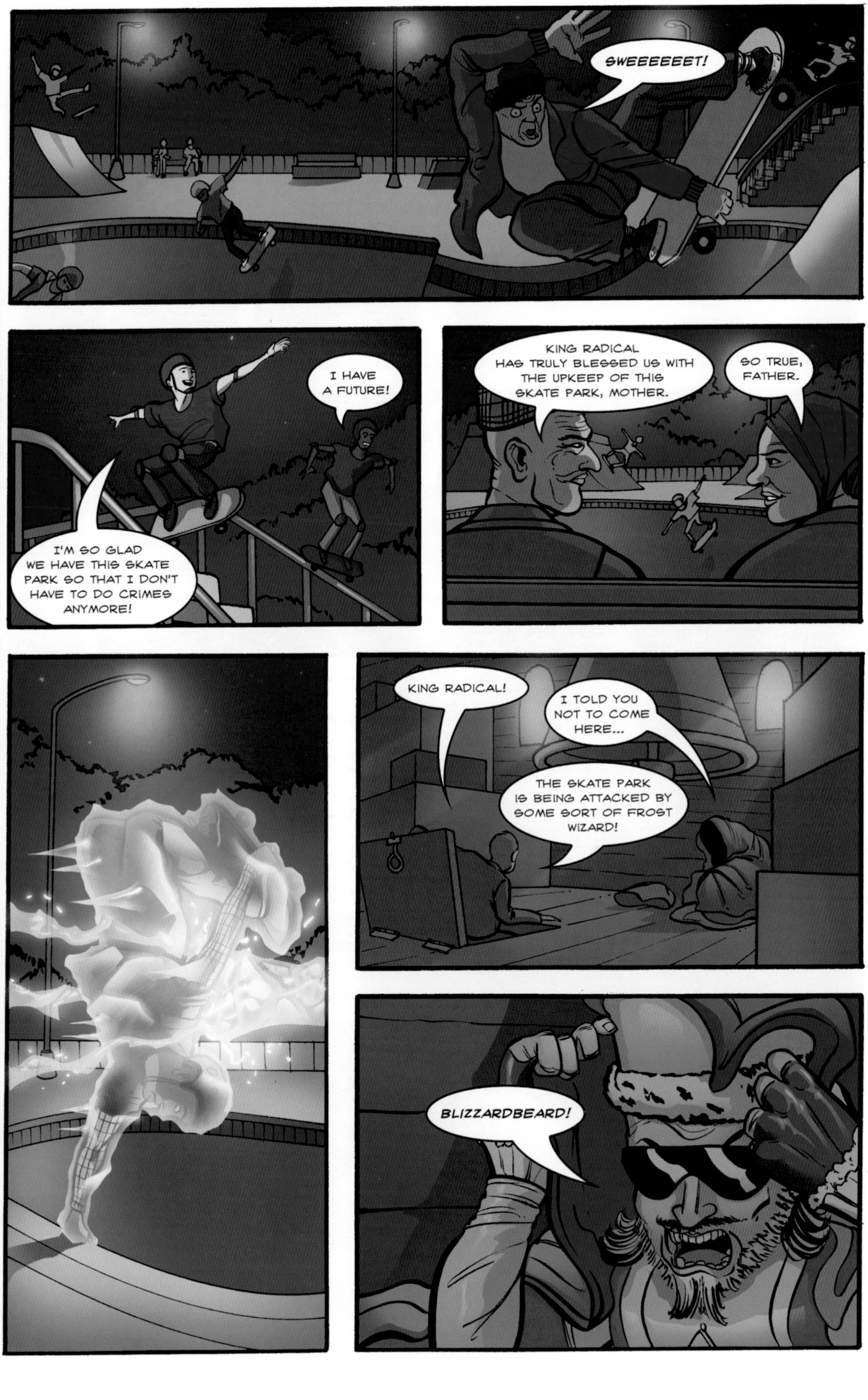
SWEEEEEET!
I HAVE A FUTURE!
I'M SO GLAD WE HAVE THIS SKATE PARK SO THAT I DON'T HAVE TO DO CRIMES ANYMORE!
KING RADICAL HAS TRULY BLESSED US WITH THE UPKEEP OF THIS SKATE PARK, MOTHER.
SO TRUE, FATHER.
KING RADICAL!
I TOLD YOU NOT TO COME HERE...
THE SKATE PARK IS BEING ATTACKED BY SOME SORT OF FROST WIZARD!
BLIZZARDBEARD!

Go ahead and yell that yourself at different points during your day. I think you'll find it quite satisfying.

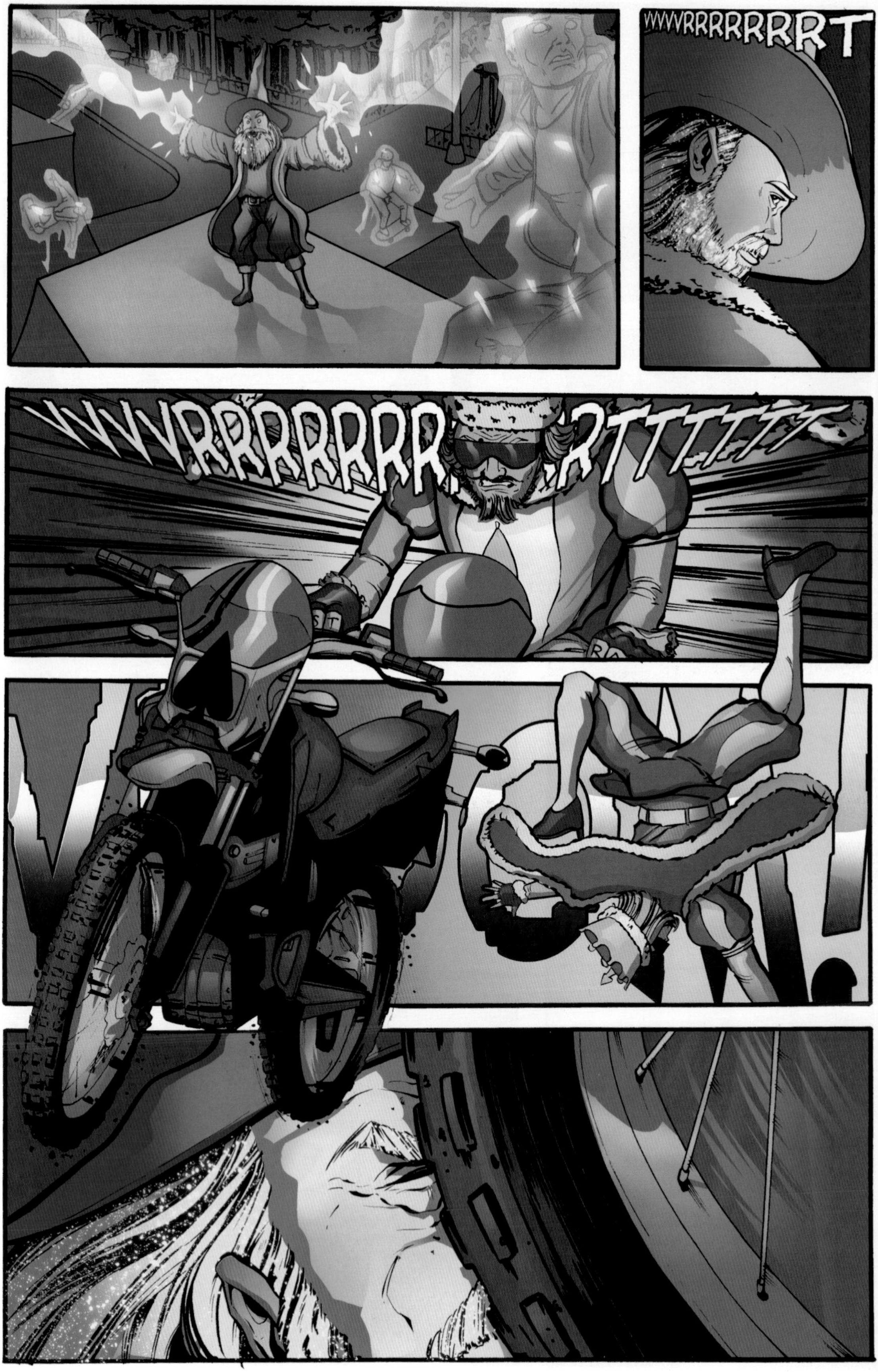
VVVVVRRRRRRRT
VVVVVRRRRRRRRRTTTTTTT

It was so tempting to give Blizzardbeard some Mr. Freeze–style one-liners, but I can't compete with Arnold, the master.

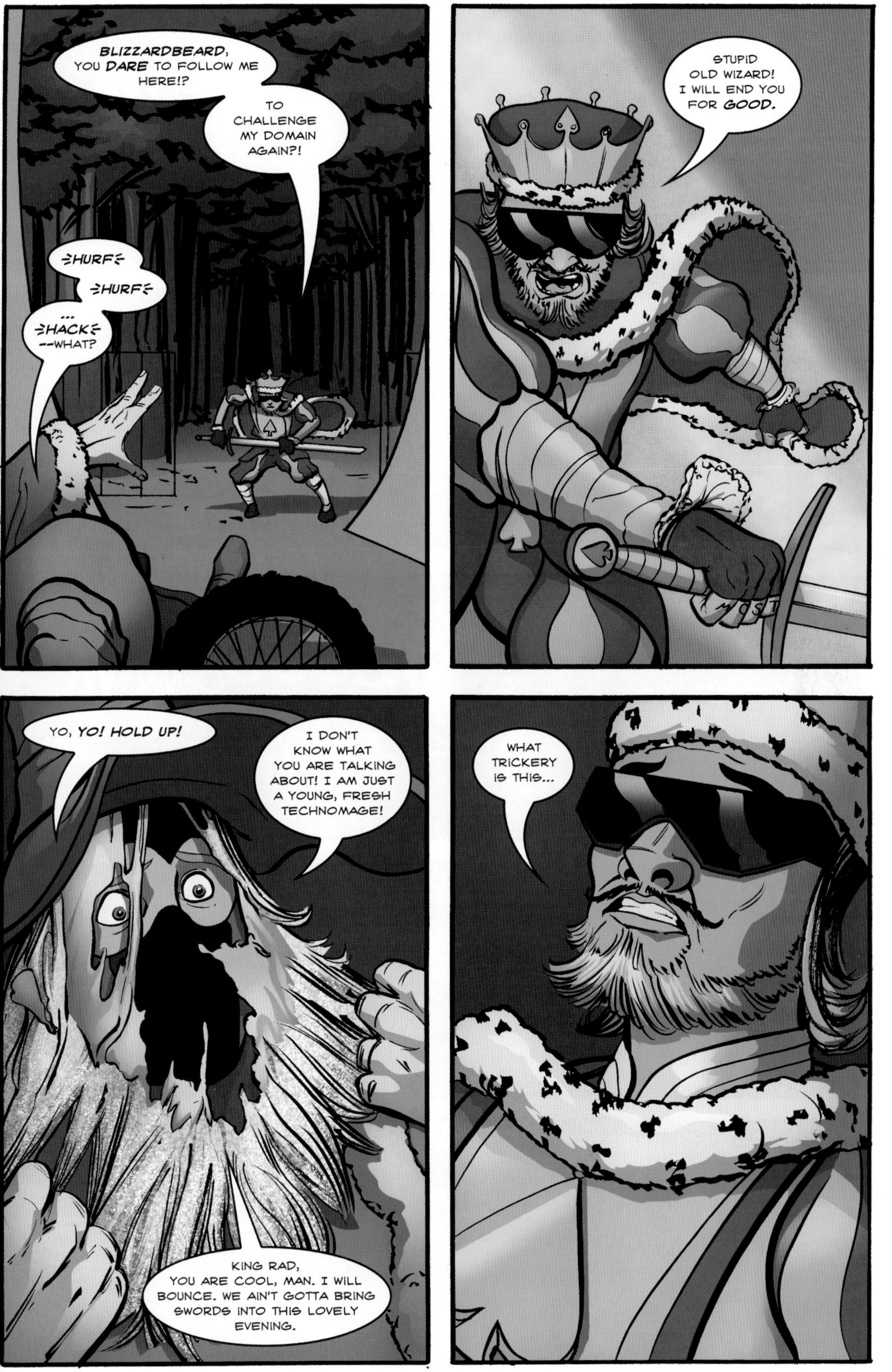

BLIZZARDBEARD, YOU DARE TO FOLLOW ME HERE!?
TO CHALLENGE MY DOMAIN AGAIN?!
HURF
HURF
... HACK --WHAT?
STUPID OLD WIZARD! I WILL END YOU FOR GOOD.
YO, YO! HOLD UP!
I DON'T KNOW WHAT YOU ARE TALKING ABOUT! I AM JUST A YOUNG, FRESH TECHNOMAGE!
KING RAD, YOU ARE COOL, MAN. I WILL BOUNCE. WE AIN'T GOTTA BRING SWORDS INTO THIS LOVELY EVENING.
WHAT TRICKERY IS THIS...

"Young, Fresh Technomage" was THE hip-hop jam of the summer of '91.

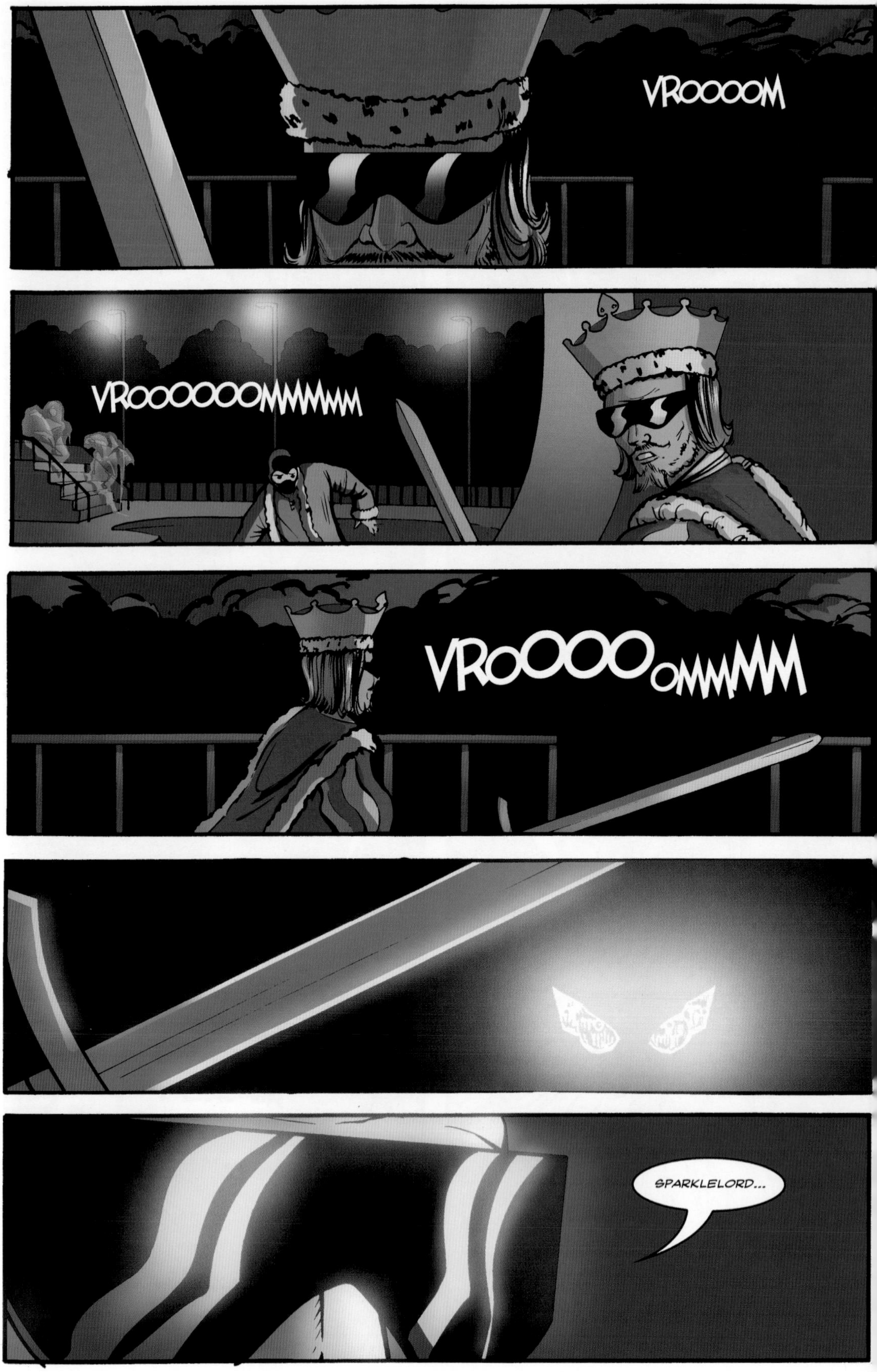
VROOOOM
VROOOOOOOMMMMMM
VROOOOOOMMMMM
SPARKLELORD...

Sparklelord is also a great name for a yogurt cup with a packet of flavor crystals attached.

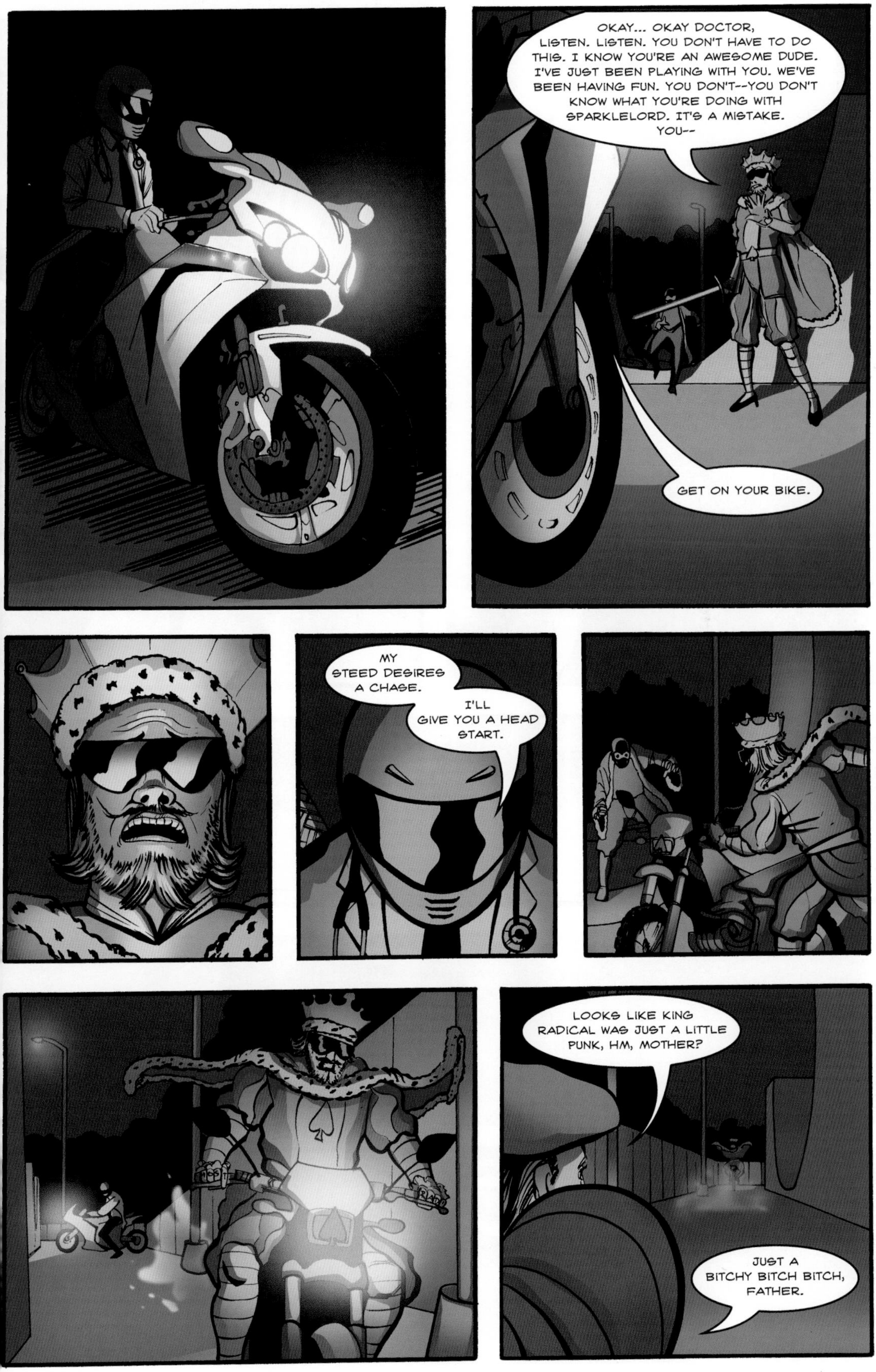
OKAY... OKAY DOCTOR, LISTEN. LISTEN. YOU DON'T HAVE TO DO THIS. I KNOW YOU'RE AN AWESOME DUDE. I'VE JUST BEEN PLAYING WITH YOU. WE'VE BEEN HAVING FUN. YOU DON'T--YOU DON'T KNOW WHAT YOU'RE DOING WITH SPARKLELORD. IT'S A MISTAKE. YOU--
GET ON YOUR BIKE.
MY STEED DESIRES A CHASE.
I'LL GIVE YOU A HEAD START.
LOOKS LIKE KING RADICAL WAS JUST A LITTLE PUNK, HM, MOTHER?
JUST A BITCHY BITCH BITCH, FATHER.

Look, I'm sorry. I know King Radical and Doc should have fought while driving their motorcycles around in one of the empty pools, but I FORGOT.

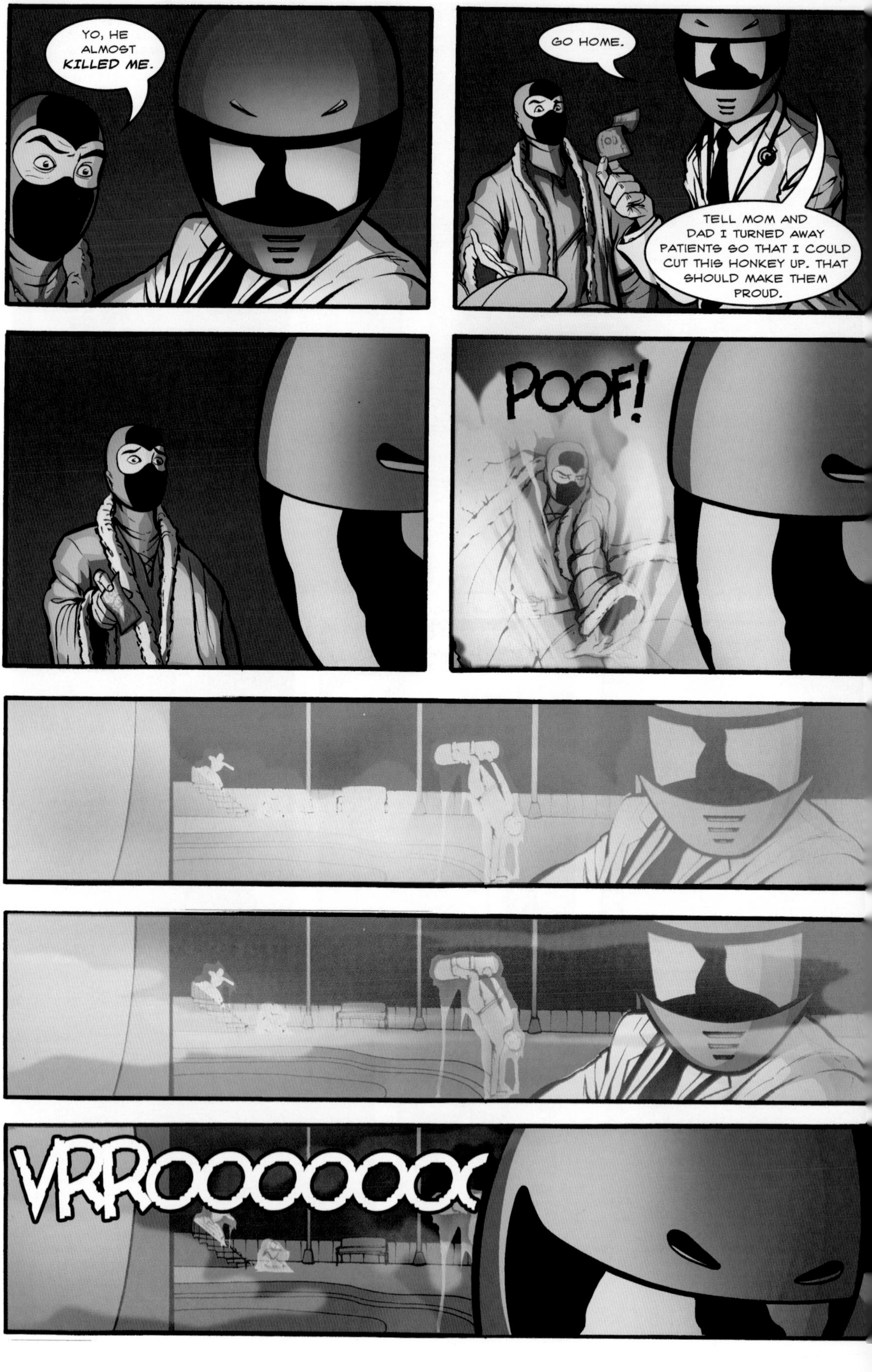
YO, HE ALMOST KILLED ME.
GO HOME.
TELL MOM AND DAD I TURNED AWAY PATIENTS SO THAT I COULD CUT THIS HONKEY UP. THAT SHOULD MAKE THEM PROUD.
POOF!
VRROOOOOOO

Dr. McNinja steps forward slightly and farts.

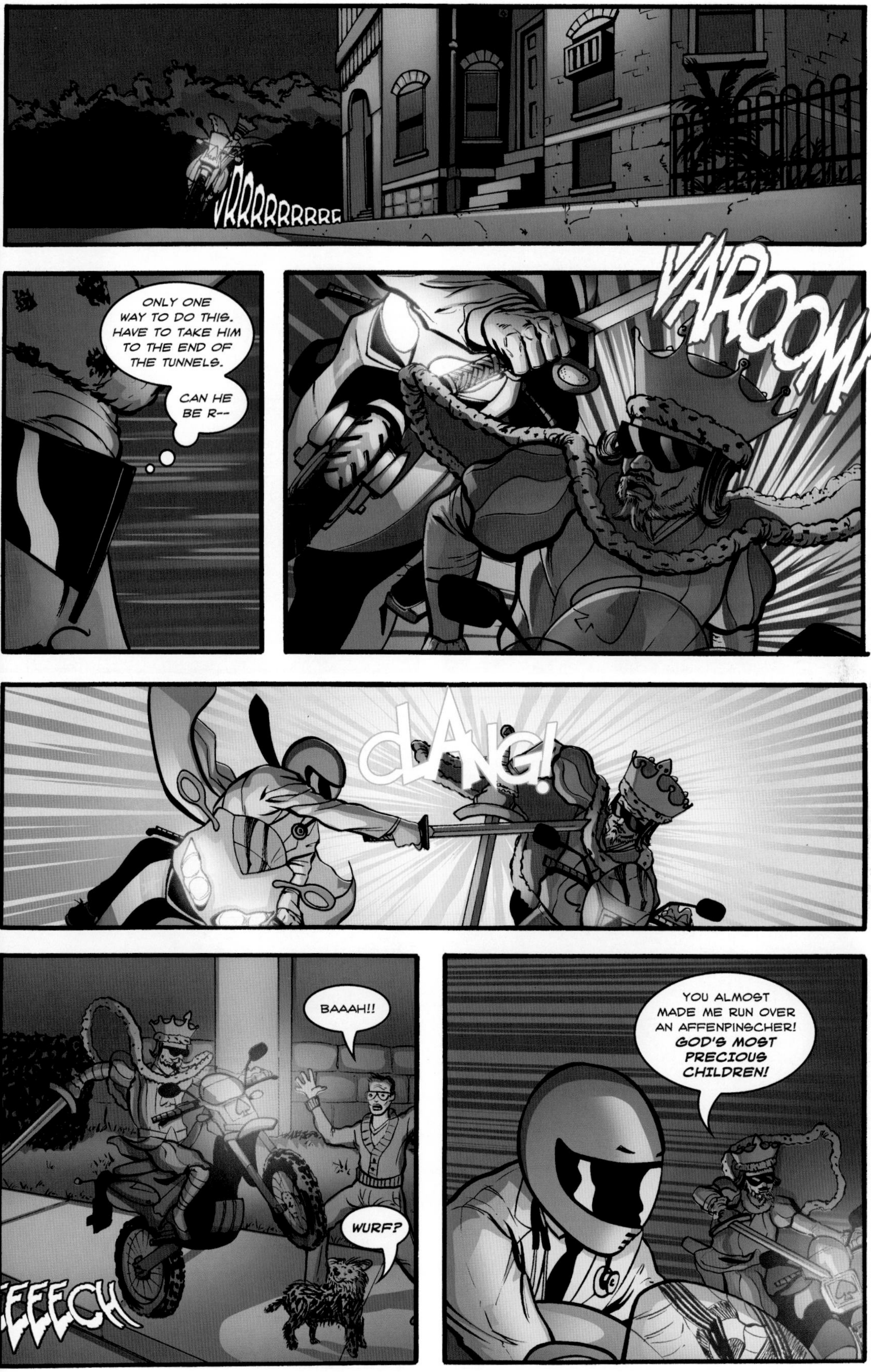
VRRRRRRRRRR
ONLY ONE WAY TO DO THIS. HAVE TO TAKE HIM TO THE END OF THE TUNNELS.
CAN HE BE R--
VAROOM!
CLANG!
BAAAH!!
WURF?
EEECH
YOU ALMOST MADE ME RUN OVER AN AFFENPINSCHER! GOD'S MOST PRECIOUS CHILDREN!

OR a DOG with a FUNNY NAME I looked up on THE WIKIPEDIA LIST OF DOG BREEDS.

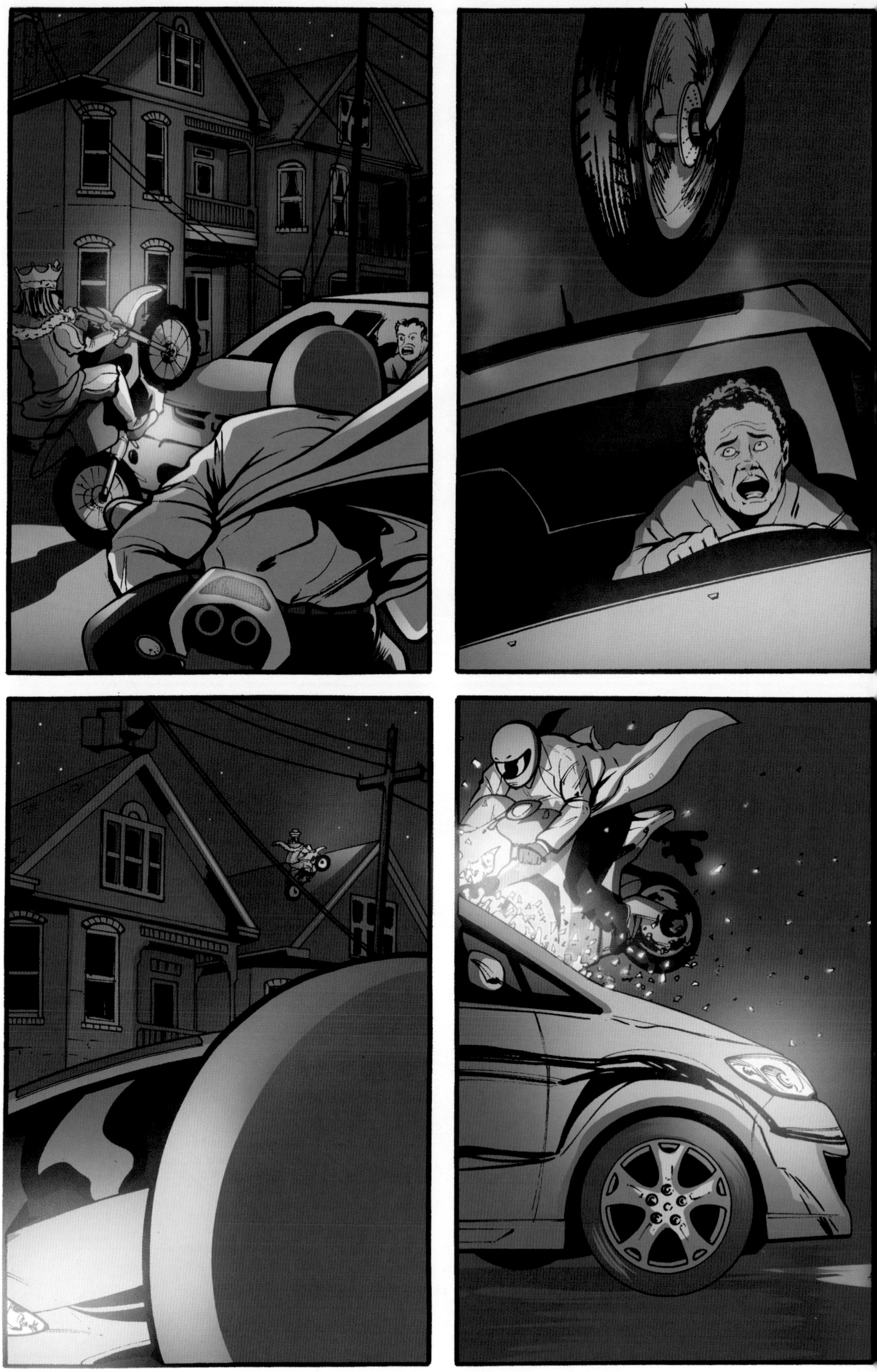

Oh, and both of the bikes are magical, and you don't need to have a hand on the throttle to make them go.

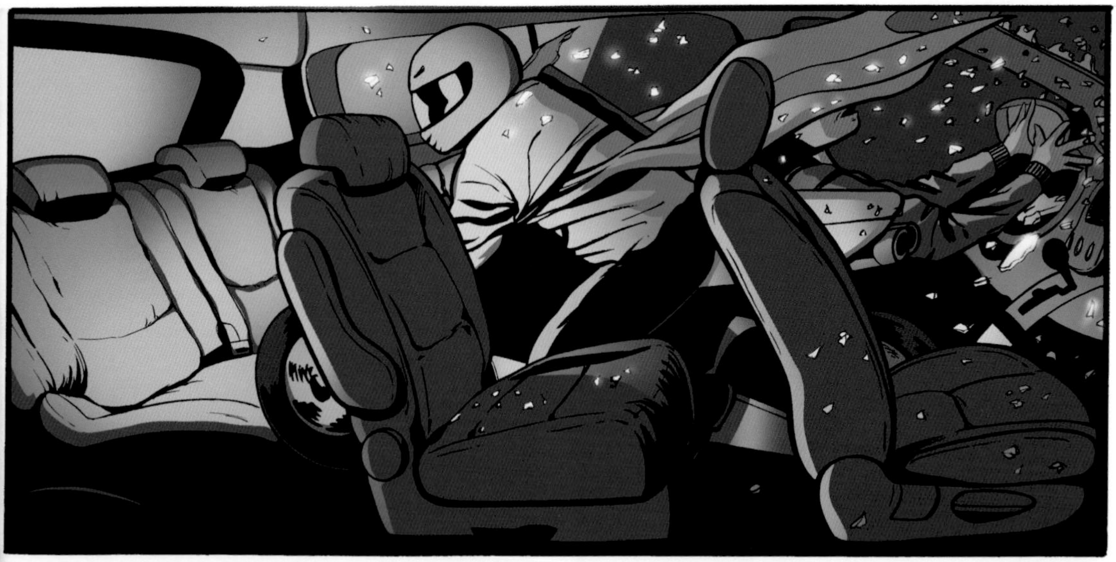

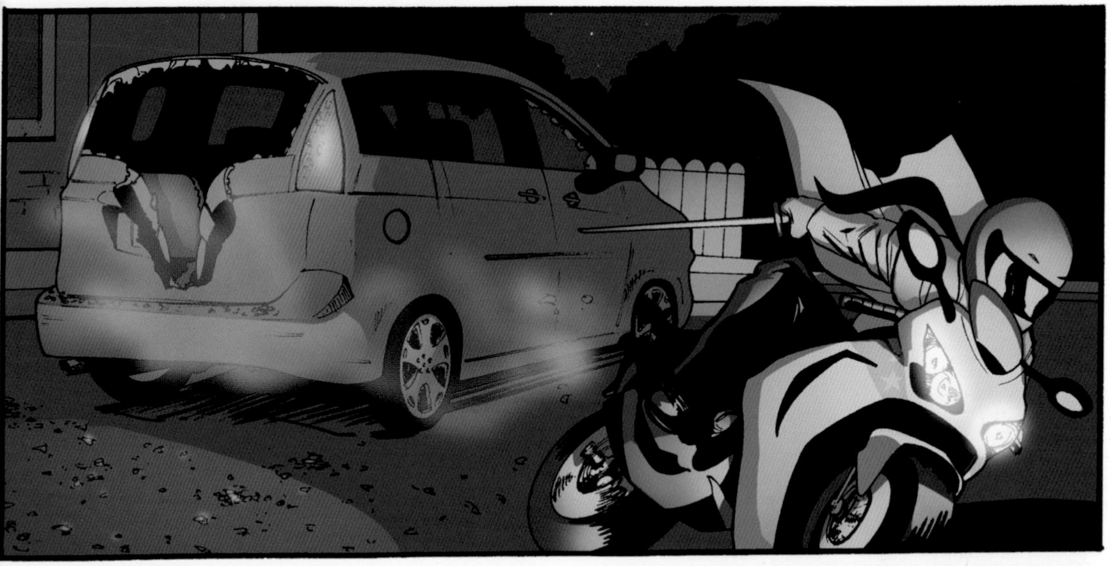

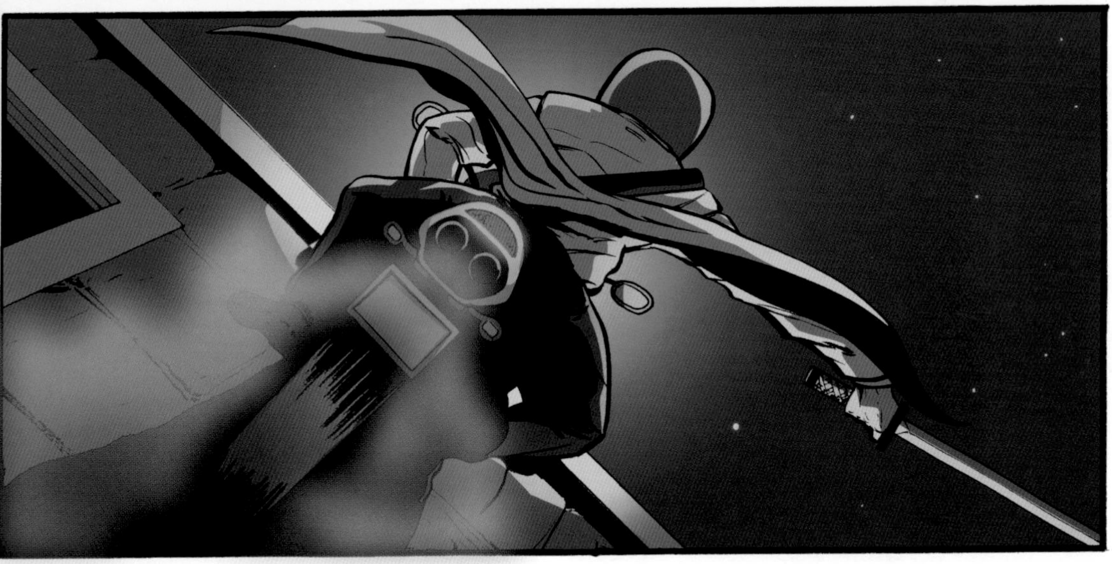

Good amount of space in that van.

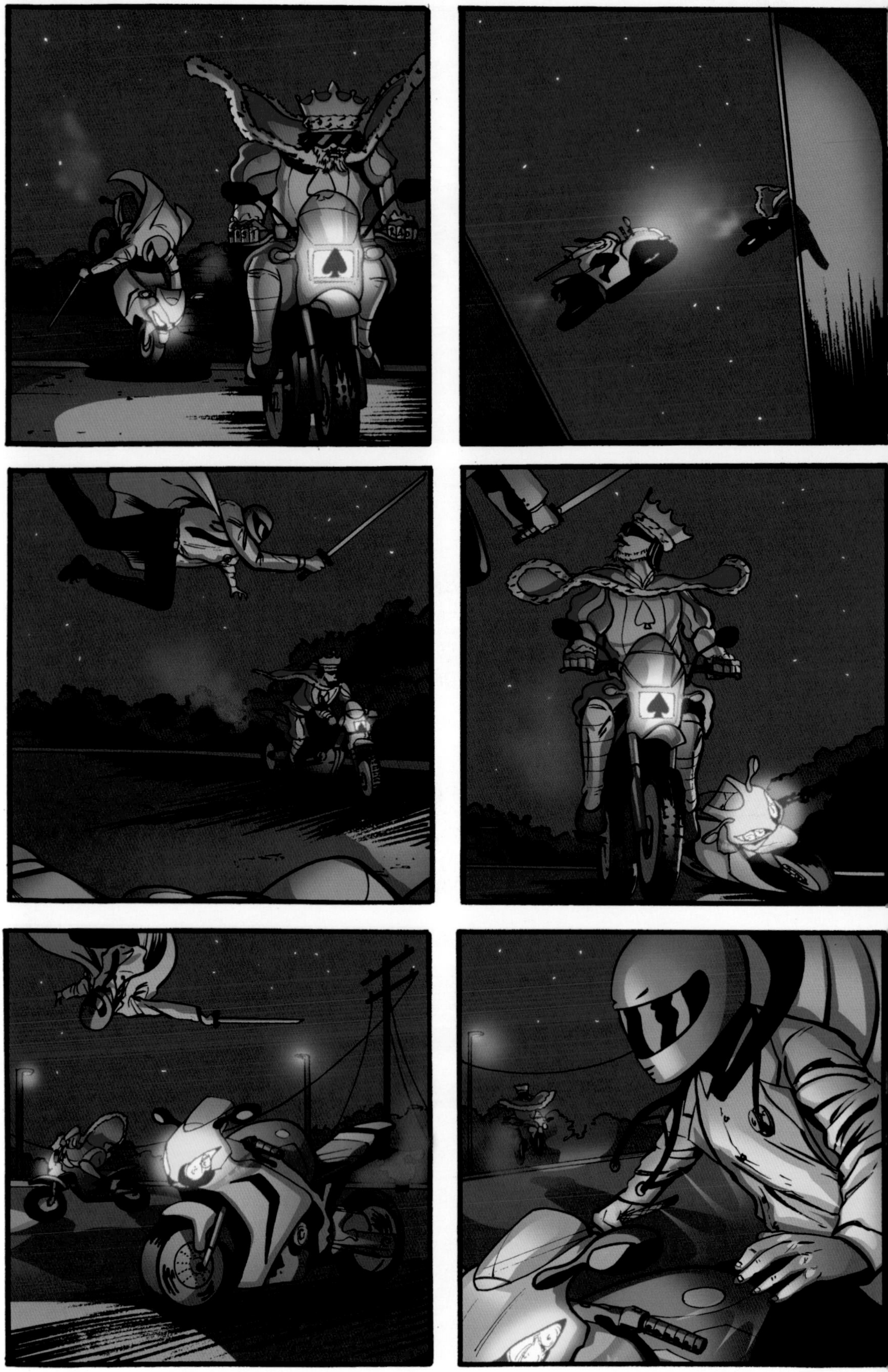

Uh, yeah, so listen. I can't come up with a good alt text here because I just got off a red-eye flight and I have "Combination Pizza Hut and Taco Bell" stuck in my head.

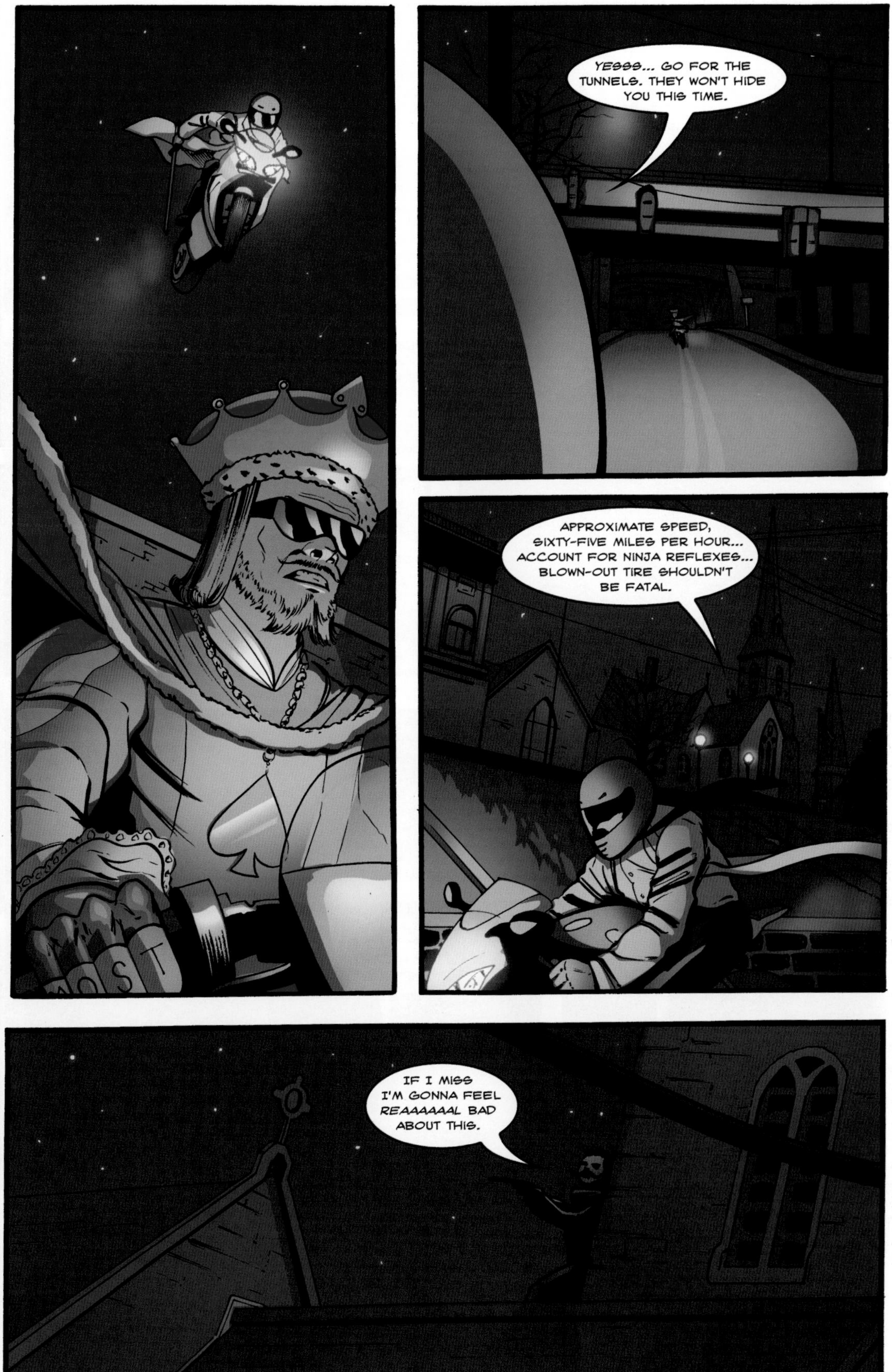

YESSS... GO FOR THE TUNNELS. THEY WON'T HIDE YOU THIS TIME.
APPROXIMATE SPEED, SIXTY-FIVE MILES PER HOUR... ACCOUNT FOR NINJA REFLEXES... BLOWN-OUT TIRE SHOULDN'T BE FATAL.
IF I MISS I'M GONNA FEEL *REAAAAAAL* BAD ABOUT THIS.

OR King Radical is headed for the Allegany Center for Massage, which is also on that street.

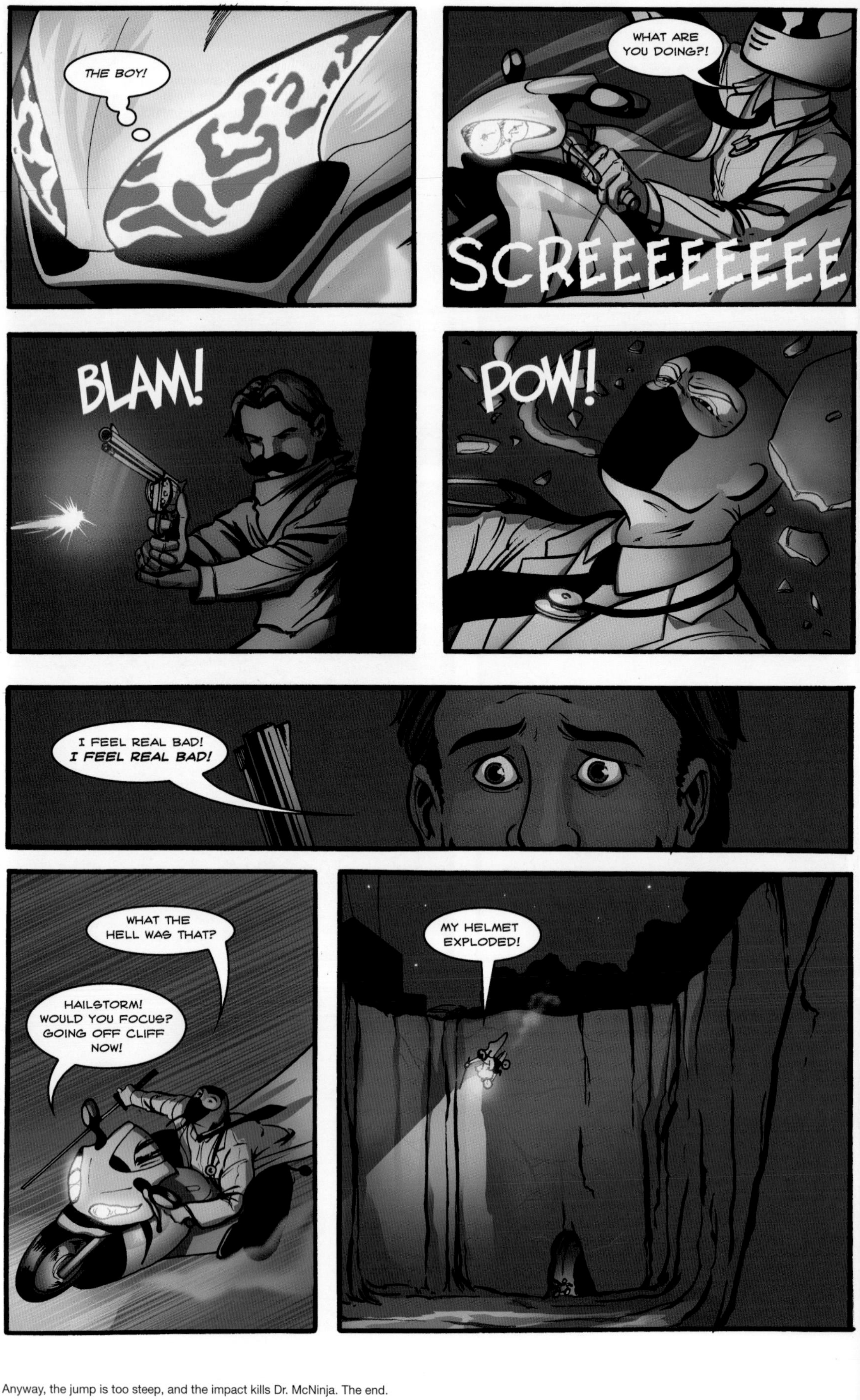
THE BOY!
WHAT ARE YOU DOING?!
SCREEEEEEEEE
BLAM!
POW!
I FEEL REAL BAD!
I FEEL REAL BAD!
WHAT THE HELL WAS THAT?
HAILSTORM! WOULD YOU FOCUS? GOING OFF CLIFF NOW!
MY HELMET EXPLODED!

Anyway, the jump is too steep, and the impact kills Dr. McNinja. The end.

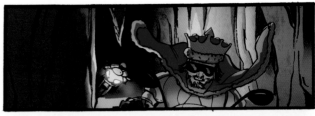

BLARALBGL.

HOPE *THAT* NEVER MAKES IT TO THE SURFACE.

MESS UP THE WHOLE ECOSYSTEM.

Hairy octopus.

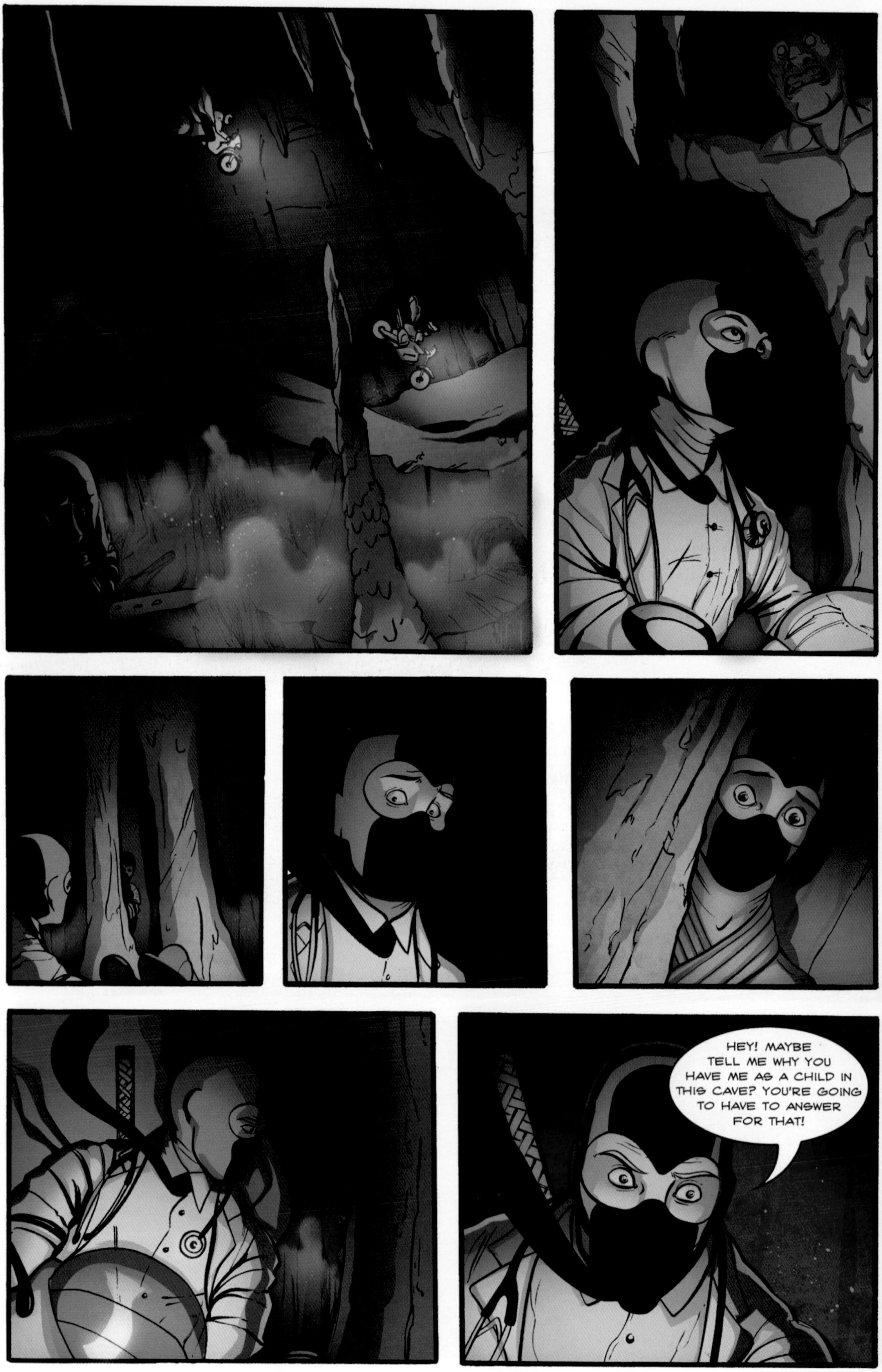
HEY! MAYBE TELL ME WHY YOU HAVE ME AS A CHILD IN THIS CAVE? YOU'RE GOING TO HAVE TO ANSWER FOR THAT!

I . . . I don't want him to have to fight that hairy octopus!

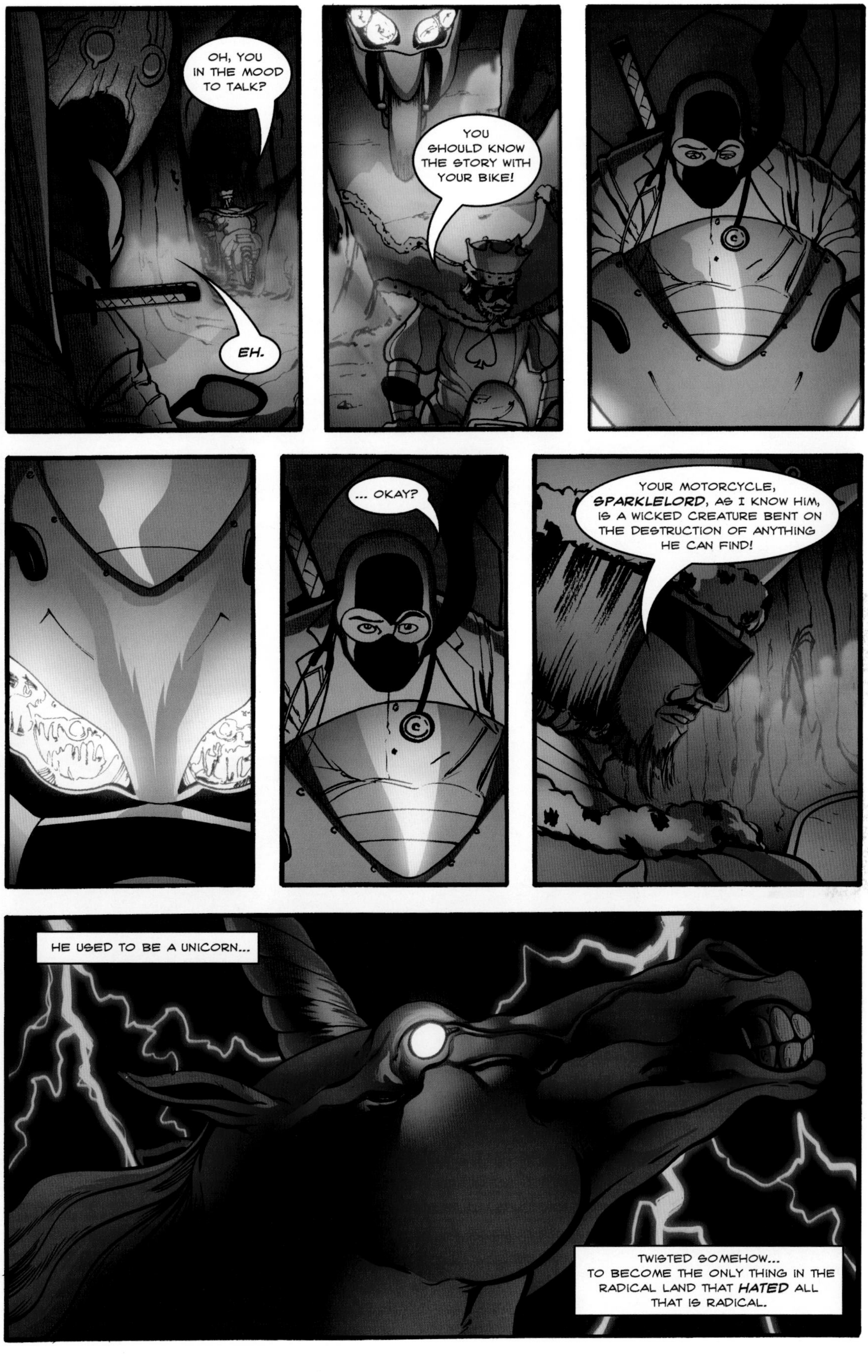
OH, YOU IN THE MOOD TO TALK?
EH.
YOU SHOULD KNOW THE STORY WITH YOUR BIKE!
... OKAY?
YOUR MOTORCYCLE, SPARKLELORD, AS I KNOW HIM, IS A WICKED CREATURE BENT ON THE DESTRUCTION OF ANYTHING HE CAN FIND!
HE USED TO BE A UNICORN...
TWISTED SOMEHOW... TO BECOME THE ONLY THING IN THE RADICAL LAND THAT HATED ALL THAT IS RADICAL.

I am absolutely positive that nobody saw this coming.

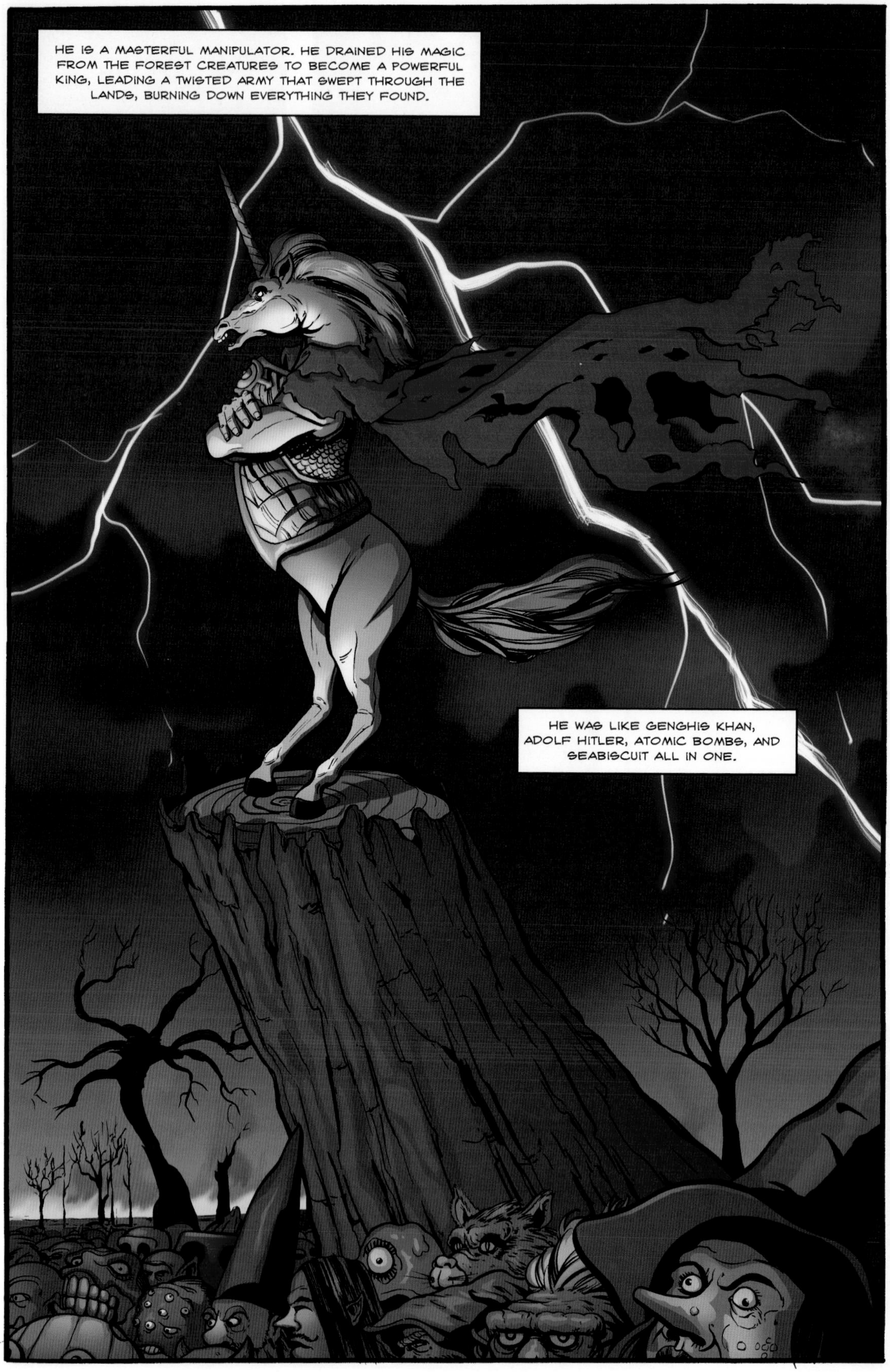
HE IS A MASTERFUL MANIPULATOR. HE DRAINED HIS MAGIC FROM THE FOREST CREATURES TO BECOME A POWERFUL KING, LEADING A TWISTED ARMY THAT SWEPT THROUGH THE LANDS, BURNING DOWN EVERYTHING THEY FOUND.
HE WAS LIKE GENGHIS KHAN, ADOLF HITLER, ATOMIC BOMBS, AND SEABISCUIT ALL IN ONE.

Somewhere, somebody has my lost notepad that describes this page, "evil horse king, all bipedal." Also they are a jerk because my name and number are in the notepad.

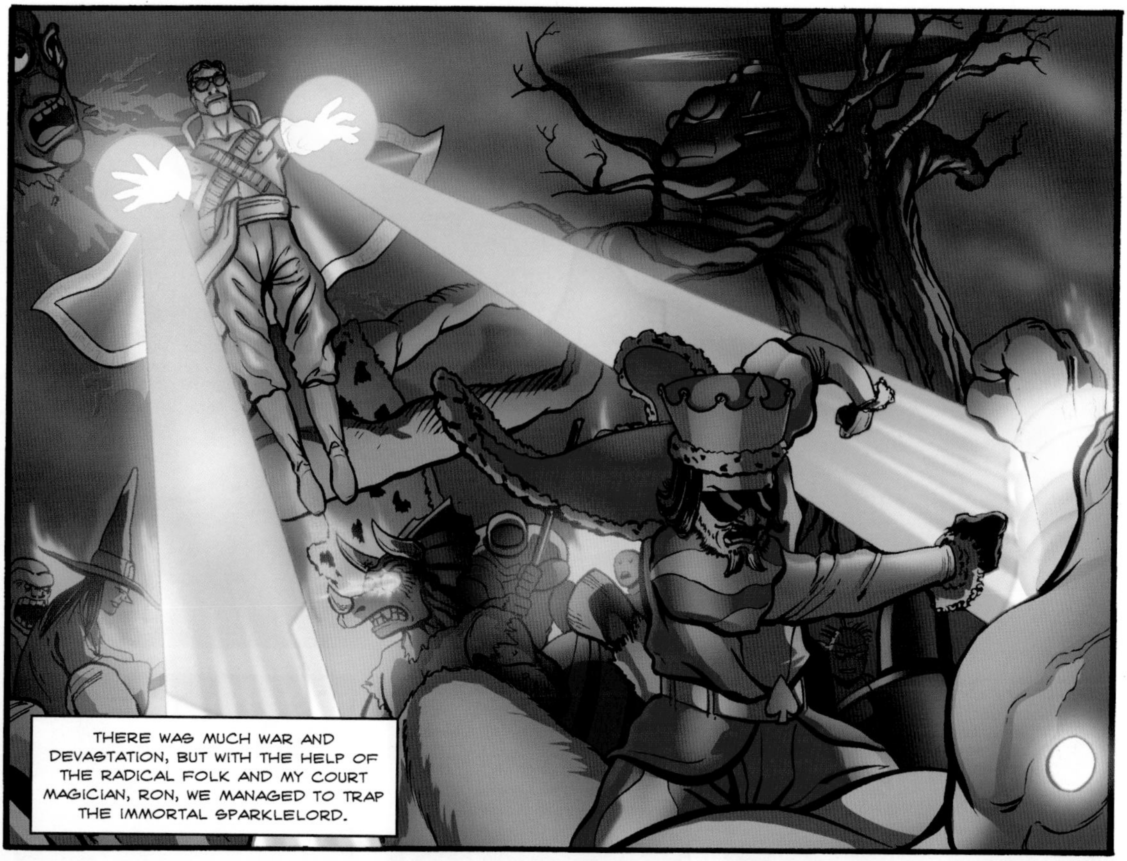
THERE WAS MUCH WAR AND DEVASTATION, BUT WITH THE HELP OF THE RADICAL FOLK AND MY COURT MAGICIAN, RON, WE MANAGED TO TRAP THE IMMORTAL SPARKLELORD.

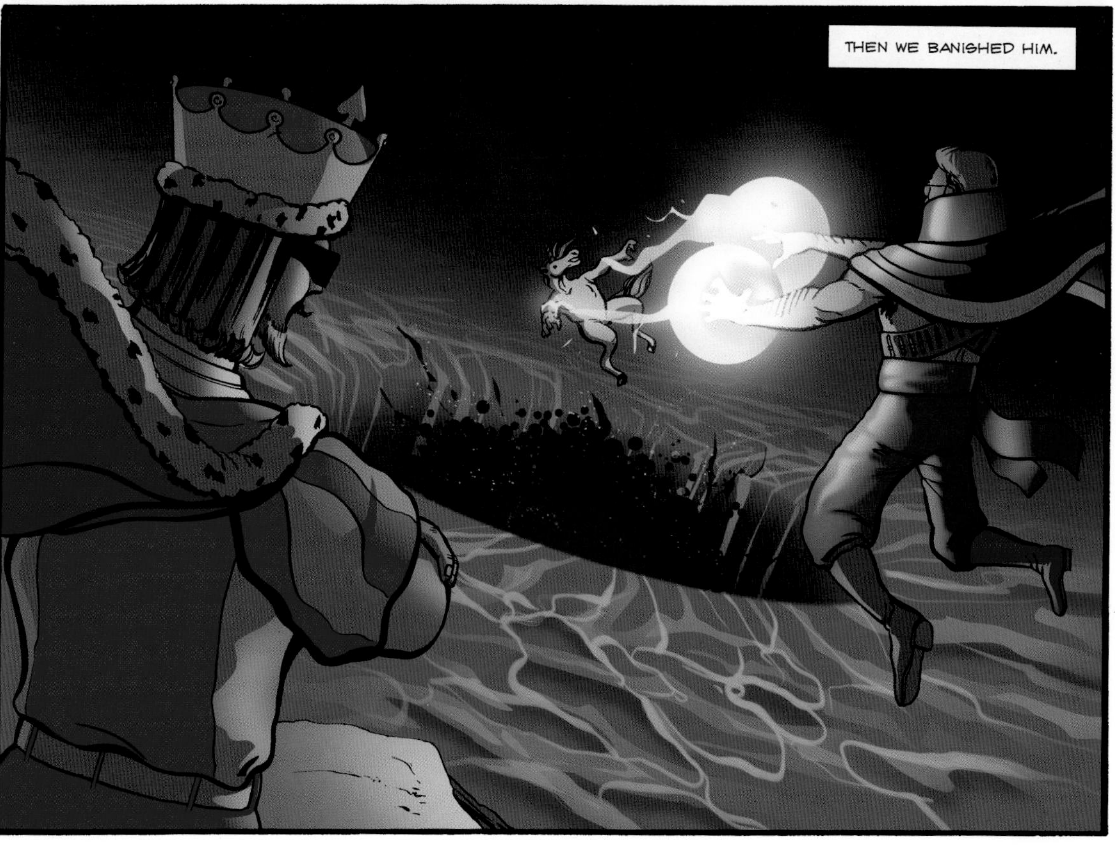
THEN WE BANISHED HIM.

Two things. First, Ron Wizard is my *City of Heroes* character, and he's a badass. Second, top right, that's an ent with a helicopter head.

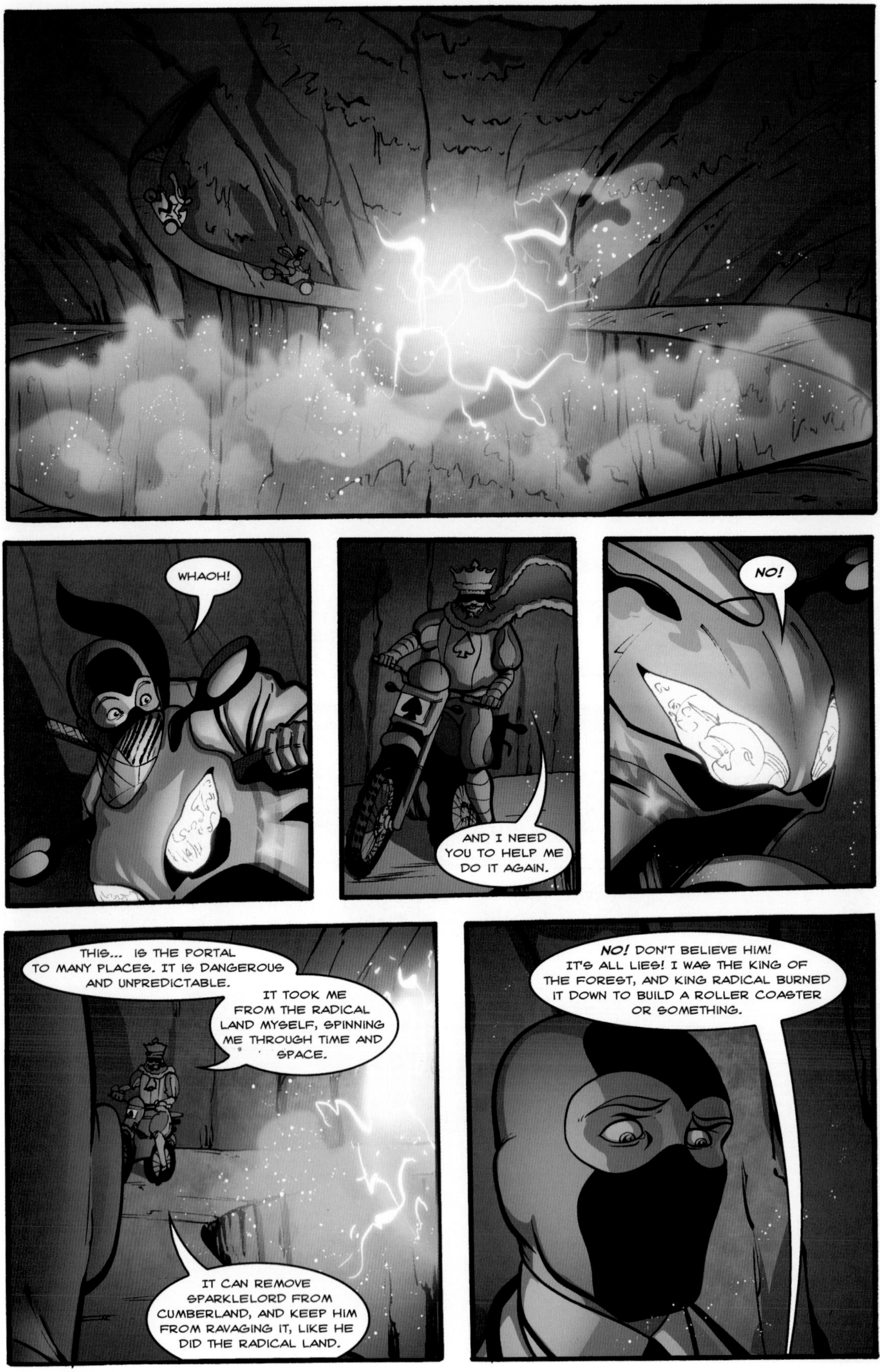
WHAOH!
AND I NEED YOU TO HELP ME DO IT AGAIN.
NO!
THIS... IS THE PORTAL TO MANY PLACES. IT IS DANGEROUS AND UNPREDICTABLE.
IT TOOK ME FROM THE RADICAL LAND MYSELF, SPINNING ME THROUGH TIME AND SPACE.
IT CAN REMOVE SPARKLELORD FROM CUMBERLAND, AND KEEP HIM FROM RAVAGING IT, LIKE HE DID THE RADICAL LAND.
NO! DON'T BELIEVE HIM! IT'S ALL LIES! I WAS THE KING OF THE FOREST, AND KING RADICAL BURNED IT DOWN TO BUILD A ROLLER COASTER OR SOMETHING.

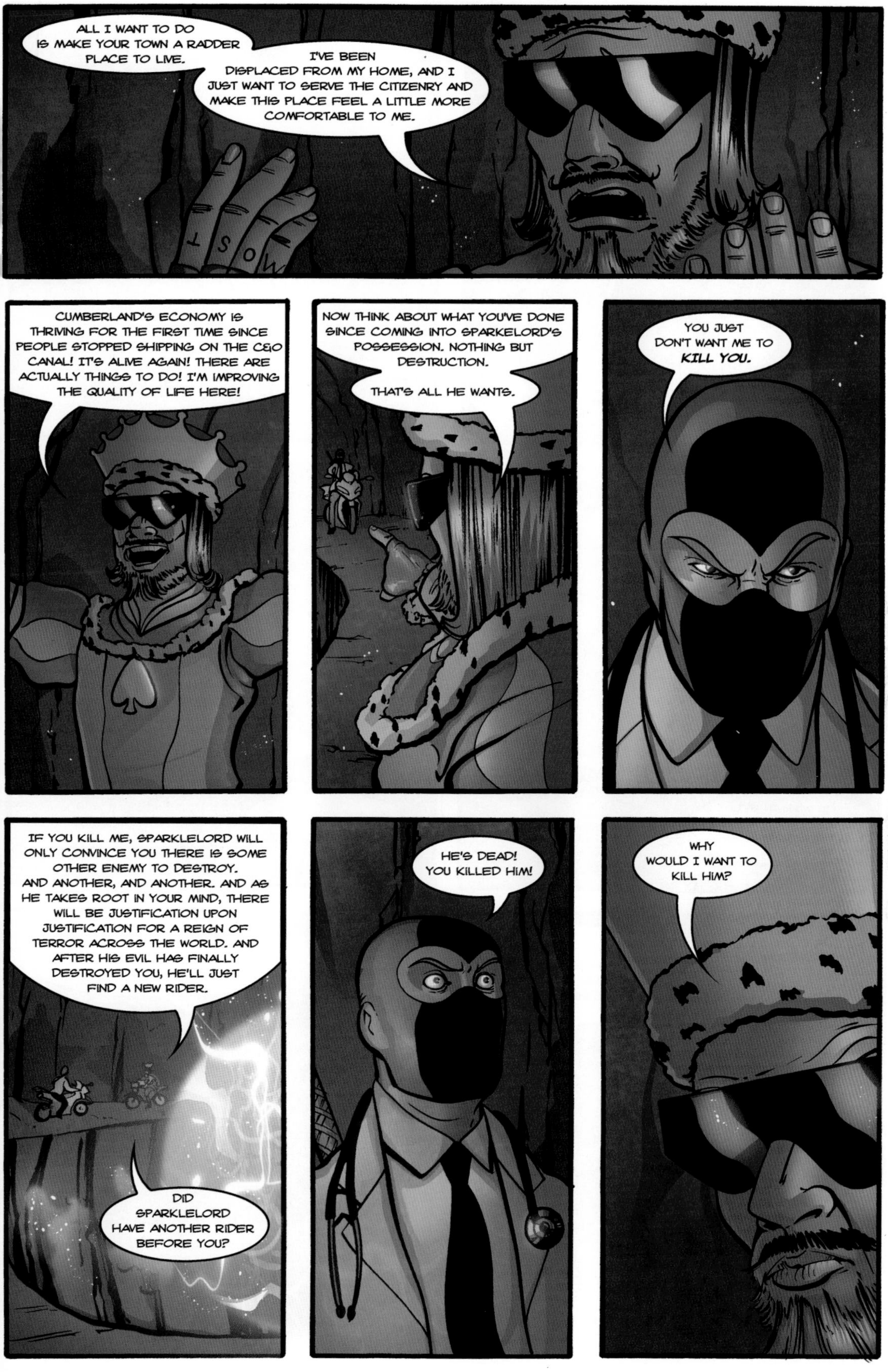
ALL I WANT TO DO IS MAKE YOUR TOWN A RADDER PLACE TO LIVE.
I'VE BEEN DISPLACED FROM MY HOME, AND I JUST WANT TO SERVE THE CITIZENRY AND MAKE THIS PLACE FEEL A LITTLE MORE COMFORTABLE TO ME.
CUMBERLAND'S ECONOMY IS THRIVING FOR THE FIRST TIME SINCE PEOPLE STOPPED SHIPPING ON THE C&O CANAL! IT'S ALIVE AGAIN! THERE ARE ACTUALLY THINGS TO DO! I'M IMPROVING THE QUALITY OF LIFE HERE!
NOW THINK ABOUT WHAT YOU'VE DONE SINCE COMING INTO SPARKELORD'S POSSESSION. NOTHING BUT DESTRUCTION.
THAT'S ALL HE WANTS.
YOU JUST DON'T WANT ME TO KILL YOU.
IF YOU KILL ME, SPARKLELORD WILL ONLY CONVINCE YOU THERE IS SOME OTHER ENEMY TO DESTROY. AND ANOTHER, AND ANOTHER. AND AS HE TAKES ROOT IN YOUR MIND, THERE WILL BE JUSTIFICATION UPON JUSTIFICATION FOR A REIGN OF TERROR ACROSS THE WORLD. AND AFTER HIS EVIL HAS FINALLY DESTROYED YOU, HE'LL JUST FIND A NEW RIDER.
DID SPARKLELORD HAVE ANOTHER RIDER BEFORE YOU?
HE'S DEAD! YOU KILLED HIM!
WHY WOULD I WANT TO KILL HIM?

Why dontcha take your fish-oil pills and think of THAT!

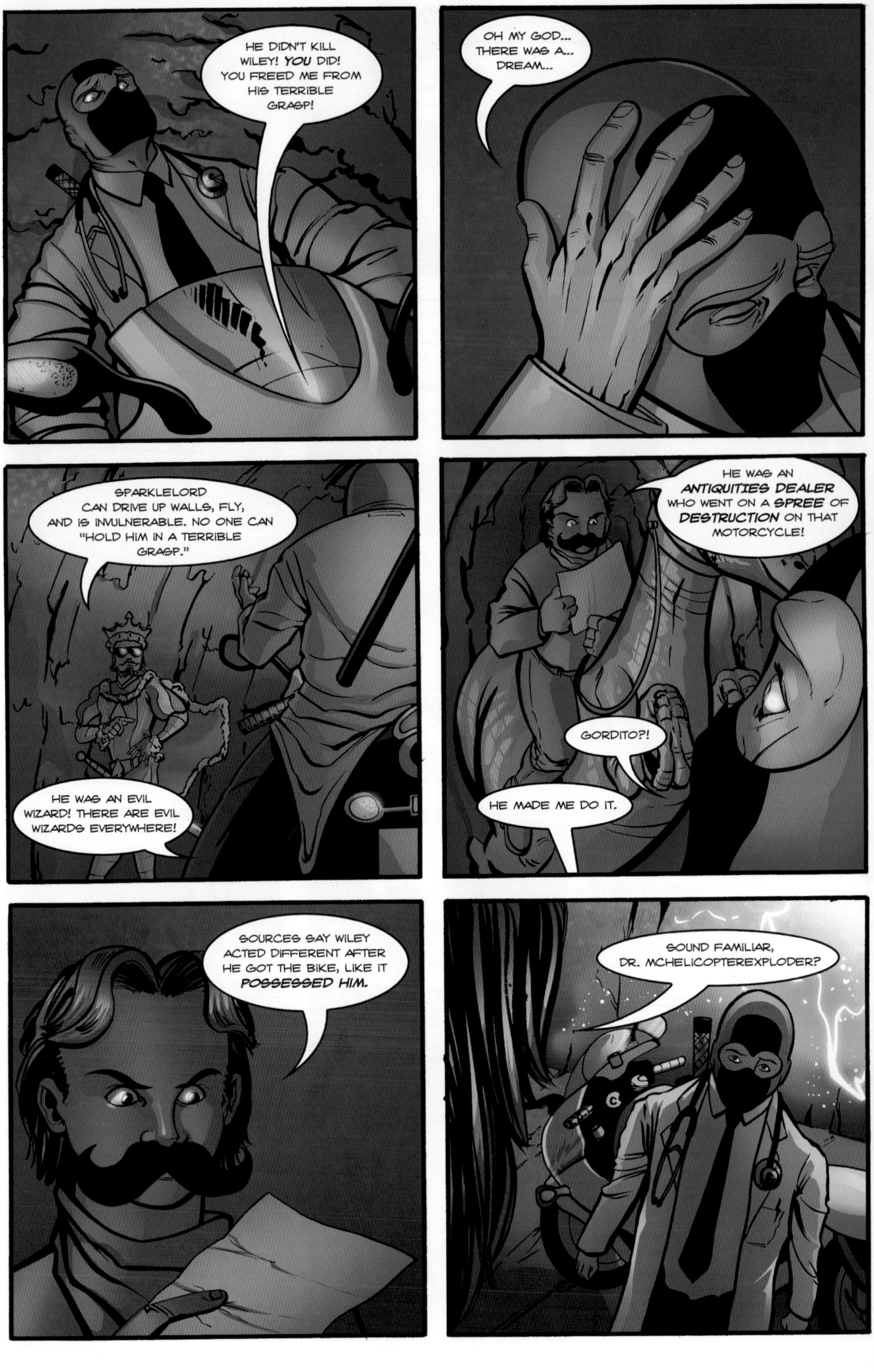
HE DIDN'T KILL WILEY! YOU DID! YOU FREED ME FROM HIS TERRIBLE GRASP!
OH MY GOD... THERE WAS A... DREAM...
SPARKLELORD CAN DRIVE UP WALLS, FLY, AND IS INVULNERABLE. NO ONE CAN "HOLD HIM IN A TERRIBLE GRASP."
HE WAS AN EVIL WIZARD! THERE ARE EVIL WIZARDS EVERYWHERE!
HE WAS AN ANTIQUITIES DEALER WHO WENT ON A SPREE OF DESTRUCTION ON THAT MOTORCYCLE!
GORDITO?!
HE MADE ME DO IT.
SOURCES SAY WILEY ACTED DIFFERENT AFTER HE GOT THE BIKE, LIKE IT POSSESSED HIM.
SOUND FAMILIAR, DR. MCHELICOPTEREXPLODER?

To be fair, Doc always WANTED to blow up helicopters. The bike just gave him the means.

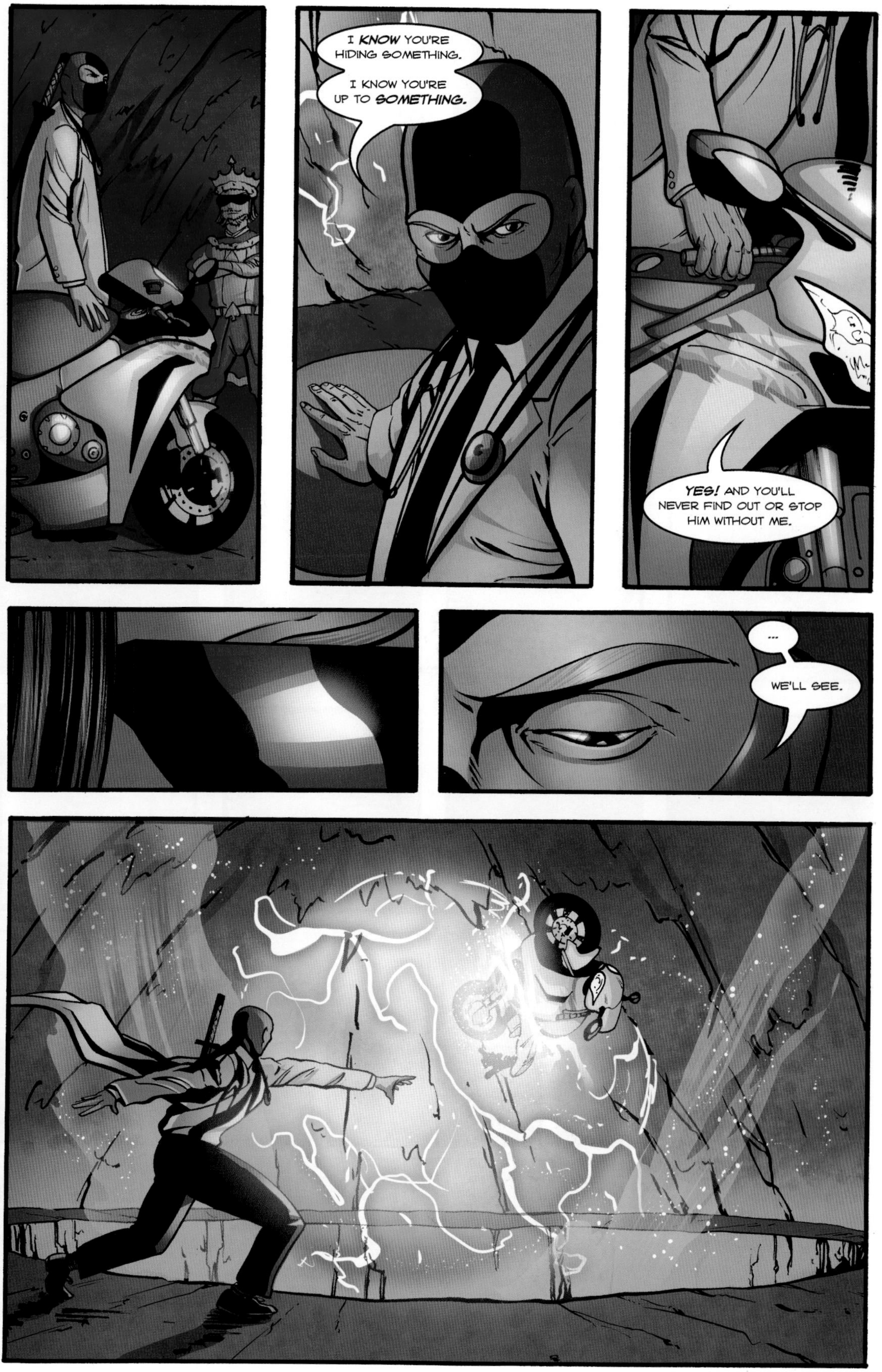
I KNOW YOU'RE HIDING SOMETHING.
I KNOW YOU'RE UP TO SOMETHING.
YES! AND YOU'LL NEVER FIND OUT OR STOP HIM WITHOUT ME.
...
WE'LL SEE.

Not exactly a church bell, but we make do.

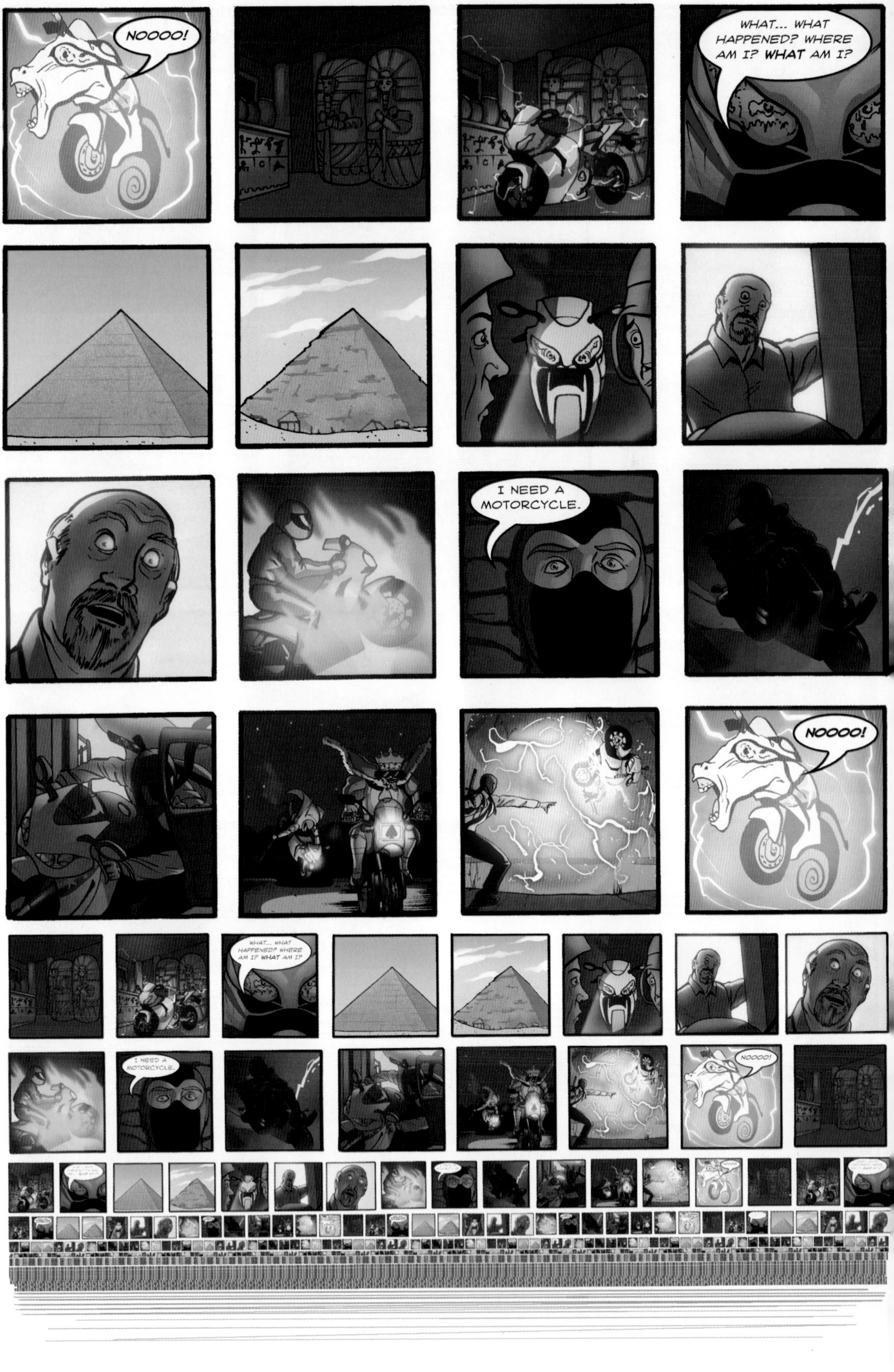
NOOOO!
WHAT... WHAT HAPPENED? WHERE AM I? WHAT AM I?
I NEED A MOTORCYCLE.
NOOOO!
WHAT... WHAT HAPPENED? WHERE AM I? WHAT AM I?
I NEED A MOTORCYCLE.
NOOOO!

There's a hilarious joke that I snuck into panel 1753.

DOCTOR...

THAT MUST HAVE BEEN EXCRUCIATING. SPARKLELORD HAS AN IRRESISTIBLE PULL. I'M GLAD YOU DECIDED AS YOU DID.

...

BECAUSE HE WAS RIGHT.

WHAT?!

HA HA!

NO MATTER HOW RAD YOU GET... YOU WILL NEVER GET RADICAL! AHAHAHAHA!

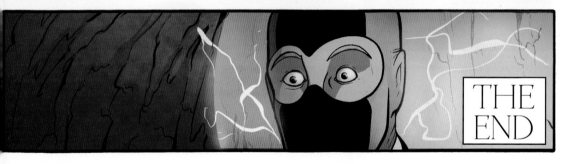

THE END

You like that? A little play on the opening title? Eh? Eh? Pretty good? I AM A WRITER.

DR. MCNINJA'S FINAL THOUGHTS

JUST... BE SURE YOUR HAND RUNS ALONG THE LEFT WALL, AND WE'LL EVENTUALLY MAKE IT TO THE ENTRANCE.

IT'S SCIENCE.

SO... YOUR MOTORCYCLE WAS A UNICORN, HUH?

YEP. TURNED OUT IT WAS A UNICORN.

DON'T UNICORNS ONLY APPROACH VIRGINS?

UH... WELL, SPARKLELORD WAS *TWISTED*. SO YOU KNOW, THAT HAS TO MAKE ME LIKE TOTALLY...

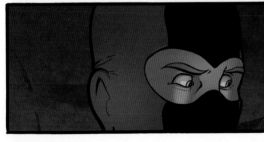

I DON'T LIKE ADDRESSING MATURE ISSUES IN MY COMIC.

Also you're twelve.

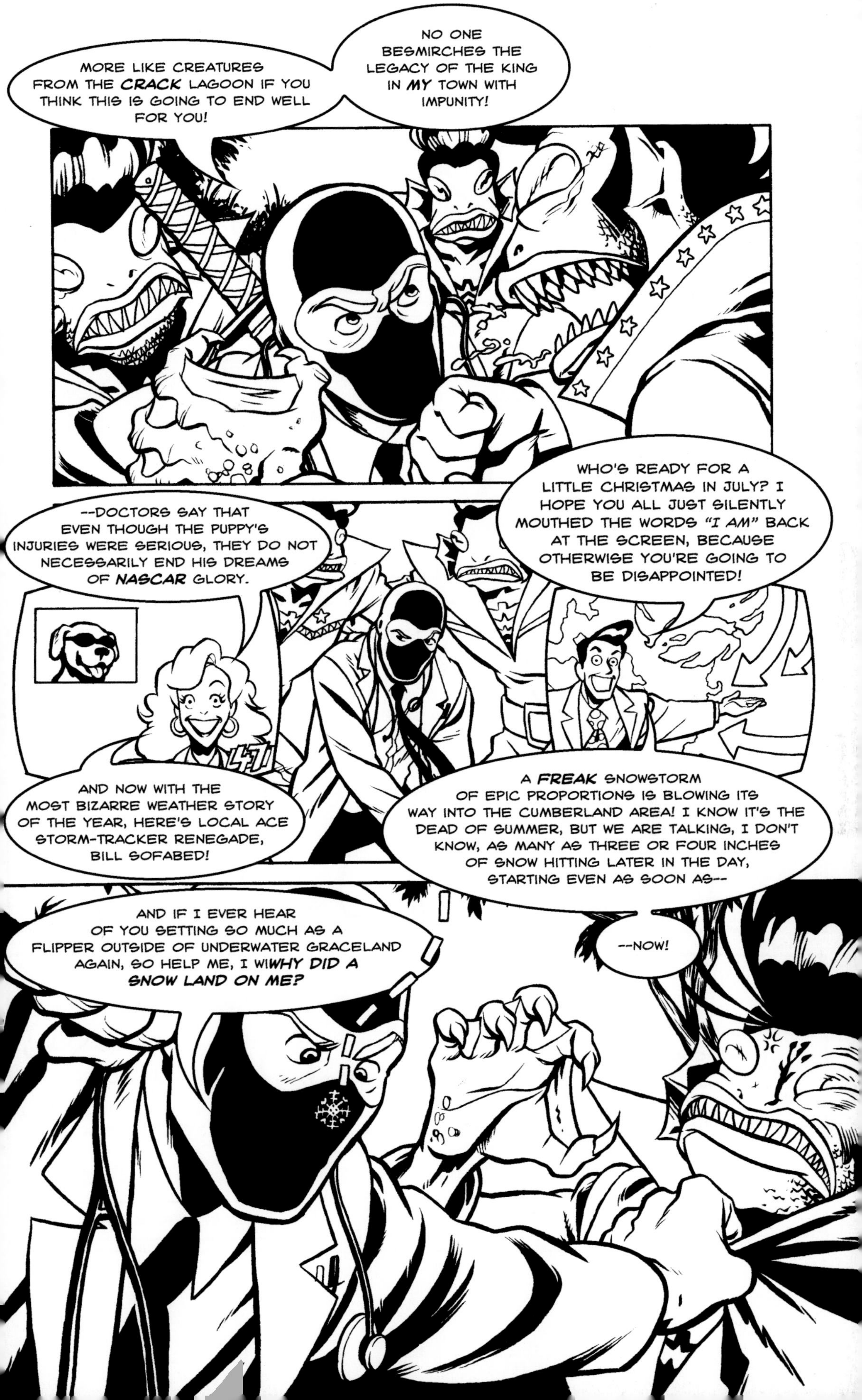
MORE LIKE CREATURES FROM THE *CRACK* LAGOON IF YOU THINK THIS IS GOING TO END WELL FOR YOU!
NO ONE BESMIRCHES THE LEGACY OF THE KING IN *MY* TOWN WITH IMPUNITY!
--DOCTORS SAY THAT EVEN THOUGH THE PUPPY'S INJURIES WERE SERIOUS, THEY DO NOT NECESSARILY END HIS DREAMS OF *NASCAR* GLORY.
AND NOW WITH THE MOST BIZARRE WEATHER STORY OF THE YEAR, HERE'S LOCAL ACE STORM-TRACKER RENEGADE, BILL SOFABED!
WHO'S READY FOR A LITTLE CHRISTMAS IN JULY? I HOPE YOU ALL JUST SILENTLY MOUTHED THE WORDS *"I AM"* BACK AT THE SCREEN, BECAUSE OTHERWISE YOU'RE GOING TO BE DISAPPOINTED!
A *FREAK* SNOWSTORM OF EPIC PROPORTIONS IS BLOWING ITS WAY INTO THE CUMBERLAND AREA! I KNOW IT'S THE DEAD OF SUMMER, BUT WE ARE TALKING, I DON'T KNOW, AS MANY AS THREE OR FOUR INCHES OF SNOW HITTING LATER IN THE DAY, STARTING EVEN AS SOON AS--
AND IF I EVER HEAR OF YOU SETTING SO MUCH AS A FLIPPER OUTSIDE OF UNDERWATER GRACELAND AGAIN, SO HELP ME, I WI*WHY DID A SNOW LAND ON ME?*
--NOW!

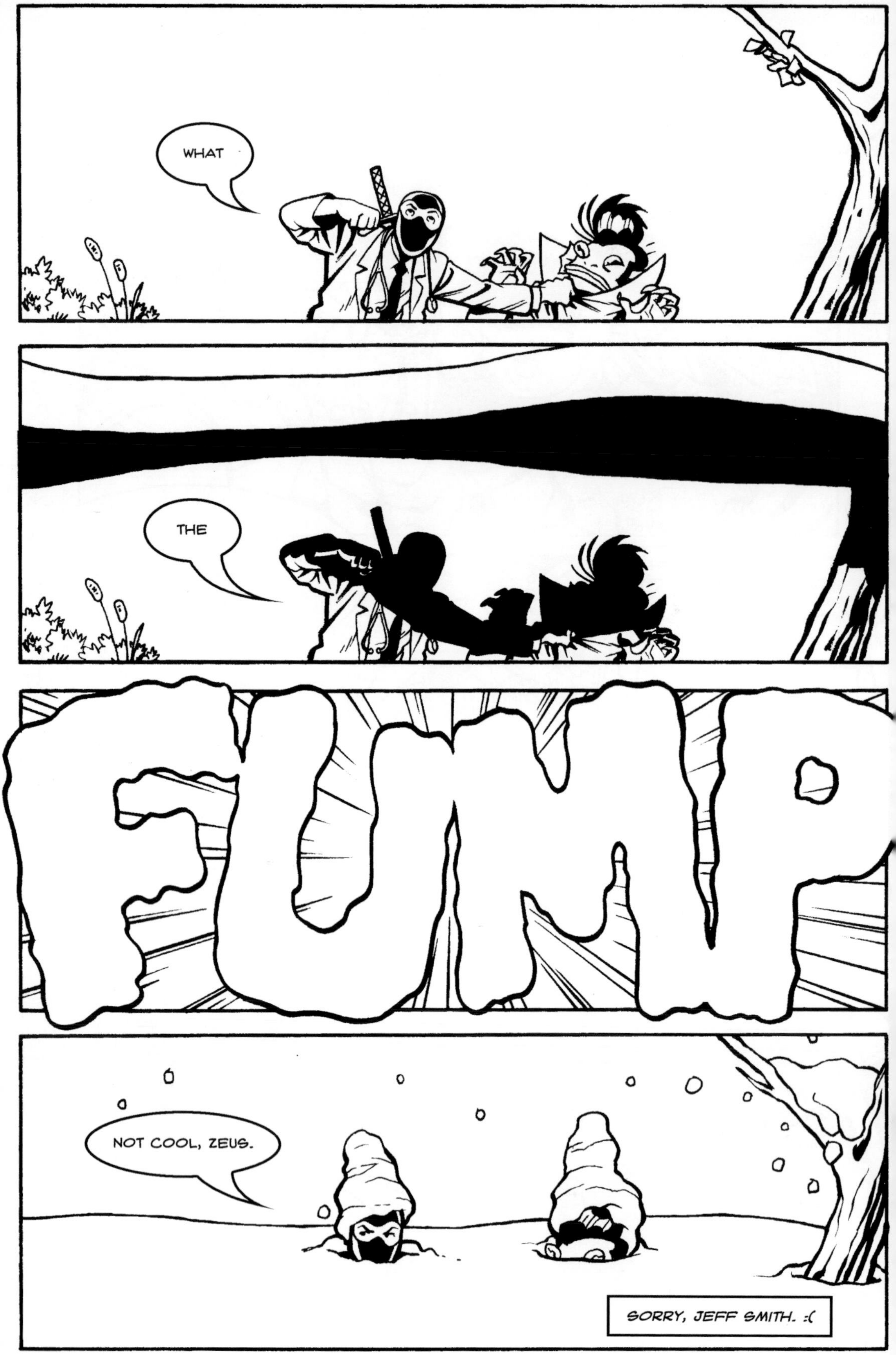
WHAT
THE
FUMP
NOT COOL, ZEUS.
SORRY, JEFF SMITH. :(

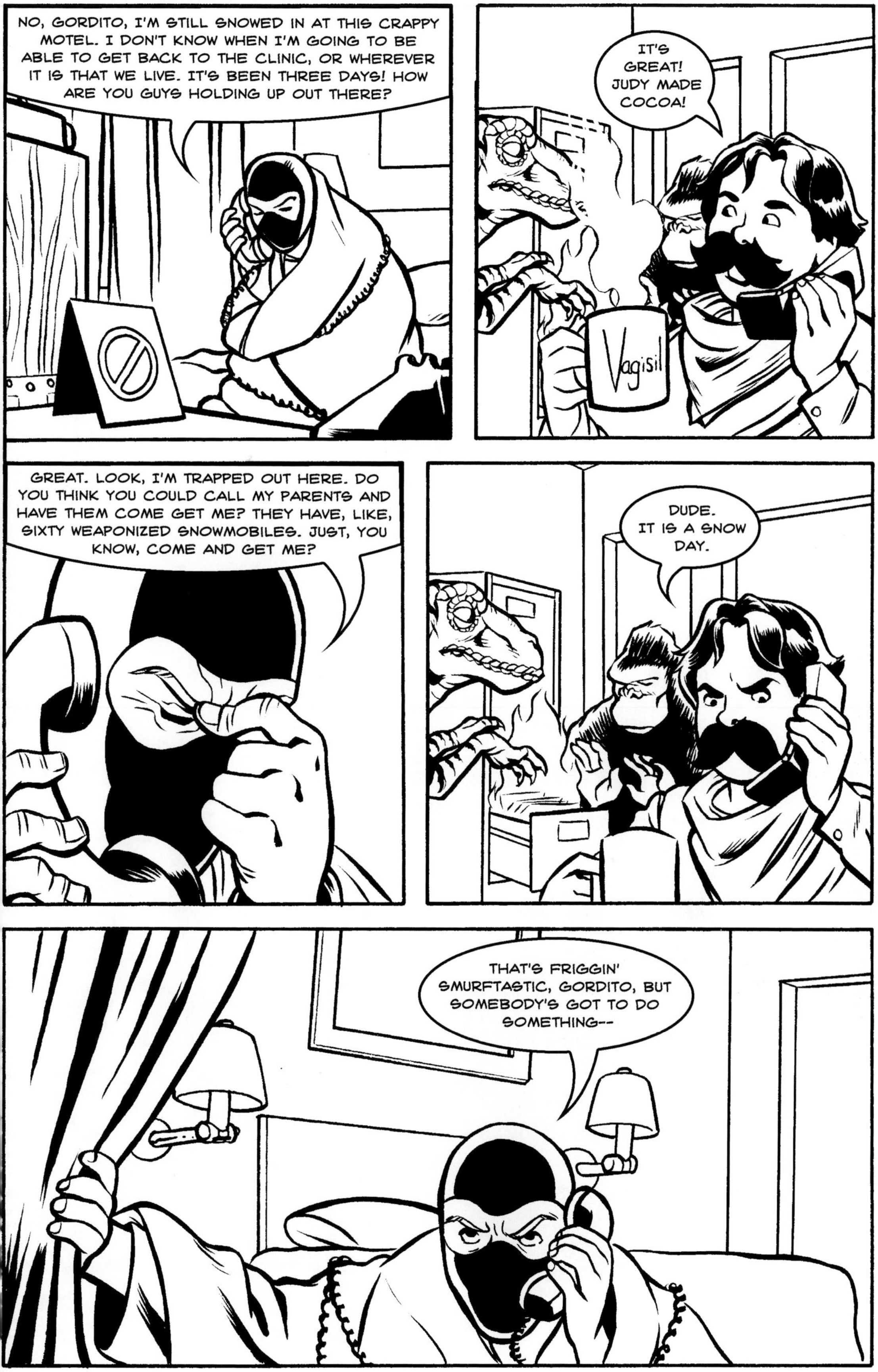
NO, GORDITO, I'M STILL SNOWED IN AT THIS CRAPPY MOTEL. I DON'T KNOW WHEN I'M GOING TO BE ABLE TO GET BACK TO THE CLINIC, OR WHEREVER IT IS THAT WE LIVE. IT'S BEEN THREE DAYS! HOW ARE YOU GUYS HOLDING UP OUT THERE?
IT'S GREAT! JUDY MADE COCOA!
Vagisil
GREAT. LOOK, I'M TRAPPED OUT HERE. DO YOU THINK YOU COULD CALL MY PARENTS AND HAVE THEM COME GET ME? THEY HAVE, LIKE, SIXTY WEAPONIZED SNOWMOBILES. JUST, YOU KNOW, COME AND GET ME?
DUDE. IT IS A SNOW DAY.
THAT'S FRIGGIN' SMURFTASTIC, GORDITO, BUT SOMEBODY'S GOT TO DO SOMETHING--

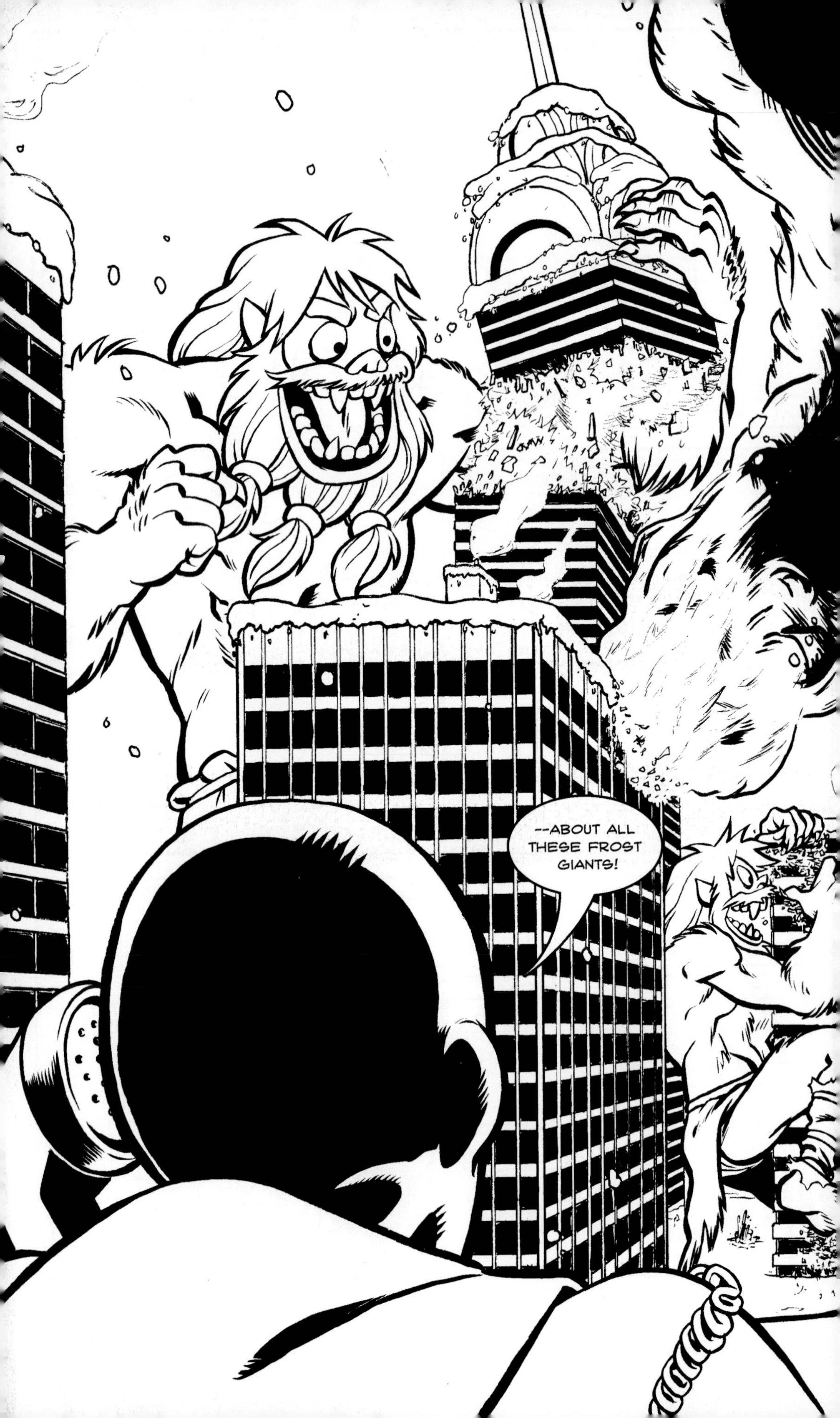
--ABOUT ALL THESE FROST GIANTS!

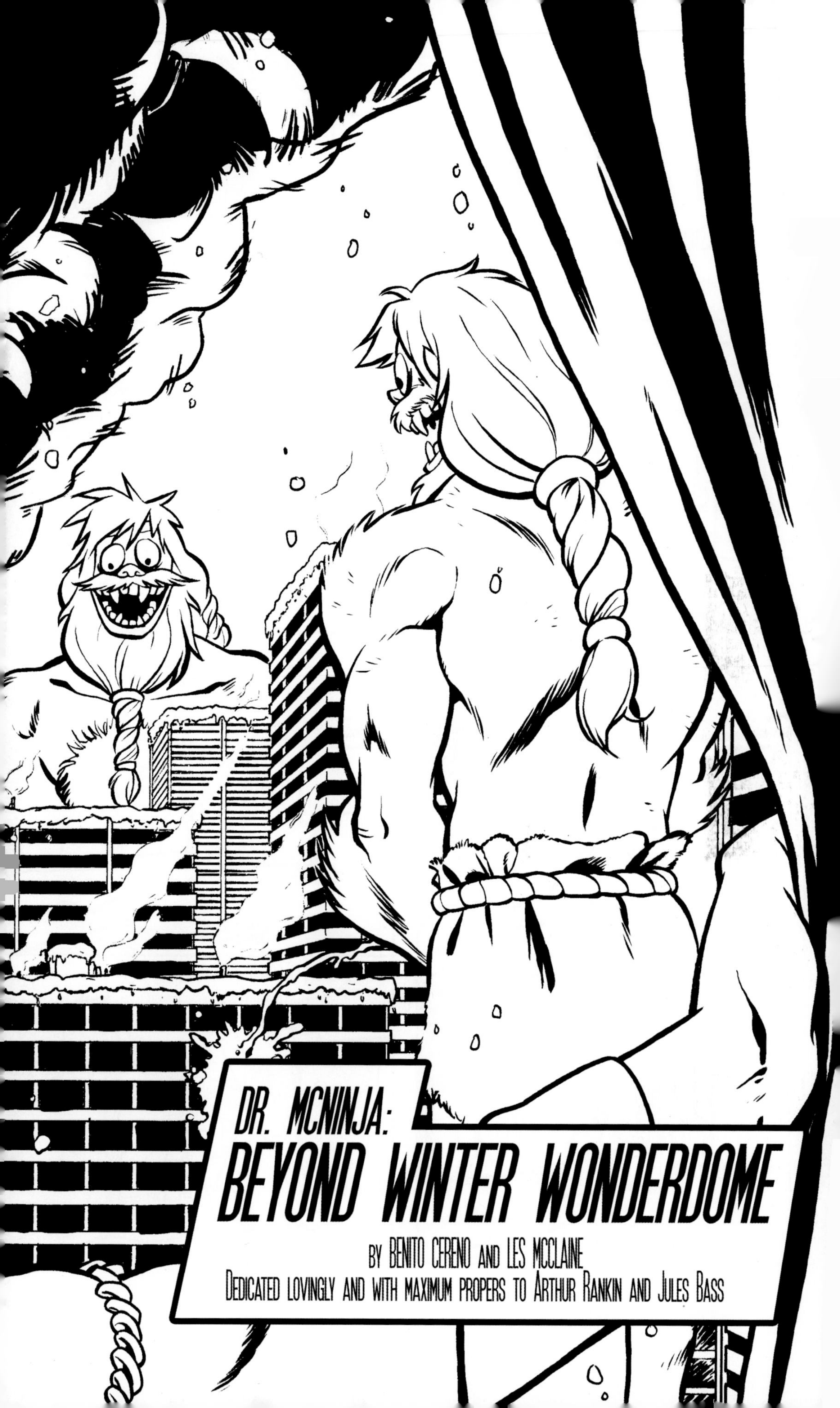
DR. MCNINJA:
BEYOND WINTER WONDERDOME
BY BENITO CERENO AND LES MCCLAINE
DEDICATED LOVINGLY AND WITH MAXIMUM PROPERS TO ARTHUR RANKIN AND JULES BASS

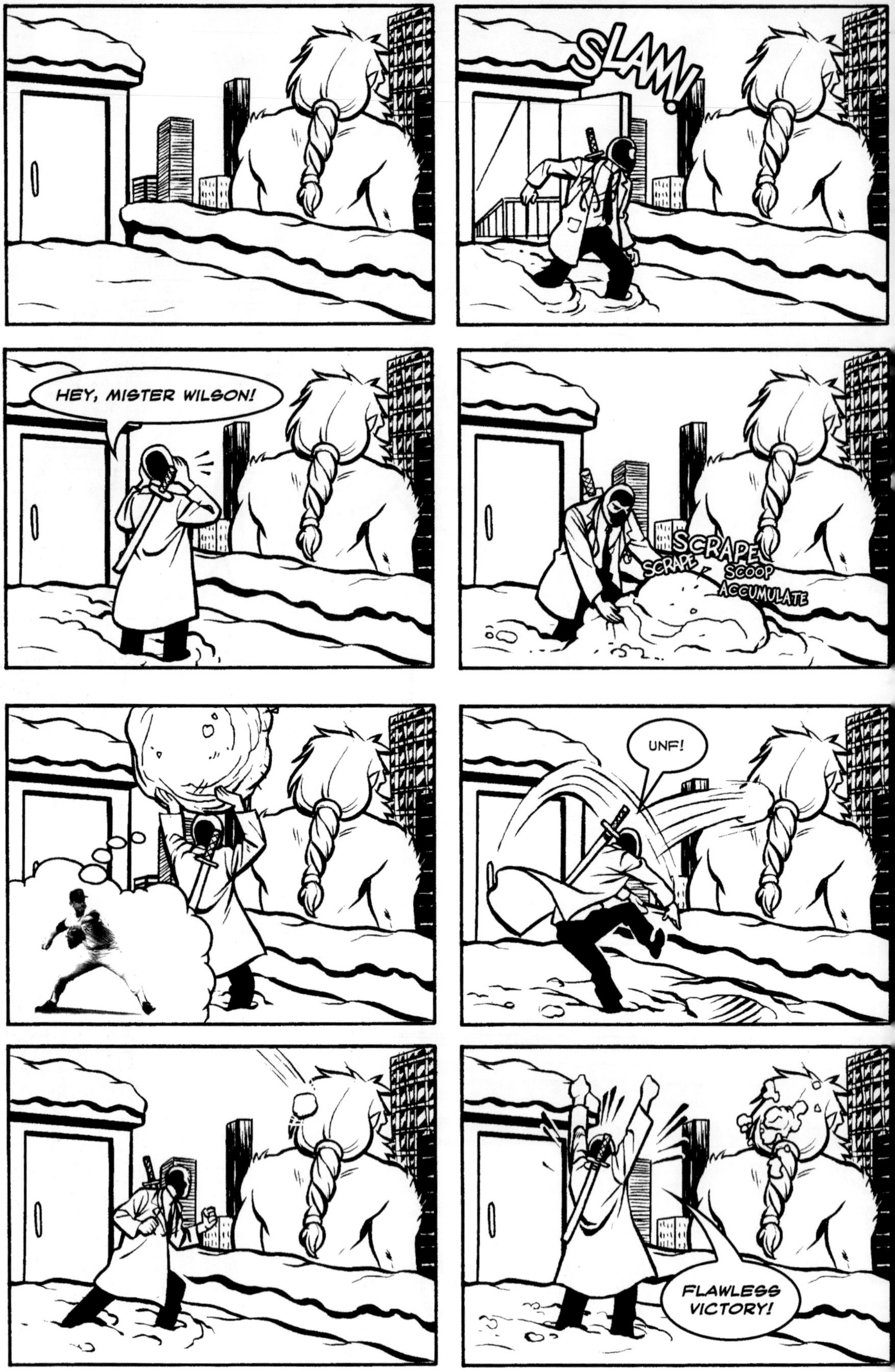
SLAM!
HEY, MISTER WILSON!
SCRAPE
SCRAPE
SCOOP
ACCUMULATE
UNF!
FLAWLESS VICTORY!

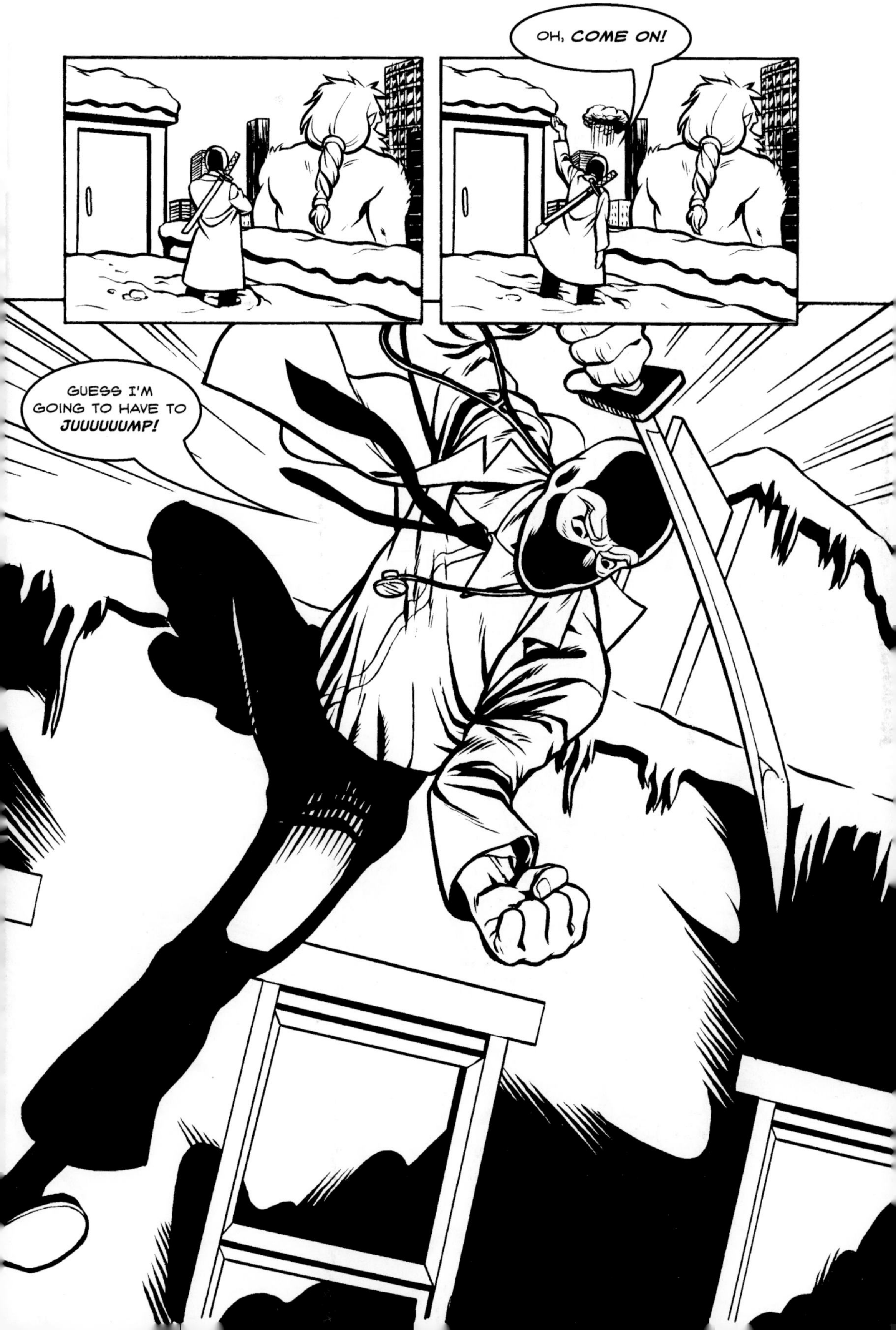
OH, COME ON!
GUESS I'M GOING TO HAVE TO JUUUUUUMP!

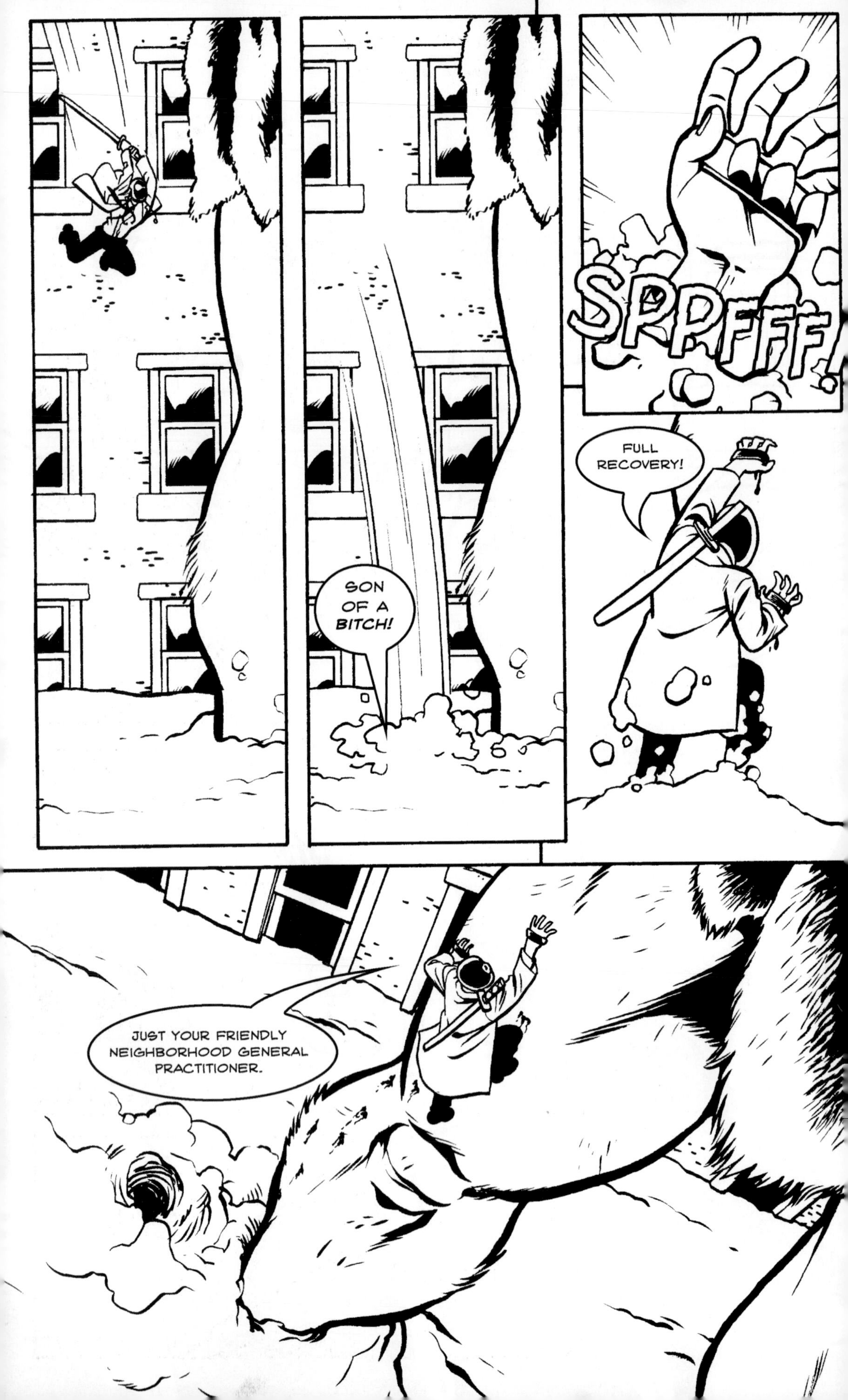
SON OF A BITCH!
SPRFFF!
FULL RECOVERY!
JUST YOUR FRIENDLY NEIGHBORHOOD GENERAL PRACTITIONER.

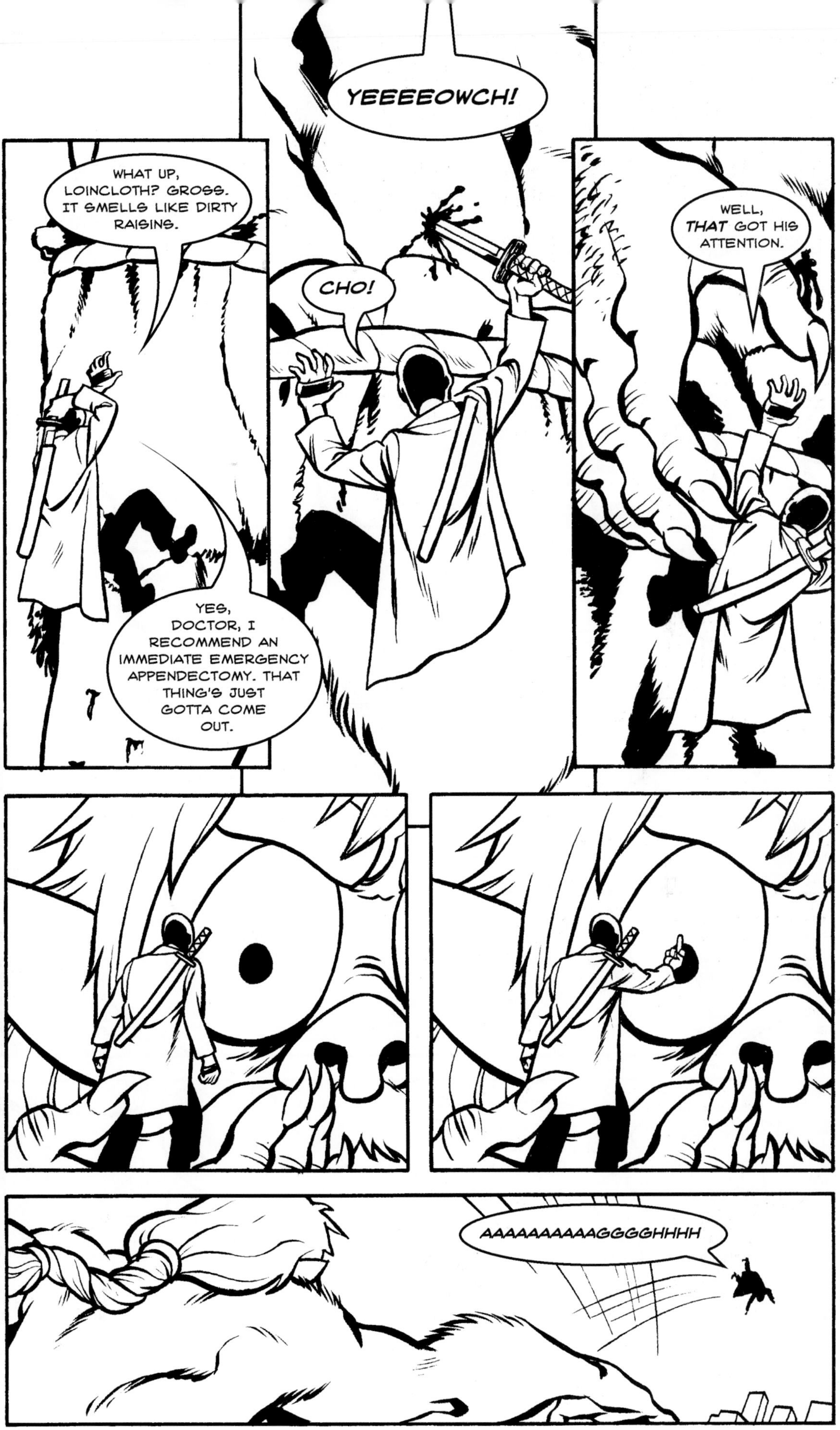
YEEEEOWCH!
WHAT UP, LOINCLOTH? GROSS. IT SMELLS LIKE DIRTY RAISINS.
YES, DOCTOR, I RECOMMEND AN IMMEDIATE EMERGENCY APPENDECTOMY. THAT THING'S JUST GOTTA COME OUT.
CHO!
WELL, *THAT* GOT HIS ATTENTION.
AAAAAAAAAAGGGGHHHH

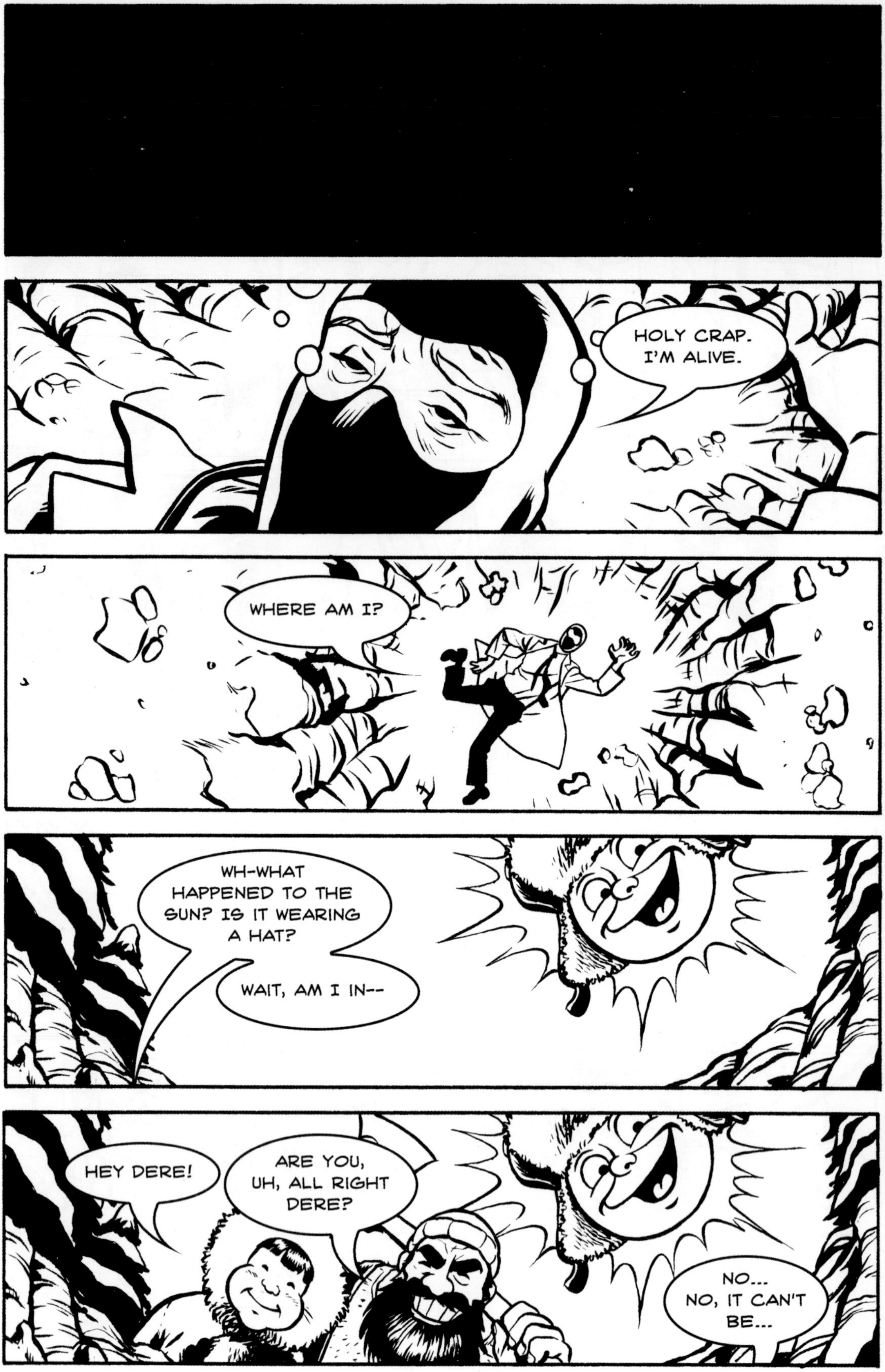
HOLY CRAP.
I'M ALIVE.
WHERE AM I?
WH-WHAT HAPPENED TO THE SUN? IS IT WEARING A HAT?
WAIT, AM I IN--
HEY DERE!
ARE YOU, UH, ALL RIGHT DERE?
NO... NO, IT CAN'T BE...

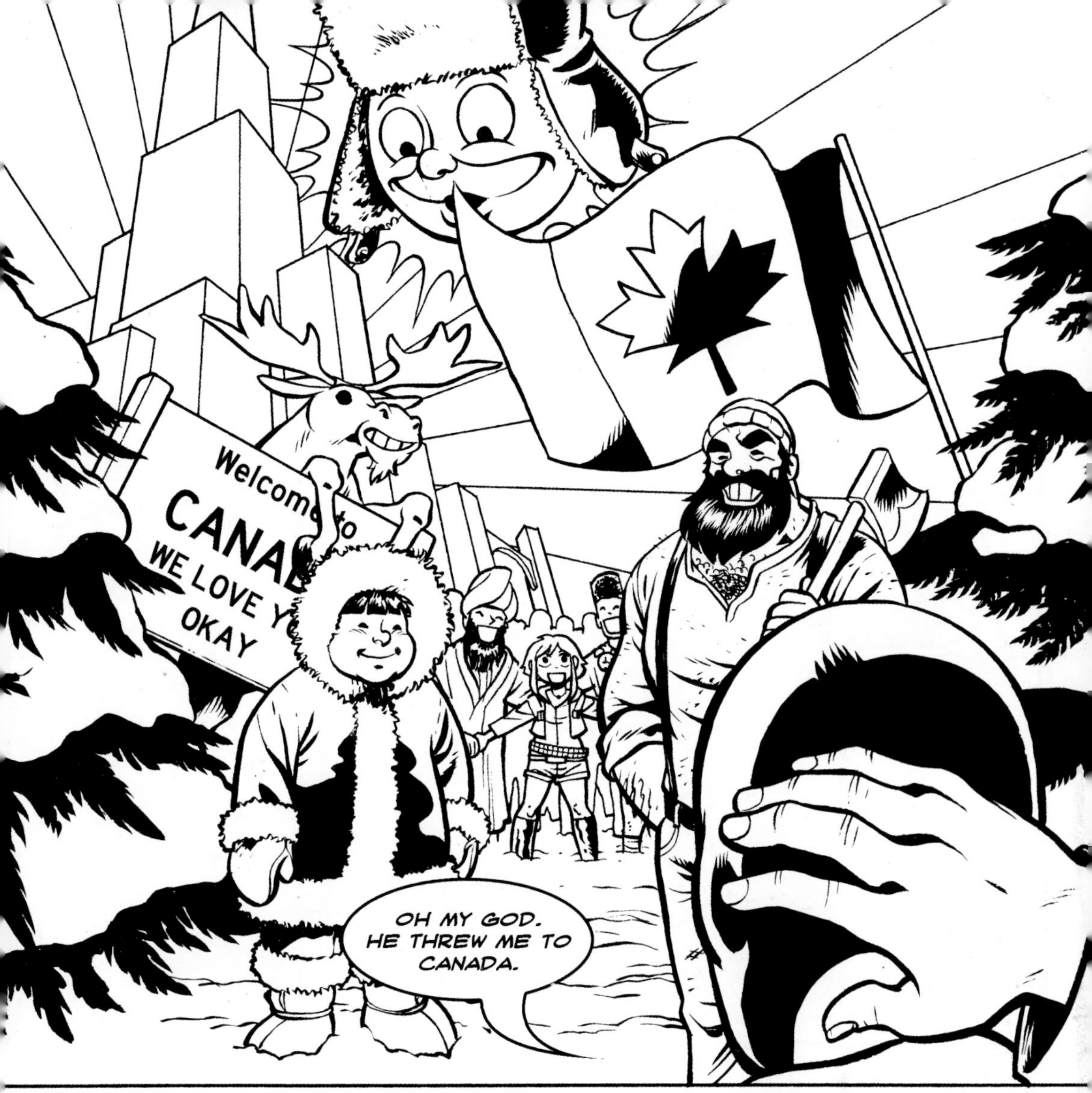
Welcome to
CANAD
WE LOVE Y
OKAY
OH MY GOD. HE THREW ME TO CANADA.
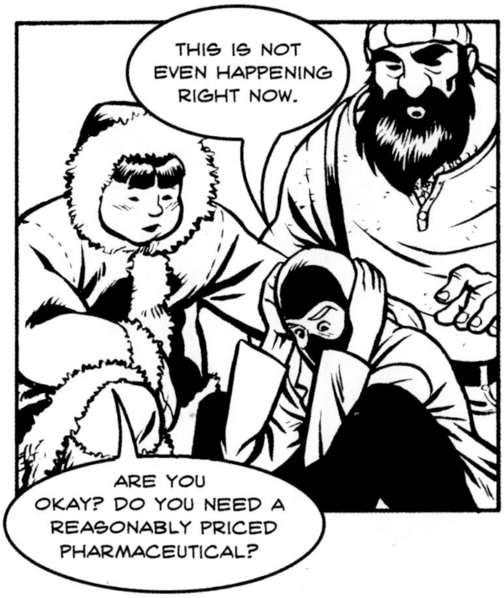
THIS IS NOT EVEN HAPPENING RIGHT NOW.
ARE YOU OKAY? DO YOU NEED A REASONABLY PRICED PHARMACEUTICAL?
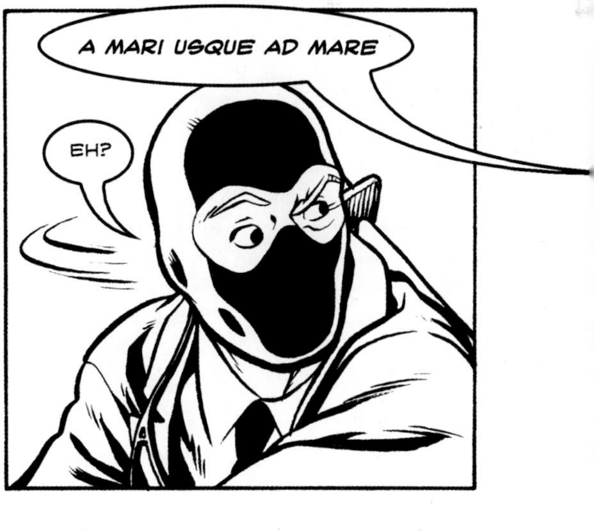
A MARI USQUE AD MARE
EH?

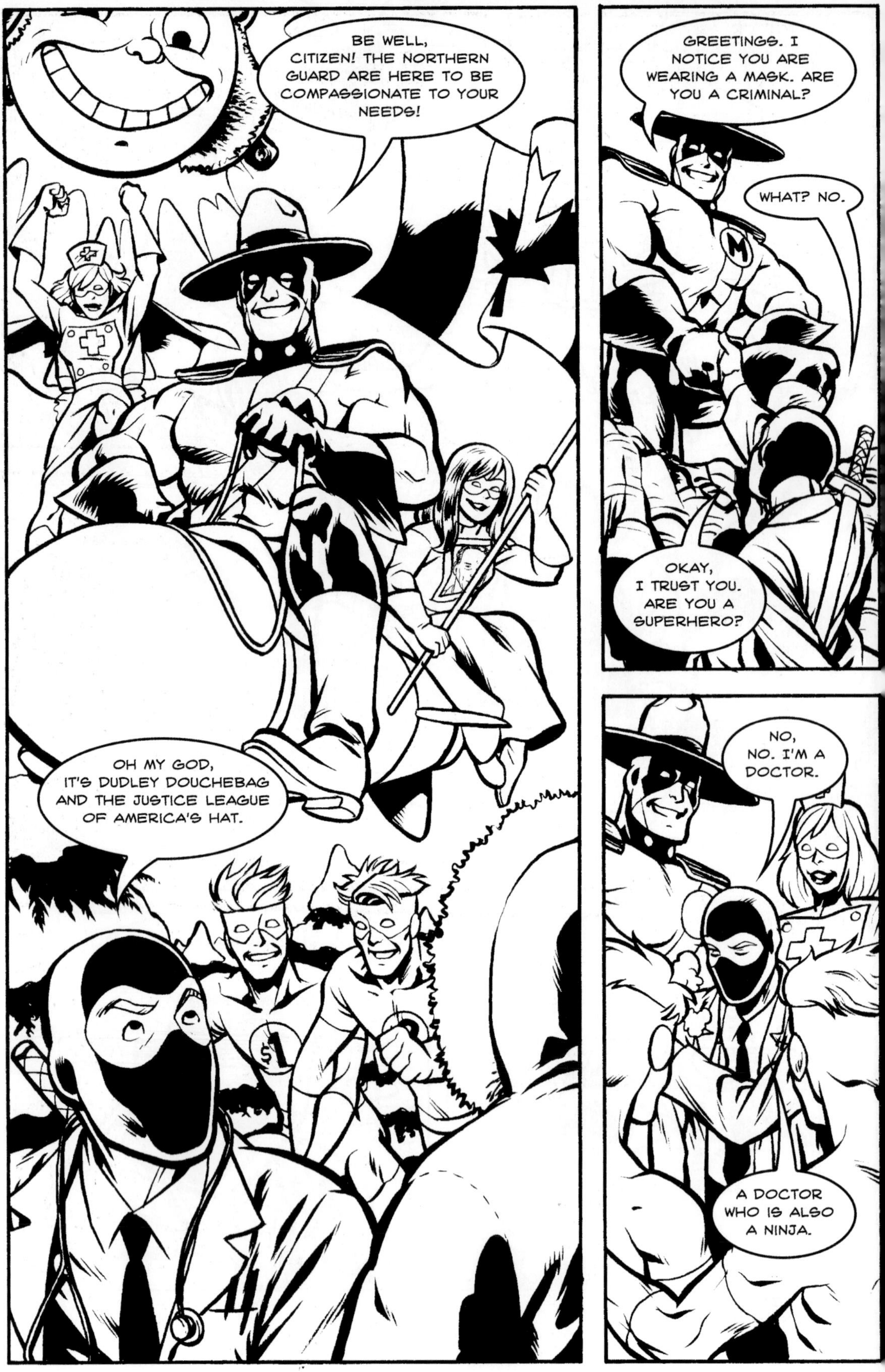
BE WELL, CITIZEN! THE NORTHERN GUARD ARE HERE TO BE COMPASSIONATE TO YOUR NEEDS!
OH MY GOD, IT'S DUDLEY DOUCHEBAG AND THE JUSTICE LEAGUE OF AMERICA'S HAT.
GREETINGS. I NOTICE YOU ARE WEARING A MASK. ARE YOU A CRIMINAL?
WHAT? NO.
OKAY, I TRUST YOU. ARE YOU A SUPERHERO?
NO, NO. I'M A DOCTOR.
A DOCTOR WHO IS ALSO A NINJA.

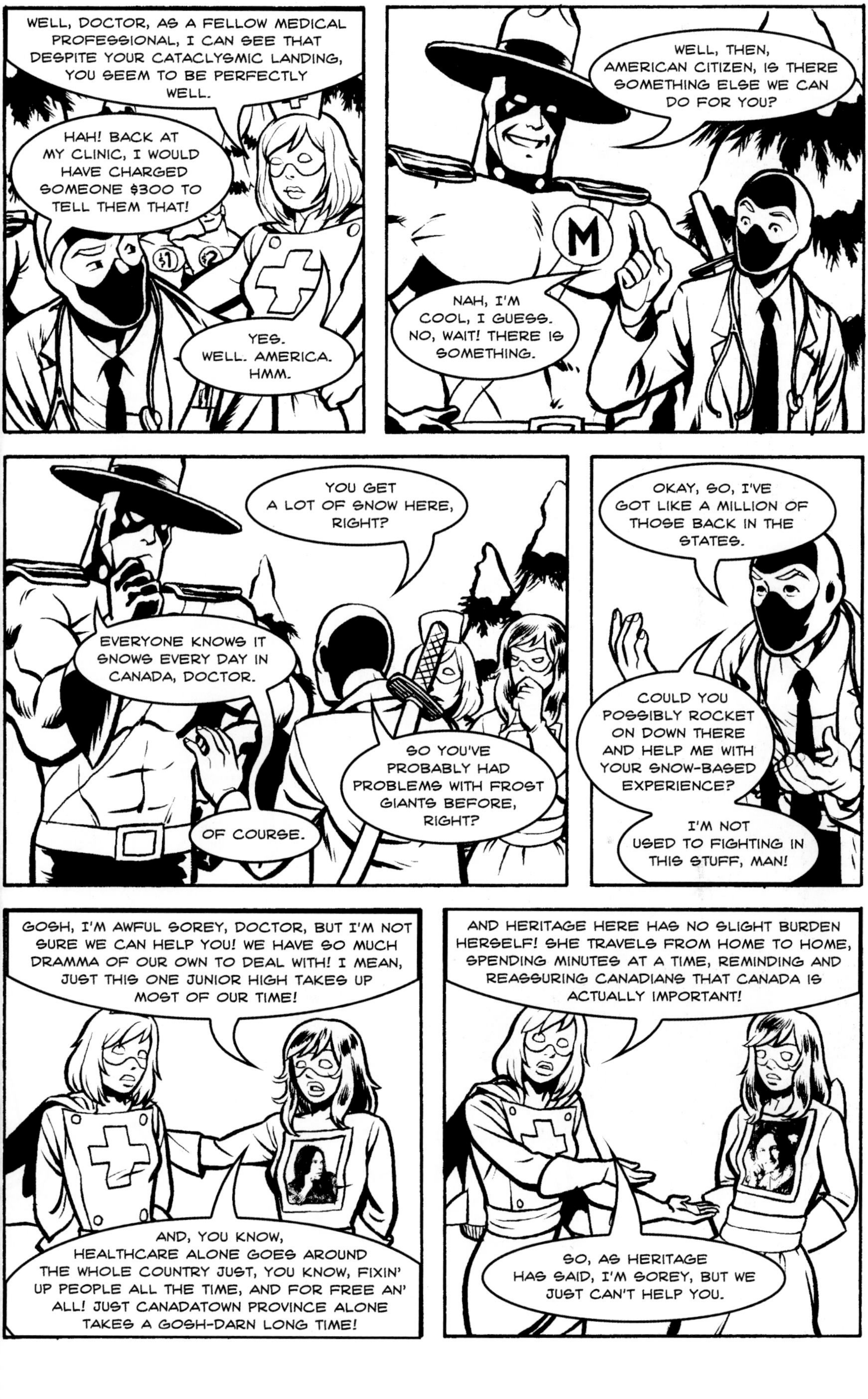
WELL, DOCTOR, AS A FELLOW MEDICAL PROFESSIONAL, I CAN SEE THAT DESPITE YOUR CATACLYSMIC LANDING, YOU SEEM TO BE PERFECTLY WELL.
HAH! BACK AT MY CLINIC, I WOULD HAVE CHARGED SOMEONE $300 TO TELL THEM THAT!
YES. WELL. AMERICA. HMM.
WELL, THEN, AMERICAN CITIZEN, IS THERE SOMETHING ELSE WE CAN DO FOR YOU?
NAH, I'M COOL, I GUESS. NO, WAIT! THERE IS SOMETHING.
YOU GET A LOT OF SNOW HERE, RIGHT?
EVERYONE KNOWS IT SNOWS EVERY DAY IN CANADA, DOCTOR.
SO YOU'VE PROBABLY HAD PROBLEMS WITH FROST GIANTS BEFORE, RIGHT?
OF COURSE.
OKAY, SO, I'VE GOT LIKE A MILLION OF THOSE BACK IN THE STATES.
COULD YOU POSSIBLY ROCKET ON DOWN THERE AND HELP ME WITH YOUR SNOW-BASED EXPERIENCE?
I'M NOT USED TO FIGHTING IN THIS STUFF, MAN!
GOSH, I'M AWFUL SOREY, DOCTOR, BUT I'M NOT SURE WE CAN HELP YOU! WE HAVE SO MUCH DRAMMA OF OUR OWN TO DEAL WITH! I MEAN, JUST THIS ONE JUNIOR HIGH TAKES UP MOST OF OUR TIME!
AND, YOU KNOW, HEALTHCARE ALONE GOES AROUND THE WHOLE COUNTRY JUST, YOU KNOW, FIXIN' UP PEOPLE ALL THE TIME, AND FOR FREE AN' ALL! JUST CANADATOWN PROVINCE ALONE TAKES A GOSH-DARN LONG TIME!
AND HERITAGE HERE HAS NO SLIGHT BURDEN HERSELF! SHE TRAVELS FROM HOME TO HOME, SPENDING MINUTES AT A TIME, REMINDING AND REASSURING CANADIANS THAT CANADA IS ACTUALLY IMPORTANT!
SO, AS HERITAGE HAS SAID, I'M SOREY, BUT WE JUST CAN'T HELP YOU.

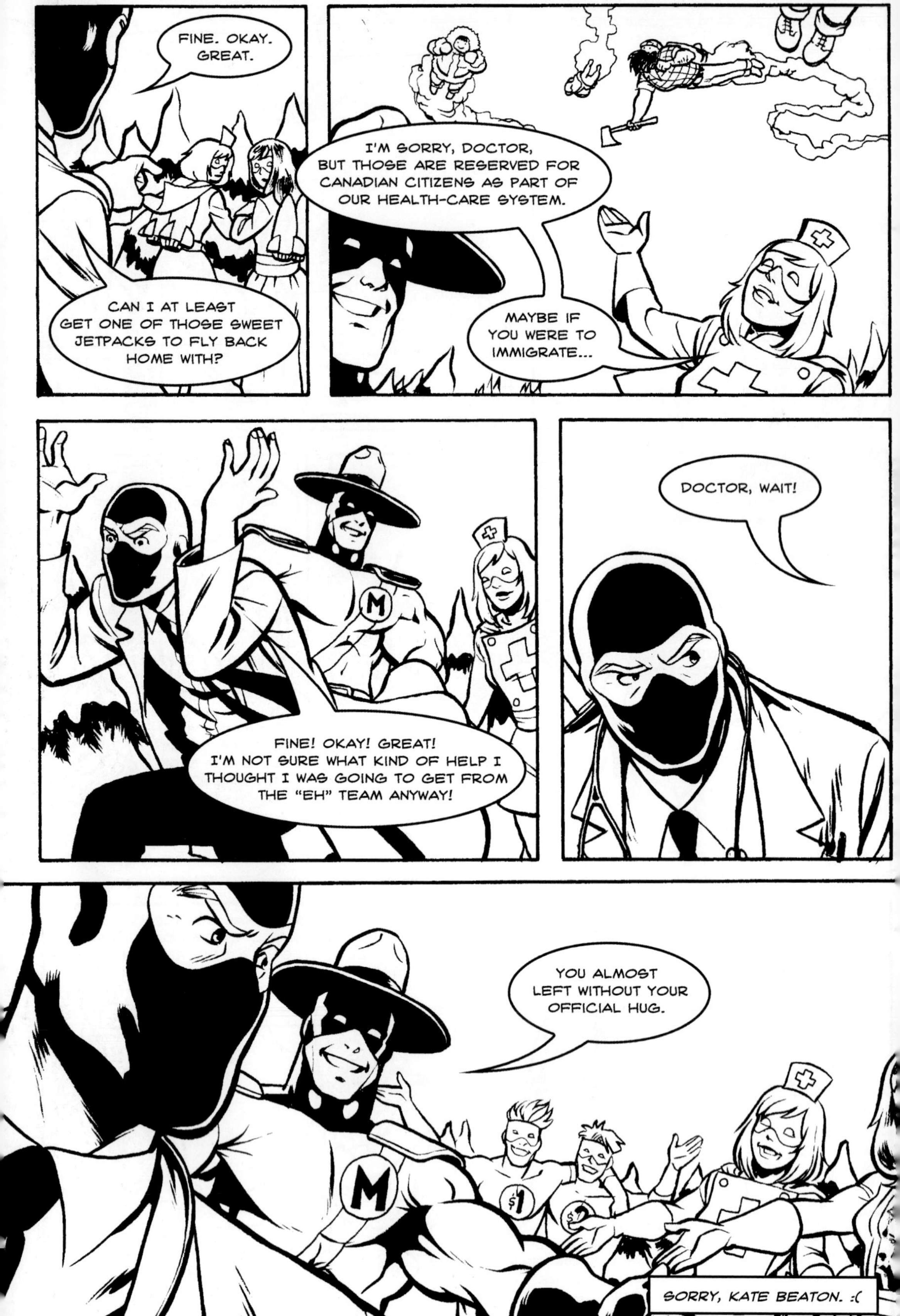
FINE. OKAY. GREAT.
CAN I AT LEAST GET ONE OF THOSE SWEET JETPACKS TO FLY BACK HOME WITH?
I'M SORRY, DOCTOR, BUT THOSE ARE RESERVED FOR CANADIAN CITIZENS AS PART OF OUR HEALTH-CARE SYSTEM.
MAYBE IF YOU WERE TO IMMIGRATE...
FINE! OKAY! GREAT! I'M NOT SURE WHAT KIND OF HELP I THOUGHT I WAS GOING TO GET FROM THE "EH" TEAM ANYWAY!
DOCTOR, WAIT!
YOU ALMOST LEFT WITHOUT YOUR OFFICIAL HUG.
SORRY, KATE BEATON. :(

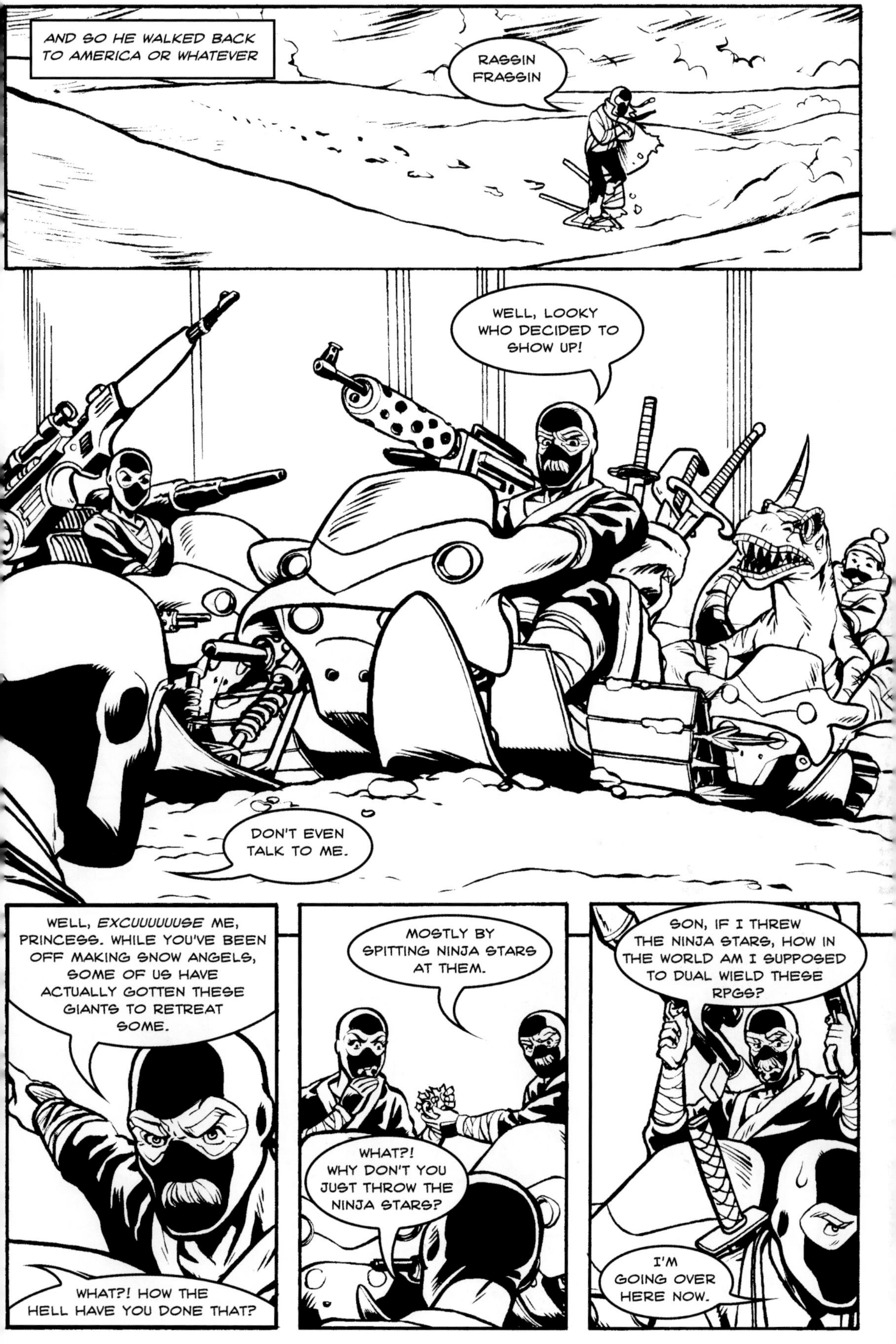
AND SO HE WALKED BACK TO AMERICA OR WHATEVER
RASSIN FRASSIN
WELL, LOOKY WHO DECIDED TO SHOW UP!
DON'T EVEN TALK TO ME.
WELL, *EXCUUUUUUSE* ME, PRINCESS. WHILE YOU'VE BEEN OFF MAKING SNOW ANGELS, SOME OF US HAVE ACTUALLY GOTTEN THESE GIANTS TO RETREAT SOME.
WHAT?! HOW THE HELL HAVE YOU DONE THAT?
MOSTLY BY SPITTING NINJA STARS AT THEM.
WHAT?! WHY DON'T YOU JUST THROW THE NINJA STARS?
SON, IF I THREW THE NINJA STARS, HOW IN THE WORLD AM I SUPPOSED TO DUAL WIELD THESE RPGS?
I'M GOING OVER HERE NOW.

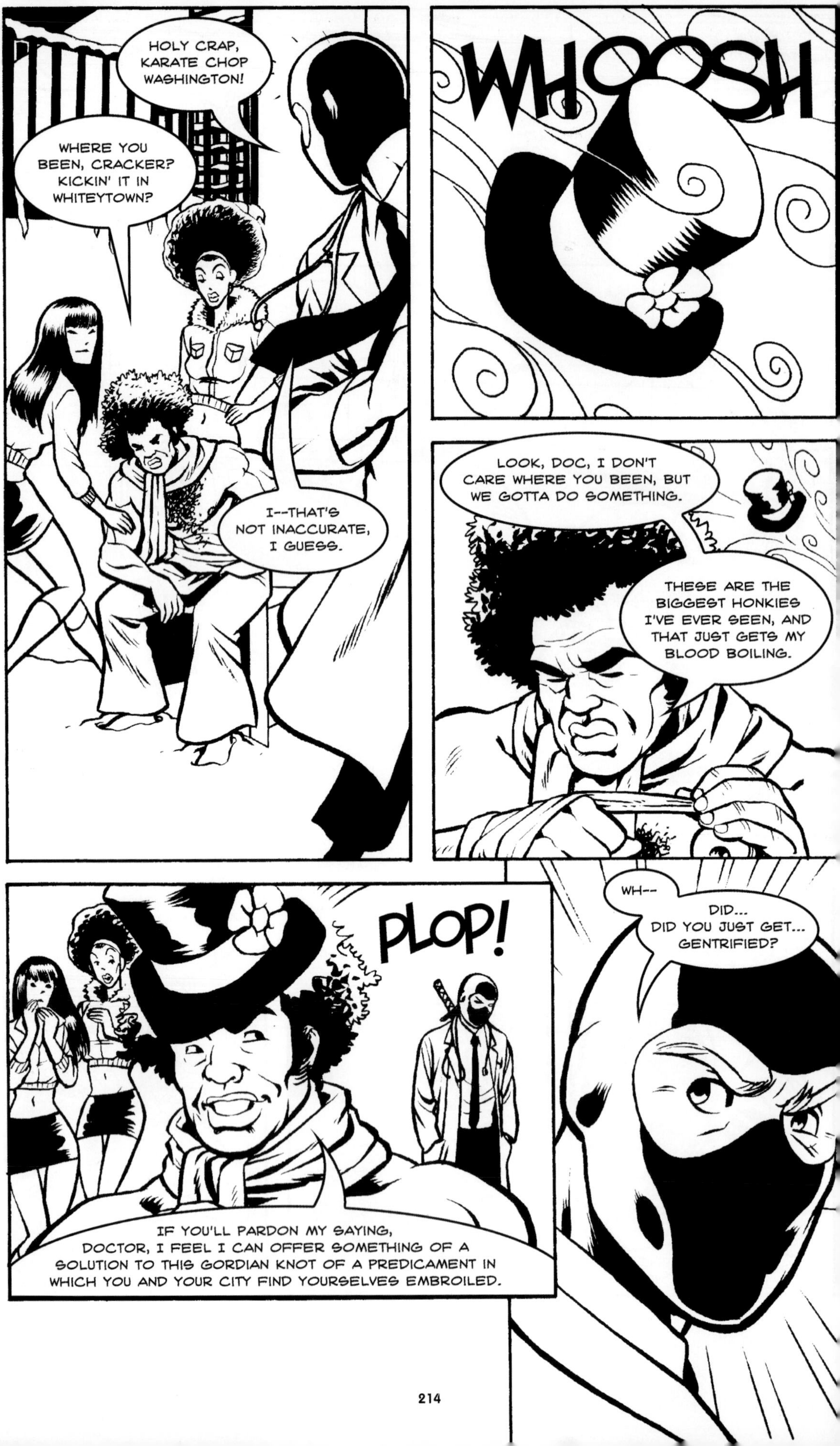

HOLY CRAP, KARATE CHOP WASHINGTON!
WHERE YOU BEEN, CRACKER? KICKIN' IT IN WHITEYTOWN?
I--THAT'S NOT INACCURATE, I GUESS.
WHOOSH
LOOK, DOC, I DON'T CARE WHERE YOU BEEN, BUT WE GOTTA DO SOMETHING.
THESE ARE THE BIGGEST HONKIES I'VE EVER SEEN, AND THAT JUST GETS MY BLOOD BOILING.
PLOP!
IF YOU'LL PARDON MY SAYING, DOCTOR, I FEEL I CAN OFFER SOMETHING OF A SOLUTION TO THIS GORDIAN KNOT OF A PREDICAMENT IN WHICH YOU AND YOUR CITY FIND YOURSELVES EMBROILED.
WH--
DID... DID YOU JUST GET... GENTRIFIED?

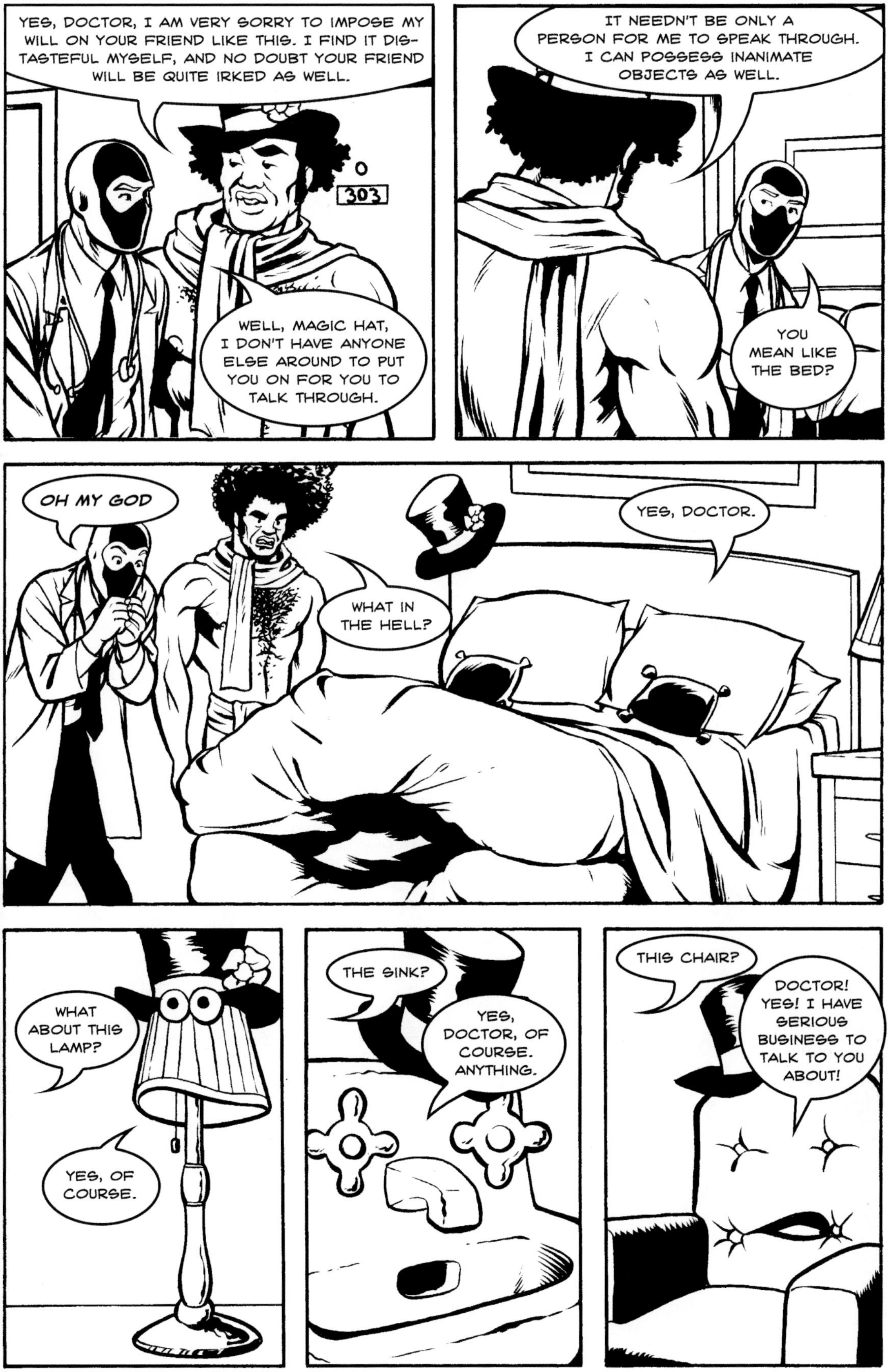
YES, DOCTOR, I AM VERY SORRY TO IMPOSE MY WILL ON YOUR FRIEND LIKE THIS. I FIND IT DISTASTEFUL MYSELF, AND NO DOUBT YOUR FRIEND WILL BE QUITE IRKED AS WELL.
303
WELL, MAGIC HAT, I DON'T HAVE ANYONE ELSE AROUND TO PUT YOU ON FOR YOU TO TALK THROUGH.
IT NEEDN'T BE ONLY A PERSON FOR ME TO SPEAK THROUGH. I CAN POSSESS INANIMATE OBJECTS AS WELL.
YOU MEAN LIKE THE BED?
OH MY GOD
WHAT IN THE HELL?
YES, DOCTOR.
WHAT ABOUT THIS LAMP?
YES, OF COURSE.
THE SINK?
YES, DOCTOR, OF COURSE. ANYTHING.
THIS CHAIR?
DOCTOR! YES! I HAVE SERIOUS BUSINESS TO TALK TO YOU ABOUT!

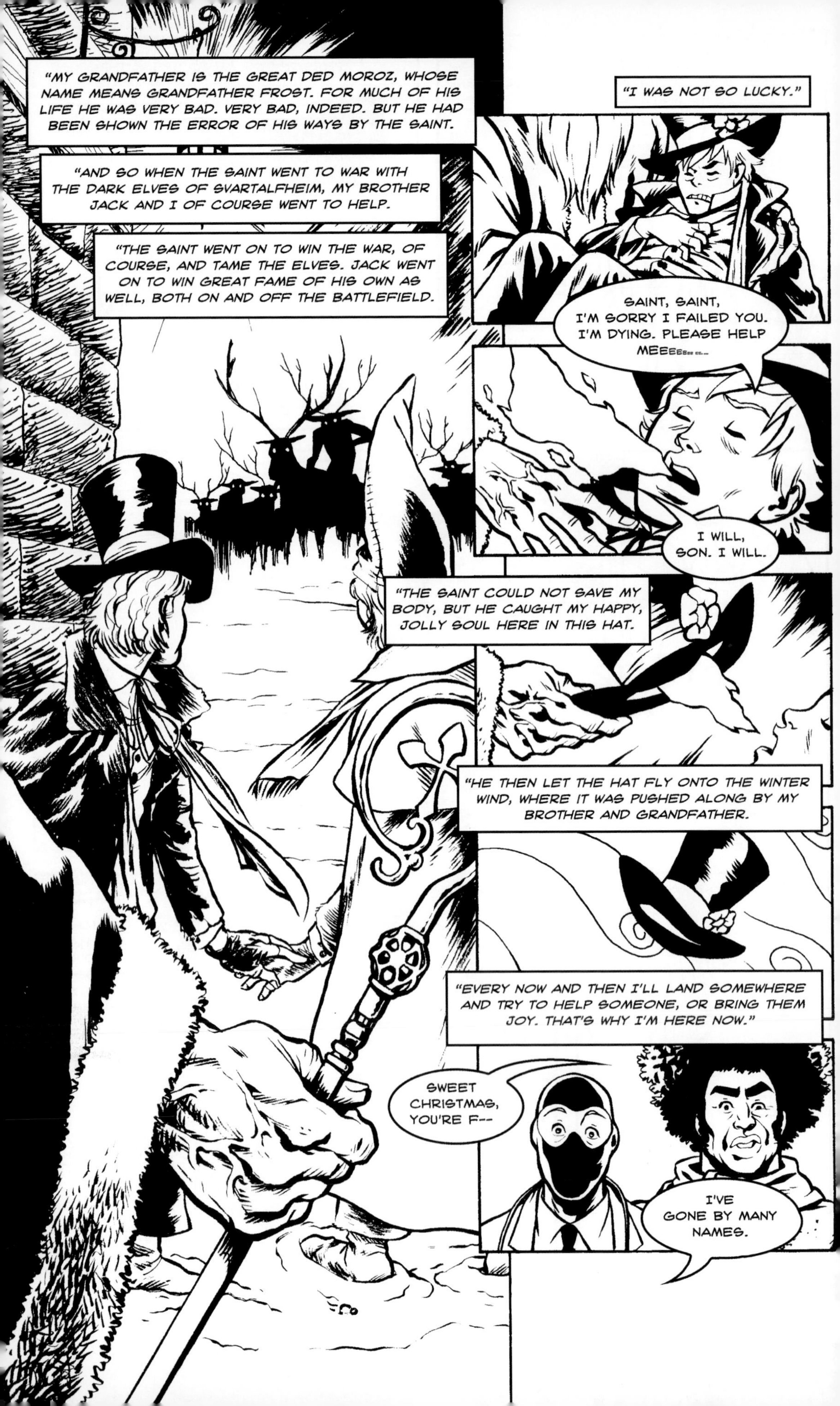
"MY GRANDFATHER IS THE GREAT DED MOROZ, WHOSE NAME MEANS GRANDFATHER FROST. FOR MUCH OF HIS LIFE HE WAS VERY BAD. VERY BAD, INDEED. BUT HE HAD BEEN SHOWN THE ERROR OF HIS WAYS BY THE SAINT.
"AND SO WHEN THE SAINT WENT TO WAR WITH THE DARK ELVES OF SVARTALFHEIM, MY BROTHER JACK AND I OF COURSE WENT TO HELP.
"THE SAINT WENT ON TO WIN THE WAR, OF COURSE, AND TAME THE ELVES. JACK WENT ON TO WIN GREAT FAME OF HIS OWN AS WELL, BOTH ON AND OFF THE BATTLEFIELD.
"I WAS NOT SO LUCKY."
SAINT, SAINT, I'M SORRY I FAILED YOU. I'M DYING. PLEASE HELP MEEEEEEE...
I WILL, SON. I WILL.
"THE SAINT COULD NOT SAVE MY BODY, BUT HE CAUGHT MY HAPPY, JOLLY SOUL HERE IN THIS HAT.
"HE THEN LET THE HAT FLY ONTO THE WINTER WIND, WHERE IT WAS PUSHED ALONG BY MY BROTHER AND GRANDFATHER.
"EVERY NOW AND THEN I'LL LAND SOMEWHERE AND TRY TO HELP SOMEONE, OR BRING THEM JOY. THAT'S WHY I'M HERE NOW."
SWEET CHRISTMAS, YOU'RE F--
I'VE GONE BY MANY NAMES.

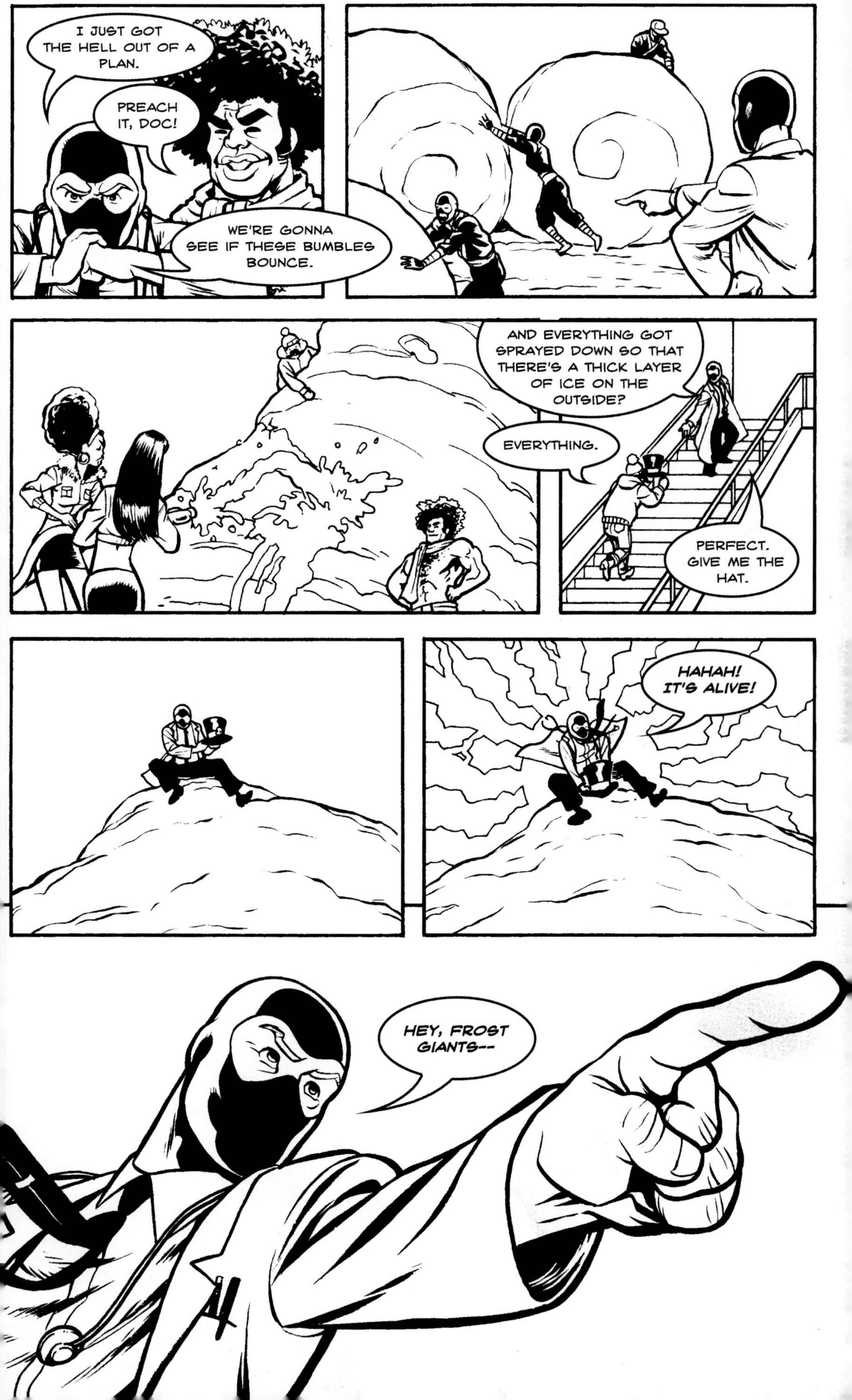
I JUST GOT THE HELL OUT OF A PLAN.
PREACH IT, DOC!
WE'RE GONNA SEE IF THESE BUMBLES BOUNCE.
AND EVERYTHING GOT SPRAYED DOWN SO THAT THERE'S A THICK LAYER OF ICE ON THE OUTSIDE?
EVERYTHING.
PERFECT. GIVE ME THE HAT.
HAHAH! IT'S ALIVE!
HEY, FROST GIANTS--

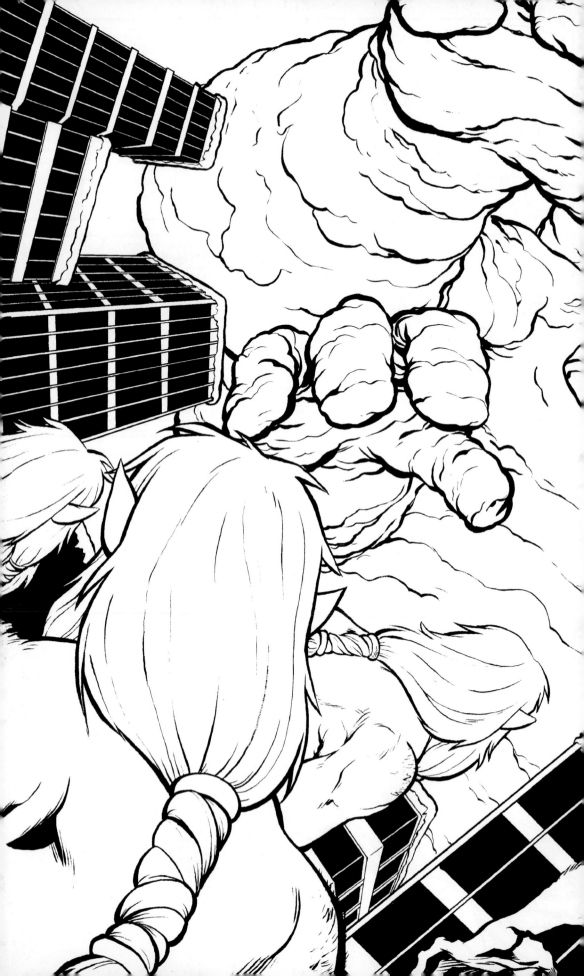

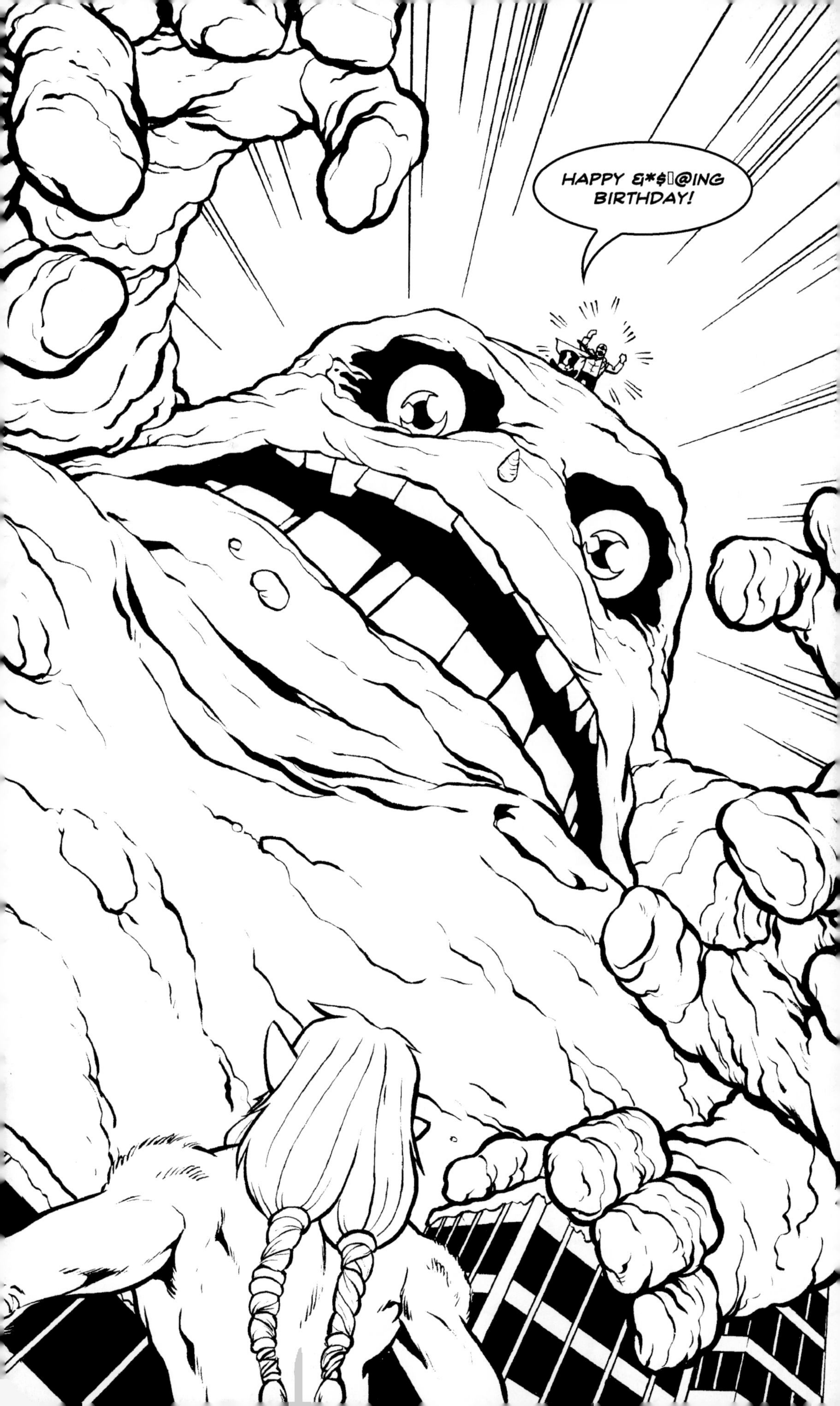
HAPPY &*$□@ING BIRTHDAY!

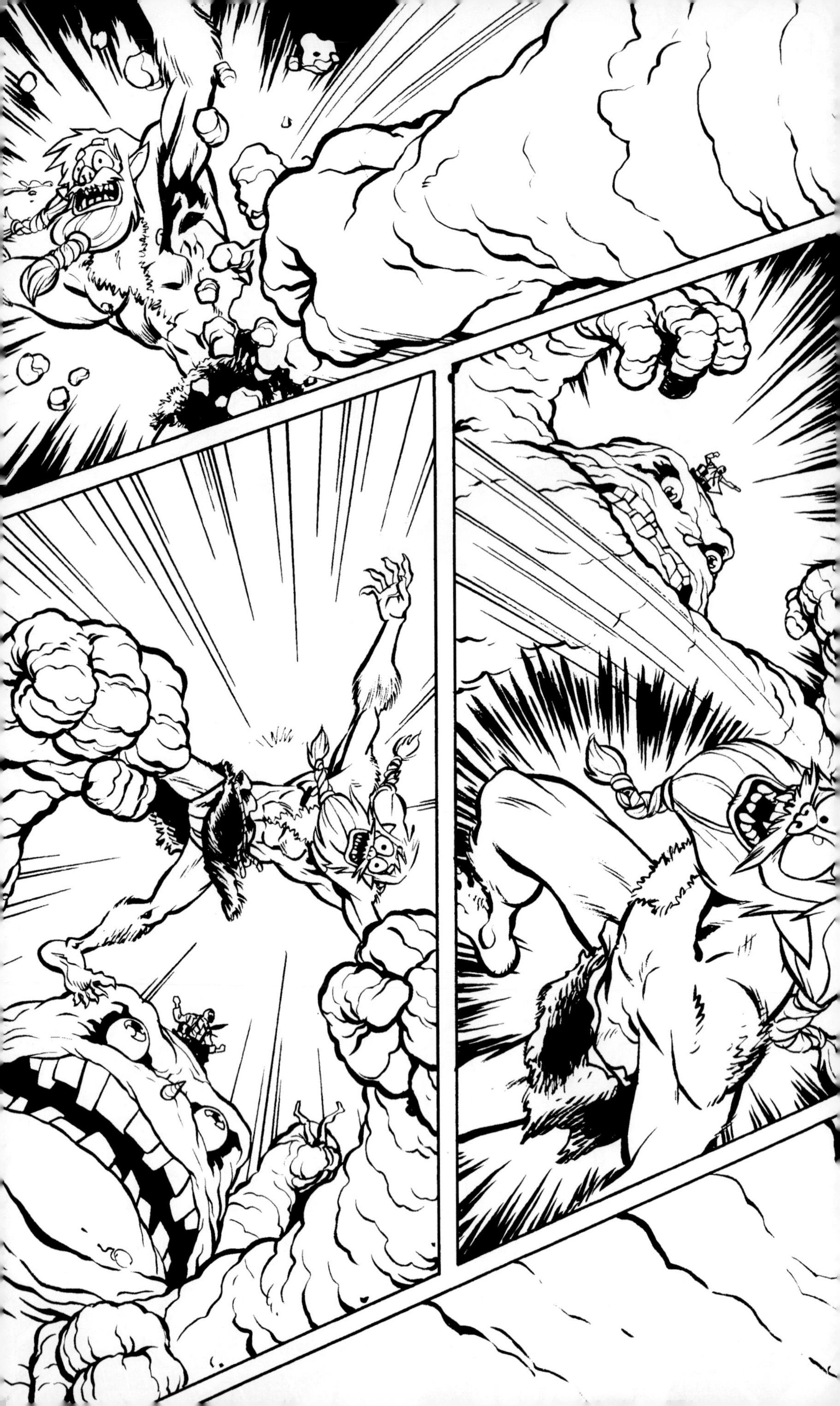

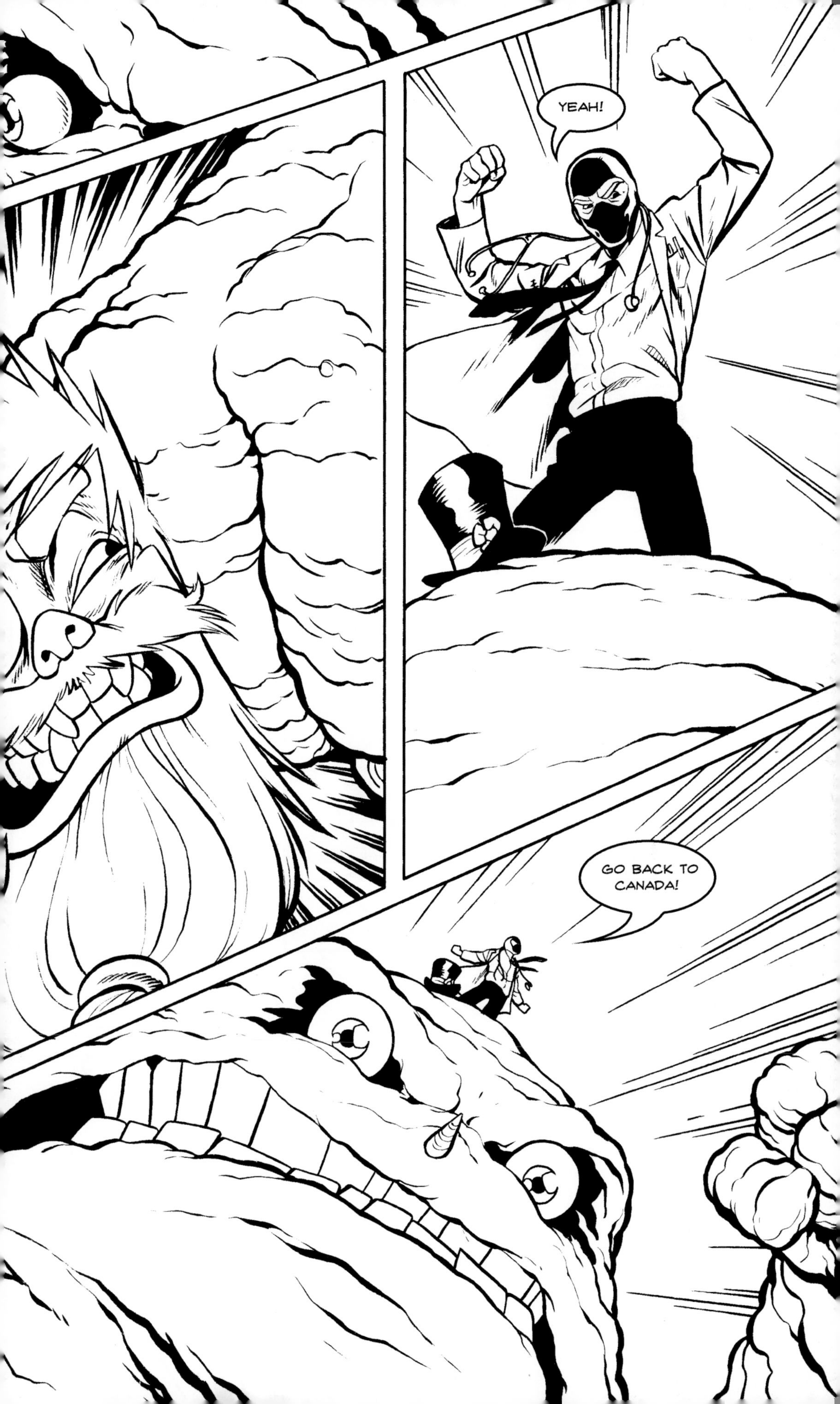
YEAH!
GO BACK TO CANADA!

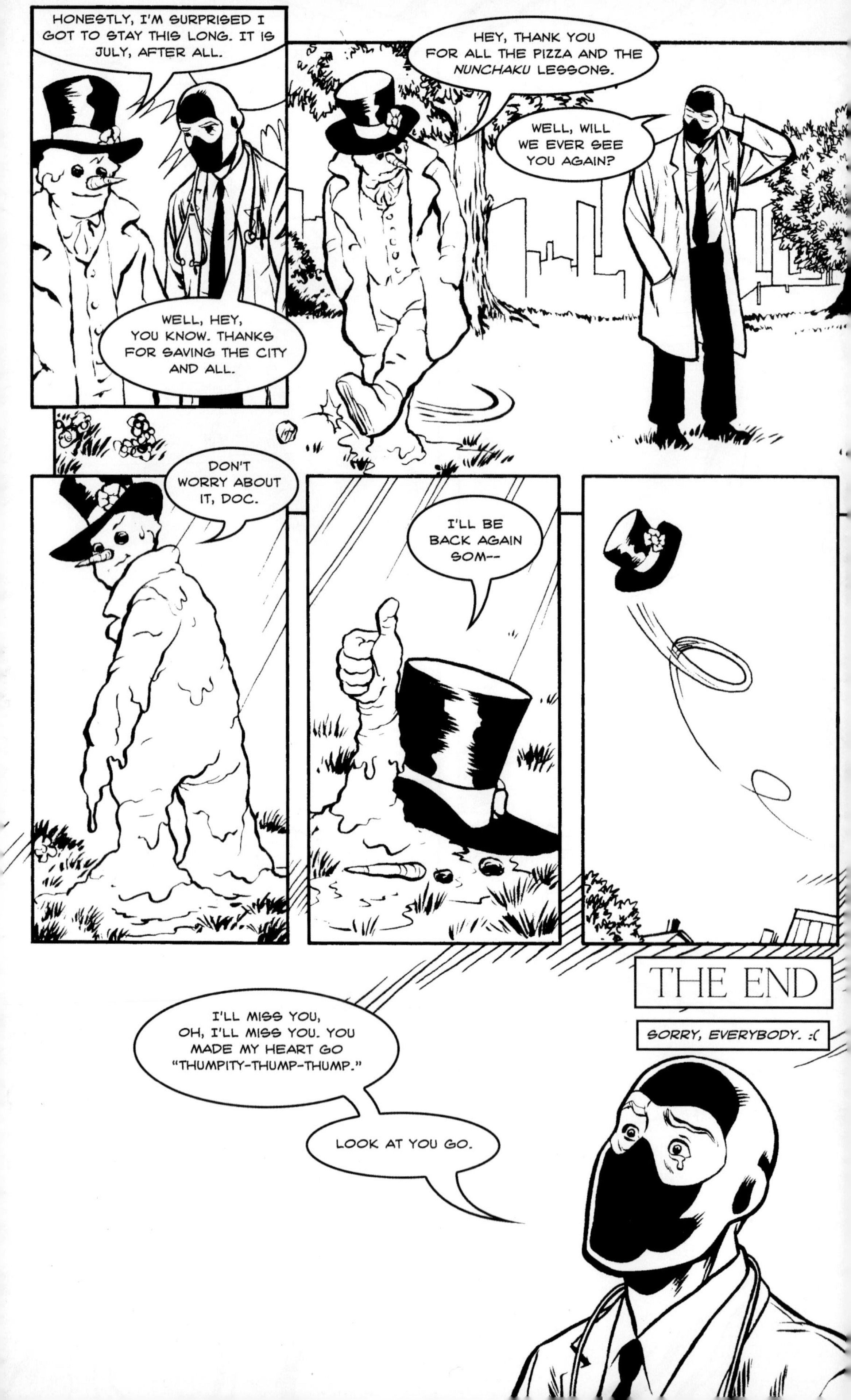
HONESTLY, I'M SURPRISED I GOT TO STAY THIS LONG. IT IS JULY, AFTER ALL.
WELL, HEY, YOU KNOW. THANKS FOR SAVING THE CITY AND ALL.
HEY, THANK YOU FOR ALL THE PIZZA AND THE *NUNCHAKU* LESSONS.
WELL, WILL WE EVER SEE YOU AGAIN?
DON'T WORRY ABOUT IT, DOC.
I'LL BE BACK AGAIN SOM--
THE END
SORRY, EVERYBODY. :(
I'LL MISS YOU, OH, I'LL MISS YOU. YOU MADE MY HEART GO "THUMPITY-THUMP-THUMP."
LOOK AT YOU GO.

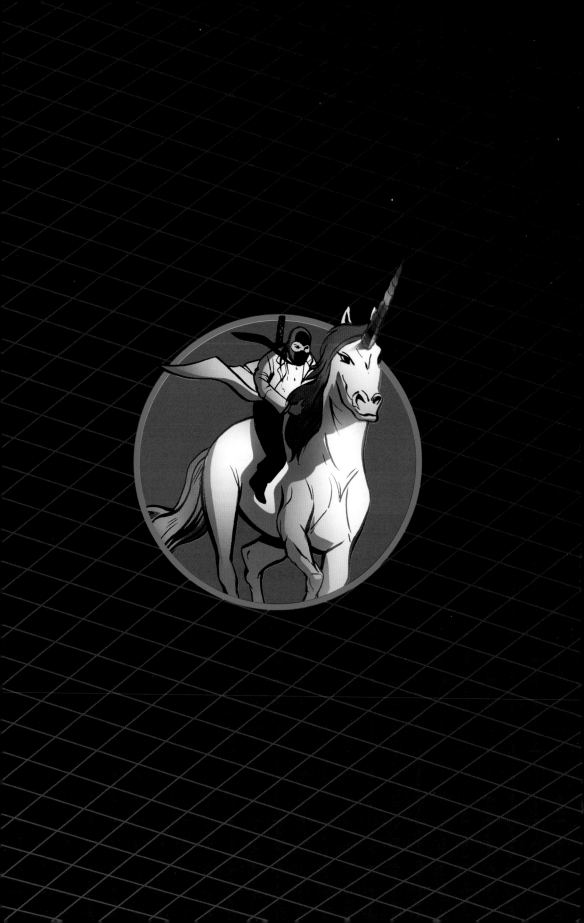